UNIVERSITY LIBRARY
UW-STEVENS POINT

UNIVERSITY LIBRARY
UW-STEVENS POINT

STRATEGIC ADVERTISING CAMPAIGNS

STRATEGIC ADVERTISING CAMPAIGNS

Don E. Schultz, Ph.D.
Assistant Professor, Northwestern University

Dennis G. Martin
Assistant Professor, Brigham Young University

Crain Books
Crain Communications Inc.
740 Rush Street
Chicago, Illinois 60611

To the late Andrew Kershaw,
former Chairman, Ogilvy & Mather Inc.

For SDS, BES, JPS, CES and LWS
Dr. JBM and DFM

Copyright © 1979 by Don E. Schultz and Dennis G. Martin.

Published by Crain Books Division of Crain Communications Inc.
All rights reserved. The book may not be reproduced in whole or in part
in any form or by any means without written permission from the publisher.

International Standard Book Number: 0-87251-043-3
Library of Congress Classification: 79-92171

Printed in the United States of America.

HF
5823
.S3636

Contents

318593

The Function of Advertising in the Marketing Plan

Advertising and marketing: who salutes whom?

From the very beginning of this text, advertising should be put in its proper place. Marketing is the master or king; advertising is one of many servants attending marketing. In spite of its extraordinary intrusiveness and aggressive posture, advertising does not and never will run the marketing show. It is at most the tip of the marketing iceberg. If a company really understands how to market its products,[1] advertising is skillfully integrated as part of a whole plan usually designed by the marketing manager. This doesn't mean advertising cannot play first violin, but it does mean that advertising should not take control of the marketing baton.

Ecosystems and marketing systems: remarkably similar

A company's marketing success or failure is heavily influenced by many forces. Few persons really understand how fragile and vulnerable a company's marketing system is, that it is dependent on what may be called a "systems law." Alarming as it may appear, the life and vitality of America's profit-making enterprises are constantly being threatened. This is a normal phenomenon. It can be expressed as a law. The secret of a company's survival is how well it recognizes and responds to the law.

The systems law

A productive system contains a collection of things (animate or inanimate) which receives both negative and positive inputs. It must act concertedly upon them to produce certain outputs. If the system is to survive, it must be committed to an objective — maximizing some sustaining function. If that commitment is not shared by all within the system, it will eventually be defeated (and replaced) by a more productive system.

To help illustrate how fragile the modern corporation's marketing system is, let's compare it to an ecosystem. Both are subject to the same kind of systems law. In theory, there is very little difference. And it's remarkable how vulnerable both really are.

Exhibit 1-1 is an illustration of a simple biological system. A 15-acre summer camp was built right in the middle of this virgin ecosystem. One might say that human intrusion was a negative input. The effect on output was not long in coming. The first group of nature lovers to stay overnight found hordes of field mice tiptoeing through their cabins, some even scampering across their sleeping bags. Why such a massive invasion? It seems a nearby nest of rattlesnakes had been nearly exterminated by the construction workers. With this local predator gone, the ecosystem responded by increasing the rodent population, a primary food supply of the rattler. Part of the system was merely compensating for the imbalance caused by human intrusion. The system was merely doing what it had to do.

A marketing system, by analogy, should be as finely integrated as such an ecosystem. Inputs and outputs must counterbalance each other. It should be remembered that an advertising campaign is only one of many internal operations affecting the marketing system's output. Exhibit 1-2 shows the marketing version of an "ecosystem."

A marketing system lives and breathes

Picture McDonald's restaurant business inside this carefully integrated marketing system. Management is continuously monitoring external inputs. The national inflation rate is an economic factor of great impor-

Exhibit 1-1. Bear Reservoir Ecosystem, High Sierra Range, Amador County, California, 6,000 feet above sea level.

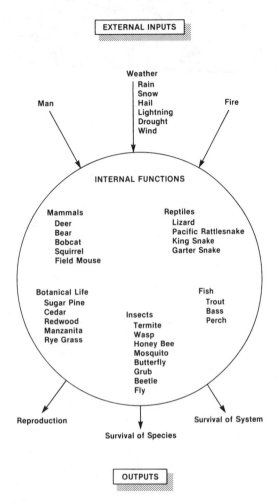

oriented organization is to grow and prosper as a result of filling consumer wants and needs, not simply through the production of goods and services.

Skeptics have sneered at the implicit idealism embodied in the so-called marketing concept. Idealism, however, is precisely what the business world needs as its standard. As altruistic as the marketing concept is, nothing better expresses the ideals of excellent service and genuine product quality to which all marketers should aspire.

Ray Kroc, founder-chairman of McDonald's Corporation, is a true believer in the principles of the

Exhibit 1-2. Marketing system.

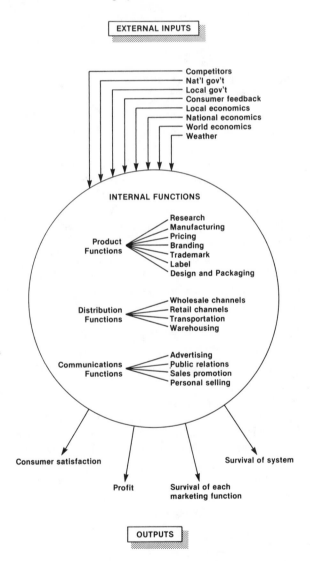

tance. Also, management interfaces with local government officials to maintain harmony with building codes and restrictions. Every day, every hour, competitors are challenging the corporation's product, distribution, and communications goals. Consumer feedback is sought through various research methods. McDonald's marketing system is indeed a living, breathing entity that is threatened daily. It must literally struggle and compete for survival, much like an ecosystem. Every internal function, based on external inputs, attempts to maximize the output—profit derived from consumer satisfaction.

Long live the marketing concept

What is this so-called marketing concept? Expressed simply, it means that the company, whether providing a manufactured product or service, seeks to fill consumer wants and needs. This is a rather dramatic change from the production-oriented philosophy on which this country prospered until the end of World War II. The contemporary view of the market-

marketing concept. Kroc doesn't dismiss the importance of profits. His philosophy, however, has been much like that of the early Gimbel's department store in New York. Focus on the product and the customer. Don't look for shortcuts to making a fast dollar. When

McDonald's started in the mid-fifties, Kroc explains, "We passed up some immediate sources of income when we needed it, such as juke boxes and pay phones, because this was contrary to our philosophy. Not too many businessmen have the courage to do this, but, in the long run, one cannot be motivated merely by dollars. The dollars come automatically when you have achieved your basic goals."[2]

Assume you are a brand manager for a major package-goods firm. How do you view your entire marketing system and your contribution to integrating it? First, remember that no two companies will integrate their marketing system in exactly the same way, nor should they. What's important is to apply creative judgment in integrating your own program for the benefit of your brand. On first glance at an integrated marketing operation (Exhibit 1-3), we may infer that each function in the system plays an equal role. That, however, is rarely if ever true. The Avon cosmetics firm, for example, is heavy on personal sales and spends considerably less in the mass media than many other cosmetics companies. Avon's in-home "push" distribution strategy is designed to move products through the distribution channels by personally delivering product samples and promotional materials to the consumer's doorstep, to literally "push" the product through the channels with supplementary support from advertising.

By contrast, Revlon and Procter & Gamble employ a heavier "pull" strategy by relying on the mass media. Those firms' heavy advertising support builds a "consumer franchise," or demand, for their products. As a consequence, retailers find they *must* stock those products to please their customers. Thus, the product is "pulled" through the distribution channels by consumer demand created by advertising.

As in both examples, most firms use a combination push-pull strategy. The budget weight behind each strategy is where the largest differences are found. Every successful company must discover its own best formula that satisfies the consumer at a profit. Indeed, the possible variations in integrated marketing systems are as manifold as the musical compositions attainable with 12 basic notes of the scale. There is virtually no limit to the possibilities.

A formula for integrating your marketing people

Genuine integrated marketing does not come easily. General Foods discovered this in the early seventies. The company found that new-product success had declined, that the cost of each had increased markedly, that the average life span of a new product was declining, and that, in many cases, the competition had introduced improvements ahead of General Foods in

Exhibit 1-3. Integrated marketing; advertising integrated into the system.

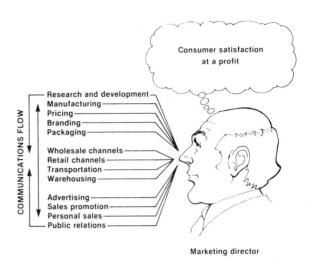

product categories where, historically, that firm had been the leader.[3]

General Foods' strategy was to integrate the firm's brand-management team with the technical research and development staff. The firm called it the "portfolio plan." *The plan assumed, for example, that the sales and promotional needs of a given product could be summarized on one side of a sheet of paper, while the technical efforts designed to meet those needs were listed on the opposite side.* Thus, for the product in question, the brand management/technical R&D interface was reduced to a single line running down the middle of the page. With the material displayed in this way, the technical people, the "left hand," found it easier to understand what the brand-management people, the "right hand," were doing. Now, the two groups could mesh and balance their collective efforts.

Specific advertising problems can be solved with the same method. The advertising and public relations departments could interface much more effectively with side-by-side objectives. Advertising specialists could be of greater help to sales personnel if the two groups could line up opposite each other with written objectives. Advertising agency account teams could more easily communicate with client brand managers on marketing questions that related directly to media selection and creative strategies.

The campaigns approach—the need for greater integration and continuity

An effective advertising campaign represents a masterpiece of marketing coordination. In fact, the written advertising plan prepared by the company or its agency contains more marketing data than communications or advertising information. The advertising plan is

Exhibit 1-4. Interlocking marketing components affecting an advertising plan.

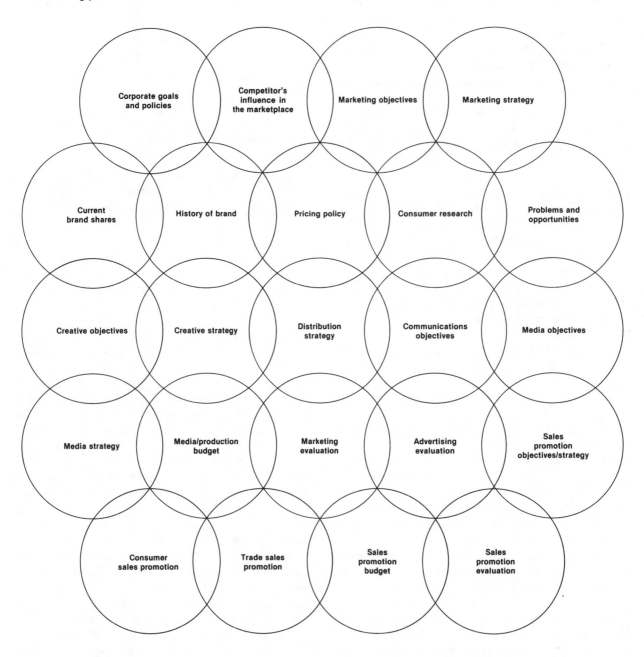

often part of a more comprehensive annual document called the company marketing plan.

What are the actual components of an advertising plan? Exhibit 1-4 shows how the many different marketing components affect the writer of an advertising plan. (Subsequent chapters will treat these variables in detail.)

An advertising campaign is a complex set of interlocking functional areas (circles) that must somehow be merged (integrated) into a system which will function successfully in its particular marketing environment. Of course, there is a logical sequence in which these individual circles should be handled. Marketing problems must be clearly defined before marketing objectives can be on target. Advertising or communications objectives would be hard to formulate without clear marketing objectives. Similarly, media objectives may be obscured without clear-cut creative objectives and strategies.

Continuity holds a campaign together

The actual advertisements or commercials seen or

Exhibit 1-5. Typical marketing organization of the fifties.

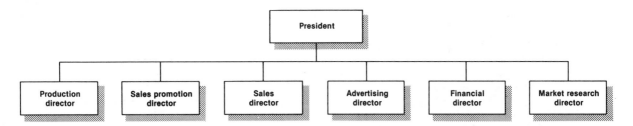

heard by the target audience are tied together by a common thread. It's called *continuity*. In essence, the campaigns approach to advertising management demands a coordination of functions from marketing problems all the way through the creative strategy. All parts must blend together so that the final campaign works like a family—individual members who bear a striking resemblance to each other, yet function in separate roles.

Brand manager, the one who makes the marketing moves today

Typical marketing organizations of the fifties

Before the brand management concept evolved in the 1960s, many package-goods firms succeeded with only a handful of products. They didn't need a marketing specialist for each brand. One person took the whole line. The line may have consisted of three or four brands, and the company organization looked something like that shown in Exhibit 1-5.

As illustrated, the president had a very direct relationship with each of the directors. He was, essentially, the marketing director with the title of "president." Depending on the president's philosophy, the directors below him or her could function as agents or pawns to be dictated to or manipulated. The latter form of management occurred more often than not.

Brand management for the 1980s has come a long way. In today's larger package-goods firms, the brand manager is entrusted with a particular brand and becomes responsible, as an independent agent, for its success or failure. The brand manager answers directly to the division brand manager who in turn reports to the marketing director. Some of the management levels may be eliminated in smaller firms, e.g., division brand manager. Exhibit 1-6 shows how many major package-goods companies such as Procter & Gamble and General Foods might be organized today.

If you examine the lower part of Exhibit 1-6, you will see how the brand managers are separated from the service personnel on the right side of the chart. Each

Exhibit 1-6. Hypothetical marketing organization in the eighties.

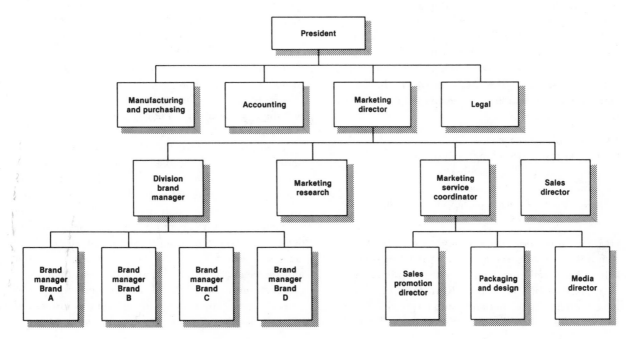

Exhibit 1-7. How advertising communicates.

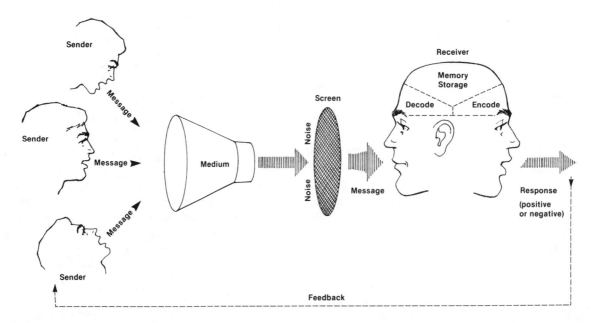

brand manager must work through the marketing director to get the support services to adjust to the particular needs of the brand. Here's where the brand manager's talents and skills will be put to the test. He or she must literally compete for the same support resources used by the other brand managers. By usurping the president's role, the brand manager is now functioning as a responsible agent (or "president") of the brand. The manager may delegate much of the writing of the advertising plan to an agency account executive. The manager, however, is still responsible to the marketing director for everything in the plan. Other responsibilities include the coordination of advertising with sales promotion and the guidance of marketing research activities. Even package design, logo design, and other details relating to the brand are directly under the guidance of today's brand manager.

Here are some of the areas in which the brand manager reports regularly to the marketing director, usually monthly:

- Current brand share
- Progress toward reaching sales goals
- Competitive activities against brand
- Changes, if any, recommended
- How support services can help brand achieve sales goals

It is clear that today's advertising specialist, whether in account service or creative or media functions, is likely to be directly involved with the brand manager. It is important for you, as the advertising specialist, to understand how much authority and responsibility that person has. The brand manager's success will depend on how well you understand all the marketing variables affecting his or her brand and how well this knowledge is applied in promoting and advertising the product. In effect, you will be working for a brand "president."

Communication as a method of selling

How mass communication works

Etymologists trace the origin of the word, "communication," to the Latin prefix, *communis*. The word is in the same family as words like "communism" and "commune," meaning "in common." When two or more people exchange an idea or concept and they understand each other, they have something "in common." They have "communed" with each other. Successful advertising copy develops this commonality between the seller and buyer. In the mid-1960s, John D. Maloney conceived an excellent model to illustrate how advertising communicates. Exhibit 1-7 is a modified version of Maloney's well-known "Communifunction Model."

As you study Exhibit 1-7, notice how the receiver is bombarded with more messages than he or she can handle. How much exposure does the average consumer get? Estimates range from two or three hundred to over a thousand advertising exposures a day. However, as with the mumps or measles, exposure doesn't mean "catching it." It simply means an *opportunity* existed for the receiver to "catch" it, or notice it, and respond. To defend himself, the consumer learns to screen out material that is not "in common" with his or her needs. Three things must occur before a consumer will catch or respond to a message:

1. At exposure, the message must gain his or her attention. It must get past the noise of competing stimuli.
2. The sender must use common symbols understood by the receiver. If the symbols are "in common," the receiver can easily decode the message. Verbal language, body language, color, shape, typography, and music are among the many symbols used in advertising communications.
3. The message must stimulate the needs or wants of the receiver if positive response is to occur.

Notice that the receiver has a memory storage capacity. Even if a need is not immediately stimulated, information may be stored for future use. In that case, a positive response may be encoded. National advertisers of high-ticket items such as cars or TV sets work hard to develop advertising messages that will be retained, that will get inside the receiver's memory storage to be retained for future retrieval, since such products are not frequently purchased.

Advertising as a different form of mass communication

During the past two decades, Americans have been getting an increasingly richer diet of information through the mass media. As our ability to gather information has grown and as our facilities for sending out messages through the various media have increased, differences have appeared in the measured effects of various types of communication. Indeed, some authorities have suggested that the American public may well be on the verge of drowning in a sea of information simply because it cannot be physically processed and assimilated.

Traditionally, we have thought of advertising as working in the manner illustrated in Exhibit 1-7. That is, the message is sent out by the advertiser through the media. If the message is clearly communicated, i.e., gets through the noise in the channels and passes the screen erected by the consumer, the receiver will likely receive and process the information. In our model (illustrated as Exhibit 1-7), we assume that the receiver is an active, seeking individual who wants information.

With the advent of television, there is increasing evidence that advertising may not go through this traditional mass communication process model at all. Herbert Krugman of the General Electric Company and others have suggested that advertising messages, particularly those appearing on television, may be the result of learning without active involvement. While watching television, for example, the audience may be in a very relaxed physical and mental state. The traditional screen which has been used to control messages may not be in use by consumers at this time. What

results is learning by the audience without active participation. Krugman calls it "passive learning." The result is that consumers may process advertising messages appearing on television which they would have ignored or totally rejected in some other medium. There is evidence that a form of learning occurs at a level lower than that which has been traditionally measured.

If indeed this form of advertising communication does exist, that in which the audience is not the supposed active seeker of information or is not at all times consciously processing information for later use, advertising may well be a unique form of mass communication. It may, in fact, depart from the traditional learning patterns which have been previously studied.

Much work remains to be done in this area. Yet there is increasing evidence that paid, persuasive messages in the form of advertising are a unique form of communication and should be treated as such in future research.

What advertising can and can't do

With enough advertising dollars behind a new product, it can be presented to over 90 percent of all U.S. households in about four weeks. However, advertising alone cannot make the new product a success. Other marketing variables have as much or perhaps more to do with the product's success as does advertising. (See Exhibit 1-2.) Distribution policy, manufacturing and quality control, the product concept itself—these variables are crucial in launching a successful product.

Behind every great advertising campaign is a great product

Bill Bernbach, noted advertising executive, believes there is one principle more important than any other, even more important than believability of the message. That is the principle of a good, solid product. This truism is illustrated by Bernbach's experience with a problem product.

> Seagrams owns Calvert. Calvert had gone down in sales to a point where [the company] was concerned. Edgar Bronfman asked me if we could work together on it. We got an idea for this Calvert whiskey and the idea was . . . introducing "soft whiskey."
>
> The important thing about this is that if we had run this ad with the whiskey they had, it would have been a complete flop. Calvert was a good whiskey but not softer than all other whiskies. *Great advertising just makes a bad product fail faster.*
>
> Bronfman—and I can't pay enough tribute to him—spent millions calling in every bottle of Calvert on the market, getting a new bottle, and putting a new whiskey into that bottle. When we launched this campaign, we had a great soft whiskey behind it. When people tasted it, they said, "That advertisement is right." The advertisement didn't make the product work; the product made the advertising work.

Then Bernbach said something that endorses the idea of getting advertising and product development people together:

> I think it behooves us as advertising people, since the product is the most important element in the success of a campaign, to get more involved in the planning of a product.[4]

What a perfect testimonial for General Foods "Portfolio Plan" (see previous section). Communications people can make a great contribution to a company's product development if that company will have enough vision to bring different people together, different managers of different marketing functions. It's called *integrated marketing*. And it works.

Notes

1. For economy of language, the word "product" will be used in the broad sense meaning all types of package goods, hard goods, and services.
2. Robert F. Hoel, *Marketing Now* (Glenview, Ill.: Scott, Foresman, 1973), p. 81.
3. *Advertising Age*, 23 February 1976, p. 123.
4. *"Some Things Can't Be Planned,"* Speech to the Western Region Annual Meeting of American Association of Advertising Agencies, Pebble Beach, California, 1965. By permission, William Bernbach, chairman of the Executive Committee, Doyle Dane Bernbach Inc. Advertising, New York.

2

Anatomy of an Advertising Plan

As we said earlier, an advertising plan is so filled with marketing information that it is often integrated into a more comprehensive document called the *marketing plan*. The advertising plan is, in fact, a direct descendant of the marketing plan. Since this text is oriented toward the development of advertising campaigns, we are more concerned with the *advertising plan*. The plan can be defined as:

> A concisely written document giving the company or brand's relevant history, current situation in its marketing environment, problems and opportunities, marketing and communications objectives, and strategies.

Before you begin to think of the advertising plan as a rigid blueprint devoid of flexibility, let's look at it from a practical viewpoint. Isn't advertising both an art and a business? Great advertising cannot be stamped out of a universal mold. Yet, the very existence of an advertising plan suggests this false syllogism:

(a) A carefully written and well-organized plan precedes great advertising campaigns.
(b) Great advertising campaigns have a solid research foundation.
(c) Therefore, solid research and careful planning will result in great advertising.

The false logic here is disarming. There is no magic recipe for creating great advertising campaigns. *Application* of the marketing information is where the true genius occurs. The "magic" is added by the brilliance of the marketers. They reduce the maze of research and statistical data to a statement of clear direction. The result—communication.

The marketing (or business) part of the advertising plan leads into the expression of the creative objectives and creative strategy. With this clear statement of direction from the marketing experts, creative experts have a much better chance of achieving greatness.

Still, this paradox persists: *A great, clearly written advertising plan does not guarantee great advertising. However, we believe advertising campaigns conceived without carefully written plans will surely fail.*

Some tips on style

Plans traditionally avoid the use of first-person pronouns, namely, "I" and "we." The plan represents the entire group, not just one person. Also, if a plan is written in simple objective language, you have an automatic advantage. Those involved in executing the plan will understand what you expect them to do. The odds for success are greatly increased when the writer communicates. Remember, to communicate means to be "in common" with your readers—all of them. Also be brief. Use the outline form liberally. "The plans that almost killed marketing plans used to run from one to two inches thick, not counting the impressive bindings. If yours goes much over ⅜ inch thick, put it on a diet."[1]

Perhaps the best way to visualize the development of the advertising plan is by examining some of the actual steps in the advertising decision process. David W. Cravens, Gerald E. Hills, and Robert B. Woodruff offer a framework for identifying the advertising areas requiring managerial decisions (see Exhibit 2-1). In this instance, the diagram also illustrates the various steps required in the development of the advertising campaign.

As the illustration suggests, the development of an advertising program is actually a series of interrelated steps dealing with most of the factors that affect advertising decisions. None of the steps is made in isolation, and certain decisions must be made in one area before moving to another.

The Cravens, Hills, and Woodruff model is excellent, but a more specific outline for the advertising

Exhibit 2-1. An analytical advertising decision process.

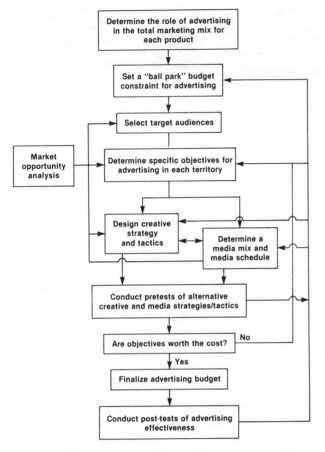

Source: Cravens, Hills and Woodruff, *Marketing Decision Making, Concepts and Strategy*, 1976.

plan is necessary. The following outline has proved to be successful for many advertisers and advertising agencies.

The components of an advertising plan

Here are brief descriptions of the major parts that make up an advertising plan. Following this section is a working model in outline form. Use that model when you're ready to start writing. We'll assume that you are preparing this plan either for the management of your company or as the representative of an advertising agency for a client company.

Executive summary

(See example in the working model.)

As the title suggests, this is a brief digest or abstract of your entire plan. You should also write a summary for each major section of the plan. The purpose is to save the precious time of management. After reading the summary, the marketing director may go directly to the sections of the plan most pertinent to his or her interest.

Situation analysis

(See example in the working model.)

Company and product history

It is traditional to include a brief sketch of the company's history. A single paragraph will usually do. Your history of the product or brand is also quite brief (usually a page or so), and it sticks to the key issues relevant to the brand's future success. Above all, avoid the temptation to stroke the client with a verbose, yawn-producing "century-of-progress annual report."

Relevant history may relate to the sales history of all manufacturers in the given industry. Equally important is the past market growth for this particular brand. Gross-profit history (net before taxes) may also be significant.

Consider the creative approaches used by the client over the past five years. Are there significant changes or shifts in direction? How did past creative efforts affect the success of the brand? How does that effort compare with the creative direction of major competitors?

Product evaluation

(See example in the working model.)

Here's where your written plan gets down to serious business. Imagine you are writing a report for the chairman of the board. He's smart and quick. He wants the facts about the product's current personality—*in order of importance*. Do not, repeat, do not write this section (or any section) of your plan using deductive logic, that is, moving from the general to the specific. The last thing a brilliant marketing executive wants is an advertising plan written like a novel that leads up to the climax or surprise. Write inductively. That is, put the most important evidence up front. This kind of writing entails the most difficult labor human beings have ever engaged in. It's called *thinking*. Pre-digest the information for your client to save time and energy.

Let's take an example. Suppose distribution is the most important part of the product story. Begin there. Don't feel obligated to treat product, packaging, and price in that order merely because they are listed that way on some academic outline. Feed the client the main course first. He or she will not only stay awake; but will also thank you for respecting his or her intelligence.

The consumer (target market evaluation)

How do you analyze the buying behavior of twenty or thirty million target prospects? You don't. To keep the cost within reason, you resort to statistical tools like probability sampling. (Tools and techniques for doing primary research are given in chapter 3.)

Getting an accurate picture of your primary target consumer is your first crucial task. The prospect should be described in demographic terms, i.e., age, sex, race, household income, education, occupation, and locality. This information is essential for everything from copy strategy to media planning.

Most advertising agencies and clients rely heavily on psychographic research to better understand the life styles and attitudes of the prospect. This kind of information is usually most helpful to the creative department people. If they can picture the prospect as a *person*, they can communicate with much more sensitivity.

Competitive analysis

Modern marketing language was borrowed from ancient military strategists. As any commanding officer knows, accurate intelligence on the enemy is crucial if he is going to succeed in launching a successful military campaign.

As a plans writer, you must insist on thorough research into the competitive environment of your market. Even though the activity of competitors is an uncontrollable factor in your "battle," knowing the other side's strengths and weaknesses can give you a real advantage. For example, if the introduction of your product in the media needs to match up with the competition's introduction, investigating last year's media records may put you one-up with your timing plans. If you discover weak spots in your competitor's distribution network, you might succeed where he or she didn't. Good marketing intelligence on your competitor's activities is priceless.

Marketing goals

Today's successful and most aggressive marketing firms are very goal oriented. It's a philosophy, almost an obsession, with companies like Procter & Gamble and most other package-goods firms. The reason is quite simple. These companies know their most valuable resource is not raw goods—it's brilliant, motivated people. They select their management personnel based on their ability to set realistic marketing goals and achieve them. The advertising plan writer must demonstrate the same quality throughout his or her plan.

Marketing goals are often expressed in both short-range and long-range goals. Short-range goals are planned typically for one year. The time period for long-range goals may be three to five years. The time frame is very flexible. It should be based on the needs of the company and brand. Express goals quantitatively, if possible, so they can be measured.

Advertising recommendations
Advertising objectives

These are measurable communications goals that are limited to a specific time period, usually one year. (See chapters 4 and 6.)

Advertising strategy. This is companion to the advertising objective. It clearly states how the measurable goals will be attained. The strategy lists the tools and methodology that will be employed. (See chapters 4 and 6.)

Creative objective (key advertising problem)

This spells out the single major issue that must be addressed in creating the advertising messages for the brand. It is a brief, one-or-two-sentence statement that articulates the naked truth. It may often be posed as a question. (See chapter 6.)

Creative strategy or positioning strategy—The answer to the advertising problem. A companion to the creative objective, the creative strategy is an answer to the advertising problem. It is a brief description of the idea, the creative force that will fulfill all your advertising objectives. (See chapters 4 and 6.)

Copy platform

Now, your client wants to know how you plan to execute your brilliant strategy. There are many versions of copy platforms. The following is recommended for its conciseness. For further details, see chapters 4 and 6.

Promise. A clear, straightforward statement of the major consumer benefit your product has to offer. It can be either a "Unique Selling Proposition" or a position. Whatever the promise, say it loud and clear. If you have trouble articulating it, it's probably not an honest promise.

Target audience. A brief description of whom you are talking to in your ads based on the research described in your situation analysis.

Execution. After the creative strategy is fixed, there are usually dozens of ways to execute the idea. Here, you give a brief description of the single approach you have decided on and the theme or slogan that will express your strategy. In the case of Grumman American (see later section, this chapter) it was the "Private Fighter" theme.

Product features. A list of the product qualities that support the promise.

Media recommendations
Key media problem

The media director must articulate the major issue he or she faces. Here's an example from a media plan for Sprite soft drinks:

Considering that Sprite's major competitor (Seven-Up) has a national advertising budget five and a half times larger than Sprite's current budget, how can we allocate precious media dollars to effectively win additional brand shares and increase Sprite consumption?[2]

Media objectives

These are specific goals established by the media planner (see chapter 8). They must be stated as quantitative measurable goals with precise time limits.

Media strategy

A companion to media objectives, the media strategy lists the tools (media choices) that will enable you to reach the stated goals. This section tells *how* the objectives will be reached.

Media budget

By now you have presented your creative product and stated how you will advertise it in the media. The next logical question is how much the promotion will cost? That's why the budget should come right after the media plan. By now, if you have done your job, the client will be ready to approve your spending proposals.

Typically, the budget consists of four parts:
1. Estimated cost of each medium recommended
2. Total media expenditures
3. Justification for expenditures
4. Estimated production costs

Sales promotion recommendations

Complete details on sales promotion are given in chapter 9.

Sales promotion objectives

These goals should be stated in quantitative (measurable) terms as much as possible. *How much* increase in shelf facings is expected during the year? *How much* return is expected on coupon redemptions?

Sales promotion strategy. As always, the sales promotion strategy answers the question of how the objectives will be met. Specific tools to be used are listed here in general terms:
- End-of-aisle displays
- Shelf talkers
- Sampling
- Contests
- Sweepstakes
- Tie-in promotions with related products
- Coupons

Execution

Details on each strategy are spelled out for the client.

For example: *Couponing — Sprite marries the Quarter Pounder.* All McDonald's customers will receive a coupon worth 20¢ off when they buy a six-pack of Sprite cans. Conversely, at retail food stores, customers will get a 20¢-off coupon when they buy a six-pack of Sprite — to be redeemed at McDonald's on a Quarter Pounder.

Promotion budget

In no more than a single page, the estimated costs of all promotional or merchandising items are listed. Because many promotional ideas may be totally original, research into manufacturing costs is often necessary. And the client expects you to know how much your socko idea is going to cost.

Budget recap

This is a brief (single page) cost accounting summary. It is simply adding media costs together with production and sales promotion. Nothing more than a grand total of all estimated costs in creating the new advertising campaign.

Evaluation methods

See chapter eleven for a complete discussion of the evaluation of campaigns. It's essential that you spell out very clearly *how* you plan to measure the effectiveness of your campaign.

Conclusions

This is usually no more than a one-page summary of why your client or prospective client should buy the campaign. "Conclusions" may also list some of the particular strengths your agency has to offer.

If you are working with a prospective client, you should definitely "ask for the order." What kind of agency would dare to claim selling expertise if it did not close the meeting with a persuasive request for the business?

Your advertising plan — a working model

No perfect outline exists that will fit every marketer's needs. The following outline was created with three major objectives — simplicity, substance and clarity.

Be very selective in using this outline or any other. Don't let an outline intimidate or govern you. Change the sequence of ideas to suit your needs. Be concise. Resist your impulse to throw in all the facts mentioned in the situation analysis, for example. If you're not careful, you'll end up with a 200-page monster.

Advice on situation analysis: Go ahead and dig up all of the information listed here. Then cut away the fat and get down to 10 or 15 pages of lean relevant protein.

This outline follows the same order as the earlier "Components of an advertising plan." The major difference is that this outline is intended as a *working model* to be used when you understand what the components are and how they work together. If you get confused, go back to the "components" section.

Outline for developing an advertising plan

I. Executive summary

On a single side of a sheet of paper, address the key issues covered in your plan. Let your reader discover your ability to get to the point on the very first page.

II. Situation analysis

Critical examination of the facts relevant to your product's current condition. Use pie charts, graphs, and growth curves liberally to help facilitate understanding for your reader.

A. History of product—past advertising strategy
1. Relevant history of company
2. Growth curve for market (past 3 to 5 years)
3. Sales history of brand
4. Share of market history
5. Pricing history of brand, reasons for fluctuations
6. Gross profit margins (net before taxes)
7. Advertising history (e.g., media strategy, themes)
8. Past advertising budgets (graph last 5 years)
9. Personal selling history
10. Patents, technological history of brand
11. Significant political and legal influences on product or company
12. Current creative directions, campaign theme now being used
   Note: Most of the questions asked about your brand's history could also be asked about your major competitor's brand. Historical comparison with competitors can be made in this section of your plan or separately under Competitive Analysis. Either is acceptable. Do whatever is most efficient and understandable for your reader.

B. Product evaluation
1. Distribution
   a. Current distribution channels
   b. Percent penetration in market outlets
   c. Distribution geography
   d. Average retail shelf facings
   e. Where product is located or positioned in stores
   f. Do distributors like the product? The company?
   g. Do they gladly allow space for displays?
   h. Is there an out-of-stock problem among retailers?
   i. Does brand emphasize "push" or "pull" strategy?
   j. Do distributors get "deals"?
2. Current product character
   a. Current price acceptable?
   b. Product ingredients? Construction? Quality?
   c. Is packaging functional? Convenient?
   d. Label design effective?
   e. Sufficient product facts on label?
   f. Service provided with product?
   g. How does product quality compare with competition?
   h. What consumer problems does product solve?
   i. Major product benefit. Uniqueness.

C. Target market evaluation
1. Target audience (primary research)
   a. Demographic profile. Categories shown are based on the *Demographic Composition of Samples* from W. R. Simmons & Associates Research.[3]
   b. *Occupation* (for explanation, see chapter 9)
      • Professional/technical
      • Managers/administrators
      • Clerical/sales
      • Craftsmen/foremen
      • Other employed
      • Not employed
   c. *Marital status/household head* (for explanation, see chapter 9)
      • Single
      • Married
      • Divorced/Separated
      • Widowed
   d. *Race*
      • White
      • Black
      • Oriental
      • Native American
      • Other
   e. *Education* (for explanation, see chapter 9)
      • Graduated college
      • 1–3 years college
      • Graduated high school
      • 1–3 years high school
      • No high school
   f. *Age*
      • Under 12
      • 12–17
      • 18–24
      • 25–34
      • 35–44
      • 45–54

- 55–64
- 65 +
g. *Household income*
  - $20,000 and over
  - $15,000–$19,999
  - $10,000–$14,999
  - $ 8,000–$ 9,999
  - $ 5,000–$ 7,999
  - Less than $5,000
h. *Presence of children in household*
  - Under 6 years
  - 6–17 years
  - None under 18
i. *Social class* (for explanation, see chapter 9)
  - Class I. Upper
  - Class II. Upper Middle
  - Class III. Lower Middle
  - Class IV. and V. Lower
j. *Locality type*
  - Metro—Central City
  - Metro—Suburban
  - Non-metro
k. *Geographic region* (see chapter 9 for list of states)
  - Northeast
  - Central
  - South
  - West
l. Optional geographic breakdown
  Note: Many organizations use the distribution or territorial descriptions given in *Target Group Index* or a breakdown by Simmons Market Research Bureau, particularly for food and drug items.
  - New England
  - Mid-Atlantic
  - East Central
  - West Central
  - Southeast
  - Southwest
  - Pacific
m. County size (for explanation, see chapter 9)
  - A
  - B
  - C
  - D

2. User profiles—psychographics (see chapter 9 for in-depth coverage)
   Note: Usually, the psychographic or lifestyle pattern of the target consumer is written into the creative section of an advertising plan. It consists only of a paragraph or two. Here are a few of the questions that may be considered in developing a psychographic profile.
   a. Do people who like your product tend to be outward and friendly or shy?
   b. Are they typically conservative in their dress and manner or less rigid?
   c. Describe their life style—the car they drive, the home they live in, the books and magazines they read, the sports they engage in, their religious activity.

3. Analysis of target consumer behavior (primary research)
   a. Consumption facts: social influences, where consumed, how consumed, frequency of consumption, average quantity consumed
   b. Attitudes about quality, price, packaging, styling, reputation of brand
   c. Consumer purchase habits: year, month, time of day, cash, credit, who buys. Is buyer same as consumer?
   d. Percentage consumer awareness of current advertising campaign.
   e. Attitudes toward current advertising. How is advertising perceived? Believed?
   f. What problems does our product solve for the consumer? Is the consumer aware of these problem-solving benefits?
   g. How loyal are the present consumers of our brand? Does brand switching occur? How much?
   h. Who are the best prospects among non-users of our particular brand? What kind of advertising appeal will stimulate them toward trying our brand?

D. The competition
   1. Marketing strengths and weaknesses
      a. Number and type of competitors
      b. Major competitors and brand shares
      c. Minor competitors and brand shares
      d. Distribution policy, geography
      e. Retail shelf facings
      f. Location of product in stores
      g. Distributors' attitudes about competitors
      h. Do competitors get better display treatment?
      i. Is "push" or "pull" strategy used by competitors?
      j. Do competitors give better trade deals?
   2. Competitive brands
      a. Pricing policies
      b. Product ingredients, construction, quality
      c. Packaging comparisons
      d. Labeling comparisons
      e. Service comparisons

f. Quality comparisons

g. What consumer problems does product solve?

h. Major benefits. Any superiorities over our own brand.

3. Competitive advertising

a. Advertising history (media, creative themes, slogans)

b. Past advertising budgets (graph 5-year period)

c. Brand awareness for competing products. Do consumers recognize competitors' advertising slogans or themes better than our own brand?

d. Any weakness in communications—advertising, personal selling, or public relations?

III. Marketing goals for our brand

A. Marketing objectives

1. Current case sales or unit sales vs. sales goals for next fiscal year (e.g., increase case sales from X to Y in 12-month period beginning June 1.)

2. Current market share vs. market share goal for next fiscal year

3. Current market penetration (percentage of all potential distributors carrying product) vs. penetration goal for next fiscal year

B. Marketing strategy

Note: State clearly *how* these marketing goals will be reached. What specific marketing tools will be employed to get there? (e.g., increase sales force, increase advertising pressure, improve product, hire jobbers to expand distribution.)

IV. Advertising recommendations

A. Advertising objectives (communications goals)

1. Advertising strategy

B. Creative objective (key advertising problem)

1. Creative strategy (the big idea or concept)

C. Copy platform

1. Promise

2. Target audience

3. Execution (concept or idea)

4. Product features

V. Media recommendations

A. Key media problem

B. Media objectives

C. Media strategy

D. Media budget rationale

VI. Sales promotion recommendations

A. Sales promotion objectives

1. Sales promotion strategy

B. Execution

C. Sales promotion budget

VII. Budget recap

VIII. Evaluation methods

Advertising information sources

I. How to find information about a company

A. Finding what books exist on a subject

1. Library card catalog

2. *Cumulative Book Index*

3. *Books in Print*

B. Finding journal and newspaper articles

1. *Funk and Scott Index of Corporations and Industries*

2. Business Periodical Index

3. Wall Street Journal

C. Financial services

1. Moody's manuals

a. Moody's Industrial Manual

b. Moody's OTC Industrial Manual

c. Moody's Bank and Finance Manual

d. Moody's Municipal and Government Manual

e. Moody's Public Utility Manual

f. Moody's Transportation Manual

2. Standard and Poor's Corporation

a. Standard Corporation Records. A looseleaf service in six volumes with bimonthly supplements

b. New York Stock Exchange listed stock reports

c. American Stock Exchange stock reports

d. Over-the-counter and regional exchange stock reports

D. Company information

1. Annual reports (often available from stock brokerage firms)

2. House organs

3. Prospectuses

II. How to find information about an industry

A. Guides to sources

1. Wasserman's Statistics Sources

2. Encyclopedia of Business Information Sources

B. Other sources

1. Standard and Poor's Industry Surveys. Covers 49 industries and their principal companies

2. U. S. Census publications

a. Annual Survey of Manufacturers

b. Census of Agriculture

c. Census of Business

d. Census of Construction Industries

e. Census of Housing

f. Census of Manufacturing

g. Census of Mineral Industries

h. Census of Population

i. Census of Transportation

3. Survey of Current Business

C. Directories listing corporations

1. Thomas Register of American Manufacturers—includes alphabetical listing of

trademarks
2. Conover-Mast Purchasing Directory

III. How to find information about a geographical area
A. U. S. Census publications (in addition to those listed above)
    1. Statistical Abstract of the United States
    2. County and City Data Book
    3. County Business Patterns
B. State statistical abstracts
C. State industrial directories
D. "Survey of Buying Power Issue," *Sales Management* magazine (annual)

IV. Special advertising sources
A. Standard Rate and Data Service
    1. Consumer Magazines
    2. Business Publications
    3. Canadian Advertising
    4. Network Rates and Data
    5. Newspaper Rates and Data
    6. Spot Radio Rates and Data
    7. Spot Television Rates and Data
    8. Transit Advertising Rates and Data
    9. ABC Weekly Newspaper Rates and Data
    10. Print Media
    11. Directorio de Medias
    12. Newspaper Circulation Analysis
B. Standard Directory of Advertisers
C. Standard Directory of Advertising Agencies
D. National Advertising Investments

V. Syndicated marketing studies
    Note: Companies listed here will often provide "year-old" data to universities and colleges for cost of postage and handling. If you need more current studies, advertising agencies will often help out if there is no commercial application.
A. Simmons Market Research Bureau
    Audience exposure estimates and product-usage studies correlated with both broadcast and printed media. A major source of consumer research data and marketing studies for all major consumer product categories.
B. A. C. Nielsen Company
    The world's largest research company with operations in major world population centers. Several kinds of syndicated services are available:
    1. NTI (Nielsen Television Index) is a national television rating service that estimates audience size for all the network TV shows using audimeters installed in approximately 1,200 U. S. TV households.
    2. NSI (Nielsen Station Index) is the Nielsen's service for measuring local TV audiences.
    3. Nielsen Food & Drug Index is a service that measures movement of products in retail stores. From these store audits, companies are able to estimate their brand shares.

C. Target Group Index (now merged with Simmons Market Research Bureau) is best known for product-usage studies in consumer packaged goods. Consumers are matched with media exposure habits based on usage by brand. Studies include both print and broadcast.

D. LNA-BAR
    Leading National Advertiser–Broadcast Advertiser Reports provides a monthly estimate of TV commercial expenditures and gross time billing for all major national brands. Also available are estimates of production costs for programs and talent costs along with station lineups. Network Radio station lineups by program and advertiser is another service syndicated by LNA–BAR.

E. SAMI (Selling Areas—Marketing, Inc.)
    This syndicated research company estimates inventory withdrawals by major food and drug chains and stores.

How to look for the advertising problem

Chapter one built a solid foundation for the campaign superstructure. At this point you should recognize advertising's complete subordination to the marketing system and its function in that system. You should also have a clear picture of how to organize and write a campaign.

This chapter assumes you know how to do a situation analysis and are ready to define the advertising problem. At this point two separate problems must be dealt with: the primary marketing problem and the advertising problem. The method of attack is really the same for both. And since this book is aimed at advertising, the focus will be in that area.

Looking for the advertising problem is where the challenge begins. If you have a trace of Sherlock Holmes in your blood, you'll relish the job of working through the situation analysis—the digging, the discovering. After stuffing your head with facts, you face the greatest challenge of all, thinking, original thinking that will focus on the single most important issue your client must now face.

This is where the advertising plan writer can display his or her genius. You must judge which of the assembled facts are most important and how they relate to each other. What do they mean? Bare and isolated facts presented in the situation analysis are virtually sterile. They need to be clothed in understanding before you can present them to management. Again, this is the pre-digesting work you will do for the brand or marketing manager. You are expected to take risks, to dare to think in an original way. Do your deductive thinking first; then write your message inductively.

Remember, the marketing problem has a wide-angle focus on the entire marketing system of which advertising is only a part. The key advertising problem, therefore, is necessarily different from the marketing problem. A paper written for the Association of National Advertisers tells where and how to look for the marketing problem:[4]

> What is meant by problem? Well, the problem may be the product itself or its price or its packaging. It may be inadequate distribution or unsatisfactory point-of-sale support. It may be dissatisfaction on the part of the trade with the marketer's customer service, or his policies with respect to cooperative advertising or cash discount, or the markup the trade is able to take.
>
> Some of these "problems" may not lend themselves to correction or solution, but their disclosure in the plan brings them into the open and subjects them to critical examination of their potential solvability. At the same time, many of the problems are susceptible to solution, and that is the point at which the problem is converted into an opportunity. There may be problems of an entirely different nature.
>
> Maybe too few customers are aware of the product. Still more may not know of the merits or of changes that may have been made in it to make it more responsive to consumers' wants. Perhaps advertising has placed emphasis on product attributes which are of little or no concern to consumers, and conversely has failed to emphasize — or at least to "sell" — the attributes which consumers do want.

A recognition of the problem is the first step toward creating an opportunity. But singling out the key problem isn't easy. Here's how the Murray-Chaney agency did it.

Case history

The situation: major product facts

The Grumman American Aviation Corporation builds very efficient two- and four-seater private airplanes. The basic model was engineered and designed first for flying speed and fuel efficiency. The plane was not intended to be a luxury aircraft. On the contrary, it was built for the less wealthy segment of the market who loved to fly, who wished for all the status, but who couldn't afford a Beech Bonanza.

The Grumman was described in one aviation publication as the "Honda of the air." Its major competition was other builders of single engine, fixed-gear aircraft, namely Piper, Cessna, and Beech.

Although famous for World War II aircraft construction, the Grumman name was a newcomer in the smaller private-plane market, entering the field, as the company had, by buying into the American Aviation Corporation of Cleveland. So the new Grumman product not only lacked awareness, it lacked image or personality. It was a great little aircraft but it would just have to wait around until somebody noticed it. After all, Cessna, Piper, and Beech had been making light aircraft for decades. Pilots knew those planes. Who had ever heard of a Grumman small plane? And why should a potential customer buy one?

The sweet smell of opportunity

As Tom Murray of Murray-Chaney Advertising pointed out in an article in *Advertising Age*, focusing on Grumman's problem required an open-minded view of the whole marketing environment in America.[5] Grumman's fuel-stingy private airplane appeared to be the ideal product for an energy-starved world. Yet, Murray noted, after considering the energy-saving appeals used in new car advertising, it became obvious to him that a fresh approach was needed (from that in car advertising). "We have simply taken the EPA figures and jammed them into the ads, with headlines about economy never looking so good. The competitors are all making mileage claims, so what's a fellow to do but counter their claims?"

Crediting Theodore Levitt's thesis called "Marketing Myopia," Murray said, "If we stand back far enough to realize that we are moving from a centuries-old miles-per-*hour* era into a miles-per-*gallon* era, then we have got to move beyond the simple appeal of *savings* to come up with broader and more varied appeals for saving energy."[6]

This kind of thinking is what saved the Murray-Chaney agency people from leaping on the trite "Don't be fuelish" bandwagon. They rejected the "Honda of the air" approach for several reasons. Their main concern was that pilots are often very status-conscious persons and very sensitive about the image they project among other pilots and the nonflying public.

Appealing to them on the basis that they were simply saving gas money by buying a Grumman American seemed not only flimsy but downright dangerous in a market in which the big three (Cessna, Piper, and Beech) were doing very well with no appeal to efficiency whatsoever. There was no indication that anyone was interested in saving on fuel.

Here's how Murray saw the key advertising problem:[7]

> Since our primary target's first reason for buying an airplane is transportation, with strong overtones of adventure and status, how can we position the Grumman American as a simple and efficient airplane that is practical, yet address the pilot's needs for adventure and status?

With a firm grasp of the problem, the Murray-Chaney agency followed up with these objectives and strategies.[8]

Summary of objectives and strategies

Grumman American Advertising Campaign

1. Advertising objective: To achieve 90 percent awareness and identification among our primary target prospect of Grumman American light aircraft with its relatively new "mother corporation," Grumman Corporation. The reputation of Grumman is strongly based on its outstanding fighter aircraft built for the U.S. Navy, particularly during World War II. In the aviation community, Grumman is referred to as "The Iron Works," reflecting its reputation for building aircraft that could withstand extensive battle damage, yet still bring its pilots home safely.

2. Advertising objective: To achieve 100 percent awareness among our own dealers, many of whom sell other-make aircraft, of the powerful selling proposition of simplicity and efficiency that the Grumman American airplanes embody.

3. Advertising strategy: To make our airplanes highly visible in airports and to attract pilots and prospective pilots for close and careful consideration.

4. Advertising strategy: Our idea must be unusual, interesting, and appealing enough to editors to suggest to them cover photo ideas and feature possibilities. This will extend and multiply our number of exposures in the media beyond the pages that our advertising budget will buy for us.

Murray explains:

After some weeks of searching for a creative concept that would fulfill all of these advertising objectives, we came up with a far-out idea. The noblest of the flying fraternity are the fighter pilots, and more songs and poems and stories attest to their competence and bravery than to perhaps any other segment of the flying community. Why not appeal to the would-be fighter pilot in all of our prospects? And why not play up energy savings as the patriotic American cause that it is? Here's the strategy we came up with.

Creative Strategy for Grumman American

Paint representative models of Grumman American aircraft in World War II fighter colors as a way to attract attention to them and as a platform to dramatize our superior fuel and speed efficiency when compared with similarly priced models of "the big 3" in light aircraft sales, Cessna, Piper, and Beechcraft.

Four representative models of Grumman airplanes were painted in World War II fighter paint to serve as the symbols of the new approach. The campaign theme was built around "The Private Fighters," and Grumman appealed to pilots to "join the fight for America's fuel, protect America's freedom to fly fast and protest the high cost of buying, flying and maintaining airplanes."[9]

As one aviation magazine writer put it:[10]

The dramatic, romance inspiring difference was the painting . . . thrilling Navy, Army, and Air Force fighter plane camouflage designs and colors, and what that combination did to people from ex-military fliers to those who were still in diapers during World War II. They went bananas!

This campaign not only worked, it did barrel rolls around the competition. All the airplanes scheduled for production for the entire year were sold at the introductory dealer meetings. Dealers paid premium prices for the models painted in wartime paint for renting out. They reported 100 to 200 percent more rentals than for the same models painted in standard colors.

The United States Naval Academy bought flying-school airplanes from Grumman American instead of from better-known Piper, Cessna, or Beech. And within the year, Grumman American edged out Beech as the number three builder of low-wing, fixed-gear aircraft. An appeal to status, not savings, had done the job.

As expressed by Roy Garrison, Grumman's senior vice-president—light aircraft marketing,

We told people that we had the numbers—more airspeed, carrying capacity, and general performance out of low-horsepower engines than anybody else. But when we told them we could cruise at 160 mph in the Tiger with the 180-hp engine that our competitors were only getting about 130 out of, they didn't believe us. And when we told them we could almost match the numbers of the 200-hp airplanes with retractable gear that sold for thousands more than ours, they grinned unbelievingly. So we gave the Tiger to the editors to try for themselves, and the result was that we ended up on the covers of just about every aviation magazine around.[11]

How was this marketing coup executed so masterfully? First was an excellent product. Second, and equally important, was the agency's problem-solving genius. Agency writers cleared away all the fog and pinpointed the major issue facing Grumman's communications.

Murray's knack for absorbing a rich supply of marketing facts and digesting them into a single major issue demonstrates truly creative problem-solving ability. To quote him, "It is our job to mentally shift our gears and our heads to the new ways Americans are going to move and live. Next, we must clearly define the problems as we search for honest, original appeals for the new and present products our clients will be asking us to help them sell."[12]

Isolating the advertising problems

Advertising problems are communications problems. Although consumer advertising is responsible for improving sales and brand shares, can you see how the following problem statement is misleading?

Considering the serious competitive erosion of our brand share (down 35 percent) and loss of 50 key retail distributors, how can advertising be employed to regain our original marketing position?

Although something of an exaggeration, this problem statement demonstrates careless thinking. It assumes advertising is the *only* cure for sales problems. However, declining sales and loss of distribution may have nothing to do with the communications program. They may not even be the key marketing problems. They are probably *symptoms* of the problem, just as headaches and nausea are often symptoms of serious disease. If you treat only the symptoms, you may see a temporary improvement, but, ultimately, the patient (or brand) will probably die.

The real issue (or problem) may be poor quality control, inadequate transportation, overpricing, or out-of-stock problems at the point of purchase. These are marketing problems beyond advertising's direct influence. Or, all of the above could be in perfect order and the real issue is related to communications. The advertising copy may be offensive to the point that consumers stop buying. The point is, whatever the key problem, isolate it with specific language. If it is clearly a problem related to communications, zero in on its exact nature. Isolating problems is analogous to diagnosing illnesses. Accuracy in language is crucial before the right medicine can be administered. And if the wrong medicine is prescribed, results may be fatal. Like it or not, if sales go down and the agency cannot find the *real* cause, it will probably be fired anyway.

Notes

1. Roger Barton, ed., *Handbook of Advertising Management* (New York: McGraw-Hill, 1970), pp. 10-12.
2. *AAF Advertising Campaign for Coca-Cola's Brand Sprite,* Prepared by Sans Serif, Inc., Brigham Young University, 1978, p. 15.
3. *Technical Guide, 1976/77 Study of Selective Markets and the Media Reaching Them,* Simmons Media Studies (New York: W. R. Simmons & Associates Research, 1977), pp. 36-39.
4. Roger Barton, *Handbook,* pp. 10-12.
5. Thomas D. Murray, "How We Turned Savings and Sacrifice into Status Symbols," *Advertising Age,* 27 February 1978, pp. 51-52.
6. Ibid, p. 51.
7. "Creative objective" is another term used by some agencies to describe the "advertising problem." The two terms are synonymous.
8. Thomas D. Murray, personal correspondence.
9. Murray, *Advertising Age,* p. 52.
10. Dwight Boyer, "Flights of Fantasy," *Cleveland Plain Dealer,* Sunday News Magazine, 8 February 1976, pp. 20-22.
11. Personal communication.
12. Murray, *Advertising Age,* p. 52.

3

Research, the Foundation of the Advertising Campaign

What is research? An overview

A well-known saying in advertising, often attributed to David Ogilvy, is that advertising people use research much as a drunk uses a lamppost, more for support than illumination. Directional research is taken as gospel truth. A few selected results are projected to the universe. Or, worst of all, poorly conducted research is used as the basis for a campaign, often resulting in a waste of the entire advertising investment. On the other hand, sound research can provide insights into very difficult advertising problems, but there is a major difference between *sound* advertising research and what often passes as research.

Before we proceed, a few definitions are needed. The American Marketing Association defines research as ". . . the systematic gathering, recording, and analyzing of data about problems relating to the marketing of goods and services."[1] C. H. Sandage and Vernon Fryburger suggest redefining market research as "market intelligence," since the primary interest is in gathering information which can be used in the development and execution of marketing and advertising programs.[2]

Many reasons can be cited for increased market research or market intelligence. Philip Kotler suggests three: a shift from local to national and international marketing, a transition in the marketplace from buyer needs to buyer wants, and a transition from price to nonprice competition among major consumer goods companies. He summarizes by saying, "As sellers increase their reliance on competitive weapons such as branding, product differentiation, advertising, and sales promotion, they require great quantities of information on the effectiveness of these marketing tools."[3]

If we examine the entire marketing research and marketing intelligence system and the information re-

quired, we might perceive something like the model suggested by David Cravens, Gerald Hills, and Robert Woodward.[4]

Exhibit 3-1. Market opportunity analysis.

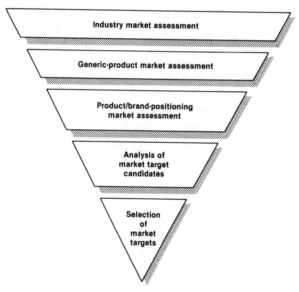

With this model, we can see how important knowledge is and how the advertising campaign must be built on a solid research base. Then we realize how dependent advertising decisions are on all types of market information.

To provide a structure for the research problem, Charles Ramond suggests that three steps are required in each of the areas of campaign development as shown on the following page.

A final note of caution on advertising and marketing research: As Kenneth Longman points out, research gives us information on a situation. Research does not tell us what the advertiser or marketer should attempt

To Make This Decision	One Must Choose a	Using Techniques Variously Known as
What to say	Theme, copy platform	Concepts tests, positioning studies
To whom	Target audience	Market segmentation studies
How to say it	Copy, commercial execution	Copy research, commercial tests
How often	Frequency of exposure	Studies of repetition
Where	Media plan	Media research models, audience studies
How much to spend	Budget level	Sales analysis, marketing models[5]

to do.[6] Thus, research may suggest a clue to the solution but it seldom if ever provides the total answer. Research is necessary for the development of a sound advertising campaign, but it should be viewed as a necessary ingredient, not a finished product.

If we only knew the question

An ancient adage—if we only knew the question, we could find the answer—is very true in advertising. Because we are dealing with people, the questions become difficult since there are so many variables in consumer purchase decisions. Often, unfortunately, the apparently obvious answer doesn't fit the question or vice versa.

Whom can we believe?

We often find advertising built on management's definitions of consumers' problems, needs, and wants. These are often fictitious problems and a campaign based on such misinformation will succeed only in providing solutions to needs the consumer doesn't have or benefits of little value to potential users. The advertising may do a great job of satisfying the needs of the advertiser but little or nothing for consumers, who are expected to respond to the message.

This problem often arises because of the assumption that questions or answers to advertising problems can be found without talking to consumers. When this happens, it is because the advertising campaign planner stopped with the first answer. It is tempting to believe, for example, a salesperson who says, "We should be advertising the larger size of our product. Competitor X is doing that." In fact, the problem may not relate to the size of the product advertised. There may be a hundred other reasons the large size of Brand X is selling better than our product. The only productive way to learn the answer is to ask consumers why they are buying the large size of Brand X. Or, better still, ask customers why they are not buying the large size of our product. Consumers frequently have answers that may have eluded both the advertising management and the sales force. Unfortunately, in some instances, even the consumer can't give his or her reason very accurately.

This example is not meant to imply that the advertiser or sales force don't know their product or their marketplace. It does suggest that, although research investigations should start internally, they shouldn't

end there. Often the manufacturer and the sales force can identify the problem immediately. But it is still worth checking with consumers to make sure they perceive the same situation. To obtain market intelligence, once must seek information at all levels, but especially from the consumer.

Yes, the client may be wrong. Yes, the sales force may be wrong. Yes, the laboratory people may be wrong. Yes, even advertising management may be wrong. True answers are to be found only with the consumers of the product. They have the final voice in the purchase decision. And that decision, after all, is what advertising is attempting to influence.

Finding the question

Our look at research for the campaign deals primarily with Ramond's first two questions, i.e., "What to Say" and "To Whom."[7] (Other questions in the development of the campaign will be dealt with in later chapters.) Having limited the questions to be asked, we can now address ourselves to what is needed. Again, following Ramond's outline, the primary research job is to find a "Theme" or "Copy" platform and a target audience. Finding those two ingredients can be a most difficult task.

Perhaps the best way to answer a question is to ask a question. R. T. J. Tuck and Jill Firth suggest five basic questions to pose in planning a campaign:

1. *Where are we now?* This usually indicates the type of information required. It is the basic question of where the brand stands now in the marketplace and in the mind of the consumer. To properly assess the future, we must know where we are today.

2. *Why are we there?* Why does our brand have the position it now has in the market and in the consumer's mind? To answer those questions, factors that have contributed to the brand's strengths and weaknesses must be determined. If there is a product problem, we should recognize it. If there is a distribution problem, why has it arisen? We must get the facts.

3. *Where could we be?* The question is not where we would like to be but the position our brand realistically could hold in the future. The answer requires a review of the market position sought, the buyers and users who must be reached with our advertising, and how they might respond to our brand. The problem is to determine not what is profitable or desirable but what

is realistic. Having determined where we would like the brand to be, our next step is creating a strategy to make the change. If consumers have certain beliefs about our brand, what must we say to make them believe something more conducive to potential sales? This leads to the next question.

4. *How can we get there?* What changes will have to be made in what elements of the product, or the consumer's image of the product, to enable us to achieve the goal we have set? With this objective, we can now begin to develop the techniques and materials necessary to reach the goal.

5. *Are we getting there?* This is the feedback component in the strategy loop. If we don't know the progress we are making, we may never know if we are moving toward the goal. We must see the advertising campaign in action if we are to know that it will work.[8]

Obviously, if we could answer these questions immediately, there would be no need for research. So we develop a research plan. Even with this approach, many research problems are not nearly as clear-cut as we would like. For example, Ramond says:

> Advertisers' choice of what to say have been aided by research on product attributes, on the benefits consumers perceive them to provide, and on the effects such messages have in favor toward the advertiser. But, deciding what to say cannot be separated from deciding to whom to say it. Different target audiences will respond differently to different messages.[9]

Thus, the clear-cut questions posed by Tuck and Firth must be tempered by what is determined to be the most important audience for the product. This is often determined by what can be said about the product. Developing an advertising campaign often appears to be a circular problem, which is why the answers do not come easily.

Finally, to complicate the matter further, we're faced with the situation Haley describes when he says, "What people do to (advertising) messages is more important than what (advertising) messages do to people."[10]

The questions are indeed hard to delineate and often less than precise. The advertising campaign planner must obtain marketing intelligence on which to base a sound program. The rest of this chapter will be devoted to outlining methods not only for arriving at the questions but also for answering them.

What do we really need to know?

The primary objective of any advertising campaign is quite simple: to reach the right target audience with the right message at the right time. Unfortunately, determining the right audience and the right message are not done easily. Sandage and Fryburger suggest that solutions to most advertising questions are found in three research areas: consumer analysis, market analysis, and product analysis.[11] By studying these areas, the proper questions quickly become apparent.

The consumer analysis

Pertinent questions to be asked in the consumer analysis are: Who buys the product? What do they buy? When do they buy? How do they use the product or service? How frequently do they buy? How rapidly is the product used up? Are there buying trends in the product category? Answering such questions requires us to define and describe the consumer.

Definitions of consumers are drawn in two distinct ways, demographically and psychographically. Demographics are hard measurable facts about a consumer such as income, education, age, sex, geographic location, urbanization, and occupation. Psychographic factors make up the person's life style. Some consumers, for example, put great emphasis on comfort; they spend a disproportionate amount of their income purchasing things that provide comfort. Then there are frugal persons, who prefer to shop thoroughly before a purchase and who pride themselves on thrifty, sound buying habits. Each group represents a type of life style. The components are the psychographics, which make up the total person.

Demographics and psychographics are equally important in consumer analysis. Demographics normally receive more emphasis simply because they are easier to measure and more closely related to media planning and purchase. Psychographics, however, are becoming increasingly important as less personal income is spent on the necessities of life.

Two advertising theories related to consumer analysis have gained widespread acceptance in the past few years. First is the "heavy-half" concept developed by Dik Twedt, which states that, in most product categories, a small percentage of the buyers of a product consume a disproportionate share of the total amount sold.[12] Studies have shown, for example, that about one-quarter of households account for 80 percent of all purchases of dog food and instant coffee.[13] If the advertiser could reach this "heavy half," sales might be increased. Increasing emphasis is being placed on locating and defining the heavy-user segment of a market for all types of products.

The second theory is that of the "evoked set of brands." This concept, based on a psychological approach by James J. Gibson,[14] suggests that, in a market of parity products, consumers usually have several brands they regard as acceptable in quality and appeal. Rather than seeking out a single brand, therefore, they make a choice among several brands. Consumers are willing to switch and substitute among this "evoked set of brands" according to minor differences, such as small price fluctuations and availability. If a product can be included in the consumer's acceptable set of brands, a much better chance of the brand being selected exists than if it were not in the "evoked set."

While other approaches and concepts of consumer behavior have been or are used to define markets, demographics and psychographics are the primary tools used by most campaign planners to identify target markets.

The market analysis

Market analysis consists of identifying the marketplace for a product. What is needed is information on the general retail category in which the product or service competes. This is not as simply defined as might be expected. It is easy to assume, for example, that a resort travel destination such as Hawaii competes against other destinations like Florida, the Caribbean Islands, and the Mediterranean. Taking a broader view, however, one might consider Hawaii competing not just against other destinations but also in the total recreation market. Membership in a local tennis club, therefore, might be just as strong competition for the consumer dollar as another resort destination. Taking the example a step further, the competition Hawaii faces is actually for discretionary consumer dollars. Competition for a resort destination may then also be a sailboat, an addition to the house, or even whether to have Junior's teeth straightened. To properly define the competition for a product or service, we must look at the broad consumer expenditure categories rather than the narrowly defined fields of direct competition.

Once the basic field of competition is defined, exactly how the product or service being investigated fits into that category must be determined. This analysis includes such areas as value of the market, sales trends of the category, actual direct share of market, distribution, market potential for the category and the product, regional or other geographic differences in product usage or sales and market share of the product.

Comparisons or evaluations of markets and products are often expressed in terms of a category-development index (CDI) or a brand-development index (BDI). Another often-used index is the all-commodity volume (ACV). These give convenient numbers to help in identifying the best markets or the proportion percentage of distribution for individual products or services.

All-commodity volume (ACV) stands for the total amount of sales in a given category. For products sold in food stores, for example, sales of all food stores would comprise the all-commodity volume. Because a small number of food stores often generate a large share of total food store sales, it is possible to achieve a high percentage of distribution of the ACV in a disproportionately small number of stores. Let's assume that total sales of canned tuna fish in Tulsa are 2,000 cans per month. That would comprise the all-commodity volume (ACV), or the total number of cans of tuna sold. Let's further assume that the sales by chain by month were as follows:

Chain	Number of Stores	Number of Cans of Tuna Sold	Percent of ACV
A	12	850	42.5
B	16	420	21.0
C	19	180	9.0
D	23	154	7.7
E	4	103	5.2
All others	116	293	14.6
Total	190	2,000	100.0

The ACV is 2,000 cans of tuna fish sold each month. Yet, these sales are not equally divided among the chains in the market nor among the individual stores. For example, Chain A has only 12 stores, yet sells 850 cans of tuna per month, an average of 70.8 cans per store per month. On the other hand, Chain D has 23 stores and sells 154 cans per month, or an average of 6.7 cans per store per month. On a store-by-store basis, sales are not equally divided. Also, by obtaining distribution in Chains A and B, whose 28 stores account for only 14.8 percent of the 190 stores in the market, an advertiser would have distribution in stores doing 63.5 percent of the ACV. This instance is not at all unusual. In some product categories, 60 percent or more ACV distribution can be achieved in less than 30 percent of the retail outlets across the country.

Category- and brand-development indices are calculated in a similar manner. For the CDI, total sales of the category may be indexed against sales for a certain geographic region or type of store. In a product category such as soft-drink mixes, for example, the category development index may be quite high in the Midwest, say, 130 (Index = 100), while somewhat lower in the Southwest, e.g., 89 based on the percentage of total sales occurring in each geographic region.

The brand-development index is the comparison of brand sales indexed against total product sales calculated on a geographic or other basis. In the above example, Brand A might have a brand-development index of 125 in the Southwest, indicating that sales are very good in that region. This, however, would be offset to a certain extent because the CDI for that area is rather low. The use of these shorthand indices helps to better identify the present sales or potential market for a brand or category. They are widely used by commercial research organizations.

A major factor in any market analysis is the sales trend for the category or brand. One cannot simply look at sales for the last year or even the year before. Five-year trends should be investigated because frequently there are wide fluctuations in the marketplace in one- or two-year periods. Trend lines are especially important for products that have shown consistent growth or decline for a number of years. Being able to spot a trend can often be very helpful in planning the campaign.

The product analysis

The product analysis is exactly what it appears to be, a look at the product and its component parts. Sandage and Fryburger suggest that the product analysis should consist of a review of the product in terms of its uses, packaging, quality, price, unit of sale, brand image, distribution, positioning, and product life cycle.[15] There are probably other factors which should be investigated depending on the product and its construction, manufacturing, and distribution. The primary consideration is how the product fits into the present marketplace and how it relates to competition.

Two areas of product analysis deserve more discussion because they have been widely used and sometimes misused. First is the concept of product quality and product image. This is directly related to the second, positioning.

It appears that advertisers often are not willing to give their competition sufficient credit for developing a product which, although perhaps technically inferior, has large consumer appeal. Advertisers, for example, sometimes evaluate competitive products on the basis of manufacturing advantages or internal qualities. The position is, "We're better than our competition because our formula includes 15 percent of ingredient J where our primary competitor's product has only 5 percent." Unfortunately, if this product difference isn't immediately perceivable or doesn't offer an important benefit to the consumer, the advertiser may be making a false assumption about product quality. The product difference may be important from the manufacturing standpoint but not from the consumer's perspective. It is crucial, therefore, to evaluate the product not just from a technical standpoint but from how the consumer perceives the product quality or difference. This, then, leads into the other major area of product analysis, positioning.

Originally proposed by Jack Trout and Al Ries[16], the concept of positioning has undergone a number of changes over the years. Positioning is now generally regarded as how the particular product is perceived by the consumer. Product positioning often is accomplished through advertising. In other instances, the consumer positions the brand based on experience, disregarding what the advertiser says about it. In either case, the result is the same. The product oc-

cupies a certain niche in the consumer's mind. Advertising must function within this positioning framework, or the advertiser must attempt to reposition the product in a way the campaign planner believes would provide a better selling opportunity. Before the decision is made on how a product will be positioned, the present market position of the brand in the mind of the consumer must be determined. That determination usually is made in a product analysis.

When the consumer, market, and product analyses have been completed, the questions to be answered should be clear. Now it is time to start gathering the data. That leads us directly to the research study.

How to get the information

Having an idea of the information needed, from the consumer, market, and product analyses, however, does not necessarily solve the research problem. Just as in most other advertising and marketing operations, a successful research study starts with a plan.

Planning the research study

There are as many ways to develop a research plan as there are marketing and advertising researchers. Each tends to use a structure or outline that works best for him. Two popular research study outlines are described below. These are followed by a plan which we recommend.

Kotler's approach is brief.[17] Note, however, the assumption is made that field work will be necessary and that the information is assumed not to be available.

1. Problem definition
2. Research design
3. Field work
4. Data analysis
5. Report preparation

Dorothy Cohen suggests a much more comprehensive approach:[18]

1. Recognize and define the research problem.
2. Make exploratory investigations of all major aspects of the problem.
3. Formulate the appropriate research design.
4. Determine the adequacy of the available (secondary) data from either internal or external sources.
5. Specify the sources and methods of gathering the needed primary data through observation, experimentation, or survey research.
6. Design the questionnaires or other forms for securing the needed data.
7. Use sampling to obtain the data from the entire defined population through either probability or nonprobability approaches.
8. Carry out the field investigation to obtain the data.
9. Edit the returned data-collection forms and tabulate the results.
10. Make a statistical analysis of the results.

11. Interpret the meaning of the data in terms of the problem and the decisions necessary for its solution.
12. Present the findings to those who require the research data.

While the proposed research outlines have their advantages and, in some cases, disadvantages, we recommend that the following format be followed. It is management oriented and has been designed specifically for the development of information to be used in the advertising campaign plan.

1. Define the problem
2. Specifically, define how research can help with the problem:
   (a) Data or particular information (e.g., target market, creative direction, message design) needed to solve the problem
   (b) Impact on the advertiser to obtain or use research
3. Project the form in which the material will be presented.
4. Determine the additional information necessary.
5. List the alternative methods available to obtain the needed information and select the most appropriate:
   (a) Secondary research
   (b) Primary research
6. Estimate the cost of each form of research and weigh the cost of each against the potential value.
7. Develop the study plan.

While this research outline contains many of the same approaches suggested by others, it confines the research project to the problems encountered in developing material needed for the advertising campaign.

Information is valuable but can sometimes become too costly. The cost-benefit relationship between precise information must be weighed against the cost of obtaining that precision. For example, it is unusual for advertisers to use a strict probability sample in an advertising research study. The costs outweigh the benefits. Thus, the tradeoff between the ideal and the practical comes into play.

Defining the research problem

Whatever research plan is used, the first step is to develop a concise statement of the research problem. Too often, research projects ask more questions than they answer. When this occurs, the root of the difficulty is often the lack of a clear definition of the problem and a failure to confine the research to solving that problem. Boyd, Westfall, and Stasch suggest that research objectives be put in written form, using the following steps:

The researchers should determine: (1) who the decision makers are, the environment in which they operate, and the resources they command; (2) the objectives or goals they hope to attain (expressed in measurable terms); (3) the possible courses of action "available" for solving the problem; and (4) the consequences of each of the alternative courses of action. In short, the researchers must first attempt to answer the questions, "What is the purpose of this study?" and "Why is the study being undertaken?" If these questions are not properly answered at the outset, the project may very well be directed at vague goals with the probable result that the collected data will be inadequate for the manager's purposes.[19]

Three elements make up a good research problem statement:

1. The information to be gathered must be measurable.
2. It must be relevant to the problem.
3. The various pieces of information or knowledge to be gained must be related.

For example, the following research problem statement clearly and concisely sums up the needed research.

Sales of the 20 oz. size of Brand M have declined 10 percent in the past six months. Is the decline in sales due to a decline in the total category, the package size, or are sales being lost to another brand? If sales are being lost to another brand, which is it and why?

This research problem is measurable, the questions asked are relevant to the problem, and the information requested is directly related.

Two basic sources of information are used in most research studies, secondary and primary. First, let's take a brief look at each type of information. Later sections in this chapter will cover the techniques for gathering the information.

What is secondary research?

Secondary research is developed from information previously gathered by another person or organization. Secondary research is usually divided into two forms of information or materials—internal and external.

Internal information is that which is available within the company, such as sales records, shipments, and profit-and-loss statements. External information is that gathered and published in some form by other sources. This might consist of government-issued materials, such as census data, or information published by chambers of commerce and banks which give broad, general information on a topic. Ordinarily, secondary data were not gathered specifically to answer the questions posed by the researcher. Extrapolation of the data, therefore, or the combining of information from several sources is usually required.

Primary research

Primary research information is original data gathered specifically to solve a research question. Four general types of primary research are exploratory (normally used to better define a problem); experimental (conducted under laboratory conditions in which a cause-and-effect relationship is sought); descriptive (the most widely used in advertising campaign development), and tracking, or performance evaluation. The last type usually is used to evaluate the effects of the campaign. It is discussed in more detail in chapter 11. Primary research data may be gathered either by observation or by survey.

In observation research, consumers or users are observed as they shop, purchase, or otherwise are involved with the product under study. Survey research entails questioning a number of consumers about the specific problem.

Secondary research: the hows, whys, and wheres

While secondary research information is usually the least expensive to obtain, the results often are not available in usable form. Secondary research is generally used to answer broad, general market questions, such as size, scope, location, and trends for a particular product category. Questions that are brand specific or that indicate how consumers feel about products or other attitudinal questions usually can't be answered through secondary research. Also, secondary data is historical; it tells only what has happened in the past. This creates a major problem, particularly when information is sorely out-of-date.

Getting and using internal secondary data

One of the major sources—and often one of the least used—is the internal records of the manufacturer or advertiser. Most companies have large sources of data available. Yet, because such data are not retained in a form which is readily usable, it is often neglected.

Most internal secondary data are controlled either by the sales department, such as sales records, sales reports, and customer records, or by the accounting department in such forms as cost of materials, invoices, and operating statements. The key to obtaining internal secondary data is to know exactly what is needed and to be able to explain that need to the proper person in the records departments. If the needed information can be adequately described, it can usually be obtained.

Getting and using external secondary data

Boyd, Westfall, and Stasch divide external secondary data into four classes: census and registration data; individual project reports publicly available through books, encyclopedias, periodicals, monographs, and bulletins; data collected for sale; and miscellaneous data.[20]

The federal, state, and local governments are particularly good sources of data on almost any subject. The federal government publishes information through the census bureau on such topics as population, housing, retail trade, wholesale trade, service industries, manufacturers, agriculture, and transportation. In addition, states also publish census data on such factors as population, retail sales, income levels, and employment. Moreover, even cities and counties issue census data on population trends and projections, income, economic and planning studies, traffic counts, and demographic factors. Virtually any large library can provide most types of census data. Because new census material is constantly being published, a thorough study of existing information is suggested before additional research is undertaken.

Secondary data on individual projects may come from a multitude of sources, such as the federal, state, and local governments, banks, foundations, trade associations, chambers of commerce, publishing companies, and foundations, to mention just a few. The major problem in using data of this sort is locating it initially and then determining its accuracy. Remember, information other than that collected by the government must have been gathered for a purpose and funded by an organization. Care should be taken in analyzing the data-gathering method, sample size, and age of the information when it is being used for a research base. Boyd, Westfall, and Stasch offer an excellent list of sources of this information.[21] Additional sources are available at most libraries or through various trade organizations.

Commercial information sources are quite extensive. For example, A. C. Nielsen Company, Audits & Surveys, and Selling Areas-Marketing, Inc. (SAMI) provide basic information on consumer-product stocking in retail stores and movement through these stores. Other groups such as Marketing Research Corporation of America (MRCA), National Purchase Diary Panel, Inc. (NPD), and National Family Opinion (NFO) provide panel or other consumer information about product usage.

The *Nielsen Retail Index* covers most of the products sold through food and drugstores. Through a process of auditing selected stores, estimates are made of such things as the amount of product stocked, the number of out-of-stocks, estimated movement at retail, and number of turns. Audits & Surveys provides the same type of information for several types of stores on a custom research basis. Selling Areas-Marketing, Inc., provides basic information on warehouse withdrawals by food stores. By knowing warehouse withdrawals, one can draw inferences on retail movement.

NPD, MRCA, and NFO primarily are panel

organizations made up of consumers who keep records on purchases and product usage or who agree to test new products. The panels are carefully selected to be representative of the total population, and projected results are considered fairly reliable.

The other major source of consumer information is Simmons Market Research Bureau which has combined Target Group Index and W. R. Simmons and Associates. This group uses large-sample survey techniques to gather data. In addition to gathering data on media usage, Simmons compiles information on product categories used, amounts, and brands. From the demographic data derived from the sample, tables are prepared which show the percentage of users by demographic categories such as age, sex, income, geographic region, media usage, and heavy vs. light users. Thus, from this information, a fairly complete profile of a product category or a brand can be developed. The research service attempts to gather some psychographic data as well. Such information is quite limited. It is derived essentially from the interviewed person's view of him- or herself, using such broad-range descriptions as innovative, brave, and economical.

All the firms mentioned and the data they gather are provided on a subscription basis. The service is often regarded as custom research. Unless a manufacturer or an agency subscribes to the service or agrees to purchase the information, it is usually not available to the campaign planner. If the campaign is large enough it is often less expensive to purchase existing data from these sources rather than conducting primary research.

Miscellaneous secondary data can come from almost any source. Many trade journals conduct surveys and gather information for use in their sales presentations. Trade associations are also a rich source of information, although much of their material is developed with a built-in bias because of specialized interest. Other commercial organizations can and do conduct secondary research studies for a fee. They are usually listed in the telephone directory or are announced in trade journals. Scanning any current marketing research text or making inquiries at the library will turn up leads on other sources of information.

Secondary research is usually not too expensive to obtain. Unfortunately, much of the material tends to be out-of-date by the time it is published or often is based on questionable research methodology or sampling techniques.

Primary research: a how-to-do-it guide

Primary research is that which is original and carried out to gather specific information about the problem being studied. Primary research may take many forms,

but there are two basic types: qualitative, or exploratory; and quantitative, or conclusive.

Qualitative or exploratory research

Qualitative research is undertaken when the information needed is to be directional or diagnostic. Such research is usually done with fairly small groups of people, and the sampling is conducted on a quota or availability basis.

Definitive conclusions cannot be drawn from qualitative or exploratory research. Instead, an attempt is made to get a general impression of the market, the consumer, or the product. Two types of qualitative research can be quite helpful in the exploratory stages of the campaign. These are intensive data gathering and the use of "projective" techniques.

Intensive data gathering. The informal approach consists of gathering information or data through discussions with interested groups or individuals such as consumers, prospects, and retailers who have knowledge about the product or service. An excellent source of information is often the sales force who are in direct contact with consumers and resellers.

The formal approach consists of a more systematic method of data gathering such as conducting focus groups or doing individual "depth interviews."

In the focus-group method, eight to twelve people, familiar with the problem, the product, or the market, are brought together to discuss in detail such topics as the product category, the specific brand, uses, and methods of sale. Group interaction usually generates a great deal of insight into the research problem and can lead to more detailed methods of information gathering.

An alternative intensive data-gathering approach is the "depth interview." Interviews are conducted in the same way as those in a focus group, except they are done on an individual basis. Respondents are asked to discuss the product, the problem, or the situation. Through asking carefully structured questions, the interviewer tries to probe the deeper feelings of the respondent rather than simply expose surface opinions, which tend to be readily offered.

Both the focus-group and depth interviews are best carried out by a trained researcher. Untrained persons may obtain general information through focus-group discussion, but errors may creep in or the group may be inadvertently led to a false conclusion unless the person directing the questioning or analyzing the data has had adequate previous experience with this form of data gathering.

Projective techniques. Many forms of projective techniques may be used. All have the same basis: The person being interviewed is asked to involve him- or herself in a situation or experience in which he or she "projects" feelings and experiences about the product, brand, or problem set up by the interviewer. The assumption in these projective techniques is that the person being interviewed, by involving him- or herself in a situation, will disclose underlying feelings, thoughts, and desires about the problem or situation that would not otherwise be revealed in direct questioning.

Projective research projects can take many forms, from word association to role playing to cartoon completion to Thematic Apperception Tests. Only skilled, experienced researchers are capable of developing successful projective research instruments. If this methodology is contemplated, a commercial research organization should be consulted.

Qualitative or exploratory research is used by the advertising campaign planner in the first stages of plan development. Qualitative research is generally inexpensive, since it can be done with small numbers of consumers, with selection based on a quota or availability sample. This type of research is often conducted to determine general trends or to identify areas that need further exploration.

Qualitative research may be sufficient to answer the campaign planner's questions. The information gathered, however, because of the limited sampling methodology, is subject to wide variations in reliability and validity. If qualitative primary research is to be used, this should be so stated in the campaign plan.

Quantitative research

Quantitative research is usually primary research. The results can be projected to various portions of the marketing universe, and the laws of statistical probability can be applied to lend support to or cause rejection of the findings. Boyd, Westfall, and Stasch prefer to use the term "exploratory and conclusive research" as opposed to "qualitative and quantitative research." The meanings, however, appear to be the same. The authorities also subdivide "conclusive research" into "descriptive" and "experimentation."[22]

Boyd, Westfall, and Stasch differentiate between exploratory (qualitative) and descriptive (quantitative) studies as follows:

Descriptive studies differ from exploratory studies in the rigor with which they are designed. Exploratory studies are characterized by flexibility, while descriptive studies attempt to obtain a complete and accurate description of a situation. Formal design is required to ensure that the description covers all phases desired. Precise statement of the problem indicates what information is required. The study must then be designed to provide for the collection of this information. Unless the study design provides specified methods for selecting the sources of information (sample design) and for collecting the data from these sources, the information obtained may be inaccurate or inappropriate.

Descriptive data are commonly used as direct bases for marketing decisions. After analyzing the data, the investigators attempt to predict the result of certain actions.[23]

Thus, we see that qualitative or exploratory research is used primarily to give direction to the advertising campaign planner, while quantitative, conclusive, or descriptive research is used in choosing between alternatives or in decision-making.

Quantitative or descriptive research is also distinguished by the method in which the data is gathered. The three types are observation, experimentation, and survey. Because the first and second are not widely used in advertising campaign planning, only a brief overview will be given. More emphasis will be placed on survey research methodology.

Observation. In quantitative research, the activities or habits of persons in the marketplace are observed either personally or through some mechanical means. However, because historical data are gathered according to what the given person was observed doing or had done in the past, predictions of what that person might do in the future are difficult to make.

Another form of observation is the so-called pantry check made in consumers' homes. Pantries are checked to determine the various brands that have been purchased and the amount of product on hand. By correlating this observed information with the demographic characteristics of the respondents, the present users (or general target market) for the product can be identified.

Observation is also used by several commercial research organizations such as Nielsen or Audits & Surveys. These groups visit retail outlets and make shelf audits of products. They might, for example, gather data on what products are being stocked, what brands are available, what sizes are available, prices, and out-of-stock. This information is used by the advertiser to determine his or her position in the marketplace.

Observation can be helpful to the advertising campaign planner, but it is usually quite expensive since a large number of observations are required for a conclusion.

Experimentation. This is a type of laboratory or otherwise controlled research in which a cause-and-effect relationship is sought. Strict controls are employed so that the variable which causes the effect can be identified. Experimentation is used only on a selective basis; since it is very difficult to control all marketing variables.

The most common form of experimental research in advertising occurs in the test market for new products or in new advertising campaigns. Here, two or more individual markets are matched as closely as possible according to such marketing variables as population and income. Using these matched markets, an advertising campaign is run in one market (or set of markets) and not in the others, and the results are observed. An alternative method is to use differing advertising campaigns in a given set or sets of markets and to observe the differences that result. A third method is to use media weight tests. Here, varying levels of media promotion are used in the matched test markets. Again, because other variables are held as nearly constant as possible, the influence of the media can be evaluated in terms of such effects as attitude changes and awareness.

Experimentation, particularly in advertising, is an expensive method of obtaining information, since the effects may not be immediate. It is widely used for new products, however, e.g., to test the viability of the product on a small scale, or to test various advertising or marketing alternatives prior to a major national introduction.

Survey. Survey research is the most common method of primary research data gathering. As the name implies, data are obtained through a survey of present or prospective consumers of the product or service. The usual goal is to obtain information necessary to develop a profile of the target audience or to determine the most effective advertising message to be used.

Survey research methodologies differ according to the method of data gathering employed. The most common forms are personal interviews, mail surveys, consumer panels, and telephone interviews.

PERSONAL INTERVIEWS. Personal interviewing may take many forms ranging from traditional door-to-door canvassing to intercepts in shopping malls and laundromats or outside food and drugstores. The key to success in personal interviewing is to find situations in which respondents have the time available to answer questions. The usual data-gathering form is a series of questions, scales, evaluations, or other devices which allow the respondent to express his or her ideas, concerns, or opinions. Interviews in the home may last one hour or more, while interviews with persons who are interrupted while shopping, such as in a mall intercept, must be confined to five or ten minutes. There is literally no limit to the type of data that can be gathered. In each case, the result depends on the kind of information desired and the situation in which the interview occurs.

The primary advantages of the personal interview are the opportunities to probe, to ask follow-up questions and to use examples or samples of the product or advertising material. The major disadvantages are the extremely high cost of personnel and diminishing cooperation, particularly in door-to-door calls.

MAIL. Much useful information can be gathered through a mail survey. Respondents tend to give more complete answers since the interview is relatively anonymous. Respondents also can indicate answers to questions which might not be readily available in a personal or telephone interview. The questionnaire form should be made as easy as possible to follow with primarily closed-end questions. The questionnaire may be any length and may cover almost any subject.

Data gathering by means of the mail questionnaire is relatively inexpensive. The main costs are for the mailing list, the questionnaire form, and postage. A nominal reward is sometimes included in a direct mail questionnaire to encourage response.

Mail questionnaires ordinarily have a fairly low return rate. A 30 to 40 percent response to a mail questionnaire is considered normal. Obtaining a return of 60 to 70 percent is exceptional. All results, however, depend on the quality of the questions and mailing lists.

CONSUMER PANELS. Pre-formed or existing panels of consumers have long been used for research data gathering. A number of commercial panels offer services that may be purchased. One example is National Family Opinions, Inc. (NFO).

Data gathering from consumer panels has the same disadvantage as do mail surveys in terms of time required. Response rates, however, often reach near 100 percent because the panels are established groups and are rewarded for participation. The representativeness of panels may be questionable because they answer many research questions during the course of of year.

The major advantage of panel data gathering is that more complete and more detailed information is obtained. The panel is accustomed to furnishing information through questionnaires and tends to be quite cooperative. Based on total expenditure, cost per response is usually lower than in most other types of interviews.

TELEPHONE INTERVIEWS. An increasingly important method of data gathering is use of the telephone. With the advent of Wide Area Telephone Service (WATS) lines, interviewing throughout the country can now be done from a central location which provides complete control over the interview. Costs of WATS line interviews are relatively low compared to other forms of data collection, and when time for data gathering is considered, this is probably the lowest cost of all research methods.

Telephone data-gathering usage has increased as samples have been improved. Originally, telephone samples were limited to persons whose names were listed in telephone directories. A new system of random digit dialing now makes all connected telephones part of the sample frame, and every telephone home is a potential respondent, including the approximately 20 percent or more unlisted numbers.

Telephone interviews are excellent for obtaining a relatively small amount of information from a large number of people. Because contact is by voice, only certain types of questions may be asked. Questions that require visuals or thorough understanding of a complex question are not practical. A telephone interview may last 10 to 15 minutes with many closed-end questions, although some questionnaire callers have kept people on the line for a half-hour or more. Surprisingly, telephone respondents may provide information they would not ordinarily give in a personal interview. Apparently, the telephone offers a certain amount of anonymity.

The major advantages of telephone interviews are low cost, a complete sample frame, the ability to call any geographic area (with WATS lines), and very rapid data gathering and reporting. Moreover, the telephone is the only practical method of conducting a coincidental survey, a study which is conducted at the same time the advertising is appearing.

Telephone surveys do have disadvantages, however. Answers usually must be shorter and not as in-depth as those obtained through other methods. There is no opportunity to use props or other materials which might help explain the questions or to display package designs, advertisements, or other items which the subject must see to be able to respond. Despite these disadvantages, more emphasis will likely be placed on telephone-data gathering, particularly as the costs of personal interviewing increase.

Sampling for data gathering

The success of any research design depends on the sample selected for data gathering. The major objective is to make sure that respondents to be interviewed are representative of the entire target population. It is important to determine who is to be sampled, the procedure to be used for selection of the sample, and the size of the sample.

Who is in the sample? Persons to be interviewed must be representative of the target population. If you want to learn about cat food, owners of cats should be interviewed. In advertising and marketing research, this is done through screening questions such as, "Do you or your family own a cat?" Those who do not have a cat would not be included in the study; they would automatically be screened out of the sample.

The research sampling frame for an advertising campaign study can be easily defined. It may be as broad as "all women 18 to 49 years of age with children in the home under 12 years of age," or it might be as restrictive as "those persons owning canaries in the state of Idaho." The sampling frame depends on the type of specific data to be gathered and a general idea of the information sought. A common definition used as a sample frame is "present users of a product category or brand."

The key point in any sampling plan is to state clearly and concisely in advance the sample universe. If this is done, no confusion will arise as to whether an individual selected for interviewing is qualified.

Sample selection. There are two types of sampling techniques. Probability samples are those in which every known unit in the universe has an equal probability of being selected for the research. For example, if the universe were defined as drugstores in the city of Dallas with sales in excess of $1,000,000 annually, a complete list of potential stores could be developed from various sources such as tax receipts and licenses. Knowing the names and locations of all the drugstores in Dallas which fit the qualifications makes possible the development of a probability sample such that each store has an equal chance of being selected.

Probability samples are used when the number of units to be measured is fairly small; a complete list of the items in the universe exists (such as all drugstores in Dallas); the cost per interview depends on the location of the items; the only information available on the universe is the list of items; and the need exists for precisely measuring the risk of sample error. Because of these conditions, the use of probability sampling in advertising and marketing research is quite limited unless the universe can be very precisely defined.

A non-probability sample does not provide every unit in the universe with an equal or known chance of being included in the sample frame. Take the requirement that only Dallas drugstores doing over $1,000,000 in sales are to be included. The restrictions might be relaxed. In the new study, any drugstore in North Texas stocking the product category is to be included in the sample frame. Also, the sampling is to be done on the basis of availability and convenience for the interviewer. This would be a nonprobability sample, since all stores did not have an equal opportunity to be selected.

Nonprobability samples are widely used in marketing and advertising research because, in many categories, no listing of the complete universe is available. Such samples are also used when the costs for a true probability sample are prohibitive (a) because of geographic dispersion, (b) when only a general estimate of the data is needed, (c) when there is a possibility of obtaining a larger sample with a decrease in the magnitude of error, (d) when the nature and size of the bias can be estimated fairly accurately.

Most advertising and marketing research studies are of the nonprobability type. For example, we don't really know the true universe (or number) of users of our product or competitive products. The dispersion of product users is normally great, particularly for those products sold on a national basis. We can estimate our error based on sample size, and the amount of bias can also be determined.[25] The primary reason for nonprobability sampling in advertising and marketing research is simply the cost of obtaining data. Once again, the advertising campaign planner is faced with the cost-benefit tradeoff. Planners are usually willing to trade some validity and reliability to avoid the large costs entailed in developing a true probability sample.

Sample size. One of the most difficult tasks in planning or evaluating primary research is determining the sample size required to achieve a given level of confidence. Statistical techniques are available for developing confidence levels of probability samples. The problem becomes more complex with nonprobability studies because the true universe is often unknown. Thus, estimating the size for a nonprobability sample becomes a difficult problem.

A number of rules of thumb exist for determining sample sizes which are helpful to the advertising campaign planner. While they lack precision, such rules do give general approximations of sample sizes for various types of nonprobability studies. In data gathering such as depth interviews or focus groups, for example, most major ideas or answers concerning a product or service will be verbalized after the first 30 or so persons have been interviewed, because most consumers have the same general ideas about various products and services. Therefore, when about 30 respondents have answered, repetition of the major ideas begins to mount rapidly. Similarly, interviews with 100 to 200 users of products or services, given a standard questionnaire in a limited geographic area, will tend to indicate the general attitudes of the population. After 100 interviews, reliability tends to mount as more and more respondents give the same answers to the questions being asked. For a regional study covering several cities or a few states, a sample of 300 to 400 qualified respondents is normally considered to be sufficient. A sample of 1,000 to 1,200 qualified consumers, selected according to a probability sample, will generally reflect the opinions and feelings of the national population on most subjects. While these sample sizes are only estimates, they have been proved to the extent that only in unusual circumstances will major errors occur.

Problems. Four major problems are usually encountered with sample respondents: not-at-home, refusals, respondent bias, and interviewer bias.

Not-at-home and refusals create more problems in a probability sample than in a nonprobability one. For a group to constitute a true probability sample, the actual persons selected in advance must be interviewed. Obviously this is not always possible. Steps should be taken, therefore, to select a large enough original sample so that substitutions for nonrespondents can be made without destroying the representative makeup of the original sample.

The biases of both the respondent and interviewer are most difficult to control. Respondent bias usually appears when the person is truly anxious to assist the interviewer; the respondent often gives answers that do not reflect his or her true feelings. In some cases, respondents, in an attempt to appear knowledgeable, give answers to questions on which they have no information.

Interviewer bias usually comes about when the interviewer, through either the question itself or the manner in which it is asked, indicates the type of answer which would be most acceptable or is generally regarded as correct. The advertising campaign planner should be aware of the bias problem, particularly if the sample is small, or if the interviewers are not professionally trained, or if the interviewers or respondents have strong feelings about the particular subject under study.

Conducting a consumer research study

Up to this point, we have looked at research in fairly broad terms. The question now, if one is faced with the need for a research study, is what to do. The following sections deal specifically with how to conduct or direct your own research study. We start with a review of the steps in conducting a consumer survey.

Steps in conducting a consumer survey

1. Develop a list of specific survey objectives. Exactly what do you want to learn?
2. Project a research timetable. How long will it take to get the information? Is the time span practical for your needs?
3. Determine the method of sampling. Should you use a probability or nonprobability sample? How precise should the results be? What level of error can you accept in a tradeoff with costs?
4. Develop the questionnaire. (See details in the following section.)
5. Determine the sampling frame. In other words, on what basis will the sample be selected?

Telephone directory? Subscriber list? Service station owners? Another basis?

6. Develop the sample. Be sure that, if a probability sample is chosen, you encompass the entire universe. If nonprobability, what is the basis on which you select the respondents?

7. Do the field work. In some instances, if you are directing the study, your job may include hiring, training, and supervising the field force or the group that will gather the data.

8. Verify the field work. Be sure arrangements are made for verification of a certain amount of the data gathered from the sample. This step is crucial if the results are to be used for decision making.

9. Tabulate the data.

10. Analyze the results. What are the major findings? Any important new information, or further confirmation of what was suspected?

11. Prepare the report. What form should it take? What charts and graphs should be included?

12. Present the survey results. To whom will the material be presented? How formal will the presentation be?

As this outline shows, several factors govern the development and implementation of a consumer survey. Many decisions will be tempered by the management level for whom the research is being prepared. If it is done for internal use, some of the steps can be deleted or condensed. For the sake of completeness, you should use this outline. Following it with each study you make will ensure that no major steps have been missed in accomplishing the research.

Developing an effective questionnaire

One of the major frustrations of inexperienced market researchers is the development of a sound questionnaire. Too often the questionnaire is prepared, the survey is started, and about half-way through the third or fourth interview, it becomes apparent that respondents don't understand what information is being sought. Even worse is the case where the survey is completed and it is then learned that an important piece of information was inadvertently left out. In either case, the problem usually lies with the questionnaire.

Entire books have been written about how to develop questionnaires. The following is simply a checklist of those things which are often overlooked or neglected by beginning researchers.

1. Explain the research objectives. Be sure the reason for the study is clear. Listing the objectives helps to prevent the inclusion of extraneous materials or questions that "would be interesting to know" but are not germane to the actual study.

2. Write the actual points to be determined by the questionnaire. Again, be sure the description of the desired information is clear and concise. Avoid long questionnaires that tax the patience of the respondent. When this happens, careless or flip answers often result, or the respondent finds reasons not to answer the questions fully.

3. Break the items to be determined down into specific questions. Be sure the questions are stated in such a way that they are clear to respondents and there is no chance for misunderstanding. Avoid generalities and ambiguous terms.

4. Write a rough draft first. Polish it after you've made all your points.

5. Use a short opening statement. Include your name, the name of your organization, and the broad purpose of the questionnaire.

6. Open with one or two easily answered, interesting, and inoffensive questions. This tends to put the respondent at ease.

7. Structure the questions so they flow logically and easily from one to another. Ask general questions before the more detailed ones.

8. Have as few "closed" questions as possible. Use open-ended questions where possible, although there are some problems with them:

- "Open-ended" questions let the respondent answer whatever comes to mind, but answers are difficult to tabulate.
- Most "open-ended" questions can be closed by providing a list of anticipated answers for the interviewer to check off. This simplifies tabulation.

9. Avoid questions that suggest an answer or that could be considered "leading" questions. Let the respondent answer fully and honestly. Don't use words with strong favorable or unfavorable connotations. They tend to bias results.

10. Make the questions easy to answer. Don't use long, detailed questionnaires which may confuse the respondent.

11. When possible, include a few questions which will serve as a cross-check on earlier answers. This aids in ensuring validity.

12. Put the demographic questions (e.g., age, income, education) and other personal questions at the end of the questionnaire.

13. Pretest the questionnaire to get out the bugs. Your primary concern is to make sure the questions are being interpreted as intended and that all information being sought is included. Twenty to 30 persons in the proposed respondent group are usually a sufficient sample for a pretest.

Yes, telephone surveys are different

Another major form of research gathering is by telephone interview. While telephone studies are similar, they are not quite the same as a personal interview questionnaire.

Telephone surveys can provide quick, fairly complete information for advertising campaign planning. The data gathered should be regarded as general confirmation of exploratory or directional information and can be most helpful. Below is a general outline of the steps to be used in developing a telephone survey in a specific market.

1. Prepare the questionnaire.
   a. The telephone survey limits the type of questions that may be asked. People cannot see what you are talking about. Your questions must be related to things they know about or about which they already have opinions.
   b. Sometimes people are reluctant to give personal information over the telephone. Keep your questions as general as possible.
2. Determine the sample size.
   a. Reliability, from a statistical standpoint, varies according to what you are measuring. Be sure you know your sample frame. If it is the telephone directory, a probability sample can be developed. If it is something else, recognize it as either a probability or nonprobability sample and proceed accordingly.
   b. If you plan to break down the data (for example, if you are going to compare users and non-users), be sure the sample is large enough for there to be sufficient numbers in the analysis cells for meaningful evaluation.
   c. Generally, 300 to 500 interviews are a sufficient sample for most telephone studies used in advertising campaign planning.
3. Select the telephone numbers to be called.
   a. The simplest way is to estimate the number of telephone numbers needed (generally twice the sample size) and proceed in a systematic way through the telephone directory. For example, if you determine that 800 numbers are needed, and you find that there are 2,400 columns of numbers in the directory, take a number from every third column. Use randomly selected numbers to determine the column and number to be chosen.
   b. Write the number selected on a control sheet.
4. Choose your interviewing hours so as to include nights and weekends. If you want to interview men, most of your interviewing must be done during the evening and weekend hours.

5. Select your interviewers.
   a. If possible, obtain professional interviewers as supervisors. They can assist in the training and help with the work of other, less-experienced persons.
   b. If professional interviewers are not available, train one or two supervisors yourself and let them train the others.
6. Train the interviewers.
   a. Conduct the training sessions with all prospective interviewers.
   b. Review the questionnaire and calling procedure.
   c. Have the interviewers practice on each other.
   d. Don't accept a questionable prospective interviewer. Get another rather than take the chance.
7. Review the work.
   a. It is generally a good idea to review the first day's or first session's interviews. If a problem has developed, it can be spotted immediately.
   b. Verify a certain percentage of all calls made. Call and make sure the interview actually took place or have this done by a supervisor.
8. Establish a procedure for getting the completed forms and control sheets ready for tabulation and analysis.

How much does research cost?

Throughout this chapter, much emphasis has been placed on the cost-benefit relationship of marketing and advertising information. While the time factor can be evaluated fairly accurately, e.g., three weeks can be spared for a research study, more needs to be said about out-of-pocket research costs. Following is a list of approximate cost figures for various types of research studies. These are estimated averages and obviously subject to wide variations. For comparison, the cost of "do-it-yourself" research is also included. The figures are not given to indicate how inexpensively research can be done on your own. They are here simply to give you an idea of the differences. Obviously, professional researchers have many advantages such as experienced interviewers, skilled questionnaire writers, and statistical and analysis experts who have done many studies for all types of organizations, which justify the cost differentials. This comparison is intended primarily to show the student what might be accomplished in an advertising campaign planning situation in which professional research organizations are not available.

Alternative costs: outside firm vs. "do-it-yourself"*

Intercept
500 interviews, 4 or 5 questions, with report:

Outside firm . . . .$2,500–$3,000
Do-it-yourself . . . .$ 350–$ 500

Telephone

500 20-minute interviews, with report:
Outside firm . . . .$4,500–$5,000
Do-it-yourself . . . .$2,000–$2,500

Personal

Would not attempt anything except very easiest program (nonscientific) unless conducted by a reputable research firm.

Mail

500 returns, with report—33% response rate:
Outside firm . . . .$3,750–$4,500
Do-it-yourself . . . .$ 700–$1,000

Exclusive interview

(Talking to business administrators)
20 interviews, with report:
Outside firm . . . .$1,200–$2,400
Do-it-yourself . . . . .Your time

Focus group

One group, 8 to 10 people, with report:
Outside firm . . . .$600–$800
Do-it-yourself $100

*Estimates based on authors' experience in research in several metropolitan markets.

Criteria for evaluation of research

In any type of research, the key question is whether the results will provide solid evidence on which advertising decisions can be based. This is especially true for the advertising campaign planner who may be proposing a new or unique approach. The crucial questions are (a) the soundness of the research, (b) the issues of validity and reliability, and (c) whether the information is germane to the recommendations resulting from analysis of the data.

The Advertising Research Foundation has prepared a guide for evaluating advertising research. The guide's recommendations:

1. Under what conditions was the study made? Problems. Sources of finances. Names of organizations participating. Period of time covered. Date of report. Definition of terms. Questionnaire and instructions to interviewers. Collateral data. Complete statement of methodology.

2. Has the questionnaire been well designed? Dangers of bias. Unreasonable demands on memory. Poor choice of answers. Monotonous questions. Lack of space for answers. Was it pretested?

3. Has the interviewing been adequate and reliably done? Familiarity with prescribed interview pro-

cedure. Training. Maturity. Were spot checks made to ensure accuracy?

4. Has the best sampling plan been followed? Random sample is preferable. Quota sample is more likely to be satisfactory for collecting qualitative rather than quantitative data.

5. Has the sampling plan been fully executed? Substitutions or other variations may destroy validity of data.

6. Is the sample large enough? If a probability sample is properly designed, reliability of results can be determined mathematically. In other samples, it is much more difficult to determine adequacy of sample size.

7. Was there systematic control of editing, coding, and tabulating?

8. Is the interpretation forthright and logical? If one factor is interpreted as cause, all others must be held constant. All basic data underlying interpretations should be shown. Validity of respondents' memory should not be overemphasized. Small differences should not be emphasized. Analysis should be clear and simple.[26]

Limitations

In addition to the question of whether the actual research conducted is reliable and valid, a more basic question is, "What answers can research provide?" Cohen suggests six basic limits to all types of advertising and marketing research:[27]

1. Research, no matter how well conducted or under what circumstances, will not provide precise answers to marketing questions.

2. All research is based on past experience and conducted under certain conditions. If those conditions change—and the marketplace is constantly changing—research results may well change with the conditions. Thus, all research is time-and-situation specific.

3. Research is a business tool, not an answer to all business questions. Research may increase the probability of success. Alternatively, it may help to reduce losses. Doing research to find the answer to the question of why a brand's sales are falling may not give the answer to how to stop the slide. Research may give an indication, though, of how the slide may be reduced.

4. Research is an out-of-pocket expense. Research costs usually are not recoverable. Most research is an investment in the brand or the business. Either way, the advertising campaign planner must recognize research costs as nonrecoverable and regard such costs as an expense against the brand.

5. Research is time consuming. There must be sufficient time in the advertising planning process to allow for the necessary development, conducting, and evaluation of research.

6. Usually, there are limited personnel available for the research task. Persons who have the ability to conduct skilled research are in short supply. Therefore, there are limits as to the amount of research which can be conducted, no matter how strong the desire for information.[27]

Boyd and Westfall warn that management should learn what to expect from research.[28] There are no complete answers to advertising and marketing problems. Because research deals only with past data, projections into the future are hazardous at best. Research in advertising and marketing usually deals with only a part of the existing problem, not all of it.

In spite of all these precautions, the advertising campaign planner must find a basis for making decisions. In nearly all instances, research information should play an important part in providing a sound foundation for the advertising campaign.

Notes

1. American Marketing Association, Committee on Definitions, *Marketing Definitions: A Glossary of Marketing Terms* (Chicago: American Marketing Association, 1963), pp. 16–17.
2. C. H. Sandage and Vernon Fryburger, *Advertising Theory and Practice,* 9th ed. (Homewood, Ill.: Richard D. Irwin, 1975), pp. 153–228.
3. Philip Kotler, *Marketing Management: Analysis, Planning and Controls* (Englewood Cliffs, N. J.: Prentice-Hall, 1976), p. 149.
4. David W. Cravens, Gerald E. Hills, and Robert B. Woodruff, *Marketing Decision Making: Concepts and Strategy* (Homewood, Ill.: Richard D. Irwin, 1976), pp. 26–27.
5. Charles Ramond, *Advertising Research: The State of the Art* (New York: Association of National Advertisers, 1976), pp. 3–4.
6. Kenneth A. Longman, *Advertising* (New York: Harcourt Brace Jovanovich, 1971), pp. 177–82.
7. Ramond, *Advertising Research,* p. 3–4.
8. R. I. J. Tuck and Jill Firth, "Can Research Join in the Creative Process?" in *Market Research to Advertising Strategy and Vice-Versa* (Estoril, Lisbon, Portugal: ESOMAR, 1973), pp. 153–58.
9. Ramond, *Advertising Research,* p. 40.
10. Russell Haley, quoted by Ramond in *Advertising Research,* p. 47.
11. Sandage and Fryburger, *Advertising Theory and Practice,* pp. 153–228.
12. Dik Warren Twedt, "Some Practical Applications of 'Heavy-Half' Theory," in *Proceedings, Tenth Annual Conference* (New York: Advertising Research Foundation, 1964).
13. Norton Garfinkle. "The Marketing Value of Media Audiences—How to Pinpoint Your Prime Prospects," paper read at Association of National Advertisers Workshop, 19 January 1965. Quoted in Sandage and Fryburger, *Advertising Theory and Practice,* p. 187.
14. James J. Gibson. "A Critical Review of the Concept of Set in Contemporary Experimental Psychology," *Psychological Bulletin,* Vol. 38, 1941, pp. 781–817.
15. Sandage and Fryburger. *Advertising Theory and Practice,* pp. 153–228.
16. Jack Trout and Al Ries, *Positioning "Positioning"* (Chicago: Crain Books, 1972).
17. Kotler, *Marketing Management,* p. 428.
18. Dorothy Cohen, *Advertising* (New York: Wiley, 1972), p. 234.
19. Harper W. Boyd Jr., Ralph Westfall, and Stanley F. Stasch, *Marketing Research: Text and Cases,* 4th ed. (Homewood, Ill.: Richard D. Irwin, 1977), p. 205.
20. Ibid., p. 150.
21. Ibid., pp. 153–54.
22. Ibid., pp. 33–58.
23. Ibid., p. 48.
24. Cohen, *Advertising,* pp. 229-51.
25. Ibid., pp. 229-51.
26. *Criteria for Marketing and Advertising Research* (New York: Advertising Research Foundation, 1953).
27. Cohen, *Advertising,* pp. 229-51.
28. Harper W. Boyd Jr., and Ralph Westfall, *Marketing Research: Text and Cases,* 3d ed. (Homewood, Ill.: Richard D. Irwin, 1972), pp. 45-62.

4 Determining Advertising Objectives

Once the problem (or opportunity) facing the brand or company has been defined and verified through research, either primary or secondary, the next steps are determining the advertising objectives and developing the plan. While the plan and objectives appear to be rather straightforward goals, they may become quite complex based on the varying results advertisers expect from a campaign. We start with a brief overview of factors that may affect the advertising plan and objectives and follow with a detailed look at how those objectives may be determined.

The corporation and its marketing: a corporate overview

Many factors influence the development of an advertising plan or the setting of advertising objectives for a brand or company. The important factors are the company philosophy, corporate objectives, and marketing objectives.

The company philosophy

There are two types of companies, production oriented and marketing oriented. The difference is quite dramatic. The marketing-oriented organization views the market from the consumer's standpoint and determines how the consumer's wants may best be met. The production-oriented organization, however, takes the opposite approach—that manufacturing and distribution of products are most important. Production-oriented organizations concentrate their efforts on developing more efficient means of producing or distributing a given product. The production-oriented company takes the view that, "If you build a better mousetrap, the world will beat a path to your door." The marketing-oriented company provides the opportunities and even the path to their product for the consumer to take.

Even in our supposedly enlightened marketing age, many companies in the United States are still production oriented. This orientation is quite evident in the industrial sector and is prevalent among many consumer-product companies which manufacture or process commodity-type goods.

In addition to the marketing or production orientation, corporate executives hold widely differing views on the value of advertising. Some executives believe the success of the firm is a direct result of advertising efforts. Other feel that advertising is conducted simply because "it's something we have to do," or it's a "cost of doing business." While the advertising campaign planner should try to impress management with the value of advertising, successful businesspeople are often reluctant to alter the approaches that have worked for them in the past. Thus, promising a total change in company direction based on a single advertising campaign may create more problems than advertising can possibly solve.

The relative sophistication of company top management also has a direct bearing on the development of advertising objectives. Those firms accustomed to strong consumer advertising campaigns with clearly defined tasks and measurements usually require very complex and detailed advertising objectives. For less-experienced advertisers, objectives may need to be stated in somewhat different terms. The advertising campaign planner should keep the company's advertising philosophy clearly in mind when he or she is developing the advertising plan and identifying the advertising objectives.

Corporate objectives

Over-all corporate objectives are also important in the development of advertising plans. Because corporate objectives vary widely, it is difficult to develop

37

hard and fast rules. General guidelines are available, however, which should be helpful in the developmental stages of the advertising plans and objectives. The following suggestions are presented from the view of a consumer products organization. They may vary for industrial or service firms but should serve as general guidelines.

Sales at a profit. Usually, the overriding objective of any company is to generate sales of its product or service at a profit. While the approaches used may vary widely from a "skimming" to an investment or developmental approach, the major corporate goal normally is to generate a profit which can be either reinvested in the business or returned to stockholders in the form of dividends. Advertising, therefore, is viewed as an expenditure which must return or increase anticipated profits either immediately or over a period of several years. All companies view advertising as a profit-making investment of some type, and this profit factor must be kept in mind when one is developing an advertising plan and setting advertising objectives.

Marketing objectives

A final area for consideration is the marketing objectives of the firm. These objectives usually play the most direct part in the development of the advertising plan and setting of advertising objectives. Five specific areas of the marketing plan appear to have the most influence. They are the type of business the company is in, the marketing strategy, the product life cycle, the competition, and market segmentation.

What business are we in? Many companies fail to recognize the actual business in which they are engaged. While this may sound unrealistic, it is too often true. For example, company management may consider themselves to be in the snowmobile business simply because they manufacture and sell snowmobiles. In more realistic terms, they are in the winter recreation business and may well be in the general competitive area of leisure-time products. As was discussed in chapter 3 under Market Analysis, a study of the entire competitive area must be made, not just the specific, direct competition.

An often-used example to illustrate how a company defines its business is attributed to Charles Revson, founder of Revlon, Inc. When asked what his company sold, Revson, rather than saying perfume, nail polish, lipstick, or any of the myriad of other beauty aids manufactured by the company, said simply, "We sell women hope." Thus, Revson positioned his company not as a cosmetic manufacturer or even a beauty house, but as a producer of products through which women could find potential happiness. Revson recognized the multitude of Revlon competitors striv-

ing for the same available dollars spent on personal-care items. Potential Revlon competition, therefore, came not just from other directly competitive cosmetic manufacturers, but from anyone who promised women a better life.

In setting advertising objectives, the actual business of the company must be defined and the natural and extended competition which it faces must be identified. This is not an easy task, but the advertising campaign planner must recognize the importance of this first step.

What marketing strategy is the brand manager or company employing? In many cases, the marketing strategy being employed by the brand or company is clear-cut and easily identified, while in others, the situation may not be quite so obvious. The firm's marketing strategy position is determined by the market in which it competes, the product areas that top management has decided to pursue, and the reaction to competitive pressure. Cravens, Hills, and Woodruff have identified five marketing strategies widely used by consumer product firms.[1]

BALANCING STRATEGY. The firm seeks to use its marketing resources against a stable, mature market which is normally well defined with established competition. Decision-making uncertainties are usually low, and high priorities are set for market segments in which the firm has a competitive advantage.

Many commodity-type manufacturers and processors such as dairies, bakeries, and sugar companies are typical users of a balancing marketing strategy. For example, consumption of dairy products is fairly stable. Consumers are well identified. Competition is usually limited to a few but well established firms. Thus, dairies tend to concentrate their marketing efforts in areas of specialty products such as yogurt, sour cream, cottage cheese, and other processed diary products rather than fluid milk. Specialty products offer an opportunity for the development of competitive advantages and potentially increased sales from marketing investments.

MARKET DEVELOPMENT STRATEGY. This strategy is typically used by a firm wishing to extend its product lines from an existing base of product knowledge and experience. A market development strategy is used by a firm when existing product-market combinations fail to provide the necessary profit goals. This strategy is different from the following two in that it builds from an existing product or market base even though the expansion may take the company into totally new areas of operation.

MARKET RETENTION STRATEGY. Much like the balancing strategy described above, the major difference here is that the firm seeks to expand its markets or to modify present product lines to gain a competitive advantage. Because technology keeps most competitive organizations in a state of semi-equilibrium, this is the strategy most firms employ. It is widely used by consumer-durable manufacturers.

GROWTH STRATEGY. The company typically has had some experience either in the product area or the market but pursues a strategy of aggressive invasion of the product category with a new marketing program. Strategies of this type usually have a high degree of uncertainty, and the payoff tends to be long term.

NEW VENTURE STRATEGY. In this strategy, the firm enters areas or fields in which it has little or no experience with either the product category or market. Here, the firm attempts to break out of an existing mode to take advantage of a perceived opportunity which may exist for only a limited time. Unusually high risks are associated with this approach, although successful entry into the market may sometimes pay very high rewards.

Product life cycle. A marketing concept that has generated much interest is the product life cycle. Specifically, Philip Kotler describes the stages in the product life cycle as being those of introduction, growth, maturity, and decline. In addition, he reports that some authors also include a stage between maturity and decline which is described as saturation.[2]

The introduction and growth of a new product generally follows Everett Roger's model of the diffusion of innovations. In a simplified way, the diffusion process means that any successful new product, idea, or custom first gains awareness by potential users, then interest, followed by evaluation, which then results in trial, usually followed by adoption.[3] This adoption process normally results in an effect which is depicted as an S-shaped product sales curve as consumers move through the various stages. (See Exhibit 4-1).

While the product life cycle has a definite conceptual appeal and has been constructed from historical data, it is most difficult, if not impossible, to predict the life cycle curve for an existing product unless it has already reached the "decline" stage. The advantage of the concept, however, is mainly as a framework for developing effective marketing strategies rather than as a forecasting tool. By evaluating the life cycles of similar or competitive products, the campaign planner may be able to develop and refine alternative marketing strategies. For example, in the growth stage, the company usually attempts to improve the product, to enter new market segments, to find new distribution channels, and perhaps to reduce the price slightly. With a product in the decline stage, however, the company attempts to identify the declining markets, to develop a particular marketing strategy for continuation while

Exhibit 4-1.

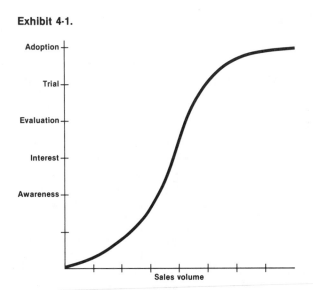

the product is being milked, and finally plans to withdraw the product from the marketplace.

Competition. While the competition has been mentioned before, it has a direct effect on the advertising plan and advertising objectives. Competition in some cases not only controls what an advertiser can and cannot do in the marketplace, it often dictates a particular strategy which must be followed simply for survival. For example, assume there are two dominant brands in the market, Brand A and Brand B. For the past several years, the two products have been at competitive parity in terms of advertising expenditures, each company attempting to gain an edge through product improvements. Suddenly, Brand A achieves an outstanding technological breakthrough which Brand B cannot match for at least two years. Competitive parity in the marketplace no longer exists. With the obvious technological edge, Brand A's company embarks on an investment spending plan hoping to capture Brand B's market before its company can react. Brand B's company has few alternatives other than to increase its spending pattern substantially, even though it is at a technological disadvantage. To remain at the present advertising level with the "same old story" in the face of strong competition could lead to serious market erosion. Thus, Brand B's company is forced to spend above its means simply to attempt to hold its share of market until it can match the technological advantage gained by Brand A.

A complete marketing plan usually will show examples of competitive advertising and spending as they relate to the product. If not, this area should be carefully studied for the potential effect it could have on the advertising plan.

Market segmentation. The final area that influences development of the advertising plan and objectives is the company's market segmentation policy. Specific

Exhibit 4-2.

Immediate past Year (actual)	Present year (budget)	Present year (forecast)	Present year + 1 (forecast)	Present year + 2 (forecast)	Present year + 3 (forecast)

groups or geographic areas may be central to the success of a brand. Such groups are often segmented for special emphasis with advertising or are considered to be key areas which advertising must reach and influence. For example, in many product categories, the "heavy users" of the product, as discussed in chapter 3, often account for a disproportionate share of the total consumption of the product. Many marketers try to segment their advertising and direct it to this "heavy-half."

In a similar vein, product usage varies widely in geographic areas. For example, instant coffee consumption is heavily skewed toward the northeast part of the country, while residents of Wisconsin consume almost half of all the brandy sold in the United States. These geographic differences can become very important when the advertising plan and advertising objectives are being developed. Most marketers practice marketing segmentation in one form or another, and this technique must be considered in the advertising plan.

While there are doubtless other factors that might influence the advertising plan and advertising objectives, those discussed seem to be the ones most applicable to consumer products.

The marketing plan

In general the marketing plan consists of all data, both physical and financial, that relates to the manufacturing, distribution, pricing, and promotion of a brand or product. Perhaps one of the best summaries of what makes up a good marketing plan was written by Herbert West:

> A marketing plan is a written document which (a) examines the major acts in a marketing situation of a product or service; (b) identifies the problems and opportunities in the situation; (c) proposes long-range strategy to meet these problems and opportunities; (d) recommends tactics of selling and advertising for the coming year to carry out this strategy.[4]

The marketing plan incorporates a look at long-term and short-term marketing needs. Most consumer product companies develop both a five-year plan and an annual plan for each brand.

The five-year plan

This plan covers the year immediately past, the present year, and a three-year look into the future. Normally, the plan forecasts only for a period of four years, using the past year as the source of known facts. For example, the typical outline of a five-year plan might

look something like Exhibit 4-2.

The year just past is used as the basis of all projections because it contains the most current actual data. The present year is viewed in two ways: what was budgeted for the year and the current forecast for the year. While the budget is usually firm, the forecast is revised up or down based on changing conditions, so that management can see how the forecast compares to the actual planned budget.

A projection of sales, expenses, and profits is forecast for the coming three years. These figures are considered firm for the present year but will be adjusted with each annual revision of the plan. The five-year marketing plan is the basis on which top management makes its major investment and spending plans. Although the plan is only a forecast of what can be expected, the marketing manager is responsible for the accuracy of information.

The annual marketing plan

In addition to the five-year plan, a separate marketing plan is prepared each year for the brand or company. This plan is much more specific. It contains details of what is scheduled for the brand in all areas during the coming year, such as how the brand manager anticipates sales will occur, how expenditures will be made, and how promotions are to be carried out. The annual plan consists of a detailed profit-and-loss sheet by month and individual outlines of various activities on a monthly or quarterly basis.

While the annual marketing plan is written for approval perhaps six months prior to implementation, it is constantly revised. Because it covers a much shorter period of time, it is expected to be much more accurate and detailed in all areas than are longer-range forecasts.

The advertising planner should not look at just the annual marketing plan in isolation. The long-term potential and effects of the five-year plan may reveal plans or situations that may impinge on the specific advertising plan under consideration.

Advertising goals, objectives, strategies, and tactics: are they all the same?

Before we proceed to advertising plan development, some clarification of terminology is needed. Because so many people write so many advertising plans using such different language, simply defining what is meant by "advertising objective" is a helpful start.

In this text the term "advertising objective" is used. Others prefer "goal" or "tactic." The definition is:

Advertising objective — A clearly stated measurable end result of an advertising message, messages, campaign, or program. Usually the objective is measured in terms of a change in awareness, preference, conviction, or other communication effect.

The terminology describing the development of the advertising message or the content of the message to be delivered to the prospect (not the specific form) also creates some confusion. The following definition is used here:

Advertising strategy — The benefit, problem solution, or other product advantage, which is the general idea of the advertising message to be delivered to the target market.

With these definitions, it becomes clear that advertising objectives must be measurable in one form or another, while advertising strategies may not. Another definition may also be helpful, that for the advertising execution:

Advertising execution — The physical form in terms of such elements as art, illustration, copy, and music in which advertising strategy is presented to the target market to achieve the advertising objective.

While these definitions may seem tedious, the basic problem in the evaluation of an advertising campaign or an advertisement often is the lack of clear understanding or agreement on the exact meaning of these terms. With these terms clearly defined, advertising results are more easily measured, and the true value of an advertising investment may be determined.

The advertising plan

The advertising plan is an integral part of the total marketing plan, and, as discussed in chapter 2, may be developed in any of several ways. Some advertisers prefer to include all promotional activities for the brand or company in the advertising plan, while others limit the plan to media advertising and direct consumer promotional expenditures. Whatever the content, the primary objectives of the advertising plan are to state clearly what activities will occur, what they will cost, and how they will be evaluated.

Setting advertising objectives for measurable results

As was shown in chapters 1, 2, and 3, the debate about whether advertising results should be measured in term of sales or communication effects has not been totally resolved. Russell Colley, in *Defining Advertising Goals for Measured Advertising Results* (DAGMAR), did much to convince advertisers that communication effects are the logical basis for advertising evaluation.[5] A second result of Colley's efforts was the general idea of establishing advertising objectives and then measuring

results of the advertising campaign against those objectives. We now look at the general function of objectives as they relate to the advertising campaign.

Function of objectives

David A. Aaker and John G. Myers have identified three basic functions of advertising objectives.

A communication device. Simply expressed, advertising objectives are a practical method of informing lower levels of management what tasks are assigned to advertising.

Decision-making criterion. Objectives can be used as a measure of the anticipated results of an advertising campaign. Management can then evaluate the potential of various advertising approaches.

Criterion for evaluating results. By providing a goal, the objectives of the campaign can then be used as the measure of results of the program.[6] Aaker and Myers also suggest that advertising objectives must be operational; they must provide a link between the strategy developed and the tactical decisions that are made to carry out the program. With operational objectives, the ultimate consumer behavior advertising is attempting to encourage, reinforce, change, or influence can then be determined.[7]

Some problems in setting advertising objectives

In the late 1960s, Steuart Henderson Britt made a study of what were regarded as successful advertising campaigns. His primary interest was the method by which these campaigns were judged to be successful. In reviewing the stated campaign objectives as developed by the advertisers and their advertising agencies, he found four primary difficulties in evaluating advertising objectives:[8]

1. Failure to state the objective(s) in quantifiable terms.
2. Apparent failure to realize that the results of the advertising could not be measured in sales.
3. Failure to identify the advertising audience.
4. Use of superlatives (which are immeasurable).

In each instance, the campaigns were believed to be very successful by the experts who judged them. Yet, no true evaluation measures were adopted and followed in most cases. Britt's main point was that the determination of advertising objectives should be precise and measurable. In his study he found that only 31 percent of the campaigns were evaluated on the basis of the objectives set for the campaign.[9]

Another example that illustrates the difficulty of setting advertising objectives was a study conducted by the National Industrial Conference Board in 1966. The NICB found the major reasons advertisers failed to set advertising objectives were:

1. Advertising was a minor element in the marketing mix of the company. This was particularly true for industrial firms.
2. The company was not oriented toward marketing planning.
3. The company made erroneous assumptions regarding the role of advertising vs. other marketing efforts.

Because of these problems, the individual companies surveyed had no way of knowing what advertising weight was required or what advertising expenditure was needed in the marketplace. The advertiser was guessing when it came to the amount to invest and the results to expect.[10] While it does not seem possible in the modern sophisticated marketplaces of today, advertisers probably exist who still don't know the value of or the method for measuring their advertising investment.

Even the determination of the advertising objectives to be measured is subject to much interpretation. If the wrong message is selected, the advertising has little or no chance of success, regardless of its ability to communicate to the target market.

In spite of all these problems, the demand for measurable results from advertising remains. The fundamental problem is finding the most practical method of evaluation.

Colley's DAGMAR approach

Since Colley developed the DAGMAR approach in the early 1960s, several authors have offered alternative approaches to setting advertising objectives. All, however, are basic variations on Colley's theme.[11] Specifically, Colley states:

> Advertising's job, purely and simply, is to communicate to a defined audience information and a frame of mind that stimulates action. Advertising succeeds or fails depending on how well it communicates the desired information and attitudes to the right people at the right time at the right cost.

Colley develops the outline for his approach to measuring advertising results using the following six principles.

1. An advertising goal is a succinct statement of the *communication aspects* of the marketing job. (It expresses the particular work advertising is uniquely qualified to perform and does not encompass results that require a combination of several different marketing forces.)
2. The goal is expressed in writing—in finite, measurable terms. (If there is agreement among all of those concerned on what advertising is expected to accomplish, then it is no great chore to reduce it to writing. If there is lack of agreement as to purpose, the time to find this out is before the advertising is prepared, not afterward.)
3. Goals are agreed upon by those concerned at both creative and approval levels. (Planning is separated

from doing. Agreement is reached on *what needs to be said to whom* before time and money is spent on *how best to say it.*)

4. Goals are based on an intimate knowledge of markets and buying motives. (They express realistic expectancy in the light of carefully evaluated market opportunities. They do not express mere hopes and desires arrived at without factual foundation.)
5. Benchmarks are set up against which accomplishments can be measured. (State of mind—knowledge, attitude, and buying propensity—are appraised before and after the advertising, or among those reached versus those not reached by the advertising.)
6. Methods to be used at a later date in evaluating accomplishments are set up at the time goals are established.

As can be seen from this outline, Colley's primary theme throughout the DAGMAR approach is that good communication objectives are both specific and measurable.

In Colley's approach, the key to measuring advertising results is one's ability to define the advertising goals to be accomplished. This decision is one of the most difficult parts of the task and suggests a "6 M" approach, which he outlines as follows:

Merchandise:	What are all the important benefits of the products and services to be sold?
Markets:	Who are the people to be reached?
Motives:	Why would these people buy or fail to buy?
Messages:	What are the key ideas, information, and attitudes to be conveyed? (To move the prospect closer to the ultimate aim of a sale.)
Media:	How can the prospects be reached?
Measurements:	What method is proposed to measure accomplishment in getting the intended message across to the intended audience?"[12]

For us to be able to measure the effect of the advertising message, we must be able to detect a change in the consumer's perceptions, attitudes, or actions. Colley proposes the following hierarchy of stages in the communication process designed to achieve the ultimate goal of advertising, which is persuading the consumer to act. The four stages of "commercial communication" suggested by Colley are:

1. *Awareness:* The prospect must be made aware of the brand or product.
2. *Comprehension:* The prospect must comprehend what the product is and what it will do for him.
3. *Conviction:* The prospect must arrive at a mental disposition or conviction to buy the product.
4. *Action:* Finally, the prospect must take action.[13]

The primary thrust of Colley's approach is that response to communication can be measured, in many cases with existing research tools and methodologies. Colley offers the following example (Exhibit 4-3) of the effects advertising might have on consumers. He uses two different products and compares the effects before and after advertising communication. This example demonstrates Colley's approach to clearly defined, measurable advertising objectives.

Exhibit 4-3. Effect of advertising on consumer response.

Product: Filter cigarette	Before advertising (percent)	After advertising (percent)
Aware of brand name:		
Unaided recall	20	40
Aided recall	40	80
Comprehended messages:		
Message A	6	12
Message B	10	20
Message C	8	16
Favorably disposed to buy	4	8
Demonstrated action	2	4
Image: Industrial chemical division		
Aware of corporate name	85	88
Aware that corporation is a leading supplier of industrial chemicals	15	30
Comprehended key messages:		
Message A	6	12
Message B	4	8
Message C	5	10
Favorably disposed to buy	5	10
Action leading to purchase . . .	3	6

Source: Russell H. Colley, *Defining Advertising Goals for Measured Advertising Results,* 1961.

Colley does not concern himself with how the benchmarks are established or the methodology of measurement. The key point is the identification of specific communication goals from the start of advertising to the close of the campaign.

In summary, Colley's DAGMAR approach can best be described as a written measurable communications task involving a starting point, a definite audience, and a fixed period of time.

A recommended approach to setting advertising objectives for measurable results

The DAGMAR approach is sound both conceptually and practically, with one exception. The hierarchy of steps from awareness to action is somewhat ill-defined. The DAGMAR approach is recommended with the exception that a model be used that has a different hierarchy of effects, specifically, the Lavidge and Steiner model as illustrated in Exhibit 4-4.

Lavidge and Steiner's model is more specific than Colley's "Four stages of commercial communication." It works like this:

Advertising may be thought of as a force, which must move people up a series of steps:

1. Near the bottom of the steps stand the potential purchasers who are completely unaware of the existence of the product or service in question.
2. Closer to purchasing, but still a long way from the cash register, are those who are merely aware of [the product's] existence.
3. Up a step are prospects who know what the product has to offer.
4. Still closer to purchasing are those who have favorable attitudes toward the product — those who like the product.
5. Those whose favorable attitudes have developed to the point of preference over all other possibilities are up still another step.
6. Even closer to purchasing are consumers who couple preference with a desire to buy and the conviction that the purchase would be wise.
7. Finally, of course, is the step which translates this attitude into an actual purchase.[14]

To summarize, advertising objectives must be stated as clearly and concisely as possible. The example Colley offers should be used as a guideline for all advertising objectives. If advertising objectives are stated in this manner, they can be measured and the results evaluated.

> To increase among 30 million homemakers who own automatic washers the number who identify brand X as a low-sudsing detergent and who are persuaded that it gets clothes cleaner — from 10 percent to 40 percent in one year.[15]

Some practical examples of sound advertising objectives

We have looked at several alternative ways in which advertising objectives may be stated. Perhaps the best illustrations, however, are practical examples. The statement of advertising objectives (A) below is taken from an actual student advertising plans book for a "real-world" client. Note how specifically the advertising objectives are stated, i.e., to achieve 70 percent awareness of the product in a very specific target market. In addition, note how the advertising campaign objectives are separated from the marketing objectives in numbers 4 and 5. These final objectives deal specifically with behavior, and, since there are intervening variables such as marketing and promotional programs, these are separated from the advertising objectives which deal only with communication effects.

Advertising objectives can also be much more complex that those illustrated above. For example, the statement of advertising objectives (B) illustrates a different set of objectives for an advertising campaign. This plan involved a national overlay program plus a heavy-up campaign in 55 additional high-potential markets. As is shown, separate advertising objectives

Exhibit 4-4. Effect of advertising on consumers: movement from awareness to action.

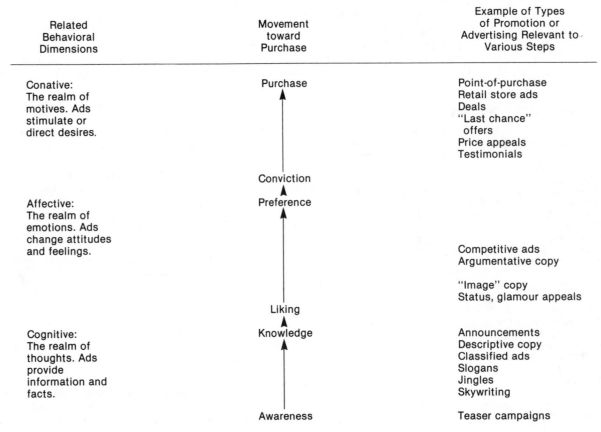

Source: Robert J. Lavidge and Gary A. Steiner, *Journal of Marketing,* 1961.

were developed for each portion of the campaign based on the differing levels of media weight and market conditions. The awareness goal nationally, for example, was set at 30 percent while, in the heavy-up markets, the objective was 75 percent.

Again, the advertising objectives and marketing objectives have been separated. Advertising is evaluated in terms of communication effects, while marketing is evaluated according to trial, repurchase rate, and franchise.

Advertising objectives—Example A

1. To create awareness of Brand X among 70 percent of our target market (primarily women in the top 100 markets, ages 18 to 49, with one or more children under age 18, and having household incomes of approximately $15,000 plus) by the end of Year 1, the introductory year of our national campaign.
2. To have 70 percent aided recall in our target market of our brand image as projected in the creative strategy.
3. To have 65 percent of our target market report a

preference for Brand X over other competitive brands.

Through a combination of advertising and marketing efforts

4. To generate a 39 percent trial rate in our target market within the designated distribution areas by the end of the introductory year.
5. To achieve a 65 percent repurchase rate (an average of five purchases per year/six packages per purchase) in our target market by the end of the introductory year.

Advertising objectives—Example B

	National Overlay (Percent)	Heavy-Up Markets (55) (Percent)
Awareness	30	75
Correct image perception	20	60
Liking	15	50

In addition to these three objectives, which can be linked directly to advertising, three behavior-related objectives of the total advertising, marketing, and promotion program are stated:

Ultimate objectives of advertising, marketing, and promotion

	National Overlay (Percent)	Heavy-Up Markets (55) (Percent)
Trial	10	40
Repurchase rate . . .	50	50
Franchise	5	20

The national objectives can be explained as follows:

1. *Awareness:* When asked to name all brands that come to mind, 30 percent of the target market will name Brand X.

2. *Correct image perception:* 20 percent of the target market will acquire the correct perception of the product image from Brand X's advertising messages. Image perception is measurable by checklists, semantic differentials, and projective techniques.

3. *Liking:* 15 percent of the target market will prefer Brand X to other brands in the product category. Liking can be measured by rank order of preference or by rating scales.

4. *Trial:* 10 percent of the target market will purchase one package of Brand X once during the first year. Trial can be measured by store audits or surveys as well as by coupon redemption.

5. *Repurchase rate:* 50 percent of those who try the product during the first year will purchase it again. This can be measured by diaries or tracking studies.

6. *Franchise:* The end results of trial and repurchase rates will constitute our market share.

Advertising objectives as illustrated by these examples can be made measurable. For proper evaluation of the campaign results, they must be measurable. Further, these measurable results greatly simplify the task of justifying to management the advertising campaign and the advertising expenditure.

Notes

1. David W. Cravens, Gerald E. Hills, and Robert B. Woodruff, *Marketing Decision Making: Concepts and Strategy* (Homewood, Ill. Richard D. Irwin, 1976), pp. 326–31.
2. Philip Kotler, *Marketing Management: Analysis, Planning and Control* (Englewood Cliffs, N. J.: Prentice-Hall, 1976), pp. 230-45.
3. Everett Rogers and F. Floyd Shoemaker, *Communication of Innovations,* 2d ed. (New York: Free Press, 1971).
4. Herbert West, "Why You Need a Master Strategy Blueprint," *Advertising Age,* 18 January 1957, p. 59.
5. Russell H. Colley, *Defining Advertising Goals for Measured Advertising Results* (New York: Association of National Advertisers, 1961).
6. David A. Aaker and John G. Myers, *Advertising Management: Practical Perspectives* (Englewood Cliffs, N. J.: Prentice-Hall, 1975), pp. 85–86.
7. Ibid.
8. Steuart Henderson Britt, "Are So-Called Successful Advertising Campaigns Really Successful?" *Journal of Advertising Research,* June 1969, pp. 3–9.
9. Ibid.
10. *Setting Advertising Objectives* (New York: National Industrial Conference Board, 1966).
11. Colley, *Defining Advertising Goals,* p. 21.
12. Ibid., p. 23.
13. Ibid., pp. 36-37.
14. Robert J. Lavidge and Gary H. Steiner. "A Model for Predictive Measurements of Advertising Effectivess," *Journal of Marketing,* October 1961, pp. 59-62.
15. Colley, *Defining Advertising Goals,* p. 7.

5 Advertising Budgeting

Advertising budgeting

One of the most important areas of campaign planning is the budget, that is, the amount appropriated for advertising and promotion. Because the budget governs all proposed expenditures, placing upper limits on what can be proposed, it is naturally paramount in the eyes of the campaign planner. In spite of the importance of the budget, there is still much discussion and disagreement in the field about how budgets should be determined and how a proper allocation should be developed.

A central problem in the determination of an advertising budget is the continuing inability of advertising or marketing managers to explain and quantify the exact effects of advertising in terms of actual sales and profits for the firm. The problem is especially serious for consumer-product advertisers who place their messages primarily in mass media. As we discussed in chapter 4, there are so many intervening market variables, it becomes almost impossible to define exactly what sales resulted from a particular advertising campaign. Without specific evidence of results, campaign planners are hard put to justify a request for advertising funds, particularly when advertising must compete against other departments for the available scarce resources. In spite of the tenuous nature of the advertising/sales relationship, a budget must be developed before the campaign can be planned. Before we discuss specific approaches, an overview of advertising as an expenditure by the firm must be examined.

Advertising: an investment or an expense

The question of whether advertising is an investment or an expense to the firm has long been debated. Marketing forces have traditionally viewed advertising as an investment, stressing that even though the funds are expended in one period of time, value will be received over the long term. In addition, in our diffused marketplace where consumers often have little personal contact with the firm, opinions and attitudes about the company and its products are often the direct result of advertising messages received. The resulting "goodwill" of the firm is often cited as a direct result of advertising expenditures.

People in accounting and finance normally hold the opposite view of advertising. Since advertising funds are normally spent in one period, there is no satisfactory way to depreciate them. The financial view, therefore, is that advertising is an expense. Advertising should be charged to the operation of the firm in the period in which it was expended. Because the federal government, for tax purposes, views advertising as an expense, the debate between expense or investment is largely theoretical.

In spite of the accounting view that advertising is a direct expense, an understanding of the investment concept is necessary to understand advertising budgeting methods.

Joel Dean, using an econometric approach, suggests that advertising be viewed as an investment in the firm, just as would an addition to a plant or other capital expenditure. Results from advertising expenditures could then be viewed as a return on investment. Advertising (and its results) could be compared to other areas to which the firm has allocated funds. Viewed as an investment, advertising would then have to compete for the dollars the firm had available with other potential expenditures on the basis of return on investment.[1]

Kenneth Longman expanded Dean's approach with development of an advertising investment model. Longman's approach, using marginal analysis, holds that advertising operates and generates additional revenue for the firm only between two sales

Exhibit 5-1. Sales related to advertising expenditure.

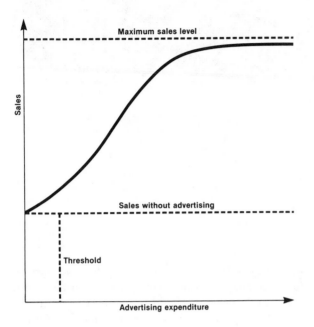

Source: Longman, *Advertising*, 1971.

points. Expressed graphically, at the bottom, a certain level of sales will occur even with no advertising. Longman labels this the "threshold" level. At the upper end, there is a point beyond which sales cannot rise regardless of the advertising investment. This upper limit may be imposed by production capabilities of the firm, saturation of the market, or other causes. It is between this upper ceiling and the "threshold" level that advertising actually contributes revenue. Using marginal analysis, a point can then be calculated where investment dollars cease to produce revenue for the firm.

Longman determines the marginal return point by plotting a series of curves. The slope of the curve depicting the value of the advertising investment is the result of a combination of the maximum sales level and advertising efficiency. Exhibit 5-1 illustrates the concept.

In Longman's scheme, the firm's production, distribution, and advertising costs are then deducted. This determines the firm's net profit before taxes. This is done in two steps. First, the production and distribution costs are deducted to obtain the "gross profit" curve (see Exhibit 5-2). This curve is then plotted along with the advertising expenditure curve to illustrate the point of maximum marginal utility. Finally, because the optimum point for an advertising expenditure is difficult to see in this relationship, the maximum profit point is illustrated in the right-hand graph of Exhibit 5-2 to show the maximum profit point for an advertising investment.

Longman carries the idea of advertising investment a step further by also calculating the "sales carry-forwards" on the advertising investment, that is, the value of the advertising in the future. He also considers the "discounted future profits" of the advertising investment, which are considered to be the "opportunity cost of the money" invested in advertising, or the value of the funds spent in advertising rather than in some other opportunity that might be available to the organization.[2] Longmans' approach, while theoretically sound, lacks widespread acceptance by pragmatic businesspeople. It does, however, give a much clearer view of the relationship between advertising sales and also indicates that an advertising budget could be calculated for every product. Unfortunately, much of the information needed for the calculation is not available at reasonable cost.

There are, of course, other views of advertising as an investment rather than an expense. Most writers and model builders in the field use the marginal analysis and marginal utility concept. All, however, are fraught with the same difficulty. While marginal analysis and marginal utility are theoretically sound concepts, in most instances the information, correlations, and effects of advertising expenditures are not known. Thus, persons attempting to use these approaches for advertising budget allocation are forced to rely on estimates or educated guesses as inputs. Under these circumstances, other methods appear to be much simpler and probably just as accurate.

With this conceptual view of advertising budgeting and its attendant problems in mind, we can discuss the more pragmatic approaches to advertising appropriations.

Where do the marketing and advertising dollars really come from?

Central to the development of any advertising budget is an understanding of exactly where budget dollars originate. In some campaign proposals, it appears that advertising budgets are conceived and even allocated in splendid isolation. Thus, their relationship to the real world is questionable. A brief discussion of the relationship of sales, profits, available marketing/advertising funds, and the calculation of various margins will illustrate how marketing and advertising funds are generated.

Exhibit 5-3 is a hypothetical combined operating statement for a typical consumer product. The letters at the left of each of the entries are used for descriptive purposes.

Assume you are the brand manager for XYZ Company. Your primary brand responsibility is canned marinated eggrolls. The eggrolls are packaged in

Exhibit 5-2. Sales and profit curves related to advertising expenditure.

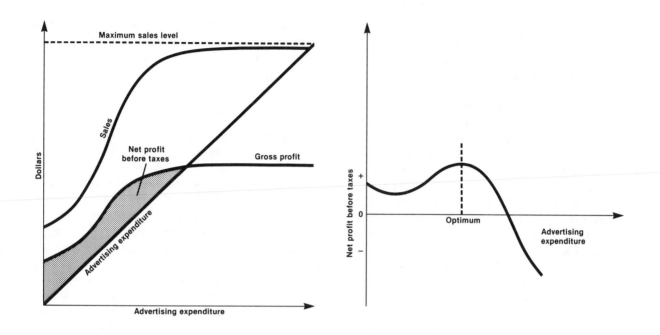

Source: Longman, *Advertising*, 1971.

Exhibit 5-3. Hypothetical operating statement for a non-durable consumer product.

(A)	Retail price 69¢ per can/12 per case		$8.28	
(B)	Retailer's margin @ 20%		1.66	
(C)	Gross price to retailer		6.62	
(D)	Less trade promotions/deals @ 2%		.13	
(E)	Net price to retailer		6.49	
(F)	Wholesale/broker commission @ 7%		.45	
(G)	Net sales price		6.04	(100%)
(H)	Cost of goods		3.32	(55%)
(J)	Fixed costs, 20%	$ .66		
(K)	Variable costs, 80%	2.66		
(L)	Gross margin		2.72	(45%)
(M)	Distribution expense		.12	(2%)
(N)	Contribution margin		2.60	(43%)
(P)	Direct expenses			
(Q)	Advertising	.36		(6%)
(R)	Consumer merchandising	.24		(4%)
(S)	Management and sales expense	.92		(15%)
(T)	Research and development	.06		(1%)
(U)	Total direct expenses		1.58	(26%)
(V)	Product margin		1.02	(17%)

14-oz. cans containing approximately 17 eggrolls and are shipped 12 cans to the case. The normal retail price (out-of-store) is 69¢ per can.

Line A illustrates the retail price of a case of 12 cans of eggrolls at 69¢ each. From the retail price of 69¢, the retailer usually obtains a gross margin of 20 percent. Thus, on a per-case basis, the retailer's gross profit is $1.66 (Line B). The Gross Price to Retailer on a case of eggrolls is $6.62 (Line C).

From the Gross Trade Price, a deduction for trade promotions or deals must be made (Line D). In this case, XYZ Company plans to offer trade promotions amounting to 2 percent of Gross Sales to the Retailer. The discount is offered on all purchases made during the year if the Retailer will run a reduced-price feature on eggrolls during the Chinese New Year's promotion. The cost of the trade promotions is deducted from the Gross Price to Retailer to give Net Price to Retailer (Line E). Thus, the Net Price (per case) to Retailer is $6.49 (Line E).

Your eggrolls are not sold directly to the retailer but through a broker or wholesaler. His or her commission, therefore, must be deducted. The average commission to a broker (or the margin required by a wholesaler) is 7 percent of the Gross Price (Line F), in this case, 45¢. This amount is deducted from the Net Price to Retailer, leaving a Net Sales Price for the eggrolls of $6.04 per case (Line G). This is what XYZ Company will receive for the sale of each case of marinated eggrolls.

The cost of manufacturing and packaging the eggrolls must be deducted from the Net Sales Price. The total Cost-of-Goods, as determined by the production and accounting departments, amounts to $3.32 per case, or 55 percent of the Net Sales Price. The Fixed Costs (Line J), your share of the company's general overhead, is calculated at 20 percent of the Cost-of-Goods, or 66¢ per case. The Variable Costs (Line K) are calculated at 80 percent of the Cost-of-Goods of the product, or $2.66 per case. The Variable Costs include such items as raw materials, manufacturing cost, filling and packaging the eggrolls, and storage and handling until the products are put into the distribution stream. Thus, by deducting Cost-of-Goods (Line H) from the Net Sales Price, we obtain the Gross Margin on the product (Line L). The Gross Margin is the amount available for transportation and marketing expenses plus any profit to XYZ Company on the sale of each case of eggrolls.

Using the Gross Margin available (Line L) of $2.72 per case, we first deduct Distribution Expense (Line M). This is the actual cost of physically moving the product from the manufacturing plant to the wholesale warehouse or retail store. Here, the Distribution Ex-

pense is calculated to be 2 percent of Net Sales, or 12¢ per case. Subtracting the Distribution Expense from the Gross Margin leaves a Contribution Margin of $2.60 per case (Line N). If there were no selling or other expenses, this Contribution Margin would be the amount each case of eggrolls could contribute to the profit of the company. Realistically, however, there are promotional expenses, which are referred to as Direct Expenses (Lines P and U).

Direct Expenses include all promotional costs such as Advertising (Line Q), Consumer Merchandising (Line R), Management and Sales Expense (Line S), and an allocation for Research and Development of new or improved eggrolls (Line T). These costs are combined as Total Direct Expenses (Line U).

While the final profit on each case of eggrolls is shown as Product Margin (Line V) and appears to be what is left after all costs and expenses have been deducted, the format is somewhat misleading. Usually, management of XYZ Company, after reviewing sales and expense forecasts for all company products and brands, assigns a profit margin percentage (or a total dollar figure) to the eggroll brand as a goal for the coming year. This goal is determined on the basis of projecting an adequate return on the company's investment in the eggroll brand and as a proper contribution to the over-all financial income and profit of the company. Thus, in actuality, using the profit goals established by management for the brand, the funds available for marketing—including advertising, promotion, sales, and R & D is the difference between the Contribution Margin (Line N) and the Product Margin (Line V) or, in this case, $1.02 per case of eggrolls sold. It is from this Total Direct Expense amount (Line U) that brand management makes the allocation for an advertising campaign.

There are, of course, circumstances that might help to increase or decrease the funds available for Total Direct Expense (Line U). As manufacturing economies of scale are realized such factors as increased sales might reduce the Variable Cost of the product (Line K). The possibility exists of reducing or completely deleting all Trade Promotions/Deals (Line D). If sales could be concentrated closer to the manufacturing plant, Distribution Expenses (Line M) might be lowered. A change in any of these costs would directly affect the number of dollars available to the product manager for Total Direct Expenses (Line U). For purposes of this illustration, however, the assumption is made that the sales forecast is fairly firm, that the trade promotions and deals are already established, and that distribution expenses will not vary. It is within this framework that product management and the advertising agency must determine how best to allocate the available marketing funds, including the cost of the advertising campaign.

In most instances, Management and Sales Expense (Line S) and Research and Development costs (Line T) are most difficult to manipulate. For example, Management and Sales Expenses (Line B) consist of the salaries and expenses of the sales force who call on the trade. In a multiproduct company, this expense is usually allocated to individual brands on the basis of total sales volume, or brand managers determine how much of the sales force's time they would like to be devoted to the brand. The cost to the brand is then determined as a percentage of over-all sales costs. In addition, the salaries of the product manager, any assistants, and the clerical staff are included in this figure. As a result, reduction of Management and Sales Expense is a difficult task, although some options are available.

The same is true of Research and Development costs (Line T). In this instance, because XYZ Company manufactures many products, a general Research and Development program for the entire company is operated under a R&D unit. Because this group works on behalf of all brands, costs of their efforts are allocated on an equalized basis. The eggroll brand pays a pro-rated share of all costs of research and development with the understanding that the group is working on behalf of the eggroll brand a proportionate share of the time. R&D expenses charged to the eggroll brand are allocated by top management and are difficult to reduce.

It quickly becomes evident that the actual funds available for an advertising campaign, using our illustration of the eggroll brand, are greatly constrained. The funds available are the result of sales and expense forecasts made by brand or top management. Any increases in funds available for advertising must be a direct result of increased sales or reduced costs.

In some cases, it appears, there is little understanding of how and where advertising funds are generated within a company or by a brand. The usual result of this lack of understanding is an unrealistic advertising campaign proposal or a request for additional advertising dollars that are not available. We hope this simplified explanation helps to clarify how advertising dollars are generated within a company and what must be done to justify proposed campaigns or to request additional funds.

There are, of course, other approaches to advertising budgeting. Sometimes the advertising agency and even the advertising manager may not be privy to the complete operating statement of a particular brand or company. Top management may prefer not to release for analysis specific profit-or-loss margins on the whole

company or even individual products. In these cases, the advertising department and the advertising agency's prime task is allocation of an approved advertising budget and execution of the approved promotion plan for the brand. Unfortunately, this approach is used more often than the brand management system where sales forecast information is used to adjust advertising levels. Therefore, the more traditional approaches to advertising campaign budgeting are now reviewed.

What goes into the advertising budget

One of the primary concerns of persons responsible only for allocation, control, and implementation of an advertising budget is the determination of which items are legitimately to be charged to the advertising budget and which expenses belong in other areas. While all expenses must eventually end up in someone's budget, those that are considered advertising must be clearly defined, or advertising budget control becomes impossible.

Exhibit 5-4 illustrates a well-accepted breakdown of charges. Various costs that do or do not belong in the advertising budget are shown, plus those regarded as borderline cases.

What is charged to the advertising budget? A *Printer's Ink* survey[3] of 216 companies shows promotional items arranged in descending order according to the percentage of firms charging the item to the advertising budget. The first group includes those charges considered advertising expenses by two-thirds or more of the companies. The second and third groups (split at 50 percent) include those items falling into the advertising budget of one-third to two-thirds of the companies responding. The fourth group comprises items considered advertising costs by one-third or fewer of the companies.

Factors that influence the advertising budget

Having determined what will be charged to advertising, let's review the factors that might affect the results of a campaign. Longman suggests two primary criteria for establishing an advertising budget: (a) it must be adequate to the task to be accomplished, and (b) the advertising investment must return a maximum profit to the advertiser. While both criteria are ideal, Longman also points out:[4]

> In practice, neither of these rules is easy to apply. Probably, the most important cause of the difficulties experienced in budgeting is the fact that the people's reactions to advertising at various spending levels must be predictable in this respect. They do not react to the fact that advertisers spend in large or small sums. Rather, they react to the particular message they receive, the place where they encounter it, and the frequency with which

they are exposed to it. These factors are only loosely connected with the amount of money being spent.

Simon Broadbent, the British media authority, takes a somewhat more pragmatic view.[5] He says there are four questions which must be answered to adequately determine an advertising budget:

1. What can the product afford?
2. What is the advertising task?
3. What are the competitors spending?
4. What have we learned from previous years?

With answers to those questions, Broadbent suggests, the manager has some understanding of his basis for setting an advertising budget.

David L. Hurwood and James K. Brown are more specific. They suggest the following considerations in budgeting for a consumer product:[6]

1. The extent of product usage, i.e., is it widely used by many people or only by a limited number who use it a great deal? (heavy vs. light users).
2. The size of the core of loyal brand users vs. the size of the market who switches from brand to brand.
3. The geographic area of the country in which the product is sold.
4. The number of people presently in the market and the number not now in the market.
5. How rapidly purchasers move in and out of the marketplace.

As can be seen, some authorities view factors that influence the budget in a very broad sense, while others are much more selective. Probably all are correct, depending on the situation. While there are many considerations, all budgets are separate and unique. What is mandatory for one brand or one product may have little or no importance for another brand, even in the same category. Budgets will even vary from one period to another. Thus, suggestions for budgeting are just

Exhibit 5-4. Department charges in descending order of importance.

Items usually charged to advertising budget
Space and time costs in regular media
Advertising consultants
Ad-pretesting services
Institutional advertising
Industry directory listings
Readership or audience research
Media costs for consumer contests, premium
  and sample promotions
Ad department travel and entertainment expenses
Ad department salaries
Advertising association dues
Local cooperative advertising
Direct mail to consumers
Subscriptions to periodicals and services for
  ad department
Storage of advertising materials

Items often charged to advertising budget
Catalogs for consumers
Classified telephone directories
Space in irregular publications
Advertising aids for salesmen
Financial advertising
Dealer help literature
Contributions to industry ad funds
Direct mail to dealers and jobbers
Office supplies

Items sometimes charged to advertising budget
Point-of-sale materials
Window display installation costs
Charges for services performed by other departments
Catalogs for dealers
Test-marketing programs
Sample requests generated by advertising
Costs of exhibits except personnel
Ad department share of overhead
House organs for customers and dealers
Cost of cash value for sampling coupons
Cost of contest entry blanks
Cross-advertising enclosures
Contest judging and handling fees
Depreciation of ad department equipment
Mobile exhibits

Employee fringe benefits
Catalogs for salesmen
Packaging consultants
Consumer contest awards

Items usually not charged to ad budget
Premium handling charges
House-to-house sample distribution
Packaging charges for premium promotions
Cost of merchandise for tie-in promotions
Product tags
Showrooms
Testing new labels and packages
Package design and artwork
Cost of non-self-liquidating premiums
Consumer education programs
Product publicity
Factory signs
House organs for salesmen
Signs on company-owned vehicles
Instruction enclosures
Press clipping services
Market research (outside-produced)
Sample for middlemen
Recruitment advertising
Price sheets
Public relations consultants
Coupon redemption costs
Corporate publicity
Market research (company-produced)
Exhibit personnel
Gifts of company products
Cost of deal merchandise
Share of corporate salaries
Cost of guarantee refunds
Share of legal expenses
Cost of detail missionary men
Sponsoring recreational activities
Product research
House organs for employees
Entertaining customers and prospects
Scholarships
Plant tours
Annual reports
Outright charity donations

Source: *Printer's Ink,* 16 December 1960.

Exhibit 5-5. Planning and evaluating the advertising budget.

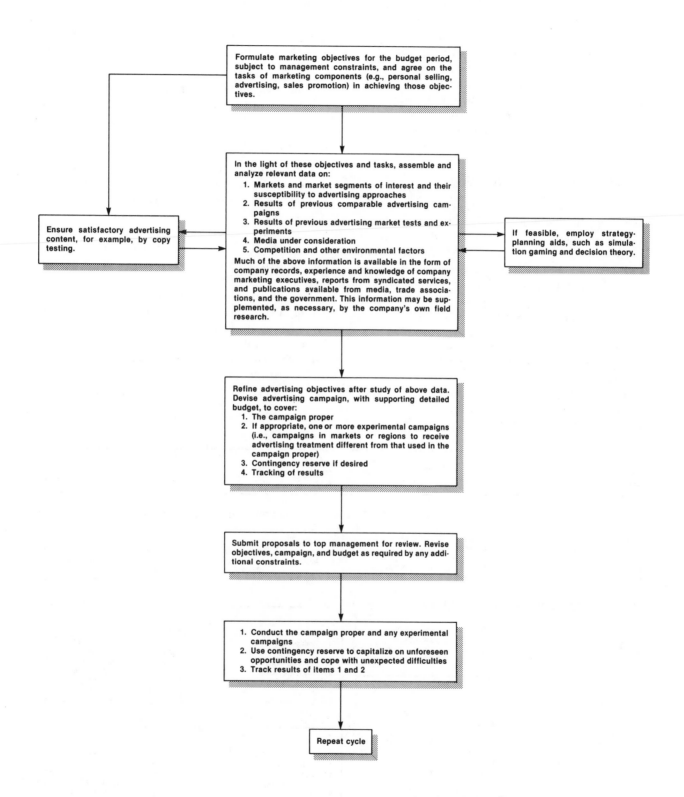

Source: Hurwood and Brown, *Some Guidelines for Advertising Budgeting*, 1972.

that, suggestions, and should be viewed as such.

If all budgets are different and all situations specific, is there a logical way to go about preparing a budget for a product or brand? An answer is presented by Hurwood and Brown in a research report prepared by The Conference Board and illustrated in Exhibit 5-5.[7]

Not all brands go through all the steps proposed. The outline proposed by Hurwood and Brown, however, is an excellent checklist for the development of an advertising budget. It should serve experienced budgeters and novices alike.

Accepted methods of budgeting

Over the years a number of methods of estimating, budgeting, or allocating an advertising expenditure have been suggested. The most widely accepted classification is that proposed by M. A. McNiven, which is based on a national survey of advertisers by the National Industrial Conference Board in 1968.[8] McNiven grouped all methods of advertising budgeting into three general categories:

Guidelines. Those methods that use historical or judgmental data on which to develop a basis for allocation.

Theoretical. Attempts to estimate the most profitable level for advertising for a specific advertiser by using econometric or marketing models based on historical data.

Empirical. Techniques built on experimental feedback from the marketplace rather than on historical data.

Using McNiven's scheme, we can give a brief description of each of the more popular methods of advertising budgeting.

Guidelines

Three primary approaches to the guideline technique are fixed guidelines, arbitrary appropriations, and the objective and task or task method.

Fixed guidelines. Percentage of sales: the most widely used method of guideline budgeting is a percentage of past or estimated future sales of a product. The ratio used is often determined by past experience or industry or category guidelines.

The computation is fairly simple. A given percentage of last year's sales or the forecasted sales for the coming year for the product determines the allocation. For example, if sales totaled $100,000 last year, and 2 percent was the arbitrary figure selected as appropriate for advertising, the budget for the coming year would be $2,000 ($100,000 × .02 = $2,000). A percentage

Exhibit 5-6. 100 leaders advertising as percent of sales

AD RANK	COMPANY	ADVERTISING	SALES	ADV. AS % OF SALES	AD RANK	COMPANY	ADVERTISING	SALES	ADV. AS % OF SALES
		Airlines					**Communications, Entertainment**		
73	UAL Inc.	$ 50,624,437	$ 3,890,298,000	1.3	30	CBS Inc.	122,322,000	3,290,052,000	3.7
84	Trans World Corp.	37,500,000	3,695,000,000	1.0	55	Time Inc.	76,348,000	1,697,585,000	4.5
92	Eastern Airlines	34,800,000	2,379,564,000	1.5	66	MCA Inc.	61,000,000	1,120,644,000	5.4
97	American Airlines	29,000,000	2,735,508,000	1.1	75	Warner Communications	47,675,300	1,309,419,000	3.6
98	Delta Air Lines	28,900,000	2,225,447,000	1.3	87	ABC Inc.	35,854,400	1,783,985,000	2.0
		Appliances, Tv, Radio					**Drugs**		
21	RCA Corp.	140,000,000	6,644,500,000	2.1	37	Richardson-Merrell	105,000,000	944,961,000	11.1
31	General Electric Co.	121,294,400	19,653,800,000	0.6	41	SmithKline Corp.	91,215,000	1,112,039,000	8.2
79	North American Philips Co.	42,100,000	2,184,011,000	1.9	51	Sterling Drug	78,000,000	724,595,000	10.8
					59	Schering-Plough	68,000,000	1,082,493,000	6.3
		Automobiles			63	Miles Laboratories	62,258,000	536,983,000	11.6
					74	Squibb Corp.	50,000,000	1,515,882,000	3.3
4	General Motors Corp.	266,346,000	63,221,100,000	0.4	80	Pfizer Inc.	38,424,300	1,042,100,000	3.7
8	Ford Motor Co.	210,000,000	42,784,100,000	0.5	85	A. H. Robins Co.	36,886,000	357,070,000	10.3
10	Chrysler Corp.	188,900,000	13,600,000,000	1.4					
61	Toyota Motor Sales U.S.A.	64,575,700	12,767,840,000	0.5			**Food**		
65	Nissan Motor Co.	61,492,200	10,437,488,000	0.6					
69	Volkswagen of America	57,000,000	14,110,000,000	0.4	3	General Foods Corp.	340,000,000	5,472,500,000	6.2
78	American Motors Corp.	43,444,500	2,585,428,000	1.7	14	General Mills	170,000,000	3,745,000,000	4.5
89	Honda Motor Co.	35,000,000	1,639,000,000	2.1	17	Beatrice Foods Co.	150,370,000	7,468,373,000	2.0
					19	Norton Simon Inc.	144,591,000	2,428,797,000	6.0
		Chemicals			20	Esmark.	141,431,000	5,863,962,000	2.4
					23	McDonald's	136,803,000	4,575,000,000	3.0
					36	Kraft Inc.	114,166,700	5,669,900,000	2.0
35	American Cyanamid Co.	115,000,000	2,745,745,000	4.2	38	Pillsbury Co.	104,000,000	2,165,983,000	4.8
57	DuPont.	70,000,000	10,584,000,000	0.6	40	Consolidated Foods.	91,500,000	4,700,000,000	1.9
72	Union Carbide Corp.	51,103,764	7,869,700,000	0.6	42	Ralston Purina Co.	91,000,000	4,058,400,000	2.2

AD RANK	COMPANY	ADVERTISING	SALES	ADV. AS % OF SALES	AD RANK	COMPANY	ADVERTISING	SALES	ADV. AS % OF SALES
	Food					**Telephone Service, Equipment**			
43	Nabisco Inc.	95,600,000	2,197,300,000	4.1	13	American Telephone & Telegraph Co.	172,822,100	40,933,356,000	0.4
49	Kellogg Co.	79,600,000	1,690,600,000	4.7	28	International Telephone & Telegraph Co.	122,700,000	15,261,178,000	0.8
52	Nestle Co.	77,919,000	1,306,000,000	6.0					
56	H. J. Heinz Co.	74,111,000	2,150,027,000	3.4		**Tobacco**			
58	Quaker Oats Co.	69,312,000	1,685,600,000	4.1					
60	CPC International.	65,901,700	3,221,800,000	2.0	6	Philip Morris Inc.	236,851,000	6,632,463,000	3.6
70	Campbell Soup Co.	56,400,000	1,983,659,000	2.8	12	R. J. Reynolds Industries	182,596,300	6,622,100,000	2.8
74	Borden Inc.	50,000,000	3,802,559,000	1.3	47	B.A.T. Industries.	82,397,500	1,361,700,000	6.1
86	Morton Norwich	36,182,000	656,733,000	5.5	53	American Brands	77,270,500	5,176,700,000	1.5
94	Standard Brands	34,191,000	2,400,000,000	1.4	54	Liggett Group	77,000,000	970,695,000	7.9
99	Carnation Co.	28,500,000	2,576,047,000	1.1					
	Gum and Candy					**Toiletries, Cosmetics**			
67	Mars Inc.	60,180,000	837,400,000	7.2	7	Warner-Lambert Co.	211,000,000	2,878,496,000	7.3
83	Wm. Wrigley Jr. Co.	37,771,852	445,639,000	8.5	9	Bristol-Myers Co.	192,850,000	2,450,429,000	7.8
					11	American Home Products Corp.	183,000,000	3,276,605,000	5.6
	Oil				38	Gillette Co.	99,000,000	1,710,471,000	5.8
					39	Revlon Inc.	92,000,000	1,451,669,000	6.3
15	Mobil Corp.	$163,043,300	$37,331,000,000	0.4	45	Chesebrough-Pond's	84,747,600	969,833,000	8.7
82	Exxon Corp.	38,000,000	64,886,000,000	0.6	62	Avon Products	63,800,000	2,014,706,000	3.2
					91	Noxell Corp.	34,902,400	156,408,000	22.3
	Photographic Equipment				96	Alberto-Culver	32,391,872	172,537,684	18.8
					100	Beecham Group	27,656,500	1,910,817,000	1.4
44	Eastman Kodak Co.	86,071,700	7,012,923,000	1.2					
71	Polaroid Corp.	52,752,500	1,376,590,000	3.8		**Wine, Beer and Liquor**			
	Retail Chains				32	Seagram Co.	120,000,000	2,272,584,000	5.3
					33	Heublein Inc.	118,000,000	1,620,112,000	7.3
2	Sears, Roebuck & Co.	417,934,900	17,946,000,000	1.9	34	Anheuser-Busch	116,599,000	2,701,611,000	4.3
5	K mart.	250,000,000	11,695,539,000	2.1	68	Jos. Schlitz Brewing Co.	58,213,000	1,083,272,000	5.4
27	J. C. Penney Co.	125,000,000	10,845,000,000	1.2	89	Brown-Forman.	35,000,000	560,000,000	6.2
	Soaps, Cleansers (And Allied)					**Miscellaneous**			
1	Procter & Gamble	554,000,000	9,329,306,000	5.9	24	Johnson & Johnson	134,000,000	1,991,307,000	6.7
18	Unilever	145,000,000	1,812,000,000	8.0	25	U. S. Government.	128,452,200	—	—
29	Colgate-Palmolive Co.	122,500,000	4,312,054,000	2.8	26	Gulf + Western Industries	126,787,000	4,311,956,000	2.9
77	S. C. Johnson & Son.	43,903,400	550,000,000	8.0	50	Loews Corp.	78,885,800	3,455,644,000	2.3
93	Clorox Co.	34,645,000	1,046,577,000	3.3	64	American Express	62,000,000	4,084,500,000	1.5
					76	Greyhound Corp.	45,742,500	4,589,765,000	1.0
	Soft Drinks				81	Kimberly-Clark Corp.	38,139,000	1,910,600,000	2.0
					88	Mattel Inc.	35,629,600	493,563,000	7.2
16	PepsiCo	156,000,000	4,300,006,000	3.6	95	Scott Paper Co.	33,274,000	1,724,897,000	1.9
22	Coca-Cola Co.	138,805,300	4,337,900,000	3.2					

Source: *Advertising Age,* 6 September 1979.

of forecasted sales can also be used; the calculation is done in the same way.

While the percentage-of-sales method is quick, easy, and accepted by many firms, it has an inherent weakness. When sales are good, the advertising budget increases. When sales are bad, advertising is reduced. The basic principle at work is that advertising becomes a *result* of sales, which is contrary to the basic concept of promotion. Advertising should increase sales not the other way around.

An additional problem in the percentage-of-sales budgeting approach is the lag effect in planning. For example, a 1983 marketing plan would be developed in 1982. The advertising budget would be based on the last full year sales; in this case, that would be 1981. As a result, the advertising budget for 1983 would actually be based on sales figures that would be two years old by the time the budget was implemented—another inherent weakness in the percentage-of-sales approach.

Exhibit 5-6 illustrates examples of the budgeting approach using advertising as a percentage of past sales for the top national U. S. advertisers in 1976. As can be seen, the percentages used in various industry categories vary widely as does the percentage of sales allocated by individual companies.

Percentage of gross margin: Another popular method of advertising budgeting is a percentage of the gross margin (net sales less cost of goods) of the company or

Exhibit 5-7. Estimates of average advertising sales and advertising to gross profit margin by industry.

INDUSTRY	SIC	A&P AS % Sales 1978	% Margin 1978	INDUSTRY	SIC	A&P AS % Sales 1978	% Margin 1978
Agriculture production-crops	100	4.2	8.2	Rubber & misc. plastics prods	3000	1.3	4.9
Agriculture production-livestock	200	1.0	4.9	Fabricated rubber prods NEC	3060	1.9	7.0
Metal mining	1000	0.1	0.2	Misc. plastic products	3070	0.9	3.3
Copper ores	1020	0.2	0.9	Footwear except rubber	3140	2.3	7.1
Lead & zinc ores	1030	0.0	0.1	Leather goods NEC	3190	1.6	3.9
Gold ores	1040	0.0	0.0	Flat glass	3210	0.8	2.4
Bituminous Coal & Lignite Min	1210	0.0	0.0	Glass containers	3220	5.9	16.1
Crude petroleum & natural gas	1310	0.1	0.3	Cement hydraulic	3240	0.1	0.2
Drilling oil & gas wells	1380	0.1	0.3	Structural clay products	3250	1.1	10.0
Misc. nonmetallic minerals	1490	−0.0	−0.0	Pottery products NEC	3260	2.5	6.8
General building contractors	1520	0.8	5.5	Concrete gypsum & plaster	3270	0.4	1.6
Operative builders	1530	1.0	4.2	Abrasive asbestos & misc. min.	3290	0.5	2.1
Construction-not bldg. constr	1600	0.3	1.2	Blast furnaces & steel works	3310	0.2	1.1
Construction-spl contractors	1700	0.5	1.9	Iron & steel foundries	3320	−0.0	−0.0
Food & kindred products	2000	3.3	9.8	Prim smelt-refin nonfer. mtl.	3330	0.5	2.1
Meat products	2010	1.2	7.7	Second smelt-refin. nonfer. mtl.	3340	0.2	0.9
Dairy products	2020	1.7	11.6	Rolling & draw nonfer. metal	3350	0.5	2.3
Canned-preserved fruits-vegs	2030	2.3	10.2	Misc. primary metal products	3390	0.6	1.9
Flour & other grain mill prods	2040	1.9	10.8	Metal cans & shipping cont.	3410	1.9	8.8
Bakery products	2050	1.6	3.8	Hardware NEC	3420	1.7	5.0
Cane sugar refining	2060	2.4	6.4	Heating equip. & plumbing fix.	3430	1.3	4.7
Fats & oils	2070	2.5	20.1	Misc. metal work	3440	0.9	3.2
Beer, alcoh bev & soft drink	2080	5.1	14.8	Bolts-nuts-screws-riv-washrs	3450	0.5	1.6
Food preparations NEC	2090	1.2	3.1	Ordnance & accessories	3480	2.9	29.6
Cigarets	2110	6.2	14.7	Valves-pipe fittings ex brass	3490	1.2	3.7
Cigars	2120	2.3	8.2	Engines & turbines	3510	1.0	2.8
Textile mill products	2200	0.8	3.7	Farm & garden machinery & eqp.	3520	1.1	4.3
Floor covering mills	2270	1.3	4.5	Construction machinery & eqp.	3530	0.8	3.0
Apparel & other finished prods	2300	1.7	6.0	Metalworking machinery & eqp.	3540	0.8	2.7
Lumber & wood products	2400	0.7	3.2	Special industry machinery	3550	1.3	3.4
Wood buildings-mobile homes	2450	0.9	5.2	General industrial mach. & eqp.	3560	1.1	3.4
Household furniture	2510	1.7	7.2	Office computing & acctg. mch.	3570	1.3	2.8
Office furniture	2520	0.9	3.0	Refrig & service ind. machine	3580	1.8	6.9
Paper & allied products	2600	0.9	3.0	Elec. & electr. mach. eq. & supp.	3600	1.4	4.8
Convert paper-paperbd pd NEC	2640	1.7	4.1	Elec. transmission & distr. eqp.	3610	1.1	3.3
Paperboard containers-boxes	2650	−0.0	−0.0	Industrial controls	3620	0.7	2.1
Printing publishing & allied	2700	4.4	11.5	Household appliances	3630	3.9	12.9
Newspapers: publishing-print	2710	2.8	13.7	Electric lighting-wiring eqp.	3640	1.9	4.8
Periodicals: publishing-print	2720	3.9	14.4	Radio-tv receiving sets	3650	3.8	11.8
Books: publishing & printing	2730	4.2	7.6	Tele & telegraph apparatus	3660	1.6	6.2
Commercial printing	2750	0.9	2.7	Electronic components & acces.	3670	1.1	3.2
Manifold business forms	2760	0.6	1.5	Electrical machy-equip NEC	3690	1.7	4.6
Greeting card publishing	2770	2.3	4.0	Motor vehicles & car bodies	3710	1.6	8.0
Service indus for print trade	2790	0.7	1.3	Aircraft & parts	3720	0.8	4.0
Chemicals & allied prods	2800	1.9	5.0	Ship-boat building-repairing	3730	2.1	9.6
Indl. inorganic chemicals	2810	1.9	4.3	Railroad equipment	3740	0.1	0.7
Plastic matr-synthetic resin	2820	5.6	8.8	Motorcycles bicycles & parts	3750	−0.0	−0.0
Drugs	2830	6.4	12.5	Guided missiles & space vehc.	3760	0.3	1.7
Soap, detergents & cosmetics	2840	10.4	19.1	Travel trailers & campers	3790	0.9	6.9
Paints-varnishes-lacquers	2850	1.8	5.9	Engr. lab & research equip.	3810	1.4	3.3
Industrial organic chemicals	2860	−0.0	−0.0	Measuring & controlling inst.	3820	1.5	3.7
Agriculture chemicals	2870	1.4	3.0	Optical instruments & lenses	3830	1.7	4.3
Misc. chemical products	2890	2.2	5.1	Surg. & med. instruments & app.	3840	1.5	3.7
Petroleum refining	2910	0.6	3.0	Photographic equip. & suppl.	3860	1.9	4.6
Paving & roofing materials	2950	1.0	3.3	Watches clocks & parts	3870	1.7	6.9

| INDUSTRY | SIC | A&P AS | | INDUSTRY | SIC | A&P AS | |
		% Sales 1978	% Margin 1978			% Sales 1978	% Margin 1978
Jewelry-precious metals	3910	5.6	12.4	Retail-jewelry stores	5940	3.0	8.6
Musical instruments	3930	2.1	5.9	Retail-mail order houses	5960	13.4	27.9
Toys & amusement sport goods	3940	5.2	16.3	Retail-stores NEC	5990	3.0	10.0
Pens-pencil & other office mat.	3950	3.8	10.1	Savings & loan associations	6120	0.9	2.0
Misc. manufacturing	3990	1.1	4.2	Personal credit institutions	6140	1.7	4.0
Railroads-line haul operating	4010	1.3	5.9	Business credit institutions	6150	1.2	2.1
Trucking-local-long distance	4210	0.4	2.0	Finance-services	6190	1.7	7.8
Water transportation	4400	0.1	0.2	Security & commodity brokers	6200	1.9	9.4
Air transportation-certified	4510	1.5	5.9	Insurance agents & brokers	6400	1.0	11.0
Pipe lines ex natural gas	4610	0.0	0.0	Real estate	6500	1.9	7.0
Transportation services	4700	0.9	6.8	Subdivid. develop. ex cemetery	6550	2.0	7.7
Telephone communication	4810	0.5	1.3	Miscellaneous investing	6790	2.6	14.3
Radio-tv broadcasters	4830	2.6	4.8	Hotel-motels	7010	2.5	11.2
CATV	4890	1.6	6.0	Serv-personal	7200	3.0	10.5
Natural gas transmission	4920	0.1	0.2	Serv-linen supply	7210	0.4	1.4
Sanitary services	4950	0.2	0.5	Serv-advertising agencies	7310	1.6	5.1
Whsl-autos & parts	5010	1.3	7.1	Serv-clean & maint to bldg NEC	7340	0.2	1.2
Whsl-lumber & constr. matl.	5030	0.8	5.0	Serv-computer & data process	7370	0.9	4.1
Whsl-sporting & recrea goods	5040	4.3	13.6	Serv-R&D labs & profess serv	7390	2.7	10.7
Whsl-metals & minerals	5050	0.2	1.2	Serv-automotive repair & serv.	7500	1.2	5.1
Whsl-elec. apparatus & equip.	5060	3.8	12.2	Serv-motion picture production	7810	7.6	32.3
Whsl-hardwr. plum. heat. equip.	5070	0.3	1.5	Serv-motion picture theatres	7830	3.7	30.5
Whsl-machinery & equipment	5080	1.0	3.4	Serv-racing incl. track oper.	7940	3.1	19.0
Whsl-scrap & waste materials	5090	5.7	13.7	Serv-misc amusement & recreat.	7990	3.5	11.4
Whsl-drugs & proprietary	5120	1.9	4.1	Serv-nursing & personal care	8050	2.2	4.2
Whsl-groceries & related prods	5140	0.6	2.9	Serv-hospitals	8060	0.6	1.7
Whsl-nondurable goods NEC	5190	0.7	2.8	Serv-educational	8200	6.3	18.5
Retail-lumber-other bldg. mat.	5210	3.2	9.3	Serv-engineering & architect	8910	0.4	1.8
Retail-mobile home dealers	5270	0.8	4.9	Conglomerates	9990	1.2	4.4
Retail-department stores	5310	2.9	9.9				
Retail-variety stores	5330	2.3	8.9				
Retail-grocery stores	5410	1.3	5.8				
Retail-auto dealers gas stat.	5500	2.1	8.9				
Retail-apparel & access. store	5600	2.6	7.2				
Retail-women's ready to wear	5620	2.0	12.1				
Retail-shoe stores	5660	2.1	5.0				
Retail-furniture stores	5710	5.8	17.6				
Retail-hshold. appliance stores	5720	3.5	15.3				
Retail-eating places	5810	2.9	15.4				
Retail-drug-propriet. stores	5910	1.8	8.3				

Legend:
A&P = Advertising & promotion.
−0.0 = No data available for this value.
NEC = Not Elsewhere Classified
SIC = Standard Industrial Classification
A&P % SALES = A&P EXPENDITURES/NET SALES
A&P % MARGIN = A&P EXPENDITURES/(NET SALES—COST OF GOODS SOLD)

SOURCE: Schonfeld & Associates Inc.
120 South LaSalle Street
Chicago, Illinois 60603 (312) 236-5846

Source: *Advertising Age,* 23 July 1979.

brand. The calculation is a straightforward one in which the advertising budget is simply determined as a percentage of past or anticipated gross margin. For example, if a company has a gross profit margin on a product of $1,000,000 and invested 5 percent in advertising, the A/M (advertising as a percentage of gross profit) ratio would dictate a budget of $50,000.

Exhibit 5-7 illustrates the method of using advertising as a percentage of net sales (A/S) and the A/M by industry for the year 1976.

Unit of sales: similar to but not quite the same as the percentage-of-sales method is the allocation of advertis-

ing dollars on a per-unit basis. For example, an affordable advertising cost per unit is determined by the advertiser. By estimating the number of units which will be sold, the advertiser determines the advertising budget. The automobile industry is usually cited as an example for the use of this type of advertising budgeting. If an advertising investment, for example, of $25.00 per automobile was believed to be sufficient, and 50,000 units were forecast to be sold, the advertising budget would be $1,250,000 (50,000 units × $25 = $1,250,000). This method has the advantage of tying the advertising appropriation directly to the unit of sale but, again, suffers from the difficulty of determining whether advertising creates sales or is the result of sales. In this case, the advertising budget is not actually generated until the unit is sold.

Per outlet: Many durable goods manufacturers or service firms that rely heavily on the retailer for a personal selling effort set advertising budgets according to the number of outlets through which the product will be sold. For example, suppose a consumer loan organization determines that the company can invest $100 per loan office per year to generate personal loan applications. If it is assumed that there are 5,000 loan offices across the country, the advertising budget would be $500,000 (5,000 loan offices × $100 = $500,000).

The per-outlet approach has simplicity and is easily calculated. It does, however, ignore, the fact that all loan offices are not alike. Some offices may need considerably more than $100 per year in advertising support, and others less. In effect, the approach suggests that the cost of supporting an office in New York City is the same as that in Seminole, Oklahoma. A major difference, if only in media costs, makes the technique somewhat suspect.

Competitive expenditures: Some advertisers base their budget on what their competitors are spending, either on a dollar-matching basis or on a percentage of what is spent in the entire category. An advertiser, for example, may determine from published sources that his or her major competitor in the field is allocating $450,000 for advertising over a certain period of time. The advertiser would then appropriate the same amount to achieve a competitive parity or allocate a percentage amount which equalizes market share. Thus, if the competitor against whom the plan were developed had a 20 percent share of the over-all market and our advertiser had only a 10 percent share, the appropriation would be $225,000 (20 percent share vs. 10 percent share = 0.5 ratio; $450,000 × 0.5 = $225,000).

Another budgeting technique reflecting the competitive-parity approach is to budget as a percentage of the total advertising investment by all competitors in the same category. In most instances, this percentage is related to perceived market share or sales in the category. For example, if all advertising in the tulip bulb category amounted to $200,000, and Advertiser X had a 10 percent share of sales in that market, the advertising budget would then be established at $20,000 ($200,000 all advertising × .10 share = $20,000 budget). In some cases, advertisers will set their budget at a figure above or below their market share in hope either of capturing a larger portion of the market or of achieving advertising effectiveness at a slightly lower cost.

The competitive approach has the advantage of keeping the budget in line with competition so that advertising "wars" are kept in check. Further, the ability to tie the expenditure directly to the market share is appealing to many advertisers. On the minus side, the competitive-parity approach assumes that one's competitors know the best level for advertising expenditures in the category whether they actually do or not. Another problem is that the determination of competitive or total advertising expenditures in the category may be difficult or inexact.

The chief disadvantage is that the advertising budget is determined outside the company by competitors whose problems and opportunities may be entirely different. While there appears to be a correlation between share of advertising and share of market (which will be discussed later), the concept itself may be a self-fulfilling prophecy.

Minimum campaign: Broadbent has suggested a guideline approach, which, although lacking empirical evidence, appears to be quite well accepted among certain advertisers. He suggests that some advertisers believe there is a minimum campaign level, particularly in television, below which any investment is of little value.[9] Cohen suggests the same idea with the "noise-level approach." Her suggestion is that a minimum amount must be invested to be heard above the "advertising noise" of others in the marketplace.[10]

Regardless of the label, there is probably some value to the idea that, below a certain level, an advertising investment may not be heard in the marketplace. Unfortunately, that minimum level is largely a matter of judgment, and there appear to be no hard-and-fast rules to determine the minimum level or even prove it exists. Thus, advertisers following this approach apparently determine the budget level entirely on judgment.

Media inflation: With rapidly increasing media costs, several authorities have suggested that one guideline method for advertising budgeting is simply to use a percentage increase figure with each new budget to cover rising costs. No doubt, rapid rises in media costs have seriously eroded the buying power of all types of advertising budgets over the past few years. Media rate increases of 15 to 20 percent per year are not uncommon. Advertisers using a fixed percentage of their sales are probably actually losing message penetration as compared with a few years ago; i.e., unless brand sales are increasing at the same rate as media inflation, the advertisers' real-dollar investments must be declining. While this is certainly an area to be investigated, advertisers who attempt to budget on the basis of media inflation may find the required allocation beyond their means. Thus, they may be spending more and still getting less.

Arbitrary appropriations. Arbitrary allocations of advertising budgets are probably quite widespread in U.S. companies. Management determines the amount to be invested in advertising by some formula which is usually based on the financial situation of the entire company rather than an individual brand.

Because arbitrary appropriations are widespread, the basic methods used will be briefly reviewed here.

Management decision: The budget is established by top management and is simply allocated as the amount available to be spent. It may or may not be tied to the needs of the brand or the company. The campaign planner is concerned only in the allocation and control of advertising, not in budget determination.

What can be afforded: Top management allocates the advertising budget on the basis of what is believed to be affordable either by the brand or the company. The overriding factor in this management decision is usually the total profit desired as a return on investment. In other cases, the need may be to revitalize an existing brand or to attempt to halt declining sales of a product or brand by investing advertising funds. Since each case is individual, there may be rationales for the decision of what can be afforded. Here, too, advertising management is involved only in allocation and control of the budget, not in determination.

Go for broke: In rare instances, management may make a decision that advertising can be used either to capture a market or to attempt to save a dying brand. Advertising funds are then allocated with no relationship to sales, profits, or even return on investment. The basic plan simply is to overwhelm consumers or competition in the marketplace with advertising. Although rare, the approach is sometimes successful. Top management is usually responsible for the budget allocation, since the plan has a direct bearing on the over-all financial stability of the company.

The objective and task or task method. To develop a more scientific approach to advertising budgeting, the Association of National Advertisers commissioned a study by Russell Colley.[11] Published as a text, *Defining Advertising Goals for Measured Advertising Results* (DAGMAR) proposed that advertising should be budgeted to accomplish specific predetermined advertising goals. The approach is by far the most practical and scientific of the guideline methods. Yet, in spite of its appeal and soundness, the DAGMAR budgeting plan is apparently not widely used.

The DAGMAR approach suggests that specific advertising campaign objectives be set in advance. Based on those objectives, whether they be awareness, brand trial, or other results, the amount of advertising necessary to accomplish those goals can then be determined. The advertising budget is built from the ground up to achieve the predetermined goals rather than through the use of past or future results. The DAGMAR approach offers the opportunity to measure whether the goals set for the advertising campaign are achieved, something other guidelines approaches often ignore.

The major difficulty in using the DAGMAR budgeting method is that, although advertising goals and objectives are set in advance, it is most difficult to determine how much money is needed to achieve those goals. The objective, for example, of achieving 20 percent awareness of the advertising campaign theme is easily set by the planner. It is quite another task, however, to determine how much media reach and frequency will be needed to achieve that 20 percent awareness goal among consumers. While the objective-and-task method of advertising budgeting is more scientific and solidly based than other guideline methods, the chief advantage may be in determining whether the money was well spent after the fact, rather than in setting the original budget. The lack of information again hinders what seems to be a solid approach to advertising budgeting.

Theoretical methods

Theoretical approaches to advertising budgeting are usually based on some form of mathematical model using historical data as input. Most models are proprietary or require information which is not obtainable at a reasonable cost. Although often they are not practical for many companies, a brief discussion of the more popular models is presented in the interest of completeness.

James F. Engel, Hugh G. Wales, and Martin R. Warshaw[12] identify the primary quantitative methods as follows:

Sales model. Advertising is regarded as the only variable affecting sales. Thus, an optimization approach is used to determine the ideal advertising budget.

Dynamic models. These models attempt to account for the effects of advertising on sales over time. A typical approach is to incorporate the carry-over effects of present advertising into the future through modeling.

Competitive models. Another approach is to create a model of the activities of one's competition. Most such models are based on some form of game theory, in which it is assumed that all players are interdependent and that uncertainty results from not knowing what the others will do. A strategy is then developed for reducing and controlling this uncertainty through the model.

Stochastic models. Two major approaches using the laws of probability have been developed. One is based on Markov Chains; the other on the Stochastic Learning Model.

Simulation. Several computer models have been developed that simulate consumer behavior from stored data. Through experimental approaches, various levels of budget allocations are tested to determine the most effective return based on investment. While some success has been achieved, much work remains before this becomes a practical budgeting option.

Engel, Wales, and Warshaw believe that quantitative methods have three basic problems: (1) necessary information usually cannot be obtained at a reasonable cost; (2) most models assume that advertising is the only variable in the mix; and, (3) many assumptions in the various models appear to be quite arbitrary.[13]

One of the most successful commercial theoretical techniques is the Hendry model.[14] It has been used by many companies apparently with great success. The details of the model, unfortunately, are secret, but it is believed to be based on a mathematical model containing the "fundamental laws of consumer behavior which have been deductively derived." Developed in 1962, the Hendry model correlates the relationship between varying levels of advertising expenditure and the resulting share of market and contribution to profit. Because inputs (the direct manufacturing margin, the advertising expenditure level, and share of market) are easily obtained, the system has a number of followers who believe strongly in the approach.

Empirical approaches

McNiven's final advertising budgeting estimation technique is the empirical approach.[15] This method is different from others since it is built on experimental feedback rather than historical data. This budgeting approach is sensitive to specific characteristics of a given product class and to the marketing factors acting on the product at the time the concept is set.

Because experimentation requires trial and evaluation over time, it can be used only for specific brands and cannot be projected to other product classes or even to other brands in the same category. Most empirical approaches to budgeting are highly proprietary, and little is known of them.

A typical example of an experimentation approach might be the use of a series of test markets. Assume the product for which the budget is being evaluated is a brand of frozen orange juice. Initially, in several test markets of equal population, frozen orange juice usage and brand share would be selected and matched as closely as possible. Varying budget expenditure levels would be set for the markets. For example, Market A might be budgeted at the current national program level for that particular brand. Market B might be set at 50 percent of that amount and Market C at 150 percent. Advertising results in terms of both brand and total frozen orange juice category sales would be measured. In addition, communications effects would be tracked. Through a comparison of the results obtained over time, estimates of how the varying budget levels might perform on a broad-scale basis could be made. As a result of these experimentations, budget levels for the frozen orange juice brand could be established with more precision than with other less-sophisticated approaches.

How do most advertisers set advertising budgets?

A number of alternative advertising budgeting choices are available to the advertising campaign planner. Some are obviously better than others. Because our primary concern is application of existing theory, the question arises, "What method do most advertisers use to set an advertising budget?" Andre J. San Augustine and William Foley provide the answer.[16]

In 1975, San Augustine and Foley personally surveyed two persons, one a financial executive and one an advertising executive, from each of 25 firms in *Advertising Age's* annual list of 100 leading consumer advertisers. They also talked with two persons each from 25 firms selected from the 100 leading advertisers in business publications from a list developed by the American Business Press, Inc. The results appear in Exhibit 5-8.

Percentage of anticipated sales was the most popular budgeting method among both groups surveyed. Interestingly, there was substantial disagreement between the advertising executive and the financial executive surveyed as to which method was used by their company to set advertising budgets. San Augustine and Foley summarize their results by saying, "Budgeting by ear seems to be the rule rather than the exception of how large advertisers set budgets."[17]

Profit planning approach to advertising budgeting

So far, many alternative approaches to advertising budgeting have been reviewed. Advantages and disadvantages of each have been listed. What follows is an approach that fits the current marketing concept, especially for those firms employing the product management system. We recommend its use.

The profit planning approach consists of four basic steps:

1. The accurate forecasting of predicted sales for the coming budget period. This assumes the budgeter has a reasonably firm estimate of fixed and variable product manufacturing costs.

Exhibit 5-8. Methods used to set advertising budget.

	Nonconsumer Advertisers			Consumer Advertisers		
	Financial Executives	Advertising Executives	All	Financial Executives	Advertising Executives	All
Percent of sample	25	25	50	25	25	50
Method						
Quantitative models	0	0	0	0	4	2
Objective and task	0	20	10	0	12	6
Percent anticipated sales	24	32	28	48	52	50
Unit anticipated sales	8	12	10	4	12	8
Percent past years' sales	4	28	16	12	16	14
Unit past years' sales	4	4	4	0	12	6
Affordable approach	24	28	26	32	28	30
Arbitrary approach	44	24	34	8	16	12
All others	8	12	10	32	20	26
Don't know	4	0	2	4	0	2

Note: Figures exceed 100 percent because of multiple responses.

Source: Andre J. San Augustine and William Foley, *Journal of Advertising Research*, 1976.

2. The conversion of the sales forecast into a contribution margin for the product or brand (see figure 5-3).

3. Knowledge of the desired profit margin for the product, company, or brand either in total dollars or as a percentage of net sales price or gross margin.

4. The allocation of the available direct expense funds for marketing into advertising, promotion, selling expense, and research and development budgets.

This method permits an approach to advertising budgeting from a managerial standpoint. Emphasis is on achieving the desired profit margin for the firm based on adjustments of sales forecasts or direct expenses as necessary for achieving those goals. Each step of the profit planning approach is now outlined in concept and practice.

Accurate forecasting

Profit planning budgeting places primary emphasis on the ability of the manager to know three basic things: what the fixed and variable manufacturing costs for the product are at all levels of sales, the specific percentage or dollar amount desired as a profit margin for the company, product or brand, and a clear picture of the competitive market situation and consumers so an accurate sales forecast can be made.

Reviewing Exhibit 5-3 we can see that the product manager can manipulate only a few variables in developing an advertising budget. Once the desired profit margin has been established, assuming a competitive pricing situation, the only true variables are the number of units forecast to be sold, the variable product cost, and the direct expenses to be allocated. With a top line established by the sales forecast and a bottom line dictated by the desired profit margin, the manager's manipulative control over those costs in the middle is limited. Thus, primary emphasis in the profit planning approach to budgeting is on developing of the sales forecast.

Initially, the sales forecast should be made in units rather than dollars. The unit forecast can then be converted into dollars based on the selling price less the necessary dicsounts, which leads to the second step.

Estimating the contribution margin

Once the net sales price of the product has been determined, the cost-of-goods on the forecasted sales is deducted. This gives the Gross Margin. Distribution Expense is then deducted, leaving the Contribution Margin (see Exhibit 5-3). This Contribution Margin truly defines the funds available for all marketing, including advertising.

Deducting the desired product margin

Once the Product Margin has been established, either as a lump sum or as a percentage of Net Sales Price, it is deducted from the Contribution Margin of the product. The result is the total amount available for marketing (Direct Expenses).

Allocation of the marketing funds

The total available marketing funds (Direct Expenses in Exhibit 5-3) are now established. Based on that amount, the manager then allocates the available funds among sales expense, advertising and promotion investments, and research and development to achieve the best return. This is the point at which the budgeter knows the true alternatives available. It is also the point where the effects of various expenditures for sales vs. advertising, or advertising vs. promotion, can be estimated with some accuracy.

The major differences between the profit planning method and more traditional budgeting approaches is viewing the advertising budget within the framework of the entire product operating sheet rather than as a separate entity. Advertising is a function directly related to the profit margin and is a part of the total mix of product income and expense. Advertising is no longer theoretical. It is a practical device to be used by the campaign planner.

In the profit planning approach—because advertising is directly related to the sales forecast—effective advertising results in increased advertising dollars. Advertising and sales are inextricably intertwined. Also, the advertising budget is in the hands of the person responsible for the sale and profit of the product. By developing the sales forecast, estimating sales and costs, and knowing other expenses charged against the product, that person can justify the advertising investment to management.

The profit planning approach may not be feasible for some advertising budgeters because of lack of information on such factors as costs and profit margins desired. It is strongly recommended, however, as a sound real-world approach to establishing an advertising budget.

Budgeting for existing products

A definite difference exists between budgeting for an existing product and for a new product. First, we discuss establishing a budget for an existing product.

Budget allocation factors

While historical data provide a base for future sales forecasts for existing products, other factors in the marketplace also have a direct effect on the advertising budget. For marketers using percentage of last year's sales, per-unit allocation, and other traditional methods, these factors are extremely important. Advertisers using the recommended profit planning approach should consider these factors primarily in the context of how they will affect the key element in this budgeting method, the sales forecast.

Long-term vs. short-term goals. Determination of the goals for the existing product has a direct effect on the development of an advertising budget. If the product is declining in popularity, for example, and being "milked" by the manufacturer for profits, the advertising investment would be viewed differently than if the product were being managed for long-term growth. This question usually is answered according to the profit margin or contribution requested by management.

Competitive activity. Often, advertising budgets must be established which are based on competitive activity. If competition, for example, is succeeding with very heavy expenditures, consideration should be given to investment spending over and above the previously established budget. (Investment spending is budgeting advertising above that which could be anticipated as sufficient to provide an adequate return. In effect, management is "investing" in the brand by giving advertising support now in the hope that the investment will be returned in the future.) Competitive activity also often dictates whether available funds should be invested in advertising, promotion, or direct sales efforts.

Type of product. Exhibits 5-6 and 5-7 illustrate the established general levels of advertising expenditures for product categories and individual advertisers. The current situation in the general product category should be reviewed so the advertising planner can determine whether available funds are above or below the norm for the type of product to be advertised or the category in which it competes. Exhibit 5-7 shows the wide variance of advertising investments by product category.

Existing markets/target markets. Geographic location of product sales is often a major factor in advertising budgeting for existing products. If the bulk of the sales are made in large cities, more advertising funds are usually needed than if the sales are concentrated in smaller cities where media costs and competition may be lower. Likewise, if sales are concentrated in a few areas, media opportunities may be present that are not available to advertisers whose product sales are spread thinly over wide areas.

The brand's target market is another consideration. More funds are generally required for new markets as opposed to a policy of strict maintenance in existing markets. The same is true if increased efforts are to be used to offset competition or to make inroads in what is regarded as an opportunity market.

Distribution. The physical distribution of the product may also influence the advertising budget level. Where distribution has been achieved and where it is desired are often major budgeting considerations.

Frequently additional advertising is planned for certain regions or markets in an attempt to increase distribution of the brand. The advertising may appear to be directed to the consumer, but the true thrust of the campaign is aimed at influencing dealers to stock the product, thus obtaining additional distribution. Where this occurs, advertising budgets may actually be used as a form of direct sales efforts toward dealers.

Noise levels. As was previously discussed, an advertising "noise level" is thought to exist in the marketplace, although it has never been proved. The "noise level" is an issue of considerable debate and little fact. The advertising planner is left to determine in his own mind if such a "noise level" exists and if it is applicable to the product under consideration.

Budgeting procedure

Three primary budgeting procedures are available for existing brands.

Historical or traditional. The first and most common approach is through history and tradition. Using what has been done before has certain appealing characteristics which usually result in fairly rapid management approval of the planned expenditure. Unfortunately, past methods or approaches may not fit the marketplace in the future. If marketing is a dynamic system, history and tradition offer only limited assistance in determining future actions.

Guidelines. A multitude of guideline approaches are available to the advertising budgeter, as was discussed earlier. The method using straight percentage of past or future sales is probably the most widely practiced.

Profit planning approach. The profit planning approach is strongly recommended for the development of budgets for existing products. The sales forecast is

the key element in this budgeting method.

Budgeting for new products

Budgeting advertising for a new product or brand takes an approach different from those methods previously discussed. The most common technique is based on a payout plan. The payout plan rationale is as follows:

A new brand or product requires a heavier investment in advertising and promotion to get started than do existing brands. Because the new brand has no sales income to pay for the advertising, the company must forego profits on the brand until it can pay its own way. The parent company should invest funds in advertising and promotion for the new brand until it is established. As the new brand achieves sales and profits in the market, the investment money and previously lost profits are repaid to the parent company. Because the procedure usually cannot be accomplished in one budgeting period (ordinarily one year), a payout plan is developed in which the advertising planner for the new brand budgets the payoff of the parent's investment over a period of several budgeting periods, usually two to three years for a consumer product.

The procedure for developing a payout plan consists of four steps which are discussed below and illustrated in Exhibit 5-9.

Estimation of share goal.

The total market must be determined for the product category the new brand is entering. This estimation

Exhibit 5-9. Three-year payout plan: hypothetical consumer product.

		Theoretical Marketing Years		
		Year 1	Year 2	Year 3
(A)	Total market in units	20,000	22,000	23,000
(B)	Average percent of market-share goals	8	10	11
(C)	Market sales in units	1,600	2,200	2,530
(D)	Pipeline in units	288	50	28
(E)	Factory shipments in units	1,888	2,250	2,558
(F)	Net trade sales @ $6 per unit	$11,328	$13,500	$15,348
(G)	Less fixed and variable cost of goods			
(H)	@ 3.50 per unit	$ 6,608	$ 7,875	$ 8,953
(J)	Gross margin	$ 4,720	$ 5,625	$ 6,395
(K)	Less distribution expense @ 10¢ per unit	$ 189	$ 225	$ 256
(L)	Contribution margin	$ 4,531	$ 5,400	$ 6,139
(M)	Advertising	$ 3,000	$ 2,500	$ 2,000
(N)	Promotion	$ 5,000	$ 1,000	$ 1,000
(O)	Product margin (or loss)	$ (3,469)	$ 1,900	$ 3,139*
(P)	Product margin as a percent of sales	—	14.1	20.4
(Q)	Cumulative product margin	$ (3,469)	$ (1,569)	$ 1,570

*Product pays out at Month 30

usually is made after searching trade or research sources. Based on the estimated total market, a growth projection based on the budget period is developed. This usually covers three to five years.

As illustrated in Exhibit 5-9, the total market for the hypothetical product illustrated is estimated at 20,000 units in Year 1. The market is expected to grow by 10 percent to 22,000 units in Year 2 and by 4½ percent or to 23,000 units in Year 3 (Line A).

The new brand's estimated share of the total market must then be determined. Because a new brand's sales typically start slowly and increase until reaching a certain level, an average share for the year is often used. For example, the average market share goal for Year 1 is 8 percent (Line B). For the company to achieve that goal, brand share would probably have to be above 8 percent at the end of Year 1 to average out to that level. Most new brands reach their peak sales share between three and nine months after introduction. After that time, they may slowly decline to a stable position as new tryers either become loyal users or switch again to another brand.

Determination of trade inventories (pipeline)

In addition to consumer sales, an estimate must be made of the sales that will be made to the trade to stock the shelves at retail. This is called the "pipeline." Typically "pipeline" sales occur only at introduction. However, as a brand's distribution increases or more product is stocked on retail shelves, additional sales may be made into the "pipeline." All "pipeline" sales are one time only and usually decline dramatically after Year 1 (see Line D).

When a new product is introduced, several methods of estimating the amount of product going into the "pipeline" are used. One method is to use a straight-line projection based on the percentage of estimated sales of the product for the year. This figure varies widely depending on the speed with which the product sells and how large a display is normally found in the store.

A more widely used method is to estimate the number of units of the product that would be on display plus the amount stocked as "back-up" (or that found in the storeroom of the retail outlet) and then multiply that amount by the number of stores in which distribution is expected to be achieved. For example, assume we are introducing a new line of packaged dry soup mixes. The soup mixes are packed 24 packages to the case. We have three flavors. Normal retail display is one case of 24 packages per flavor per store. Because the sales volume of dry soup mix is fairly high, the retail store usually maintains one additional case per flavor per store in the back room for restocking the shelves. In other words, we estimate that, for all the stores in which we obtain distribution of our product, there will be two cases per flavor in the "pipeline." If our estimated distribution volume of 10,000 stores is achieved nationwide, we would have 60,000 cases of the product in the "pipeline" (2 cases per flavor × 3 flavors = 6 cases per store × 10,000 stores = 60,000 cases of the product). While there are alternative methods of determining the "pipeline," this is a common approach.

Determination of advertising/promotion expense

No hard and fast rules exist for budgeting advertising and promotional expenditures for a new product. There are, however, some rules of thumb which have proven successful for a number of marketers.

As shown in the hypothetical example (Exhibit 5-9), advertising and promotion expenditures are heavier in the introductory year than in the following years (see Lines M and N). This is logical since the product is unknown to the consumer and the trade. It simply costs more to launch a new product than to support an existing known product.

Three basic approaches to budget allocation are used: buy-your-way-in, competitive expenditure, and profit planning.

Buy-your-way-in. This approach entails allocating enough money in dealer incentives, such as promotional discounts or price allowances, to achieve anticipated distribution. At the same time, heavy advertising and consumer promotion are used so that, once the product is on the dealers' shelves, consumers are encouraged to try it. The budget is set essentially by estimating the cost of required advertising and promotion and allocating that amount. In effect, this budget plan is a form of the go-for-broke approach previously outlined. While the method is expensive and not always successful, in some instances it is the only method that can be used.

Competitive expenditure approach. The competitive expenditure approach to budgeting is widely used. The rule of thumb used is that the advertiser must spend at one and one-half to two times the annual advertising rate of competitors who have a share equal to that of the company or to its brand share objective. For example, assume our brand V has an 8 percent market share goal for the first year (Exhibit 5-9). Studies are made of the competitive market shares for the purpose of learning which brand has approximately that share of the total we seek. Assume brand Z had an 8 percent market share. Based on that, an estimation would then be made of the annual advertising expenditure for brand Z. Assume our competitor is estimated to be spending approximately $1,500,000 on brand Z. On that basis, using our rule of thumb, we should invest

Exhibit 5-10. In marketing a new brand, it's your *share* of advertising (marketing effort) that counts.

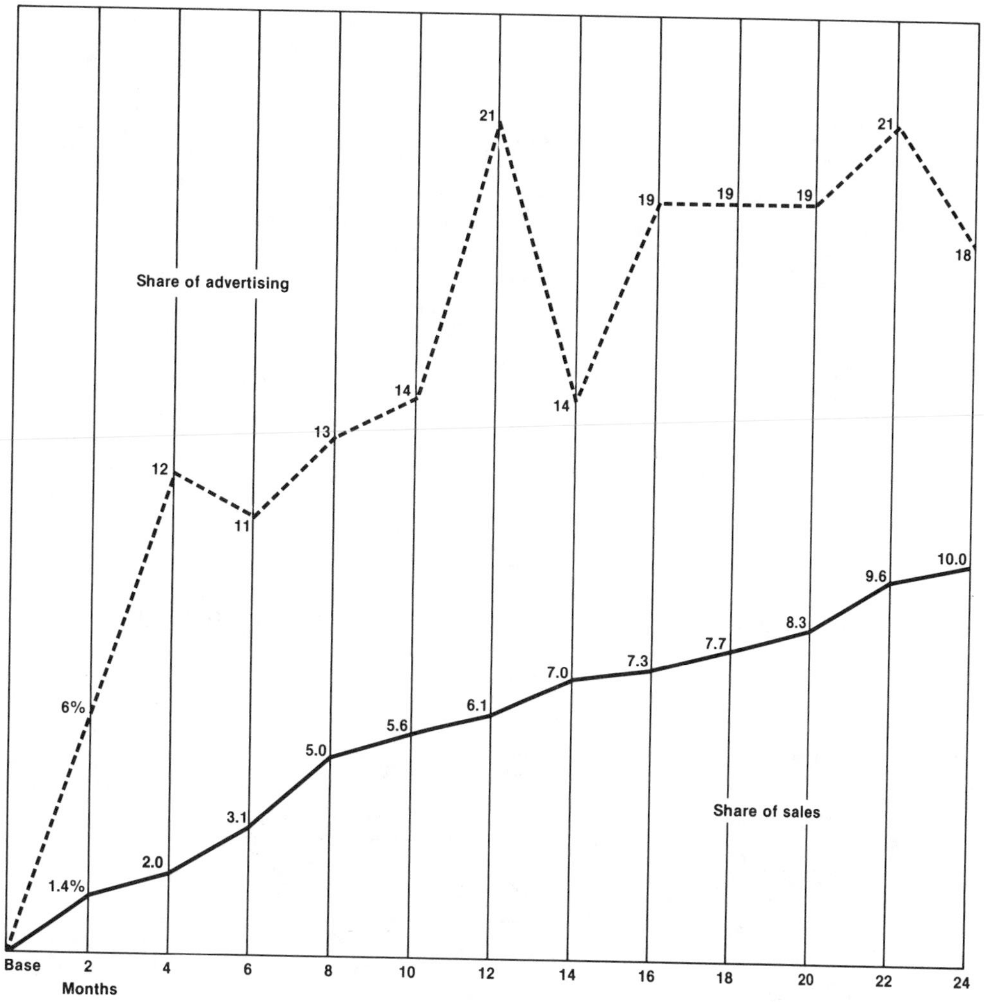

Source: Peckham, *The Wheel of Marketing,* 1975.

between $2,250,000 and $3,000,000 for our brand V, or approximately one and one-half to two times the annual rate for competitive brand Z.

Surprisingly, a high correlation seems to exist between competitive expenditures and achieved brand shares for new products over a period of time. J. O. Peckham, formerly of A. C. Nielsen Company, has charted this correlation for a number of products over a number of years. Exhibit 5-10 illustrates the actual experience of a new product in the food category over an initial two-year introductory period. The ratio of share of advertising to share of marketing was 1.6.

Peckham further illustrates the same situation with several brands in the food and household-products categories in Exhibit 5-11. The first set of bars illustrates the share of sales attained by each brand over a two-year introductory period. The second set of bars illustrates the share of advertising for each brand over

the same two-year period. The ratio is obtained by dividing share of advertising by share of sales. For the food-product category, the average ratio of share of advertising to share of sales is 1.7 and the median 1.5. In the toiletry-product category, the average ratio of share of advertising to share of sales is 1.5 and the median 1.5.

While the cases illustrated here are only examples, Peckham offers more than 40 years' experience with Nielsen figures to substantiate the general rule of thumb of a ratio of approximately 1.5 to 2.0 share of advertising to share of sales, which is needed for the successful launching of a new brand in the marketplace. The approach is often called "Peckham's Law."[18]

The profit planning approach. While the two methods described above are used by many marketers, another approach is suggested here. While the methods labeled

Exhibit 5-11. Two-year summary. Share of advertising—share of sales relationships for new brands of food products.

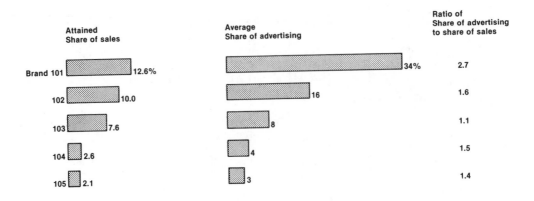

Two-year summary. Share of advertising—share of sales relationships for new toiletry brands.

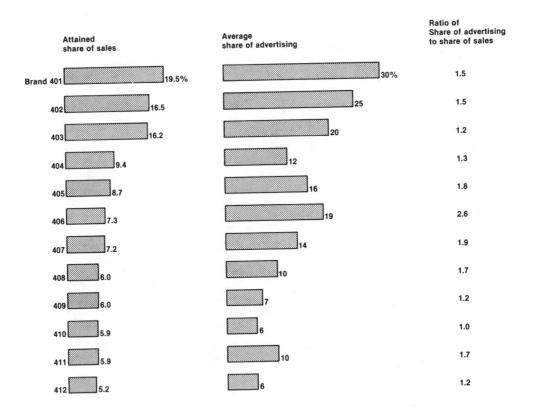

Source: Peckham, *The Wheel of Marketing*, 1975.

buy-your-way-in and competitive-expenditure have been successful, they ignore the basic reason for the payout planning program, namely, the payout. In most companies, there is an acceptable payback period for new products, usually between 12 and 30 months for consumer nondurable goods. With this guideline, the same approach can be used to determine the introductory budget as was recommended for existing products, the profit planning approach.

The profit planning approach suggests that the length of the payout period be determined first. Based on that time span, the advertising budget for the new-product introduction can be calculated. For example, in Exhibit 5-9, the hypothetical product illustrated has a payout or break-even point at approximately Month 30. (Sufficient profit will accrue in the sixth month of Year 3 to erase the carryover deficit from Years 1 and 2, as illustrated by Lines P and R.) Had there been a management decision that the new product had to pay out in 24 months, the only options would have been to raise the Market Share Goal (Line B) or reduce the advertising or promotion expenditures during the introductory periods (Lines M and N). Either step should allow an earlier payout as required by management.

The profit planning approach is suggested, although it is a more complex budgeting procedure for a new product than the alternatives discussed previously. The profit planning approach adopts a management viewpoint, dictated by the needs of the brand and the entire company. Other allocation methods lack this profit-oriented view, particularly the buy-your-way-in approach, which conceivably could end up as a major expense to the company rather than a payout.

Determination of the payout period

The final step in the development of a payout plan is determination of the length of the payout. The actual calculation is a straightforward one. The Cumulative Product Margin (Line R) is carried from period to period until the Product Margin (Line P) exceeds the amount previously invested. At the point the Product Margin gains exceed the Cumulative Product Margin losses, the product has returned all the initial seed money to the company and is now on a profit-making basis.

The calculation of the payout period is a result of the competitive-expenditure and buy-your-way-in budgeting methods. In the profit planning approach, however, it is an integral part of the development of the advertising and promotion budget, since the payout time is the basis on which the available funds are determined. This is another reason the profit planning approach is suggested for a new product.

While the payout plan requires many assumptions and estimates of what can or might occur in the future, it is the soundest method of determination and allocation of an advertising budget for a new product. Although the method is subject to variations in estimates, management is given a clear picture of exactly what is proposed, the amount of money involved, and the length of time deemed necessary to recoup the investment.

Management decisions on new-product introductions are usually based on (a) the amount of money risked the first year should the goals not be achieved and an absolute disaster occur; and (b) the sales and brand share the first year after the payout is achieved. This is usually indicative of the return that can be expected from the new brand on an on-going basis. Using these two figures, management can then determine the ratio of the risk to return when the plan is compared to alternative uses of the funds.

Determination of an advertising budget for a new product is probably the least precise of that for any budget a company might develop. There is no past experience on which to base one's plans, and there is no successful way of knowing the future. The only option is to approach the problem in the most logical and systematic manner possible. At this time, that approach appears to be the payout plan.

Notes

1. Joel Dean, *Managerial Economics* (Englewood Cliffs, N. J.: Prentice-Hall, 1951), pp. 368-69.
2. Kenneth A. Longman, *Advertising* (New York: Harcourt Brace Jovanovich, 1971), pp. 230-38.
3. Everett Rogers and F. Floyd Shoemaker, *Communication of Innovations,* 2d ed. (New York: Free Press, 1971).
4. Longman, *Advertising*, pp. 230-31.
5. Simon Broadbent, *Spending Advertising Money,* 2d. ed. (London: Business Books Limited, 1975), pp. 156-57.
6. David L. Hurwood and James K. Brown, *Some Guidelines for Advertising Budgeting* (New York: The Conference Board, 1972), pp. 22–23.
7. Ibid., p. 38.
8. M. A. McNiven, *How Much to Spend for Advertising* (New York: Association of National Advertisers, 1969).
9. Broadbent, *Spending Advertising Money,* p. 165.
10. Dorothy Cohen, *Advertising* (New York: Wiley, 1972), pp. 272-73.
11. Russell Colley, *Defining Advertising Goals for Measured Advertising Results* (New York: Association of National Advertisers, 1961).
12. James F. Engel, Hugh G. Wales, and Martin R. Warshaw. *Promotional Strategy,* rev. ed. (Homewood, Ill.: Richard D. Irwin, 1971), pp. 213-23.
13. Ibid., pp. 223-24.
14. McNiven, *How Much to Spend,* pp. 47-61.
15. Ibid., pp. 67-71.
16. Andre J. San Augustine and William F. Foley. "How Large Advertisers Set Budgets," *Journal of Advertising Research,* October 1975, pp. 11-16.

17. Ibid., pp. 11.
18. J. O. Peckham Sr., *The Wheel of Marketing* (Privately printed, 1975), pp. 73-76.

Creative strategy overview

Until this point, the development of the campaign has been rigorous labor. There's nothing glamorous about digging for the marketing facts so badly needed for the campaign foundation. It's often difficult, taxing work requiring a tremendous amount of discipline. But the time comes when, as the late Leo Burnett so eloquently put it, "Somebody has to get out the ad." And this can be a time of work or play, depending on your point of view. Either way, be ready to invest a lot of energy.

The first thing to do is to aim your energies directly at the product. Get an accurate reading. Examine all the research in the situation analysis. Become intimate with the product personally, and then look for something unique. Leo Burnett would say, "Look for the inherent drama in the product; it's there somewhere."

Is the USP an endangered species?

Are there really any Unique Selling Propositions left in the world? Yes. But they are limited. When an agency finds a client who has developed a clearly different product to fulfill a consumer need or want, the job is simpler. Not necessarily easier, but simpler, because less time and energy are spent in deciding on the creative strategy.

Procter & Gamble is famous for developing products with honest, unique selling propositions. For example, Crest toothpaste with flouride received on-the-package approval from the American Dental Association. Not only was Crest a great product, it was so special that it caught the marketing leader, Colgate, off guard. Within months, Crest was the new leader with the only acknowledged flouride on the shelf.

Procter & Gamble currently is testing a new wet bathroom tissue that comes on the familiar perforated toilet paper roll. The wetness is impregnated into the tissue (it's oil based—an emolient) so the roll can be left in the open without drying out. Not a very glamorous product, but it promises a unique consumer benefit. The agency's biggest creative job will be to determine how to say "wet toilet paper on a roll is finally here" in a tasteful way.

Another famous Procter & Gamble product that hit the top of the sales charts is Pringles. Sales are now over $100 million a year. It's the most successful new package goods product introduction since 1971. Why? Sure, good creative advertising helped immensely. But having a truly unique selling proposition (promise) to make to the consumer was invaluable. No other potato chip on the market offered the promise of freshness and long shelf life in the home. Procter & Gamble filled that need and made millions by providing an easy-to-store package that was fresh for parties or picnics. In essence, the company took a convenience food and made it significantly more convenient.

It's a law in advertising: look for an honest USP. If there is one in your product, you have the best strategy possible.

What if there is no USP?

Be honest. That's the first rule. Don't try to promise a quality as unique or special if it's available in other products. Invention of a pseudo USP may fool the consumer on the first trial, but actual usage probably will make enemies for the product as well as the whole advertising industry. Deceptive advertising will merely speed up the product's death if it is used, not to mention the moral aspects of such practices.

Look for your product's consumer strength

Let's assume your agency is assigned to develop the

creative strategy for a parity product, canned peas. Your product has a consistent track record as a fancy, high-quality product, but it is not significantly different physically from some of your competitor's fancy brands. What's your first step? Check to see if the research experts have been able to discover *why* people like your brand. Or, learn what specific qualities they look for in the generic product itself. You still want to find a promise that is genuine and believable, that will persuade the target consumer to try your brand of peas.

Both formal and informal research is crucial at the grassroots consumer level when you have parity products. You must listen very carefully to your prospects. Focus studies will often bring out the important product advantages which may have been ignored in previous creative strategies.

Own your discovery by advertising it

Jolly Green Giant owns the idea of the sweet tender pea. Not because this is the only sweet tender pea in America, but because Leo Burnett writers and researchers discovered a few simple important facts. They discovered why consumers like Green Giant peas, not why copywriters like them. Then they made that promise come alive in their advertising copy. They positioned Green Giant as a consistently sweet tender pea picked and packaged at just the right moment. The promise is honest. It's presented in an interesting charming way. Consumers have put Green Giant among the top brands of sweet peas in America. But, obviously, it's not the only good, tender sweet pea available. So, the secret to advertising parity products is *discovery*. Discover (un-cover) your product's major strength from the consumer's viewpoint. Then, if you consistently advertise it in an interesting and compelling way, you'll soon own that product strength, exclusive or not.

How to launch a new parity product

From a marketing viewpoint, the shampoo product Agree could be classified as a parity product. This is because Agree is not the only brand of shampoo capable of reducing the natural oil buildup in hair and scalp. Several brands of shampoo and conditioner, in fact, claim this benefit in their ads and on their labels.

Listening to the consumer

S. C. Johnson & Son discovered a simple fact overlooked by their competitors. Nobody fully realized how important the oily hair problem was. Agree's primary target group, women 14 to 20, had real problems controlling oil accumulation in the hair and on the scalp. And no other manufacturer was focusing on that problem either in product development or in advertising copy. Other products hit around the problem, but not directly on it. The rest is history. S. C. Johnson & Son formulated a product to help solve the oily hair and scalp problem. But that was only half the task. Needham, Harper & Steers, the advertising agency for Agree, had the even bigger task of penetrating what Larry Jackson, product manager for Agree, called "a real dogfight, heavy-deal market."[1]

How did they succeed? Their now famous blitzkreig product sampling strategy showed true marketing brilliance. But before that, they listened. They did blind product tests with consumers before introducing the brand to make sure Agree was *perceived* as effective in reducing oily hair problems.[2] Then they hit on a brilliant copy idea that clearly communicated their product's solution to the young woman's biggest hair problem. And the genius was in how they said it: "helps stop the greasies" expresses the problem in the consumer's own language.

Remember, the first secret in successfully advertising a parity product is discovery. In this case, S. C. Johnson & Son discovered a real consumer problem. It had been there for years, but no one had capitalized on it. The company developed a product to solve that problem and clearly expressed it in their advertising. If they continue to advertise "helps stop the greasies" in a compelling way, they will *own* that promise, no matter how many other similar products try to claim it. Another way to express this strategy is to say Agree owns the "helps-stop-the-greasies" position. Positioning has to do with two things: the consumer's mind and the competitive environment of the brand.

Positioning—renting mind space

The dictionary defines a position as a point in space occupied by a thing or object. Consider the human brain as a *point in space*. When you position your product, you actually stake out a claim (advertise) for a space in the consumer's mind. Trouble is, very few spaces exist for each product category. "No Vacancy" signs are always up. Who can blame the consumer; he or she's blitzed with hundreds of advertising exposures every day. According to Harvard psychologist George A. Miller, the average human mind cannot deal with more than seven units at a time.[3] (Luckily phone numbers don't exceed the seven digits.) Most people can't recall more than five or six brand names in any given field.

Positioning a product is like renting space in the consumer's brain. There are lots of would-be renters, but few vacancies. Do you see the great challenge facing you? To gain a position or space, you must usually evict a present renter. A good example is the battle now being staged by Shasta cola in the top 50 U.S.

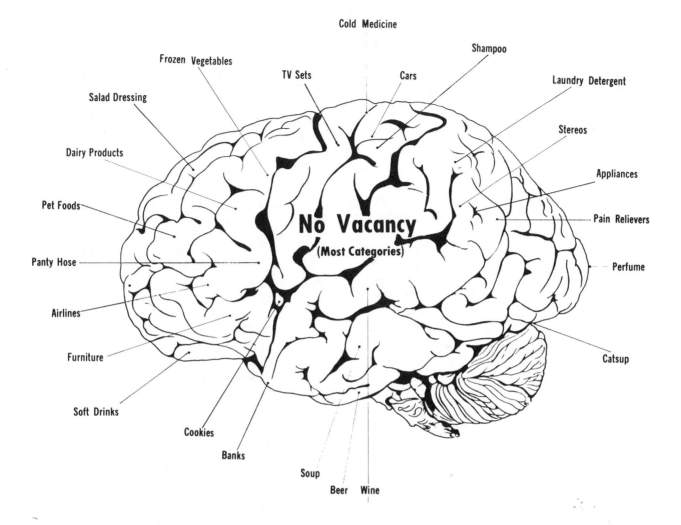

Cold Medicine

Shampoo

Frozen Vegetables

TV Sets   Cars

Laundry Detergent

Salad Dressing

Stereos

Dairy Products

Appliances

Pet Foods

No Vacancy
(Most Categories)

Pain Relievers

Panty Hose

Perfume

Airlines

Furniture

Catsup

Soft Drinks

Cookies

Banks

Soup

Beer   Wine

markets. The company's positioning strategy is to rent spaces now occupied by Coke and Pepsi. That's a mighty big job since Coke, Pepsi, and Royal Crown have had long-term leases on cola drink mind spaces. Nevertheless, if Shasta continues to advertise with messages that break through the consumer's screen, some consumers may be willing to give up part of that precious space to the new brand. If that occurs on a wide scale, Shasta will have a new position in the marketplace.

A negative position is often best

According to Trout and Ries,[4] a positioning strategy is often negative. It tells the consumer what the product is *not* rather than what it is. That's because the human mind tends to remember things better through association. Seven-Up's "Uncola" campaign is a classic example of negative positioning. Suave brand shampoo is another. In the Suave TV commercials, competitive brands are lined up and praised for their qualities. Suave is also shown and praised for the same qualities. Then the negative factor, price, is intro-

duced. "Theirs costs $1.89," the ad says. "Ours does the same thing for 99¢."

Another classic positioning coup was executed by Datril, an aspirin substitute. The strategy was to position Datril directly against the market leader, Tylenol. And the strategy showed real genius, because this was a totally new concept in pain relievers. Tylenol owned the category until Datril appeared alongside Tylenol and shouted "We're twins!" The result? Instant awareness for a former nobody. This comparative positioning strategy worked so well that the Tylenol company threatened lawsuits and other counterattacks.

How does positioning relate to brand awareness

Very closely. As we discussed in chapter 4, there are seven steps in Lavidge and Steiner's model of the buying process. The bottom step is awareness; the top step is purchase. Once a product rents a space in the consumer's mind, all seven steps must be climbed (some may be skipped) until purchase occurs. Obviously, if advertising succeeds in renting mind space for a product and then fails to help move the product up the seven steps from awareness to purchase, the space will soon be lost to a competitor. That's why you can only *rent* mind space. You are constantly reminded that a consumer's mind cannot be permanently bought.

USP and positioning strategies can work together

Datril's positioning strategy was to take over the mind space being rented by Tylenol. A USP was clearly stated in the first wave of Datril's attack on Tylenol. Datril was priced lower—in some areas more than 50 percent lower than Tylenol. That was a solid USP. And it worked until Tylenol stole the pricing thunder by knocking its price even lower than Datril.

The Grumman American light airplane was *positioned* by the Murray-Chaney agency *against "the big 3,"* Cessna, Piper, and Beechcraft. The company also had a unique selling proposition: "The Grumman American can fly faster and greater distances than 'the big 3' using the same horsepower engine and the same quantity of fuel."

Don't be caught in the either/or trap, i.e., positioning vs. unique selling propositions. Most often, positioning will prevail as the best strategy since truly unique products are not common in today's market. However, whenever the two can be used together, they pack a powerful wallop. In effect, load both barrels if you can.

Developing the copy policy

Discipline helps

The essence of a copy policy is discipline. The word "policy" comes from "police," meaning to control and regulate. Copywriters are not stifled by order and form; on the contrary, firm direction inspires and challenges most writers. Masters of poetry wrote within the confines of the sonnet: "fourteen lines of iambic pentameter rhyming in three quartrains and a couplet," as David Ogilvy reminded his creative people.

Leonardo Da Vinci's lifelong motto—and his daily practice—was obstinate rigor.[5] This is the key to successful copy strategy—rigorous discipline and the ability to endure obstinately until the infant "big idea" is conceived, delivered, and nourished into a mature selling campaign.

Here is a suggested format for your copy policy:

1. Product fact sheet
2. Advertising objectives
3. Advertising strategy
4. Creative objectives

5. Creative strategy
6. Copy platform

Ideally the advertising objectives and strategy and the creative objectives and strategy should be sharp, lucid, and brief enough to fit on one page.

The product fact sheet: a compost of marketing data

The first part of a copy policy should focus on key issues about the product. A "fact sheet" is a one-page summary of everything that has already been said. The writer is required to discipline him- or herself to reduce 98 percent of all the marketing data into a neat, easily digestible compost of rich information. From this fertile soil, healthy creative concepts can spring.

Here is a suggested outline for a product fact sheet. Use it with caution. Adjust it to your needs and establish your own pattern, your own discipline.

Sample product fact sheet

1. Product advantages
2. Product disadvantages
3. Key research results:
   (a) Product tests
   (b) Consumer attitudes about product
   (c) Consumer attitudes about current advertising
4. Ingredients and construction of product
5. What problems and needs does product solve?
6. What product changes, if any, are recommended?

Advertising objectives

This definition of objective is simple and direct. It applies not only to advertising, but to marketing, media, creative, and sales promotion objectives as well.

Objective: An aim or end of action. A clearly stated position you wish to attain. *What* you plan to do, not how.

In stating your advertising objectives, simply say what your communication aims are. What is the hoped-for end of your advertising messages?

Once you have written your advertising objectives, see if they measure up to these professional standards.

Have you stuck to communications objectives? There's a big difference between advertising objectives and marketing objectives. Marketing objectives state the goals for the product in the marketplace, e.g., garner a 25 percent brand share by end of 1985. Advertising objectives state the communications goals, e.g., achieve a 25 percent brand preference by end of current fiscal year.

Quantify objectives whenever possible. If progress toward meeting the objectives can be measured, say how much progress is expected over "x" period of time. Also, tell how it is to be measured, e.g., Gallup Phone Survey or Starch or other.

State realistic objectives. If you expect to win new customers or keep present ones, set realistic goals. Don't be afraid to take a reasonable risk, but be ready to back it up with sound logic.

Study the following set of advertising objectives for a major package goods brand.

Advertising Objectives To Be Achieved in One Year

- Increase brand awareness from 58 to 70 percent nationally.
- Increase brand awareness to 80 percent in ten key metro markets that show the highest Brand Development Index (BDI).

Advertising strategy

The advertising strategy is the action, the how behind your campaign. It clearly states how you plan to reach the advertising objectives to which you are already committed. The following definition can apply to marketing, media, creative, sales promotion, and any other kind of strategy.

Strategy: The art of employing objectives. Strategy tells how the objectives will be attained and what specific tools will be used to do it.

Here are guidelines to help you keep your advertising strategy in line with objectives.

Does the advertising strategy mesh with your marketing? This is a major purpose of a campaign—continuity between all marketing activities. If the true personality of your product is "ugly but functional," be honest in your advertising strategy. Call the VW a bug and don't try to make it something it isn't. That was Doyle Dane Bernbach's strategy to accomplish the objectives of awareness and credibility for early Volkswagen advertising. The creative tools used in this strategy were honesty, openness, and tongue-in-cheek humor.

Demand a promise in your strategy. This is covered in the section on copy platform. Don't depend on people buying your brand because you have cute or humorous ads. Cute or funny may help but, if you fail to make a meaningful promise, you're doomed. The company selling Pampers has a strong promise in its advertising strategy:

> Keeps your baby drier and happier. Pampers are superior to other diapers because they help keep wetness away from your baby's skin.

Create a personality for your product. An outstanding example is Orville Redenbacher's Gourmet Popping Corn from Hunt/Wesson Foods. Redenbacher's earthy homespun personality has been put right inside the jar. The campaign was all carefully planned from Reden-

bacher's portrait on the label to his folksy grin on television. The effect is an honest personality for an honestly superior product.

Focus on key product benefits. Kodak's new instant film processing camera has a lot of technical benefits including speed. Polaroid, however, has already educated the consumer to these advantages. Kodak has wisely focused on its known strength—color quality. Their strategy: position Kodak's instant picture as superior in brilliant natural colors compared to the market leader, Polaroid.

Creative objective (the problem)

An advertising plan needs to isolate the copy problem. And a proper place is needed for the problem, integrated with the copy policy. This is where the Foote, Cone Belding/Honig agency (famous for the Levis campaign) puts it: right after the advertising objectives and strategy.

The creative objective focuses on the single (main) copy problem. An example we discussed in chapter 2 promoted the Grumman American private airplane. The Murray-Chaney agency stated the creative objective or copy problem this way:

> Since our target audience's first reason for buying an airplane is transportation, yet with strong overtones of adventure and status, how can we position the Grumman American as a simple and efficient airplane that is practical, yet address the pilot's needs for status and adventure?

Here's how the creative objective (or problem) was stated for Frito-Lay's Rold Gold Pretzels:

> In light of Rold Gold's low brand awareness and name misassociation, how can Rold Gold best be positioned (a) in the consumer's mind and (b) against competition?[6]

And, for Coca Cola's brand Sprite:

> Considering the increasing consumer demand for lemon-lime flavored soft drinks, and since no other major soft drink is clearly calling itself a lemon-lime, should Sprite keep its current "Lymon" positioning strategy?[7]

Creative strategy—the answer

Once the creative objective is clearly defined, you are ready to tackle the biggest job of all, the concept or the idea. The creative strategy is an *answer* to the creative objective. Notice the writing style for the creative objective; it's posed as a question. It cries out for an answer. In the case of the Grumman American light airplane, here's the answer:

Creative Strategy

Paint representative models of Grumman American aircraft in World War II fighter colors to dramatize our superior fuel and speed efficiency when compared with similarly priced models of "the big 3" in light aircraft sales, Cessna, Piper, Beechcraft.

Here's an outline for your creative strategy. When you think you've got the "big idea," measure it against these criteria:

Strive for excellence. Don't marry your first idea or your second. Or perhaps even your third. Resign yourself to do whatever it takes. Don't settle for any concept short of greatness. (Greatness means a compelling, *selling* idea.) And this idea must be so brilliant that your target audience will be blinded by its light. (Not to mention the client.)

Stake out a competitive position. Remember that advertising "rents" mind space. Your creative strategy should clearly spell out the position you expect to occupy in the consumer's mind. If you plan to erode a competitor's brand share, be blunt in your language.

> Lean Strips, a meatless bacon, is positioned as a less expensive bacon replacement. This product, which looks and tastes like bacon, will get its business from people who like bacon, not from people looking for a new kind of taste.[8]

It's quite clear how the consumer is expected to perceive this product (mind position) and where the business will come from (competitive position).

Look for a USP. If your product has a unique consumer benefit which is unavailable in competitive products, this may be your strongest possible creative strategy.

Use clear simple language. Manicure the creative section of your plan until it literally sings with clarity. Of all parts of an advertising plan, the client expects this to be easiest to understand.

The copy platform

This is a controversial tool that's been bandied about in textbooks for decades. Some professional copywriters still use a platform. Often it is used today as a teaching device. The copy platform is a mechanical tool that will discipline creative people to articulate a promise before they write. The device will help you to police your copy to make sure it has substance, weight. It's also a security check on your creative objectives and strategies.

The most important idea behind a copy platform is to focus on the promise of the product—what it will do for the man or woman who buys it. The promise is the heart of the copy platform, a device to make sure that effective selling arguments are marshaled in clear and logical order before the copy is written. This copy platform model consists of five statements:

Target audience. A definition of the customer we are trying to reach, so that we may beam copy directly to the customer's interests. (Both psychographic and demographic profile. See chapters 2 and 8.)

Promise. One simple, short sentence that expresses the product's key consumer benefit. It tells what you can promise to the consumer that he or she considers important, not what you consider important.

Support. A list, in order of importance to the customer, of the reasons behind the promise. This may include product features.

Execution. A description of how the print or broadcast messages will get the point across. How will the promise be executed?

Mood. The emotional tone or feeling to be conveyed by the advertising.

Once the advertising copy is written, go back and test yourself on these three checkpoints:

1. Does the copy follow the copy platform? If not, throw the copy out. No exceptions. Be brutally honest in your judgment. Don't bend.

2. *Study advertising objectives, one by one.* Is the copy compelling enough, powerful enough to reach these goals? If not, start over. Don't compromise the copy or the objectives.

3. *Review creative strategy.* If the copy does not do everything you expect it to, burn it.

Don't expect to achieve excellence on the first draft, or even the second. Greatness is usually achieved only after great effort—writing and rewriting, thinking and rethinking. For most, "obstinate rigor" is the secret to successful creative work. So put on your work clothes and ignore the clock as long as possible.

Creative leadership

Five years ago, Foote, Cone & Belding/Honig, the advertising agency that handles the Levis account, issued a memo. The purpose was to tell both agency and client personnel how to achieve creative leadership, how to set the trends in advertising creativity, and how to avoid following other agencies like sheep. They have distinguished FCB/H as a creative leader. Extracts from the memo tell how you can do it. The heading for the memo is:

Advertising creative leadership: method of operation

A client's call for creative leadership is a heavy demand. It requires the very best performance from all concerned. It also usually includes a clear commitment to procedure different from that which exists.

The goal: To achieve creative leadership for all client, trade, and consumer advertising.

The ground rules—general

The following are essential ingredients for fulfilling the ambitious objective of creative leadership:

Ignore competitive creative approaches. To lead means to

break new ground. Preoccupation with competition produces sameness.

Assume the realistic risk of creative leadership. Original thinking, by definition, breaks rules but not always successfully.

Delegate final responsibility and authority to those whose primary job is advertising, i.e., for a division, the advertising department should have final say. For advertising execution, the agency should have final say. This does not represent license to ignore others. To the contrary, the onus is on the responsible party to perform in line with clearly set divisional objectives/strategies.

The opposite of the above procedure is nitpicking and subjectively overriding those who are being held responsible. The effect is to create an atmosphere of "play safe," "please everyone." Therefore "reach out" attitudes are discouraged and caution is fostered. These are the antithesis of creativity.

The ground rules—specific

Client and agency must agree to and abide by a firm system in writing, as follows:

Marketing objectives/strategy. Where do you aim to take the division? What is the attitude that you need? On what main tools are you counting to get there? What is the time schedule? These statements are the responsibility of top management.

Advertising objectives/strategies. Who is advertising to influence? What attitude is to be developed or changed? What results constitute advertising success? These statements are the responsibility of the advertising department, consulted by the agency, approved by top management.

Creative objectives/strategies (by ad or series). What is the single (main) problem to be solved? This statement is the responsibility of the [client's] advertising department, consulted by the agency, approved by management. It must be written in 25 words or less.

Caution: This written statement must be the *last* client directive to the agency. The greatest enemy to creative problem solving is false starts which come about when a client keeps changing or modifying the original problem.

Judging the creative. These standards should be used in judging an ad:

- Is the ad on or off written strategy?
- Is the ad honest and in good taste?
- Is the ad clear?
- Is the ad an unconventional solution to the problem?
- Is the ad arresting to a consumer of the medium?

This judgment should be the responsibility of the advertising manager.

Caution: An ad is an entity, a whole. Its parts mesh like pieces of a jigsaw puzzle. Tampering or force fitting easily breaks down the interlocking relationships. This is not to say an ad is inviolate. But, rather,that reworking it is a job for the original craftsman. Therefore, when one encounters problems with an ad, he should concentrate on trying to best explain his troubles with it and refrain from solutions. Because the new solution will have to be in-

serted to replace and smoothly blend with existing elements.

Another viewpoint on judging creative work

Almost all agencies have a creative philosophy, a "constitution" that expresses the standards they reach for in all their advertising. As you begin to feel that your creative work is right, check it against the following standards. If you still feel it's right, you're in good company.

Some thoughts on ad-making
by Bill Bernbach

1. Make your people and products close and real—not just a picture of something, but the actual thing. This will give a lifelike effect and therefore gain greater believability.

2. Where possible, make your merchandise an actor in the scene, not just a prop. This will get your product remembered—because the provocative element in your advertising is also the element that sells your product. This is so simply stated—so difficult to execute!

3. Merchandise, artfully presented, has inherent interest. it can often be, and often should be, the *very device* that attracts attention. People are materialistic. They like nice things. Make yours look so good they'll want to own it. It's not necessary to include a baby or dogs to get attention—nor even a pair of crossed nylons!

4. Be sure that the advertisement has a physical focal center—one big area that dominates and therefore attracts.

5. This total concept applies both to print and to television advertising.

6. We insist that copy and art must be fully integrated. They must be conceived as a unit—developed as a unit. We have no problem here of which comes first—copy or art. They both come simultaneously in our workshop. They are two instruments which make a single melody.

7. We insist on advertising with vitality; with exuberance. This is the vague thing called "personality." When advertising has a personality—it is persuasively different.

8. *The device that attracts attention must also tell the product story!* An artificial device just used to get people to look can antagonize—people will see it as a trick. Your attention getter must be relevant. You are wrong to stand a man on his head, unless you are selling a product that will keep things from falling out of his pockets.[9]

How to stimulate your creative glands

The Italian sociologist, Pareto, divided the world into two camps, the innovators and the sheep.[10] The innovators are nimble of mind and ready to risk new, untried settings on their compasses. The sheep follow them. It would hardly be fair to pigeonhole the entire population in one or the other of Pareto's categories. This is the theory's weakness. Almost all of humankind is capable of speculation and invention. Most minds, in fact, are capable of much more originality than they ever produce or believe they are capable of producing. Psychologists have postulated for some time that we use only a tiny fraction of our brain's real creative potential. Nevertheless, as Pareto suggests, most people allow themselves to drift into the camp of the sheep. They allow others to invent, to experiment, to dream, to risk, to exercise their creative potential. It matters not what field you choose, be it science, agriculture, medicine, marketing, or advertising. Innovative creative problem solving is absolutely vital for success in any field today. If you choose advertising, you *must* develop your creative potential, even if you do not want to be in the "creative" department. You have creative potential; that is absolute. True, some are further advanced than others in applying creativity to problems. But all areas of advertising rely on imagination. Wherever you stand on the creative ladder, you must always be stretching out for higher levels.

Einstein: simplicity, not sophistry

Journalist Alton Ketchum tells a revealing story on the subject of creativity.[11]

> Always your true creative genius clarifies the complex and sophisticated into the simple and obvious. During his lifetime the name of Einstein came to signify some of the greatest ideas of all time. His whole career was an effort to reduce celestial mechanics to one universal pattern. When Einstein wrote $E = mc^2$ he did much more than to usher in the atomic age. He announced the staggering fact that matter and energy are one and the same.
>
> I was thinking about such things one day in 1950 just after the professor had announced his Unified Field Theory—bringing electricity, magnetism, and gravitation into a single web of cosmic force. He had told the newsmen to come back in twenty years, but a little magazine sent me to see him on a subject close to his heart—Federal World Government—and he gave me the interview. For half an hour I talked with him, there by the low round table in his study, deep in papers covered with miniscule equations. That was the farthest frontier of human knowledge; you could almost feel the chill of the unknown out beyond. You knew this gentle, friendly old man was one of the immortals of all history—and yet there was a human warmth about him that bespoke the great philosopher, too. Afterwards, as I waited for a train at Princeton Junction, his assistant, Dr. John Kemeny, told me of a series of difficult equations they had completed that day. These had gone well; the professor was pleased. He turned to Kemeny, and said: "You see, God always takes the simple way." And that, Kemeny said, was one secret of his genius.

Simplicity, a sign of genius

Why this love of simplicity? Because a person's mind naturally seeks the path of least resistance. Einstein, and apparently the Almighty, prefers efficiency to waste. Why waste mental or physical energy in any endeavor? Advertising, more than any other form of mass communication, has learned to communicate efficiently by searching for the simple way to make a point.

Ray Bradbury on creativity

There is no scientific equation for creativity. In the following essay, however, Ray Bradbury gives the criteria for the creative process. As you read his essay, watch for the five steps Bradbury uses in conceiving ideas.

Stuff your head. In advertising, this means studying the product and marketplace in great detail. It also means educating yourself as much as possible. Try to be a truly liberally educated person and never stop. As Bradbury says, your mind should become this "fabulous trash heap" of information so that an integration of idea components can occur.

Associate freely. Flex your mind. This is where the chemistry begins. You'll consciously work at the problem trying to fit together different pieces of the puzzle that you acquired in the first step. You'll be trying to create new combinations from existing elements and facts your mind has stored away.

Relax the mind. Delegate the problem to the subconscious. On being named "Man of the Year" by the International Advertising Association, David Ogilvy declared, "Unless advertising contains a big idea, it will pass like a ship in the night. As a copywriter, I have had only nine. They don't come from rational thoughts but from the unconscious. Of course, the unconscious must be informed by a lot of factual input, but that isn't enough. The big idea comes from the unconscious."[12]

Illumination. When the idea or the solution to your problem presents itself, it may come suddenly or with unexpected calm. But you'll know it. The advertising executive who named the Crockpot for Rival Manufacturing Company was asleep when the idea came. He awoke with the name and wrote it down immediately. Where did it come from? The unconscious. He had been watching a television news program that covered an instance of civil disorder. The newscaster referred to a group of demonstrators as "crackpots." It passed right over his conscious mind. The illumination came *after* he stopped trying, for he had spent most of the day consciously working at the problem.

Testing the idea. A writer should not rely exclusively on his or her judgment as to the worth of an idea. In a large agency, most writers go to people they can trust to get honest reactions to their ideas. That's a necessary kind of feedback. Next, it's a good idea to let research people pre-test a new campaign concept.

Touchstones of creativity

by Ray Bradbury[13]

I got the job of writing the screenplay for *Moby Dick* from John Huston twenty years ago. It came as a great surprise. I had met him only very briefly two years before. I'd given him all my books. I said I love you; I love your films. Someday we must work together. Read these. Respond, and some day we'll do something. We corresponded once or twice in Africa when he was making *The African Queen*. He came back, sat me down with a drink in my hand, said, Ray, how would you like to write the screenplay of *Moby Dick*? I said, I don't know, I've never been able to read the damn thing.

So, what do I do? I go home that night. Do I start to read *Moby Dick* from the beginning? No. That's not the way to read a book. You read a book the same way you use the library. At least, I hope you use libraries this way.

When was the last time you used a library the way I use one? You know how to use a library? You go in like this. You take books off the shelf—anywhere, anywhere! But especially in the children's section. How much time have you spent in the children's section of your library recently? Or in the bookstore? Are you in bookstores every day of your life? If not, why not? Feeling, looking, smelling . . . books smell good, huh? That's the first thing you do with books; you smell them. Gorgeous! I can identify the ink, the paper, blindfolded, from almost any country in the world. The paste is different from every country of the world. You start with that. That exhilaration of the smell of books, the feel of them. If you don't have that as touchstone, you're sunk. You're sunk.

Okay, starting today, it's libraries and books for all of you at least three or four days a week for half an hour. Okay? So you know the stock better than the salespeople. Because I want you to be educated on every single level—where you've gotten tired, where you've gotten poisoned, where you've gotten stupid with lack of knowledge in all the various fields.

So, I jumped into the middle of *Moby Dick*. I didn't start at the beginning of the book. And I began to read various sections. I read the section where the great fountains of resile somehow are put to sea . . . the great jets of the whale at night. The spirit spout appearing in the deeps. I turned to a section on all the whitenesses of panic and terror. All the descriptions that Melville had of the nightmares of the world. All arctic and antarctic nightmares. Then I turned back toward the end, where Ahab stands at the rail and looks at the sky and says it's a mild, mild day and a mild looking sky; and the wind smells as if it blew from the shadow of the Andes where the molars have lain down with their sighs.

And I turned back to the beginning and I read, "Call me Ishmael." And I was hooked. On the poetry of *Moby Dick*. On Shakespeare in *Moby Dick*. Because that was the influence.

The whole book was changed, transmuted by the gold that Melville borrowed from his hero, William Shakespeare. Some sections of the novel are written like a play.

I went to Ireland. I read the book nine times. John Huston and I were equally ignorant, equally ignorant about what we were doing. I made 35 outlines. I wrote two thousand pages trying to figure out what the book was all about.

But it took about nine months of stuffing my head—with Shakespeare and Conrad as well as Melville. Until one morning I got out of bed in London, I looked in the mirror and said, "I am Herman Melville." And on that morning I wrote the last 35 pages of the screenplay and everything came right. Emotionally! Emotionally! It vomited out onto the paper.

That's what I wish for each of you. That you stuff yourself with so much from so many fields, you finally become this fabulous trash heap of things that can integrate and give you ideas. But you can't think your way there. I have had a sign by my typewriter for 25 years now that says, "Don't Think."

Feel! Feel! Feel! Make lists of hatreds. Write about them. Make lists of your loves. Write about them.

I was on a bus in Westwood twenty years ago. A boy ran down the street, jumped on the bus, ran down the aisle, flopped into the seat across from me. I looked at him and I said, if I had that energy, I would write ten novels a day, forty-two poems every week, sixteen billion articles a year. What's the secret of his energy? I looked down at his feet and he was wearing the brightest new pair of cloud white, cream tennis shoes I've ever seen in my life.

I said, that's it. I remember in Waukegan, when I was ten years old, at the end of winter you went downtown with your parents, first day of spring, skies are blue, go in the shoe store, take off ten tons of winter boots and throw them on the floor. And they disappear out of sight, right through the woodwork. So heavy they go right through the center of the earth.

And then you put on these cream white, light antelope tennis shoes. And then you bounce on them, huh? And then, boy, you get the heck out of there. And you can run away from all your enemies and run toward your friends waiting for you on the green hills of summer. And the magic lasts for two or three days, so that you can jump over houses and rivers and buildings and even sidewalks and bushes and dogs.

And I went home and wrote that story. The sound of summer running . . . part of *Dandelion Wine*. An exercise in word association. Felt, not thought, not thought. I want you to stuff yourself in such a way that these ideas begin to pop around like popcorn in your head. They happen.

I had an experience in the middle of *Moby Dick* with Huston. We had a problem we couldn't solve. There was a scene that wouldn't be written. And I sat with John Huston for two or three nights and he brought in his friend, Peter Vertel, to help us. And we talked, and we talked and we talked. You've been through this sort of thing . . . and it never works. You try to gang bust an idea, right? And it just can't be busted that way. Occasionally you'll have a breakthrough. But, I finally got exhausted about the third night around two in the morning. And I said to John, you don't know the first thing about creativity, not the first thing.

Now, I'll tell you what we're going to do. I'm going to walk out on this meeting right now. I'm going back to my hotel in Dublin. I'm going to put a pad and pencil by my bed. You do the same John and Peter you do the same. In the morning one of the three of us will wake with the solution to the problem. Now, before we go to sleep tonight, each of you review very quickly what the problem is . . . one of us will wake with it. They laughed at me. They laughed at me. I got out of there. I went back to Dublin. At seven in the morning my phone rang. It was Huston. He says, "Ray, Ray, I've got it!" I said, "Never give me that trouble again." And he never bugged me again. Never, ever, ever. Because that's the way you do it. You feed everything in that you need. You don't go to art galleries. You don't go to bookstores. You don't go to libraries. You don't go to plays. You don't go to movies. You tell me you don't have time. Make it! Clear away the unnecessary people that fill up your life with trash of the worst sort. The people that don't believe in you, or your ideas. Clear them out and make room for these things I'm telling you about. Books, movies, plays, walking, getting rid of lunches as of today. Okay?

What about naps in the middle of the afternoon? I've been taking naps since I was fifteen. Take at least fifteen to twenty minutes in the middle of the afternoon. Some of my greatest ideas come in that beautiful twilight suspension between thinking and dreaming. Give it a try. You can watch the ideas floating like clouds through the top of your head.

I'll give you a job to do to improve your minds and aerate your skulls tonight. From now on every night before you go to sleep, this simple process of reading every night, one poem, one essay and one short story. At the end of the year you'll be very well educated in the best poetry of our time, the best essays, and the best short stories. These ideas moving around inside your head will be of use to you in your own field.

You're speaking to someone who has had a huge interest in advertising. I've written some ads. I could easily shift and come into your field and make trouble for you. I've been thinking of running for Pope, too.

It isn't creative unless it sells

The Benton and Bowles Advertising Agency made this line famous with its own advertising campaign. And it's a fitting note on which to close this chapter. Advertising copy must be powerful enough to *move* the consumer to buy, to reach into his or her pocket and part with limited cash or credit. That's a staggering responsibility. Don't forget *your* purpose when you sit down to write your client's copy. As a famous copywriter put it,

> You measure the success of any work of art by how well it's achieved its purpose. And anybody in advertising who doesn't say his purpose is to sell that piece of merchandise is a phony. How, this is difficult. This is sweat. This is working. (From an interview with Bill Bernbach)[14]

Notes

1. William A. Robinson, "There's Something to Appeal to Everyone in Windup of 'Best Promotions of 1977,' " *Advertising Age,* 8 May 1978, p. 54.
2. Ibid., p. 55.
3. Jack Trout and Al Ries, "The Positioning Era Cometh," in *Readings in Advertising*, edited by James E. Littlefield (St. Paul, Minn.: West Publishing, 1975), p. 259.
4. Ibid., pp. 259-61.
5. M. Lincoln Schuster, *The World's Great Letters* (New York: Simon and Schuster, 1940), p. 69.
6. *AAF Advertising Campaign for Frito Lay's Rold Gold Pretzels*, Prepared by Gabardine, Herringbone & Tweed, San Jose State University, 1977, p. 7.
7. *AAF Advertising Campaign for Coca-Cola's Brand Sprite*, Prepared by Sans Serif, Inc., Brigham Young University, 1978, p. 10.
8. Kenneth Roman and Jane Maas, *How to Advertise* (New York: St. Martin's, 1976), p. 6.
9. By permission, William Bernbach, chairman of the Executive Committee, Doyle Dane Bernbach Inc. Advertising, New York.
10. James Webb Young, *A Technique for Producing Ideas* (Chicago: Crain Books, 1940), p. 18.
11. James D. Scott, ed., *The Creative Process* (Ann Arbor: University of Michigan, Bureau of Business Research, 1957), pp. 54-67.
12. "Ogilvy IAA Man of the Year," *Advertising Age,* 22 May 1978, p. 97.
13. This text was excerpted from a talk Ray Bradbury delivered to the annual convention of the American Association of Advertising Agencies in Santa Barbara, California, in October 1973. Copyright © 1979 by Ray Bradbury; reprinted by permission of the Harold Matson Co.

    Whether writing an article on Halloween for the *Reader's Digest* or scripting the screenplay for the film, *Moby Dick*, Ray Bradbury's mind is a geyser of boundless energy and imagination. Known for his versatile writing talents, he has authored over 700 novels, short stories, poems, articles, and plays. Best known as a visionary into the future, Bradbury's science fiction work includes such famous titles as *Farenheit 451, The Martian Chronicles*, and *The Illustrated Man*.
14. Denis Higgins, *The Art of Writing Advertising* (Chicago: R. R. Donnelley Advertising Publications, 1965), pp. 17-18.

7 Pretesting the Advertising Campaign

An overview of pretesting

"The purpose of an advertisement is not just to get itself seen. It is not just to get itself heard or read. The purpose of an advertisement is to convey information, an attitude about a product (service, company, cause) in such a way that the consumer will be more favorably disposed toward its purchase. The purpose of an advertisement is to bring about changes in knowledge, attitudes and *behavior* of people with respect to the purchase of the product."[1]

So said Russell Colley in 1961 in *Defining Advertising Goals for Measured Advertising Results*. The ideas expressed are as important today as they were then. Colley had yet to see the "advertising creative revolution" of the mid-1960s when it became more important to be creative than to be understood. Unfortunately, traces of that attitude are still prevalent.

With rapidly rising media costs, overwhelming numbers of advertising messages, and more and more "advertiser voices" seeking to be heard, the advertiser can't afford to wonder if his or her campaign message is heard and understood. Yet, pretesting is still one of the least developed areas of campaign planning.

While most authorities agree that advertising should be pretested—preferably at the strategy stage, before execution—there are those who don't. Before we explain the various pretesting techniques, let's look at the reasons "why advertising should be pretested and why it should not."

Should we?

Many practitioners and theoreticians agree that pretesting is an important step in the success of an advertising campaign. For example, Kenneth Roman and Jane Maas in *How to Advertise* recommend that pretesting be done before the advertising is even writ-

ten. Research money should be spent in identifying prospects, pretesting strategy, and pretesting the advertising promise before a word goes on paper. Roman and Maas summarize by saying, "What advertising says about the product is more important than how it says it. Pretest the strategy first."[2]

C. H. Sandage and Vernon Fryburger take a slightly different view. They suggest, "The principal reasons for testing (pretesting advertising) are: to avoid costly mistakes, to predict the relative strength of alternative strategies and tactics, and to increase the efficiency of advertising generally."[3] Stanley suggests that advertising pretesting be done to select the best appeals, advertisements, and campaigns so that advertising communications can be measured.[4]

Or shouldn't we?

In spite of the strong case made for advertising pretesting, there are those who disagree. "Little or no significance should be attributed to respondents' opinion of the advertising unless there is an indication that the advertising is considered untruthful, misleading, in bad taste, insulting to the intelligence, or in some other way repels rather than attracts." So says Clarence Eldridge.[5]

Charles T. Dirksen, Arthur Kroeger, and Francesco M. Nicosia suggest that many people, especially those in industry, have serious doubts about the validity of tests designed to predict success for advertising strategies and executions. The most serious question they raise is the cost-to-benefit ratio of advertising pretesting, i.e., whether the investment in pretesting provides enough solid answers to offset the cost in time and money.[6]

Finally, practicing professionals, especially those in creative, are often strongly opposed to advertising pretesting. They reason their background and experience enable them to develop and execute successful advertising campaigns for all types of products. This experiential knowledge overshadows any form of pretesting, particularly those which ask uninformed consumers to evaluate advertising for products about which they may have little of no knowledge or interest. Some creative people also believe that ordinary consumers are creatively inferior.

Yes we should!

We strongly support the idea of advertising pretesting although we're not completely satisifed with the methodologies presently available. The basic advantage of advertising pretesting is the rather modest investment required to gain some measure of assurance in the creative product. The cost-benefit ratio seems favorable when compared to the media investment. For example, assume an advertiser is planning a $5,000,000 media campaign for the coming year. A pretesting investment of as much as $50,000 would amount to only 1 percent of the media expenditure; yet the pretest could give an indication of whether the campaign would be successful. In this example, the cost-to-benefit ratio is definitely on the side of pretesting.

Similarly, Roman and Maas's suggestion that creative research money be spent "up front," or prior to the actual development of the advertising, appears to be sound.[7] It seems much wiser to invest creative research funds before using the material rather than conduct lengthy post-tests to determine if the advertising was successful. Indeed, if sufficient pretest information could be gathered, a post-test would seem almost unnecessary.

While the case for pretesting can and has been strongly argued, major problems arise in present pretesting procedures, chief of which is lack of agreement on a pretesting methodology. There appear to be almost as many pretesting approaches as there are advertising campaigns, and each has its supporters. One advantage, however, it that in any form major flaws in thinking or presentation become apparent. Thus any pretest should spot potential disaster.

One of the other major problems in all forms of pretesting is using people to evaluate the advertising. As D. L. Malickson and John N. Nason point out, unfortunately there appears to be a major difference between what people say and what they mean. Likewise, there is a problem with what people say they will do and what they actually do in any given situation.[8] When we compare our knowledge of advertising pretesting against our knowledge of what makes people buy, large common gaps appear. A major problem is that many people cannot verbalize why they purchased a particular product. There is little reason to believe

they should be able to say in advance with any more conviction or authority what they would do.

What to pretest: strategies or executions?
Test concepts and strategies—not executions

Unfortunately, most advertising research methodologies concentrate primarily on methods of evaluating advertising executions rather than advertising strategies. The reason usually given is that it is easier to obtain consumer response to advertisements in a familiar form, such as an execution, than the advertising strategy. The advertising strategy is basic. Once a sound strategy is developed, literally hundreds of ways to execute it may be available. If the strategy is wrong, no execution can save it.

Returning to the Grumman example in chapter 2, we see the advertising strategy stated as:

> Dramatize the superior fuel and speed efficiency of Grumman American airplanes when compared with similarly priced models of "the big 3" in light aircraft sales; Cessna, Piper, and Beechcraft."

The strategy is very clear-cut. The benefit is "superior fuel and speed efficiency." Out of this strategy, a multitude of executions are possible. For example:

1. We might plan, carry out, and use the results of a fuel economy run between "the big 3" and Grumman.

2. We might plan and conduct a speed test among the four planes and use that comparison.

3. We might plan and conduct a climb test between the planes and use the results in support of our claim.

4. We might fly all four planes on the same route under the same conditions and use the results as a basis for advertising.

5. We might contact new purchasers of Grumman planes who had switched from one of "the big 3" and use their testimonials as evidence of our claim.

Any of these executions and many more are possible from this single strategy. It is therefore clear that determining whether the strategy of "superior fuel and speed efficiency" is a salient message for our market, we must test the strategy, not how it is executed.

Results must be measurable

Regardless of the methodology, both strategy and execution testing have one thing in common: the results must be measurable. Definite objectives must be stated which are measurable in quantifiable terms. It is not sufficient to say, "The respondents in the pretest liked the advertisement." There must be a measurable result such as communication of the primary selling message, believability, persuasion, or a change in attitude. The pretesting technique used must be designed so that communication goals can be set and measured. Through this approach, the mere popularity of an advertising execution or the entertainment value of the commercial can be placed in proper perspective. More will be said about these topics as the various available pretesting methodologies are discussed.

No matter the results, pretesting is usually directional

While pretesting results are intended to bring real truth, in fact most information is only directional. While pretesting can often detect real "bombs," the methodologies used are not ordinarily able to determine the level of success which might be achieved. Pretest methodologies are usually conducted with small samples of consumers, often in artificial situations. Advertising pretesting, therefore, is still designed primarily to prevent disaster rather than to predict success. While the advertising campaign planner may be pleased with a high pretest score, he or she should remember that the results simply mean the likelihood of success is good, not guaranteed.

Concept, strategy, and promise testing

An important pretest area is that of product concept testing. By way of review, a product concept is usually the physical description of the product or service or an outline of the benefits that may be obtained from a particular product. For example, the product concept statement used to describe the first latex house paint might have read like this:

> This new paint covers as well as ordinary oil paints and dries in 30 minutes. It comes in a wide variety of colors and mixes and blends easily. Unlike regular oil-based paint, however, it requires no mixing or stirring. In addition, brushes and spills clean up with soap and warm water.

The benefit of the new type of paint should be obvious to the consumer. The statement describes the product and gives the advantages compared to ordinary (at that time) oil-based paint.

By contrast, the advertising strategy statement is the appeal that is made in the advertising message. An advertising strategy for the latex paint mentioned above, for example, could be based on any one of several available benefits:

1. Latex paint cleans up with soap and warm water, not turpentine.
2. Latex paint dries to the touch in just 30 minutes.

3. Latex paint is so easy to use it enables the inexperienced to achieve "professional painter" results.
4. Latex paint requires no stirring or mixing.

The list could go on and on. While the product is the same, the strategy is based on the strongest appeal to consumers.

Another approach often pretested is the "promise statement." This is similar to the strategy statement but is used primarily to determine how important or how special the claim for the product or service is to the consumer. The standard format of the "promise statement" is: "If you use this product, you will get this benefit." Roman and Maas believe that pretesting an appeal with a "promise statement" is effective for most products except those which have an emotional appeal normally requiring an execution to be understood. Competitive appeals may also be included in "promise statement" testing for determining how the proposed appeal for the product fares against the competition.[9]

With this brief review of concept, strategy, and promises in hand, we now consider actual testing methodologies.

Where do we start?

The place to start with product concept statements is with the product itself. The concept statement should do a thorough job of describing the product and the product benefits. Because concept statements are often developed to describe products or ideas that may not have been manufactured, they must be clear concise statements of exactly what the proposed products consist of, offer, or do. An easy way to determine if a concept statement is clearly written is to show it to several persons who are not familiar with it. Then ask them to describe the product in their own words. If the concept statement is clear, there should be little or no confusion or difficulty when the product is interpreted by the reader.

A bit more work is required with the advertising strategy or the "promise statement." John S. Wright, Daniel S. Warner, Willis L. Winter, Jr., and Sherilyn K. Zeigler believe the best place to start pretesting an advertising strategy statement is to thoroughly review the primary and secondary appeals being made by the competition. Competitive products often will have preempted the market for certain advertising strategies or "promise statements."[10] For example, some advertising approaches have become so closely identified with a specific advertiser they cannot be used even if the competitor is not specifically using that appeal in present advertising. A fast-food chain would have difficulty attempting to develop a clown spokesperson when competing with "Ronald McDonald." Even if the clown were totally different from "Ronald," the idea of a clown and fast-food chains has probably been well established by McDonald's in the minds of consumers. Similarly, other product ideas and appeals are "owned" by various manufacturers, such as Volkswagen and the ugly automobile, Avis being Number Two in the auto rental business, and Ivory as the bar soap "that floats." Make sure the strategy being tested isn't already being used or associated with your competition.

Next, a clear and concise statement of the strategy or strategies to be tested must be written. If "promise statements" are used, the benefit being offerred or the problem the product can solve must be clear. A preliminary test with a few consumers is often helpful for assurance that there is complete comprehension of the strategy statement. A simple preliminary test can be done by having a few people unfamiliar with the strategy read it, then play back their understanding of the strategy in their own words. This helps in determining if the statement is clearly written.

How do we test?

By using the prescreened concept statement or advertising strategy, one can begin field testing. This type of testing is normally done with relatively small groups of people in one of two ways—through personal interviews or focus groups. The key ingredient is the sample group in which the concepts will be tested.

People who evaluate an advertising concept or strategy should always be users of the product or potential members of the target market. As obvious as it may sound, professional advertising people sometimes fall into this trap and test a new product concept with the wrong audience; e.g., an idea designed to appeal to teens is tested on women in their forties. The first step is to make sure those who are evaluating the concept or strategy logically and potentially are customers.

Personal interviews. Conducting personal interviews is the traditional way to pretest concept statements or advertising strategies. The procedure may take many forms. The most common sites for interviews are the home, shopping malls, in or near retail outlets, or even major airports. The primary objective is to find persons fitting the target market description and conduct the interviews. For example, interviews for a new food product concept might be conducted in the food store with persons waiting in the check-out line. The prospects usually have time to answer questions; they are in a shopping situation and have their minds on food and food products.

A typical concept test method is to have the various ideas written on cards which are handed to respondents. After reading the cards, respondents are asked to summarize the concept in their own words.

This confirms that the statement is interpreted as intended.

After reading all the concepts, the respondent is asked to rank-order them based on their appeal. Frequently, questions are asked such as why the particular selection was made. Demographic data are also gathered to ensure that the respondent is a member of the selected target market. A sample of 50 to 100 respondents is usually sufficient to identify the most salient concept or strategy among those offered. With this number of respondents, responses tend to stabilize and little beyond verification is gained with larger groups.

Focus groups. An alternative to the personal interview is the "focus group," so called because the attention of an entire group is focused on the product category, concept, or strategy being evaluated.

A group of 8 to 12 respondents from the prospective target market are asked to meet to discuss a particular topic. Led by a trained interviewer, the respondents are shown the material to be tested. The interviewer then guides the group in a discussion. The purpose is to obtain information on the subject, not necessarily direct answers. Discussions are usually tape recorded. After the session, the interviewer or an interpreter analyzes the conversations and develops a summary or consensus of the group. This interpretation gives valuable insight into the deeper feelings of the group members. It also determines how they talk about the product and discloses the language they use.

As in the personal-interview technique, small samples such as two or three focus groups from the target market are sufficient to give an indication of the value of various concepts or strategies being tested.

The results of both personal-interview and focus-group methods usually are directional only. Since the sample is small and subject to error, the result of either type of testing should be regarded as a "prevention of disaster" test, or directional guidance for further research rather than absolute truth.

Testing advertising executions

Much has been said in the preceding pages about the value of pretesting concepts and strategies as opposed to executions. The fact remains, however, that most advertising pretesting today is of the latter variety. One reason appears to be that more faith can be placed in one's ability to test finished or nearly finished advertising executions than in testing simple concept statements or advertising strategies.

Some common problems in pretesting advertising executions

Certain problems arise when one is pretesting advertising executions. Some of the difficulties are inherent in the research problem, while others may be reduced or avoided if known in advance. Some of the more common problems encountered are described here.

Test against prospect. Pretesting of advertising executions is sometimes done with samples that are not valid. Because pretests are often used directionally, a common fault is to assume that one person's opinion is as good as another's. We find advertisements directed to farmers being pretested with suburban commuters simply because they are convenient and inexpensive to contact. For there to be an effective pretest, the persons evaluating the advertising must be members of the proposed target market.

Try to prevent the development of "experts." One of the most difficult tasks in advertising pretesting is preventing sample respondents from becoming "advertising experts." This simply means that rather than evaluating the advertising as consumers, respondents begin to suggest improvements. When this occurs, the opinions given are often worthless. While "advertising expertise" is a difficult problem to overcome, efforts should be made to confine respondent opinions and comments to their proper role as consumers of advertising, not as advertising directors. Some suggestions are given in the next section on how to avoid this problem.

"Halo effect." Another problem in advertising pretesting is the "halo effect." Once a person develops a liking for a particular advertisement or commercial, he or she tends to overlook any faults it might have. Then, when asked to cite the best headline, illustration, or other part of the test ads, the respondent tends to name something in the advertisement he or she previously selected. In effect, the advertisement he or she prefers can do no wrong, even though there may be other advertisements with stronger individual components. Little can be done about this problem except to recognize that it exists and to use a different technique such as testing different body copy with the same headline. If the "halo effect" becomes quite obvious, the respondent's answers to other questions should be deleted.

Can't test campaigns. Philip Ward Burton suggests that, because of the nature of advertising execution pretesting, only individual advertisements can be evaluated, not the entire campaign. The synergistic effect of several executions all giving the same general message or repetition of the same advertisement is not measurable in a pretest.[11] Generally, pretests cannot be extended beyond the individual execution. Thus, the generalizability of the result is quite limited.

Testing the "best of the worst." Only the best of the executions tested is found in a pretest, not the best possible execution. All the advertisements tested may be poor. The test panel may have selected only the best of the worst. While not always present, this potential problem should be kept in mind. Results obtained are projectible only to the advertisements or commercials tested and not all executions possible.

Some obvious errors. James F. Engle, Hugh G. Wales, and Martin R. Warshaw identify three obvious errors that occur frequently in pretesting:

1. Negative advertising appeals traditionally score poorly in pretests; yet they are sometimes successful in the marketplace.

2. Advertising that is entertaining, humorous, or light usually scores best in advertising pretests. The entertainment value of the advertisements is usually much more appreciated in a pretest than in the normal media channels.

3. "Hard sell" facts about the product or service usually score the lowest of all on pretests. Yet, there is ample evidence that "hard sell" advertisements and commercials may be most effective in communicating with the intended audience.[12]

When you are reviewing the results of advertising pretests, these common problems and limitations should be kept in mind.

Avoiding respondent prejudice

One of the major problems in advertising pretesting is that respondents begin to believe they are "experts." Part of the problem stems from the fact that advertising is very subjective, consumers usually have strong likes and dislikes about advertising approaches. Second, when an opinion is asked, the respondent naturally assumes he or she is qualified to answer whether he or she is or not. Finally, because evaluations are being asked prior to usage, respondents may interpret this to mean that the advertising may not be as good as it should be. Respondents may assume there is something "wrong" with the advertising and that the researchers are seeking their help. In spite of these situations, some ways exist in which "advertising expertise" among pretest respondents may be minimized, although not entirely avoided.

Ask direct questions, not opinions. As an example, the questions, "How do you like this ad?" usually leads to opinion answers. The more direct question, "Would this type of advertisement make you want to purchase the product?" is more specific and helps avoid opinions. Short, direct, to-the-point questions should be asked in an advertising pretest.

Ask questions that can be logically answered by the respondent. Sometimes the respondent is assumed to have knowledge he or she may not have. Thus, if a person is asked, "What do you think are the advantages of alternating current in an electric razor?" it is likely the answers would vary widely. Most people don't know the answer. When faced with this type of problem, they often make up an answer or guess rather than appear ignorant.

Don't ask respondents to project their answers to others. Even the most informed mother really can't answer how her children would feel or react to a product or an advertisement. Therefore, putting respondents in the position of guessing how others might feel or react only asks for trouble. Respondents know only about their own feelings. When you ask them to project to others, you're asking them to guess. When that situation occurs, respondents often believe it is acceptable to guess in other areas, too.

Ask probing questions. The first answer may represent the true feelings of the respondent, but, often, it is just that—an answer. Follow up by asking such questions as "Why do you say that?" and "What do you mean by that?" Try to get the truth, not merely a superficial answer. When respondents know you will probe, they will often dig a bit deeper to give you true facts and not just "top-of-the-mind" replies.

These certainly are not all the available methods of preventing respondents from becoming "advertising experts," but they may help overcome a very common problem in pretesting.

Methods: things you can do

A natural separation exists in methods of pretesting advertising executions. First are those which the advertising campaign planner can do with a bit of research help. Second are commercial advertising pretesting services. Almost all methodologies listed are available through professional research organizations.

Internal checklists, rating scales and readability formulas. One of the easiest and most common methods of advertising pretesting is through internal evaluation by the advertiser. This may be done by means of a checklist or rating scale system.

Checklists are used to:

1. Ensure that all the various components of the advertisement are included, such as coupon, ordering information, sizes, colors, and delivery time.
2. Ensure that the major selling points of the product or service are included in the advertisement.

Very elaborate checklists have been developed including such topics as checking for "a benefit oriented headline," "the use of the word 'you' in the copy," the inclusion of the brand name a certain number of times in the copy, or other factors believed to be important. While checklists seem somewhat mechanical, they can play an important part in ensuring that advertisements are complete and that no obvious errors are present.

Some advertisers have developed rating scales which are used to evaluate and compare ads. This might include such subjective evaluations as "Does the first paragraph follow the headline and lead to the body copy?" or "Is the brand name of the product visible at a glance in the layout?" The usual method is to develop the scale based on a five-point measure such as:

Very Good	Good	0	Poor	Very Poor

Thus, by rating different advertisements on these scales and then totaling the results for each advertisement tested, one can select a winner. These rating scales are usually completed by management of the company, the sales force, or others in a position to judge the merits of the advertisement.

The final method of internal evaluation is a readership test for print ads. Such tests are designed primarily to determine how easy the advertisement is to read and comprehend. Several formulas are available, the most common of which is the Flesch Formula developed by Rudolph Flesch. The basic computation of the formula is based on:

1. The average sentence length
2. The average number of syllables
3. The percent of personal words used
4. The percent of personal sentences in a 100-word sample of the writing

The formula determines whether the writing can be read and understood by the average person. Burton says the Flesch formula shows that the most readable copy contains 14 words per sentence, 140 syllables per 100 words, 10 personal words and 43 percent personal sentences.[13]

Checklists, rating scales, and readability levels of advertising are low in cost, easy to apply, and usually reveal glaring errors. These types of pretests, however, do little to evaluate the effectiveness of the advertisement with the consumer.

Consumer panels. A consumer panel is simply a group of prospective consumers for the product or service who are exposed to and evaluate the proposed advertising execution. Consumer panels may take many forms from prerecruited ongoing groups to persons contacted for a simple interview in the local supermarket. Regardless of the type of panel used, the primary objective is to get the considered opinion of prospective customers for the product and combine the responses to form a single opinion. Here are a few of the more common evaluation methods using consumer panels.

ORDER-OF-MERIT TEST. The order of merit is a simple ranking test of a group of advertisements by respondents. For example, consumers are asked to look at several alternative advertising executions and then rank them in some way. Rankings may be made on almost any basis, but one of the more common ones is the persuasive ability of the advertisement. Questions such as these are commonly used in the order-of-merit test:[14]

- "Which of these ads would you be most likely to read?"
- "Which headline makes you want to read further?"
- "Which of these ads convinces you most of the quality of the product?"
- "Which would be most effective in convincing you to buy?"

In addition to ranking, respondents are often asked to describe why they selected certain advertisements. This helps give the researcher a better understanding of the decisions and why they were made.

PORTFOLIO. In the portfolio technique, unidentified test advertisements are placed in a folder or portfolio with a number of other advertisements which are not being tested. Sometimes the portfolio is made up to simulate a normal magazine or newspaper and includes editorial content. Respondents are then shown the portfolio and allowed to look at it as much or as little as they like. After viewing the portfolio, respondents are asked to recall which ads they saw, what they remembered about each ad, which ad they liked best and why, and so forth. This helps determine how the advertisement will score when placed in a semi-normal environment. In the portfolio test, advertisements must be complete, or else the balance of the materials must be reduced to the completeness of the test ad to permit a fair evaluation to be made. From 5 to 10 ads can be evaluated by the portfolio method at one time. Portfolio tests are probably a stronger method of pretesting than order-of-merit tests or ranking.

RATING SCALES. Rating scales are often used for evaluation of appeals or parts of individual advertisments. They provide an opportunity to isolate dimensions of opinion. Rating scales can also be repeated with other groups for comparisons.
A semantic differential approach like this might be used:

The terms used could be applied to the product or the advertisement. Rating individual advertisements and their communicative powers makes possible an identification of the best of the lot.[15]

Other rating scales can also be used such as a scale of the important values the advertisement should contain. The inherent problem in scales of this sort is the subjective development of the factors to be evaluated.

PAIRED COMPARISONS. In this methodology, several advertisements are given to panel members. Respondents are asked to rate each ad individually against each of the others. For example, if there are three ads to be tested, A would be rated against B, A against C, and B against C. Each ad is thus rated in comparison with each of the others. With this technique, the best ad may be selected through comparison, not ranking. This technique is usually limited to approximately eight ads which require a total of 28 comparisons. Respondent fatigue often develops beyond that number.

MOCK MAGAZINES. In this method special magazines are printed or regular editions of known magazines are obtained prior to distribution. Sample advertisements are printed and inserted in place of or in addition to those regularly appearing. These specially constructed magazines are then distributed to subscribers or readers. After a suitable time, the respondents who received the magazines are contacted and are asked questions about the magazine and the advertising. This pretesting technique uses recall for determining success. The main advantage of the mock magazine is that the advertisement is tested in an actual reading situation rather than in a "forced viewing." Only finished advertisements, however, can be tested, and the investment in production must be made before testing and may be wasted on those ads that are rejected.

PUZZLE GAMES. While these are not widely used, various forms of projective techniques such as the puzzle game, word association, sentence completion, and role playing are used for pretesting. A good example is the puzzle game. Respondents are given a partially completed advertisement, e.g., the ad might be complete except for the headline and illustration. Several alternative headlines and illustrations are given to respondents, and they are asked to complete the advertisement using the parts furnished. The respondent selects the headline and illustration that he or she

	Very −3	Quite −2	Slight −1	0 0	Slight +1	Quite +2	Very +3	
Hard to use	____	____	____	____	____	____	____	Easy to use
Low quality	____	____	____	____	____	____	____	High quality
Unpleasant	____	____	____	____	____	____	____	Pleasant

thinks would be most suitable. The assumption is that the headline and illustration most often selected would be the most effective among consumers. In other forms of projective techniques, respondents are asked to fill in blanks or draw pictures that indicate what would most appeal to them.

STORYBOARD TESTS. Television storyboards are often tested with consumer juries using roughly the same techniques mentioned above. The respondents, however, are shown more than layouts. The television commercial is shown in slide form with a prerecorded audio tape. Respondents are usually able to make the transition from rather rough art and single-voice recordings to a finished commercial. Also, if needed, particular scenes can be isolated for discussion and evaluation. The major advantage, of course, is the low cost since expensive television production is not required. Artists' drawings of the various frames to be used appear to be quite satisfactory for testing purposes.

MAIL TESTS. While it is not widely used, the mail test is still effective. Alternative copy appeals are printed on postcards which are then sent to prospective customers. Offers are made on the cards using various copy approaches. The appeal that draws the most returns is judged to be best. Because this technique requires an offer and a rather long period of time for reply, it is normally used only to test direct mail or direct response advertising prior to major mailings.

FOCUS GROUPS. While not technically a consumer panel, focus groups are often used to pretest advertising. They seem to work quite well with children or younger people who often have trouble expressing themselves individually to adults but do quite well in a group setting.

This certainly does not cover the entire list of consumer jury techniques. Others that may be used are measures of predisposition to buy, forced switching tests, first- and second-brand choices and even projective buying games. All are designed to achieve the same goal, i.e., to obtain a preliminary evaluation of various alternatives by the prospective target market.

Pros and cons of consumer panel pretesting

Philip Ward Burton, Watson S. Dunn, Arnold M. Barban, and Dorothy Cohen summarize the pros and cons of the various consumer pretesting methodologies as follows:

Advantages. Consumers generally can separate the good advertisements from the bad. The advertisements are tested against consumers rather than advertising experts or other groups. Consumer pretests are fast and easy to use. Usually the cost of a consumer jury is low since samples are limited in size. Finally, the entire advertisement may be tested, not just the individual parts.

Disadvantages. It is difficult to select respondents for consumer juries to make them truly representative. The results obtained from pretests are subjective and may not represent the true opinions of the panel. The situations in which most pretesting occurs are artificial; respondents are forced to view the ads whether or not they might see them in real life. In most cases, emphasis is on simply taking note of the advertisement and not the communication power of the message. More entertaining or pleasant advertisements usually rate better on these tests than they do in the marketplace. Finally, consumer jury tests often are not very conclusive for infrequently purchased or very complex products.[16]

Over-all, the advantage of the consumer panel method of pretesting is greater than doing no pretesting at all. If the campaign planner recognizes the consumer panel for what it is—a directional guide to better advertising—then this form of pretesting can be very helpful.

Pretesting services available

A number of organizations have developed and formalized advertising pretesting services. Because many facilities and techniques are similar, with only minor methodological differences, no attempt is made here to list each specific service. We will take the general approach of giving examples of organizations offering this type of service. More specific information is available from a market research text or directly from the supplier.

Four types of pretesting services are available: objective mechanical methodologies, services specifically for print advertising, services specifically for broadcast, and sales pretesting.

Objective mechanical methods. These techniques are called objective because they rely on mechanical means for measurement rather than opinions or replies from respondents. Tests are usually conducted individually in a laboratory setting. These pretesting approaches generally have not gained widespread use and are still regarded as experimental rather than conclusive.

Engel, Wales, and Warshaw divide the various techniques into those that measure attention attraction and those that measure response.

ATTENTION ATTRACTION. There are four basic techniques:

1. The HRB-Singer test measures visual efficiency. Recognition is measured under varying conditions such as light and length of exposure and in competition with other advertisements.

2. The eye camera is used primarily to determine the effectiveness of the layout. A machine measures the movement of the eyes and the amount of time devoted to each element in an advertisement.

3. The third technique is the tachistoscope which is used to measure the perception of the ad through speed, exposure, and illumination.

4. Binocular rivalry is used to determine the effect of different elements on each eye.[17]

Because these techniques are used primarily to measure stationary objects and the perception or movement of the eye against those objects, they are usually limited to evaluation of print advertisements.

RESPONSE. Mechanical devices are also used to measure a respondent's response to advertising exposure. Most techniques measure involuntary physical response because they are believed to offer a clue to the interest or response to the advertising. The basic approaches are:

1. The psychogalvanometer which is similar to the lie-detector in that it measures sweat gland activity and other involuntary actions of the respondent.

2. The pupil dilation device measures the dilation of the respondent's eyes. A wider dilation is believed to indicate a lower interest in the material under test.

3. A salivation test is sometimes used to measure the response to advertisements for food or food products.[18]

While the above tests have the advantage of being objective, some concern has been expressed about their interpretation and the understanding of exactly what the results mean.

Print services. Two organizations, Daniel Starch and Staff, and Gallup and Robinson, Inc., offer widely used print pretesting services in which preprinted advertisements are tipped into test magazines. These magazines are then circulated to respondent groups. Following an opportunity to read the magazine, respondents are contacted and interviews are conducted concerning the magazine and the advertisements being pretested. The tests are primarily of recognition and recall and provide an effective evaluation technique prior to full-scale schedules in media.

Broadcast services. The largest number of pretesting services have been developed for broadcast advertising, particularly television. The major differences between the techniques is the situation in which the test commercials are viewed by respondents. Four broadcast pretest methodologies are used:

IN-HOME. A small-screen, self-contained projector is taken into the homes of potential target market viewers. Respondents are asked a series of questions, are shown the commercials to be tested, and then are asked another series of questions. This technique has the advantage of gaining the complete attention of the respondent. But the advantage is offset by the unnatural situation in which the viewing takes place. The technique is extremely expensive and thus not as widely used as it once was.

TRAILER TESTS. For the purpose of getting closer to the actual point of decision by the respondents, pretesting is sometimes conducted in a natural-setting/forced-viewing situation. One method is to set up a trailer in a shopping center. Shoppers are invited to enter and are offered prizes for cooperation. First, respondents are asked a series of questions about the products to be tested and are given an opportunity to select a series of brands in a simulated shopping situation using cents-off coupons or similar incentives. The respondents then view the test commercials along with other material. After seeing the commercials, respondents are given another set of coupons to be used in the stores in the shopping center. Later, coupons given the respondents are retrieved from the stores where they were used. By correlating the choices made prior to viewing the commercials with the coupons used in the actual shopping situation, inferences are drawn about the strength of the commercials in affecting purchasing behavior.

THEATER TESTS. A widely used technique for pretesting is forced viewing in a theater setting. Both Audience Studies, Inc. (ASI) and McCollum/Spielman ask respondents to come to a theater supposedly to view a potential new television series. At the beginning of the show, respondents select brands of products from among the categories to be tested. These selections are given as door prizes.

The actual test consists of showing a nontelevised pilot or other entertainment piece followed by a series of commercials and more entertainment. After the showing, respondents are again asked to make brand selections from various categories. Differences between the brand choices prior to viewing the commercials and those after the viewing are assumed to indicate the potential power of the commercials. Other evaluations are made in this type of setting through questionnaires and mechanical devices to measure such factors as attention value, effect of "clutter," persuasiveness of the commercial, and recalled sales points.

Theater testing is fast and fairly low-cost and can be replicated if necessary. Another advantage is that research organizations have tested many commercials in most consumer categories. Test commercials may be compared with previously tested commercials or the "norms" that have been established. This comparison gives an indication of the relative strength of the test commercial. A disadvantage is that the forced-viewing situation and the fact that the audience is often in the theater to be entertained sometimes leads to false assumptions of how the commercial will do in a real-world situation.

On-air/recruited natural environment. On-air commercial tests have been developed for the purpose of overcoming the problems of forced viewing and achieving as natural a setting as possible.

These tests, typified by Burke Market Research, Gallup & Robinson, and Tele-Test Co. (TTC), use an unassigned channel on a cable television system or programming on a regular UHF station as the pretest vehicle. Prospective respondents are recruited to watch the programming on the channel during the time the test commercials will be shown. Since respondents are not told which commercials are being tested, real-world viewing is simulated as closely as possible. Usually 24 hours later, the recruited respondents are called by telephone and asked a series of questions about what they saw and remembered during the time the test commercials were shown. Response to the questions and recall of the test commercials are the normal measures used to rate success.

The major advantage of this technique is the real-world atmosphere in which the commercial appears with all the normal distractions and competition from the programming and other commercials. The major disadvantage is the fairly high cost of the technique and the lack of projective ability in respect to what will happen in repeated viewings.

A variation of these techniques has been developed by AdTel, Ltd. Test sites are located in several communities in which matched samples of homes have been connected to cable television. Respondents keep diaries of such factors as purchases and television viewing. By controlling the source of the programming through the cable system, the research organization is able to show one commercial in one set of homes while a different commercial is seen by the other sample. Respondents are not aware of what is being tested. Through a comparison of the purchasing behavior of each group of viewers and their exposure to the alternatives, the commercials can be evaluated. While this technique completely simulates the actual conditions under which commercials are seen, it is quite expensive and only a limited number of advertisers can use the system at any one time.

Sales tests. The sales test replicates the actual response the advertisement will receive in the real world. Two techniques deserve mention, although they are not as widely used as might be expected. They are inquiries and split runs.

Inquiries. Inquiry tests are conducted by means of running advertisements in regular media and judging the effectiveness according to the number of inquiries generated. The standard approach is to run different advertisements at different times in the same publication or at the same time in different publications. Based on the number of inquiries received, the advertisement to be used on a broad scale or continuing basis is selected.

Split runs. Split-run testing simply means that different advertisements are run in the same edition of a publication. This can be done by having the publication use different ads in alternating issues or by running one ad in half the press run and a different ad in the other half. Such items as headlines, appeals, and offers can be evaluated according to the response achieved.

The major advantage of the sales test is that the advertising is being evaluated under real-world conditions. The disadvantage is that this type of approach can be used only for print advertising and is limited to those publications that have split run capabilities. Split-run testing may not work for all types of products. An appeal for an automobile, for example, would be difficult to test in an inquiry or split-run technique.

What makes a good advertising pretest?

Roman and Maas suggest that a number of factors be considered in pretesting. Following is a summary of their recommendations:

1. Determine first how the advertising should be judged. Should recall, persuasion, or communication of a specific product benefit be used and at what level? Usually, determining this need clarifies what techniques should be used.

2. When you are deciding to pretest, describe the problem to be solved, not the methodology to be used. This is especially important if outside research organizations are to be used.

3. Whenever and wherever possible, disguise the true purpose of the pretesting, the name of the advertiser, and other campaign themes. Try to have the respondent perceive the advertising as a customer and not as an advertising expert. Don't ask respondents if they like the advertising; ask if they can tell you the benefits or solutions to problems given by the advertising.

4. Be sure the right sample is selected, i.e., that the respondents logically are in the target market and are prime prospects for the product or service.

5. If possible, use several markets to avoid geographic bias in the pretest.

6. Understand the results of the study. The scores on pretests are only approximations. What is the

range of the scores? What is the confidence level of the study? Understand the statistical and methodological terminology used in the results.

7. Test only one thing, not several things at one time. If several of the test items are too varied, there is no way to know what stimulated the response. Hold everything constant in the pretest except the item to be evaluated.

8. Use good judgment. Don't rely totally on the results of pretests. If something sounds unusual or the results seem out of the ordinary, go back to the study. Check the verbatim comments. Understand what the respondents were trying to say. Use common sense.[19]

Other rules-of-thumb in advertising pretesting can be cited, but those described here seem to cover the major points. Advertising pretesting should be used primarily to guard against disasters. Guaranteed techniques and completely foolproof tests simply do not exist.

Revising—or will you accept the truth?

The most difficult things to accept in advertising pretesting are the results. Much work has gone into the development and formulation of the campaign, much research has been done, long hours have gone into developing appeals and yet, a group of 50 consumers in a period of only a few minutes can totally reject the entire premise of the campaign. One's natural reaction is to seek another jury, find another group who truly understands the campaign. Test and retest.

Unfortunately, although results of pretesting are only directional, they may uncover major flaws in the thinking behind and planning of a campaign. If that is the case, accept the truth. Determine, if possible, exactly what went wrong. Learn why the theme or appeal is weak or has little potential.

Most of all, learn to accept the fact that not every campaign will test well, not every campaign idea is a winner. If the pretest should prove that the campaign is a poor one, certainly an attempt should be made to determine why. But, a vendetta against the "dummies in the market" who don't understand the campaign approach is the fault of the planner, not the respondents. Accept the results as a guide for improvement. That is, usually one of the hardest parts of advertising campaign development.

Notes

1. Russell Colley, *Defining Advertising Goals for Measured Advertising Results* (New York: Association of National Advertisers, 1961), p. 35.
2. Kenneth Roman and Jane Maas, *How to Advertise* (New York: St. Martin's, 1976), pp. 104-105.
3. C. H. Sandage and Vernon Fryburger, *Advertising Theory and Practice,* 9th ed. (Homewood, Ill. Richard D. Irwin, 1975), p. 545.
4. Richard E. Stanley, *Promotion* (Englewood Cliffs, N. J.: Prentice-Hall, 1977), pp. 370-73.
5. Clarence E. Eldridge, *Marketing for Profit* (New York: Macmillan, 1970), p. 122.
6. Charles T. Dirksen, Arthur Kroeger, and Francesco M. Nicosia, *Advertising Principles, Problems, Cases,* 5th ed. (Homewood, Ill.: Richard D. Irwin, 1977), pp. 490-97.
7. Roman and Maas, *How to Advertise,* pp. 104-105.
8. D. L. Malickson and John N. Nason, *Advertising—How to Write the Kind that Works* (New York: Charles Scribner's Sons, 1977), pp. 197–201.
9. Roman and Maas, *How to Advertise.*
10. John S. Wright, Daniel S. Warner, Willis L. Winter, Jr.,and Sherilyn K. Zeigler, *Advertising,* 4th ed. (New York: McGraw-Hill, 1977), pp. 541-44.
11. Phillip Ward Burton, *Advertising Copywriting,* 3d. ed. (Columbus, Ohio: Grid Publishing, 1974), pp. 355-62.
12. James F. Engel, Hugh G. Wales, and Martin R. Warshaw, *Promotional Strategy,* rev. ed. (Homewood, Ill.: Richard D. Irwin, 1971), pp. 370-90.
13. Burton, *Advertising Copywriting,* pp. 366-75.
14. Engel, Wales, and Warshaw, *Promotional Strategy*, pp. 370-61.
15. Ibid.
16. S. Watson Dunn and Arnold M. Barban, *Advertising: Its Role in Modern Marketing,* 2d ed. (Hinsdale, Ill.: Dryden Press, 1974), pp. 272-78; Dorothy Cohen, *Advertising* (New York: Wiley, 1972), pp. 628-42.
17. Engel, Wales, and Warshaw, *Promotional Strategy*, pp. 370-90.
18. Ibid.
19. Roman and Maas, *How to Advertise,* pp. 104–105.

Media Planning— Matching Messages with Prospects

Media vs. creative—which comes first? Neither. Today they must be developed together. The fifties and sixties have been accused of generating a bunch of creative brats. Damn the media—full speed ahead on creative was the philosophy. Media planners had little status and were often considered pawns. They were not equals in planning campaign strategy. Yet, it worked. Because twenty years ago advertising vehicles were more predictable. *Life* and *Look* were on nearly every print schedule. Regular network television shows enjoyed fierce audience loyalty year after year. Media costs were relatively stable. The whole marketplace was much less volatile.

A media revolution occurred in the seventies. Television programming executives are now in the driver's seat. Schedules are schizophrenic. Costs are soaring. Radio has adapted to television with stunning success. Magazines have created a brand-new face and tempo to compete with television. Sophisticated research tells us much more about consumer media habits and buying behavior. And, of course, the computer has made it possible to analyze more data than we ever dreamed possible.

So, how do you start planning your media strategy for the eighties? Ground zero is the situation analysis: market research. Once research information has been gathered, media planners should clearly define the target prospect. With that in hand, both media planners and creative strategists should meet on equal ground to commit themselves to some basic objectives.

Today's market conditions have put the media experts on equal status with creative planners. Isolationist thinking simply has no place in this critical phase of campaign planning.

You must define your target zone accurately. The military practice of "spotting" targets for artillery gunners is closely analogous to media planning. If the message is fired out of the barrel with a 10 degree error, it could be 10 miles off target by the time it reaches the impact zone. The media spotters must give accurate directions if they expect the creative people to hit inside the target area, even a large target.

Using the research information gathered in the situation analysis, target markets can be segmented by using the following three methods, ranked in order of importance:

1. Demographic market segmentation
2. Product usage market segmentation
3. Psychographic market segmentation

Demographic segmentation

Which of these three segmentation methods is right for your product? Still by far the most accepted method is demographic segmentation.

Among the most valuable demographic tools in media planning today are the Simmons (including Target Group Index) market studies. This syndicated research firm draws its sample from a broad base of consumers selected from across the nation. The sample is usually large enough to be statistically reliable when broken down into product subgroups. Unlike some market studies done by media vehicles, Simmons reports are reasonably representative of the demographic categories employed by most advertising and marketing planners. Some of the following category descriptions might be helpful in developing your advertising plan.

Definitions for nine of the Simmons demographic categories[1]

Household head. This study's classification of household heads was obtained by asking the respondent whom he or she considered to be the head. Unlike the census definition, there was no requirement that the person so identified be considered the sole head.

Thus, even in a typical family unit with both husband and wife present, the wife might well have designated herself as the head because of her perceived status as co-head. If no one person in particular is considered "to be head of the household" from the questionnaire answer, or, "head of household" is unknown (designated by "don't know")—the person in the household having the highest yearly income will be classified as household head, and so tabulated.

As a result, the total number of household heads found by this study's household head classification procedure is approximately 82.5 million. This includes 60.3 million men and 22.2 million women.

Female homemaker. In addition to female respondents who designated themselves as the household head or were the only adult female in the household, this study also included in its female homemaker classification those females designated as the homemaker in the household. In this way, every household with an adult female is defined as having a female homemaker. Altogether the study found 71.3 million such female homemakers.

Professional, managerial. In this study we have clarified professional, managerial (including proprietors) to more specific dimensions: The classification includes those occupations in professional/technical, managerial/administrative (except farm), and proprietorship.

Locality types. Four types of locations are defined:

1. *Metropolitan:* Includes all counties located within standard metropolitan statistical areas (SMSA) as defined by the census as of August 1973. Each SMSA must contain at least one city of at least 50,000 inhabitants or two cities having contiguous boundaries and constituting, for general economic and social purposes, a single community with a combined population of at least 50,000, the smaller of which must have a population of at least 15,000. The SMSA will then include the county of such a central city and adjacent counties that are found to be metropolitan in character and economically and socially integrated with the county of the central city. Criteria of metropolitan character relate primarily to the county as a place of work or as a home for a concentration of nonagricultural workers. Criteria of economic and social integration relate to the extent of economic and social interdependence between the adjacent counties and the central county.

2. *Metropolitan central city:* The central city is the nucleus of the SMSA. If the SMSA contains more than one city of 50,000, then the largest city is con-

sidered to be the nucleus and usually gives its name to that area. The name may include other cities in the area if such cities have populations of 25,000 or more, and have at least one-third of the population of the largest city or a population of not less than 250,000.

3. *Metropolitan suburban:* Includes the part of the metropolitan area that lies outside the central city.

4. *Nonmetropolitan:* Includes all those counties which are not classified as metropolitan.

Geographic regions. Geographic regions were determined in accordance with standard Bureau of the Census definitions. The four regions in this report represent state groupings as shown below:

1. Northeast: Maine, Vermont, New Hampshire, Massachusetts, Connecticut, Rhode Island, New York, Pennsylvania, New Jersey.

2. South: Delaware, Maryland, Washington, D. C., Virginia, West Virginia, North Carolina, Georgia, Florida, Kentucky, Tennessee, Mississippi, Alabama, Louisiana, Arkansas, Oklahoma, Texas.

3. Central: Ohio, Indiana, Illinois, Wisconsin, Michigan, Minnesota, Iowa, Missouri, Kansas, Nebraska, South Dakota, North Dakota.

4. West: Montana, Idaho, Wyoming, Colorado, New Mexico, Arizona, Utah, Nevada, Washington, Oregon, California.

County size. The county size definitions are as follows:

1. County size A: All counties as of 23 February 1971 belonging to the 25 largest metropolitan areas according to the 1970 census of population.

2. County size B: All counties not included under A that are either over 150,000 population or in metropolitan areas over 150,000 population according to the 1970 census of population.

3. County size C: All counties not included under A or B that are either over 35,000 population or in metropolitan areas over 35,000 population according to the 1970 census of population.

4. County size D: All remaining counties.

Industry definitions. The standard industrial classifications prepared by the Federal Bureau of the Budget are combined to form five industry groups. The following defines those industries:

1. *Industrial:* Includes construction and mining, manufacturing, transportation, communication and other public utilities.

2. *Trade, repair, personal, and professional services:* Includes wholesale and retail trade, business repair services, personal services, entertaining and

recreational services and professional and related services of nongovernment employees.

3. *Business services:* Includes finance, insurance, real estate and business services.

4. *Agriculture:* Includes agriculture (farming), forestry, and fisheries.

5. *Public administration:* In prior years government employees were not further classified. This year's study conforms to census usage in that government employees are reported either as public administration or distributed among the industries they represent: agriculture, transportation, etc.

Index of social position. Advertisers, agencies, and media have long recognized the importance of social class differences in consumer behavior. Realizing that many people's incomes tend to change much faster than their habits and that income level alone can often be an unsatisfactory predictor of behavior, researchers have for years attempted to take direct account of the social class affiliation factor. Typically, this problem has been approached by means of a subjective rating system in which the interviewer makes an evaluation of each respondent or household. In the context of a large-scale comparative media study, such an approach carries with it the unfortunate implications of any methodological approach which is dependent upon subjective interpretations.

To fulfill the need for an objective and reliable classification system, suitable for use in quantitatively

sound research, Dr. A. B. Hollingshead, chairman of the Department of Sociology at Yale University, developed the *Two Factor Index of Social Position.* On the basis of extensive sociological research covering a period of many years, Dr. Hollingshead found that the class affiliation of most households could be characterized with a high degree of accuracy by a weighted index based upon the occupation and education of the head of household. In common with other operationally defined classification systems used in survey research, its merit rests upon the extent to which it makes possible important and meaningful differentiations between people who are differently classified.

The *Two Factor Index of Social Position* has been widely used in sociological studies conducted under the auspices of various universities, foundations, and government agencies; and in consultation with Dr. Hollingshead it has been used in a steadily increasing number of market and media research projects.

The Five Index of Social Position groups are here labeled: Class I, upper; Class II, upper middle; Class III, lower middle; and Classes IV and V, lower.

Education. By definition, a person who attended college must have completed at least a full year. A person who completed less than one year of college was classified as a high school graduate.

How to apply demographic data

In the actual Simmons market studies, products are

Exhibit 8-1. Hair shampoo. Regular, personal usage by brand, total adult females (in thousands).

	TOTAL ADULT FEMALES	AGE 18-24 YEARS	25-34 YEARS	35-44 YEARS	45-54 YEARS	55-64 YEARS	55-64 YEARS	35-49 YEARS	WHITE COLLAR	OTHER EMPLOYED	NOT EMPLOYED	ATTENDED/GRADUATED COLLEGE	GRADUATED HIGH SCHOOL	DID NOT GRADUATE HIGH SCHOOL	$20,000 & OVER	$15,000-$19,999	$10,000-$14,999	$8,000-$9,999	$5,000-$7,999	LESS THAN $5,000
TOTAL	77825	13906	16079	11672	12125	10677	17682	21858	11973	43994	18663	32120	27042	17279	11045	16877	7593	10078	14952
PCT DIST	100.0	17.9	20.7	15.0	15.6	13.7	22.7	28.1	15.4	56.5	24.0	41.3	34.7	22.2	14.2	21.7	9.8	12.9	19.2
CLAIROL	4767	1163	1255	601	816	488	964	1684	742	2341	1345	2089	1333	1245	696	1064	*372	664	725
PCT DEMO COV	6.1	8.4	7.8	5.1	6.7	4.6	5.5	7.7	6.2	5.3	7.2	6.5	4.9	7.2	6.3	6.3	4.9	6.6	4.8
INDEX	100	138	128	84	110	75	90	126	102	87	118	107	80	118	103	103	80	108	79
PCT DIST	100.0	24.4	26.3	12.6	17.1	10.2	20.2	35.3	15.6	49.1	28.2	43.8	28.0	26.1	14.6	22.3	7.8	13.9	15.2
HERBAL ESSENCE	2255	741	549	*252	377	**116	423	681	504	1070	693	880	683	575	*290	504	*206	*368	*312
PCT DEMO COV	2.9	5.3	3.4	2.2	3.1	1.1	2.4	3.1	4.2	2.4	3.7	2.7	2.5	3.3	2.6	3.0	2.7	3.7	2.1
INDEX	100	183	117	76	107	38	83	107	145	83	128	93	86	114	90	103	93	128	72
PCT DIST	100.0	32.9	24.3	11.2	16.7	5.1	18.8	30.2	22.4	47.5	30.7	39.0	30.3	25.5	12.9	22.4	9.1	16.3	13.8
EARTHBORN	1950	530	589	281	*292	**103	448	685	*246	1019	660	781	*509	517	*353	425	**159	**176	*321
PCT DEMO COV	2.5	3.8	3.7	2.4	2.4	1.0	2.5	3.1	2.1	2.3	3.5	2.4	1.9	3.0	3.2	2.5	2.1	1.7	2.1
INDEX	100	152	148	96	96	40	100	124	84	92	140	96	76	120	128	100	84	68	84
PCT DIST	100.0	27.2	30.2	14.4	15.0	5.3	23.0	35.1	12.6	52.3	33.8	40.1	26.1	26.5	18.1	21.8	8.2	9.0	16.5
JOHNSON'S BABY SHAMPOO	4846	1311	786	549	627	530	930	1179	777	2890	1203	1831	1812	1044	534	1140	504	647	977
PCT DEMO COV	6.2	9.4	4.9	4.7	5.2	5.0	5.3	5.4	6.5	6.6	6.4	5.7	6.7	6.0	4.8	6.8	6.6	6.4	6.5
INDEX	100	152	79	76	84	81	85	87	105	106	103	92	108	97	77	110	106	103	105
PCT DIST	100.0	27.1	16.2	11.3	12.9	10.9	19.2	24.3	16.0	59.6	24.8	37.8	37.4	21.5	11.0	23.5	10.4	13.4	20.2

*PROJECTION RELATIVELY UNSTABLE BECAUSE OF SMALL SAMPLE BASE. USE WITH CAUTION.
**NUMBER OF CASES TOO SMALL FOR RELIABILITY. SHOWN FOR CONSISTENCY ONLY.

W. R. SIMMONS & ASSOCIATES RESEARCH
a division of Stanton-Grudin-Chook Inc.
1976/77

This report is the property of W R Simmons & Associates Research a division of Stanton-Grudin-Chook Inc. and is distributed on loan to a limited group of clients, pursuant to contract, for their exclusive and confidential use. Any reproduction, publication, circulation, distribution, or sale of this report or disclosure of the contents thereof in whole or in part is strictly forbidden, and W. R. Simmons & Associates Research a division of Stanton-Grudin-Chook Inc. will avail itself of every remedy in law and equity respecting any unauthorized use.

Source: W. R. Simmons & Associates Research, 1976/1977.

matched by brand with demographics. As shown in Exhibit 8-1, users of Clairol shampoo are described in terms of age, employment status, education, and household income. Can you determine which income group has the highest number of Clairol users in Exhibit 8-1?

Exhibit 8-2 breaks out other important usage data based on the four common demographic segments. Can you tell which brand is used most often by high school graduates? Which income group is most important to Breck shampoo?

Exhibit 8-2. Hair shampoo. Regular, personal usage by brand, total adult females (in thousands).

	TOTAL ADULT FEMALES	AGE							EMPLOYMENT STATUS			EDUCATION			HOUSEHOLD INCOME					
		18-24 YEARS	25-34 YEARS	35-44 YEARS	45-54 YEARS	55-64 YEARS	18-49 YEARS	50 & OVER	WHITE COLLAR	OTHER EMPLOYED	NOT EMPLOYED	ATTENDED/GRAD. COLLEGE	GRADUATED HIGH SCHOOL	DID NOT GRAD. HIGH SCHOOL	$20,000 & OVER	$15,000-$19,999	$10,000-$14,999	$8,000-$9,999	$5,000-$7,999	LESS THAN $5,000
TOTAL	77825	13906	16079	11672	12125	10677	17682	21858	11973	43994	18663	32120	27042	17279	11045	16877		7593	10078	14952
PCT DIST	100.0	17.9	20.7	15.0	15.6	13.7	22.7	28.1	15.4	56.5	24.0	41.3	34.7	22.2	14.2	21.7		9.8	12.9	19.2
USED REGULAR SHAMPOO IN LAST MONTH	47406	9896	11202	7388	7086	5576	11085	14230	7394	25782	12155	19881	15370	10882	7116	10653		4579	6218	7959
PCT DEMO COV	60.9	71.2	69.7	63.3	58.4	52.2	62.7	65.1	61.8	58.6	65.1	61.9	56.8	63.0	64.4	63.1		60.3	61.7	53.2
INDEX	100	117	114	104	96	86	103	107	101	96	107	102	93	103	106	104		99	101	87
PCT DIST	100.0	20.9	23.6	15.6	14.9	11.8	23.4	30.0	15.6	54.4	25.6	41.9	32.4	23.0	15.0	22.5		9.7	13.1	16.8
BRAND USED MOST OFTEN																				
ALBERTO CULVER	624	**130	**141	**58	**109	**80	**118	*146	**69	410	*205	*255	**164	**120	**31	**166		**80	**130	**98
PCT DEMO COV	.8	.9	.9	.5	.9	.7	.7	.7	.6	.9	1.1	.8	.6	.7	.3	1.0		1.1	1.3	.7
INDEX	100	113	113	63	113	88	88	88	75	113	138	100	75	88	38	125		138	163	88
PCT DIST	100.0	20.8	22.6	9.3	17.5	12.8	18.9	23.4	11.1	65.7	32.9	40.9	26.3	19.2	5.0	26.6		12.8	20.8	15.7
AVON	1808	*280	594	*393	**165	*160	496	619	*217	971	401	1044	*362	380	*323	466		**86	**280	**272
PCT DEMO COV	2.3	2.0	3.7	3.4	1.4	1.5	2.8	2.8	1.8	2.2	2.1	3.3	1.3	2.2	2.9	2.8		1.1	2.8	1.8
INDEX	100	87	161	148	61	65	122	122	78	96	91	143	57	96	126	122		48	122	78
PCT DIST	100.0	15.5	32.9	21.7	9.1	8.8	27.4	34.2	12.0	53.7	22.2	57.7	20.0	21.0	17.9	25.8		4.8	15.5	15.0
BRECK	6608	1161	1300	1095	1100	937	1706	2049	1034	3525	1712	2702	2194	1643	1200	1356		712	763	934
PCT DEMO COV	8.5	8.3	8.1	9.4	9.1	8.8	9.6	9.4	8.6	8.0	9.2	8.4	8.1	9.5	10.9	8.0		9.4	7.6	6.2
INDEX	100	98	95	111	107	104	113	111	101	94	108	99	95	112	128	94		111	89	73
PCT DIST	100.0	17.6	19.7	16.6	16.6	14.2	25.6	31.0	15.6	53.3	25.9	40.9	33.2	24.9	18.2	20.5		10.8	11.5	14.1

*PROJECTION RELATIVELY UNSTABLE BECAUSE OF SMALL SAMPLE BASE. USE WITH CAUTION
**NUMBER OF CASES TOO SMALL FOR RELIABILITY. SHOWN FOR CONSISTENCY ONLY

W. R. SIMMONS & ASSOCIATES RESEARCH, a division of Stanton-Grudin-Chook Inc. 1976/77

Source: W. R. Simmons & Associates Research, 1976/1977.

Exhibit 8-3. Hair shampoo. Regular, personal usage by frequency, total adult females (in thousands).

	RACE		MARITAL STATUS			PRESENCE OF CHILDREN IN HOUSEHOLD			LOCALITY TYPE			GEOGRAPHIC REGION				COUNTY SIZE			
	WHITE	BLACK	MARRIED	SINGLE	WIDOWED/DIV./SEP.	CHILD UNDER 6	CHILD 6-17	NO CHILD UNDER 18	METROPOLITAN CENTRAL CITY	METROPOLITAN SUBURBAN	NON-METROPOLITAN	NORTHEAST	CENTRAL	SOUTH	WEST	A	B	C	D
TOTAL	68440	8160	49233	11214	17378	16023	27875	41678	23868	33052	20905	18518	20104	24718	13494	31503	21243	13895	11184
PCT DIST	87.9	10.5	63.3	14.4	22.3	20.6	35.8	53.6	30.7	42.5	26.9	23.8	27.1	31.8	17.3	40.5	27.3	17.9	14.4
+USED ANY SHAMPOO IN LAST MONTH	50069	4727	36330	8272	11040	13342	21792	26945	16382	24985	14274	13304	15167	17121	10049	22644	15640	9987	7370
PCT DEMO COV	73.2	57.9	73.8	73.8	63.5	83.3	78.2	64.6	68.6	75.6	68.3	71.8	71.9	69.3	74.5	71.9	73.6	71.9	65.9
INDEX	102	81	103	103	89	117	109	90	96	106	96	100	101	97	104	101	103	101	92
PCT DIST	90.0	8.5	65.3	14.9	19.8	24.0	39.2	48.4	29.4	44.9	25.7	23.9	27.3	30.8	18.1	40.7	28.1	17.9	13.2
USED REGULAR SHAMPOO IN LAST MONTH	42781	3927	30306	7271	9829	11078	18476	23188	14050	21246	12111	11524	12736	14693	8454	19465	13189	8454	6299
PCT DEMO COV	62.5	48.1	61.6	64.8	56.6	69.1	66.3	55.6	58.9	64.3	57.9	62.2	60.4	59.4	62.7	61.8	62.1	60.8	56.3
INDEX	103	79	101	106	93	113	109	91	97	106	95	102	99	98	103	101	102	100	92
PCT DIST	90.2	8.3	63.9	15.3	20.7	23.4	39.0	48.9	29.6	44.8	25.5	24.3	26.9	31.0	17.8	41.1	27.8	17.8	13.3
NO. TIMES USED LAST WEEK																			
LESS THAN 2	14685	1931	10642	1344	4821	2225	5504	10346	5140	6843	4824	3381	4629	6040	2757	6590	4247	3027	2943
PCT DEMO COV	21.5	23.7	21.6	12.0	27.7	13.9	19.7	24.8	21.5	20.7	23.1	18.3	21.9	24.4	20.4	20.9	20.0	21.8	26.3
INDEX	100	111	100	56	128	64	91	115	100	96	107	85	101	113	94	97	93	101	122
PCT DIST	87.4	11.5	63.3	8.0	28.7	13.2	32.7	61.6	30.6	40.7	28.7	20.1	27.5	35.9	16.4	39.2	25.3	18.0	17.5
2 - 3	16709	1437	12958	2480	2952	5588	7816	7499	5413	8486	4488	4900	5192	5111	3185	7602	5399	3136	2249
PCT DEMO COV	24.4	17.6	26.3	22.1	17.0	34.9	28.0	18.0	22.7	25.7	21.5	26.5	24.6	20.7	23.6	24.1	25.4	22.6	20.1
INDEX	103	75	111	94	72	148	119	76	96	109	91	112	104	88	100	102	108	96	85
PCT DIST	90.9	7.8	70.5	13.5	16.1	30.4	42.5	40.8	29.4	46.1	24.4	26.6	28.2	27.8	17.3	41.3	29.4	17.1	12.2
4 OR MORE	11387	559	6708	3447	2057	3266	5156	5344	3497	5917	2798	3243	2915	3543	2512	5273	3543	2289	1108
PCT DEMO COV	16.6	6.9	13.6	30.7	11.8	20.4	18.5	12.8	14.7	17.9	13.4	17.5	13.8	14.3	18.6	16.7	16.7	16.5	9.9
INDEX	106	44	87	196	75	130	118	82	94	114	85	111	88	91	118	106	106	105	63
PCT DIST	93.2	4.6	54.9	28.2	16.8	26.7	42.2	43.8	28.6	48.5	22.9	26.6	23.9	29.0	20.6	43.2	29.0	18.7	9.1

W. R. SIMMONS & ASSOCIATES RESEARCH, a division of Stanton-Grudin-Chook Inc. 1976/77

Source: W. R. Simmons & Associates Research, 1976/1977.

Frequency of usage data

Exhibit 8-3 matches demographic characteristics such as race and marital status with women who used any shampoo in the past month and how often they used it.

Sighting your target demographically

A novice media planner may be tempted to narrow his or her target market to the extremes. There is rarely a tiny bullseye in the use of mass media vehicles. Most often it is a disproportionately large bullseye. Based on the Simmons shampoo market study, the target prospects for Clairol shampoo may be demographically pictured as the large bullseye in Exhibit 8-4. (Data are taken from Exhibit 8-1 and 8-2.) The "bullseye" in an advertising target (also called a market segment) is rarely a small pinpoint. The media planner most often defines the target to include a *range* of prospects.

Product usage market segmentation

The second most valuable market segmentation tool is product usage data. From baby food to beer, product usage data are used extensively by virtually all package goods firms. Such information is a natural partner with demographic subheadings.

Both Simmons and TGI (see Exhibit 8-3) segment their users according to such factors as race, marital status, and place of residence. Selecting a target market based on product usage accepts the theory that current users of a product category are the best possible prospects.

Heavy user, medium user, light user

The heavy user is usually the most sought-after pros-

Exhibit 8-4. Target market for Clairol shampoo.

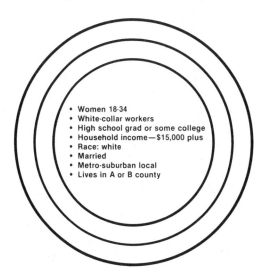

- • Women 18-34
- • White-collar workers
- • High school grad or some college
- • Household income—$15,000 plus
- • Race: white
- • Married
- • Metro-suburban local
- • Lives in A or B county

Source: W. R. Simmons Research Corporation, New York.

pect because he or she often accounts for the larger share of that product's consumption. Using Exhibit 8-3, we could define the female *heavy user* of regular shampoo with this demographic profile (based on four or more uses in the last week).

- • Race: white
- • Marital status: single
- • Locality type: metropolitan-suburban
- • County size: lives in A and B counties

The heavy user is often the most important prospect. Exhibit 8-5 shows a list of some product categories where heavy users account for the largest share of the total usage.

Exhibit 8-5. Heavy users of selected products.[2]

	Heavy User Percent of Population Group	Heavy User Percent of Total Usage
Car rentals in past year	3.6	89.6
Liquid dietary products	4.1	98.0
Air trips in past year, men	7.8	87.3
Automatic dishwasher detergents	9.0	100.0
Hair coloring rinse or tint for women	11.3	88.1
Scotch whiskey	12.6	98.6
Cigar smoking, men	17.1	98.6
Rye or blended whiskey	18.4	98.5
Bourbon	18.8	98.7
Canned dog food	19.3	99.2
Dry dog food	20.7	99.2
Canned ham	22.8	83.0

Source: Norton Garfinkle, "The Marketing Value of Media Audiences—How to Pinpoint Your Prime Prospects," Speech presented at the Association of National Advertisers Workshop, 19 July 1965.

Don't marry the heavy user theory

Blind acceptance of the heavy user theory can be hazardous. A great example is a recent development in the bubble gum market. For years, the market leaders kept pounding away at the 8- to 14-year-old heavy user who consumed approximately 80 percent of all bubble gum tonnage. Then, Life Saver, Inc., jumped into the market with Bubble Yum, a truly unique kind of soft bubble gum. The company did all its product testing with the traditional target market. Preference tests showed Bubble Yum beat the market leader by an incredible margin of 8 to 1 among kids tested.

After a highly successful product launch, Life Saver discovered early on that a growing percentage of Bubble Yum's volume came from teen/adult usage. They quickly revised their media strategy. Soon, evening prime time commercials targeted against adults hit the TV screen to supplement the daytime commercials aimed at children. The result was astounding. Now, the teen/adult group accounts for a full 60 percent of Bubble Yum's tonnage.

Bubble Yum's media strategy helped revolutionize the bubble gum market. They actually *doubled* category sales in two years and are now the number-one selling brand of bubble gum. In fact, all of Bubble Yum's combined sales are now higher than any other brand of gum in the United States.[3] It never would have happened if Life Savers marketing executives had blindly followed the heavy user theory in their media planning. They were alert enough and smart enough to break the rules.

Psychographic market segmentation

A current term used to describe a target's life style and personality traits is *psychographics*. Direct application to media planning is still quite limited. However, it can add a new dimension to the rather sterile-looking "demographic man." At present, its greatest value is adding insight to the creative effort. Applying some of the in-depth research techniques discussed in chapter 3 one can classify the target in terms of personality characteristics. Some of the most often used are:

- Leadership
- Independence
- Need for success
- Aggressiveness
- Sociability
- Conformity
- Conservativeness
- Self-confidence

In her excellent discussion on psychological insights, Dorothy Cohen describes how various "personality profiles" are used in research to single out personality characteristics which indicate a consumer preference for one product over another.[4]

Product use

A study undertaken to test the hypothesis that marketing behavior is related to personality "clearly indicated that there is a relationship between product use and personality traits." The Gordon Personal Profile was administered to a group of college marketing students along with a so-called Sales and Marketing Personality Index which included questions on the use of headache remedies, cigarettes, chewing gum, deodorants, mouthwash, and other items commonly purchased by students. Although the relationships discovered between product use and personality were not particularly strong, and although some were intuitively acceptable (i.e., one would expect that high ascendancy and high sociability would be related to the rapid acceptance of new fashions), the results indicated that this thesis merits further research.

Product acceptance

In an attempt to delineate the "Social and psychological factors associated with the acceptance of new products," one researcher divided the respondents in the study into groups: (1) high tryers or early adopters, (2) majority and laggards, and (3) low product tryers. Relationships between the trial of new food products and some distinguishing social, economic, and psychological factors did emerge—high tryers were found to be more optimistic, and more of them expected future incomes to be higher than at present. Both high tryers and low tryers appeared to be more secure than the majority in their abilities as cooks.

Product choice

Increasing attention has been focused on the relationship between personality and product choice. The thesis that personality factors are significantly associated with the selection of an automobile brand and model is the subject of continuing research and commentary. No consensus has been reached, but, as one author notes, "the anxiety, controversy, and interest raised by the research are healthy and attest to its contribution."

Arnold M. Barban, Steven M. Cristol, and Frank J. Kopec have developed an outline that may be helpful in sketching your target's personality profile.[5]

Exhibit 8-6. Psychographic classifications: definitions.

Self-concept

Classifications of self-concept are based on self-ratings with respect to groups of adjectives on a five-point scale:

1. Agree a lot
2. Agree a little
3. Neither agree nor disagree
4. Disagree a little
5. Disagree a lot

The adjectives and the scale-points that define the classifications in each case are as follows:

Affectionate, passionate, loving, romantic	1
Amicable, amiable, affable, benevolent	1
Awkward, absent minded, forgetful, careless	1, 2
Brave, courageous, daring, adventuresome	1, 2
Broadminded, open-minded, liberal, tolerant	1
Creative, inventive, imaginative, artistic	1
Dominating, authoritarian, demanding, aggressive	1, 2
Efficient, organized, diligent, thorough	1
Egocentric, vain, self-centered, narcissistic	1, 2, 3
Frank, straightforward, outspoken, candid	1
Funny, humorous, amusing, witty	1
Intelligent, smart, bright, well informed	1
Kind, good-hearted, warm hearted, sincere	1
Refined, gracious, sophisticated, dignified	1, 2
Reserved, conservative, quiet, conventional	1
Self-assured, confident, self-sufficient, secure	1
Sociable, friendly, cheerful, likable	1
Stubborn, hardheaded, headstrong, obstinate	1, 2
Tense, nervous, high-strung, excitable	1, 2
Trustworthy, competent, reliable, responsible	1

Buying style

Classifications of buying style are based on agreement or disagreement with the following statements on the same five-point scale used for self-concept:

Brand loyal.............................. 1
I always look for the name of the manufacturer on the package.

Cautious............................... 1
I do not buy unknown brands merely to save money.

Conformists........................... 1, 2, 3
I prefer to buy things that my friends or neighbors would approve of.

Ecologists............................. 1
All products that pollute the environment should be banned.

Economy-minded....................... 1
I shop around a lot to take advantage of specials or bargains.

Experimenters......................... 1, 2, 3
I like to change brands often for the sake of variety and novelty.

Impulsive.............................. 1
When in the store, I often buy an item on the spur of the moment.

Persuasible............................ 1, 2
In general, advertising presents a true picture of the products of well-known companies.

Planners.............................. 1
I generally plan far ahead to buy expensive items such as automobiles.

Style-conscious........................ 1
I try to keep abreast of changes in styles and fashions.

Using psychographics cautiously

According to Jack Sissors, psychographics are only moderately helpful in media planning. Their best use is in other areas of marketing and advertising. Psychographics may be helpful in differentiating more effectively among consumers or learning more about how consumers buy. They also are helpful in devising creative strategies, especially for very selective kinds of products. But for selecting media, psychographics tend to be weak, according to Leo Bogart, of the Newspaper Advertising Bureau.

Another person who is skeptical about the use of psychographics in selecting media is Ed Papazian, media director of BBDO. He noted, "Psychographics has some way to go before it takes on real meaning." Papazian asked about some media whose psychographics were supposed to give them an advantage over other media: "Even if the slightest psychographic edge really existed, how would it affect the reader's acceptance for the advertiser's message?" Furthermore, Papazian raised a question about the manner in which media audiences are measured: "Can adults who have sat through 50-page questionnaires, or three-hour interviews, answer questions about their psychological makeup meaningfully, and establish a relationship between their replies and the advertising or commercial impact?" He felt that the answer was no.

When psychographics was first used, there was some feeling among experts that this was going to be a means of achieving a real breakthrough in media-selection processes. Subsequent use and evaluation of psychographics indicate that it is helpful but does not replace demographic bases for selection. More research on its advantages and limitations also seems to be needed before a final evaluation can be made.[6]

How to weight target prospects

Now that you have the basic market segmentation tools in hand, how can they be used objectively? Unfortunately, there is no simple answer. The media planner must use his or her own best judgment. In most cases where a nationally distributed brand is in question, both demographic and product-usage criteria will be used by the media planner. Occasionally the brand's problems may justify the use of social or psychographic tools. If you venture in this direction, expect your client to be skeptical. An ambitious media planner will experiment with several combinations before committing him- or herself to a particular target definition.

Dennis H. Gensch has developed an excellent model for weighting target markets. He uses all three market segmentation tools; however, it works just as well with two. In edited form, his procedure follows.[7]

The target population can sometimes be defined on the basis of a single attribute; for example, denture adhesive advertisers may define their target population as only those people who wear dentures. A simple one or zero value can be attached to each individual in the vehicle's audience. Most target populations are valued over a one-variable spectrum such as past purchase behavior. A canned dog food manufacturer might assign the following weights on the basis of past purchase behavior and dog ownership:

Weight	Category
1.00	Purchased 30 cans of dog food in the last month
.60	Purchased 15 cans
.40	Purchased 10 cans
.20	Purchased 5 cans
.10	Purchased 0 cans but own dog
.01	Purchased 0 cans but do not own dog

These weights attempt to reflect the purchasing potential as well as the past purchasing record of each individual. It is hoped that light users can be encouraged to increase purchases; thus, weighting is not in direct proportion to past purchases.

Individuals can be identified on the basis of socioeconomic variables, past purchasing, and personality traits. Assuming potential customers are identified by some combination of these variables (for example, where the product in question is a new form of baby food), the potential customer may be defined as female, college educated, with traits of aggressiveness and venturesomeness, with youngest child less than 30 months of age.

To the advertiser, some variables are more important than others; also many variables can be present in various strengths or degrees. Thus, variables must be weighted on both an inter and intra basis. The table [Exhibit 8-7] shows this weighting scheme for three variables in the baby food example.

The weight indicates the importance of one variable in relation to another. The scale indicates the degree to which the particular individual possesses each variable. The .01 value is used in place of zero so that each individual will have a positive value, which is desirable when combining individual weights with other systems of weights.

Geographic ranking—weighting markets

After you've determined who your target prospect is, you need to sort out geographically the most promising marketing areas for your brand.

The first question is how well is the product distributed? Whether it be available nationally or regionally, the problem still arises: which cities, counties, or states are most important?

Simplifying the complex

With Frito Lay's Rold Gold pretzels, marketing areas are referred to as 12 heartland and 21 nonheartland divisions. (See Rold Gold Case, chapter 12.) The heartland cities in the Northeast held an 8.6 percent share of market, while nonheartland cities enjoyed a 37.5 percent share. Population in the heartland was more dense. Also, volume of pretzel consumption was higher on a per capita basis in the Northeast.

Competitive pressures were much lighter in the West. Other factors that weighed in the ranking of markets for Rold Gold were beverage consumption

Exhibit 8-7. Individual weighting system, baby food.

	Individual			
	1	2	3	4
Variable 1				
College Education				
Weight	3	3	3	3
Scale	1.00	0.01	1.00	0.50
V_1	3.00	0.03	3.00	1.50
Variable 2				
Child-30 months				
Weight	10	10	10	10
Scale	1.00	1.00	0.01	0.01
V_2	10	10	0.1	0.1
Variable 3				
Aggressiveness				
Weight	5	5	5	5
Scale	0.20	0.80	0.50	0.60
V_3	1.0	4.0	2.5	3.0
Individual's				
Value Weight				
V_1	3.00	10	1.0	30.00
V_2	10.0	10.0	0.1	0.1
V_3	1.0	4.0	2.5	3.0
Weight	30.00	1.20	0.75	0.45

Source: Dennis H. Gensch, *Journal of Marketing Research*, 1970.

and snack-food sales. Confused? Anybody would be. It's your job to digest this potpourri into simplified data that can be quickly understood by the client.

Problem: Which markets should receive heaviest advertising weight?

In reality, a host of intervening marketing variables had to be judged subjectively as well as objectively before one could develop a ranked grouping of markets for Rold Gold. No magical formula eliminated subjective, intuitive judgment. However, the place to start is with objectivity. The following method is called a multiple factor index. It's a fancy name for weighting the importance of individual markets based on available quantitative marketing data. Don't accept your first draft. Work the data in your own analysis until you know it's right.

How to build a multiple factor index

Let's assume that a total advertising budget has been determined. This index method will help you decide two things—which are the primary markets and how much to spend in each. The markets can be listed city by city, by county, by state, or by region. This example will use cities.

Exhibit 8-8. Multiple factor index (five factors).

Market	Population (000)	Annual Pretzel Sales (000)	Annual Rold Gold Sales (000)	Annual Snack Food Sales (000)	Annual Beverage Sales (000)	Sum of Factors (000)	Percent Value Index	Allocation of $975,082 Budget
City A	1,857	$ 568	$ 110	$2,666	$5,003	10,204	7.0	$ 68,256
City B	2,333	899	212	2,990	6,350	13,784	9.1	88,732
City C	986	250	89	4,060	3,865	9,250	6.1	59,480
City D	4,750	2,666	400	6,660	9,840	24,316	16.0	156,013
City E	3,255	666	450	2,770	5,707	12,848	8.4	81,907
City F	6,005	2,860	1,650	3,757	9,908	24,180	16.0	156,013
City G	1,157	450	125	2,808	4,302	8,842	5.8	56,555
City H	2,660	1,880	1,035	3,990	6,480	16,045	10.6	103,587
City I	4,860	1,669	888	4,750	9,005	21,172	14.0	136,511
City J	1,809	790	300	3,860	3,788	10,547	7.0	68,256
Base						151,188	100.0	$975,082

Example using City "A":
Sum of factors: 10,204/151,188 Base = 7.0 Percent value index × $975,082 Budget total = $68,256 Budget allocated to City A
Note how all factors are expressed in thousands. Add or delete zeros to make all factors have a common base.

Source: Jack Z. Sissors, Harry D. Lehew, and William Goodrich, *Media Planning Workbook*, 1976.

With Rold Gold Pretzels as an example, the following steps are taken:[8]

1. Select the factors. Care must be taken to use only relevant quantitative factors. For example, income is not a major factor in the purchase of snack foods. It could be left out. Important factors are:
   (a) Pretzel sales in each major market
   (b) Snack-food sales in each major market
   (c) Population in each major market
   (d) Rold Gold sales in each major market
   (e) Beverage sales in each major market
2. Find the data required in step 1 for all markets to be considered. Much of this should be available in your situation analysis.
3. Arrange the data in a table (see Exhibit 8-8).
4. Plug in the five factors across the top of the table. (Factors "a" through "e" in step 1)
5. Add the sum of factors (horizontally) for each market.
6. Divide each sum of factors for each market (step 5) by the base (base is the *total* sum of factors).
7. Multiply the percent value index (obtained in step 6) by the total available budget.

Mastering your media tools

Given the same gem, two world masters in the art of diamond cutting may create a vastly different jewel, using the same set of tools. Likewise, two masters in the art of media planning, using the same tools, may differ vastly in their strategy, yet be equally effective.

Here's a set of carefully defined media tools. They are essentially the same ones mastered by such experts as Herbert Zeltner, Ed Papazian, and Archa O. Knowlton. Now it's your turn.

Reach and frequency

Reach is the estimated percentage of a population or sample that has been exposed to a message at least once during a specific time period (usually four weeks). Note the verb *exposed* was used instead of *seen* or *heard*. That's important because an exposure is no guarantee that your message got through the consumer's defensive screen or past all the noise and clutter out there. Reach only means that the prospect was probably within range of the message. After you achieve reach, it's up to the quality of your creative effort to get your message seen or heard.

Two similar terms for reach are *cumulative audience* (cume) and *net unduplicated audience*. Here is the only difference: Reach is expressed as a *percentage* of the sample or population. Cumulative audience and net unduplicated audience are interchangeable and are expressed as *raw numbers* instead of percentages.

Example: Assume you make a spot TV buy in Las Vegas which has 105,000 TV households. The four-week reach for a media plan may be 85 percent meaning that an estimated 85 percent of the TV homes in Las Vegas were exposed at least once during the month. The cumulative audience (or net unduplicated audience) is 89,250 TV households (105,000 × .85).

Frequency is a constant companion to reach. It can be defined as the average number of times a prospect is exposed to your message over a four-week period. If we use the same example we used with reach, the frequency may be 5.5. Therefore, an estimated 85 percent of the Las Vegas TV households were exposed to our message an *average* of 5½ times over the four-week period.

Reach/frequency compromise

Reach and frequency are not unlike the cobra and mongoose. They aren't exactly out-and-out enemies, but they do battle each other since they are conversely related. As reach climbs higher every time a new prospect is exposed, frequency must fight again and again to keep up with all the new prospects. Achieving a very high frequency and high reach usually becomes outrageously expensive.

So, how do you settle the conflict? A media planner almost invariably ends up compromising because a budget is never fat enough to feed both reach and frequency to their limit.

Reach is usually emphasized for the introduction of new products. Although repetition speeds learning, the theory is that frequency should be traded for higher reach to get out the news to as many prospects as possible. Also, retail and wholesale distributors expect to see new products advertised. You have a better chance of exposing them with a reach goal of 80 or 90. Reach is also usually emphasized at the outset of a new campaign for most package-goods products. Again, the theory is that, if you are doing or saying something new, it's more important to have the whole target group hear the message two or three times rather than having only half the target hear it six times. It's simply a matter of sacrificing one for the other when the budget won't allow both.

Frequency goals are often given priority with products that are purchased frequently. Let's assume your product is Zest bar soap. Wouldn't it make sense to repeat a message frequently if a prospect buys soap every week or two and is constantly wooed to try your competitor's brand, Irish Spring? Or Dove? Or Dial? Competitive activity has a great bearing on your reach/frequency strategy. When Polaroid was the only instant camera on the market, there was no need to increase the frequency. However, once Kodak hit the market, priorities probably changed.

Ed Papazian offers some creative insight into the reach/frequency dilemma.[9]

Mediology

Structuring plans for maximum effect

A while ago we were reviewing one of our media plans with a client and everything was going well until we got to a key element in the positioning of his campaign: its reach and, as a necessary corollary, its average frequency levels.

In this case, with a predominantly TV plan, the anticipated four week reach was 70 percent while the average person in our prime prospect group would have an opportunity to see four messages over that period.

As it happened, this was approximately what we had been accustomed to attaining for a solid third-place brand (in a field of eight national entries). We had seen no reason to question or alter our media mix, nor, in fact, to analyze this aspect of the plan. But the client was studying the charts intensely and finally he asked us to justify that reach and frequency level.

In effect he was asking us how we had arrived at those particular ratios (70 percent and four). Why not 90 percent and three or 50 percent and six?, for example.

It sounds so simple, yet it was a pretty basic question and one that I fear is not being given very much attention in most media plans. Indeed, all too often, we ignore the *structure* of our schedules—the delicate, often very subtle nuances of reach and frequency overlays that vary so significantly, even if you're locked into a certain medium because everyone feels that's the only way to go.

In the case I'm describing, the resulting discussion lasted two hours and was continued at greater length some weeks later. And very honestly, we all learned a lot by going through some of the possibilities.

I'd like to share some of these deliberations with you, but first some of the basic facts about the situation.

Our brand, let's call it Brand A, had about 12 percent of the product class's business and accounted for just about that percent of its ad dollars, mostly in TV. Its competitors, Brands B and C, led with shares of 20 percent and 15 percent and commensurate spending levels. Lesser competitors split up the rest, again all mostly in TV. Over the past few years, Brand A had been gaining (up from 8 percent share) while C was down about two points, and now we were trying to build our momentum, introducing product line extensions and other improvements with a good deal of retail support.

Reflecting our recent sales increases, the budget for next year was up. This had really been what prompted the brand manager's question. Putting it differently, what he asked was this: With more dollars to spend shouldn't we be altering our thinking, trying for more reach, for example, or more frequency?

It still sounded pretty simple, but then we began to cut things apart, very finely, and discovered that there were some interesting distinctions we hadn't considered before.

For one thing, this was a package-goods product, and the average housewife replenished her stocks about every two weeks (using it on virtually a daily basis). What that meant was this: In an average week, nearly 50 percent of our prospects were making another purchasing decision and, in fact, on an average *weekday* almost 10 percent would actually buy either our brand or someone else's.

Looking at it somewhat differently, a typical housewife in the prime prospect group made approximately 26 shopping trips each year where our product class was involved, and there appeared to be some very significant differences between us and Brand C in user loyalties. While most of the products in this category were similar in repurchase rates, both we and Brand C seemed to be deficient in this respect. In fact, many more of our users (and theirs) appeared to be shopping around. For a lot of reasons that aren't relevant to this discussion, they were losing ground, *mainly to us.*

Despite all of the customary product class generalities, we were really positioned against Brand C, and boy were they vulnerable! In fact their users (who also averaged about 26 buying decisions per year) were defecting in small, but noticeable clusters—about half the time trying us and about half of that time sticking with us.

In this context the issue of reach and/or frequency became quite relevant. If we could align our weight so it pulsated against their relatively constant scheduling we might accomplish something—perhaps hypo the switching process, for example.

As we continued, it became readily apparent that generalized four-week compilations have less value than more specific comparisons of various alternatives, based more closely on the consumer's decision cycle.

What happened next is really a trade secret, so I won't divulge the procedures or techniques we utilized. But the net result was this: Without deviating from an ad TV strategy or resorting to excessive flighting, we were able to build a plan that packed in reach just before and on shopping days about 35-40 times a year with a minimal effort in between. And our reach during those short but vitally important intervals more than doubled Brand C's.

Another element was our copy approach. They ignored us in their commercials, talking mostly about themselves (mostly to themselves). Our messages were clearly directed against their users and pointed up our advantage, and by comparison, their product's weakness.

Reviewing all of these inputs, it made sense to structure a plan where small groups of Brand C users, including a growing ratio of apparently dissatisfied housewives, were exposed to our campaign just before what we assumed was another shopping trip. On those days we reached up to 25 percent of their users while (as near as we could reckon it) they reached only 10 percent of ours.

And we were hitting them harder in the copy, too.

A lot of other possibilities were evaluated including some far out ones that frankly put too many of our marbles in one basket and others that represented only minor deviations from the usual path. So we decided to try what, for want of a better description, I'll call the "pulsing" schedule.

And here's the rub. On a four-week basis, the new plot came out almost the same as the old, flat-out plan we had now discarded. Remember, we started with a 70 percent reach and a four average frequency. But now, we had a 75 percent reach and a 3.8 frequency, so by conventional yard stick we hadn't accomplished anything—or had we?

While I've used a TV-oriented package-goods illustration in this article, parallel investigations have been done in other media and, of course, with media mix. This is one of the reasons why we got into the reach and frequency business in the first place. The whole point was to use such data to structure plans, taking every opportunity to tailor our schedules so the prime target for our campaigns *was targeted* by the media we used *when we used them.*

To be sure, eventually we decide to go one way or the other based largely on subjective reasoning. But it's comforting to know how precisely we can define our alternatives, if we chose to.

That is the key to planning, or at least one of the keys.

A planner is supposed to weight and sift alternatives, to consider the impact of competitive activities, to seek out targets of opportunity—not operate in a vacuum. And his tools, reach and frequency included, are means to that

end, not the ends themselves. When four-week comparisons are more meaningful than daily or weekly or quarterly or annually, by all means use them. But only in a context where the numbers, whatever they are, have something to do with a problem or strategy.

When our client asked his simple question about reach and frequency, he asked one that most clients might ask. There are different ways to go—many of them.

But first, you have to define the situation, postulate the possibilities, and design your analytical systems to answer your questions. Instead, I fear, we have developed rigid formulas and computer data banks based on the average kind of questions and are gearing our plans to conform with the kinds of output they can generate. And that just doesn't make sense.

Just what are ratings and shares?

A common media tool is the use of ratings or rating points to express the size of the media audience in a shorthand form. Ratings are used primarily in radio and television and increasingly in outdoor. For example, in television, a rating point is computed by finding the percentage of TV households a station/program reaches compared to all TV households in the coverage area. One rating point is the equivalent of one percent of the total TV households reached. If there were 200,000 homes in a certain television market, one share point would be equal to 2,000 homes (200,000 homes × .01 = 2,000 homes). A station/program that achieves a 20 rating or has 20 rating points is being viewed by approximately 40,000 homes. Ratings for all stations/programs broadcast at any one time never reach a 100 rating simply because not every home in a coverage area has a television set on at any one given time. Usually, the maximum rating achieved by all stations/programs, even during prime time, is hardly ever over 65 to 75 rating points.

Share of audience is a totally different matter. Shares are based on a percentage calculation of all Homes Using Television (HUT) during a certain time period. The total HUT level is apportioned among the stations/programs in the coverage area based on viewership. For example, using the television market above consisting of 200,000 homes in the coverage area, assume that total HUT level for a certain time period is a 60 rating (or 60 percent of all potential homes have their sets tuned in during that particular time) or a total of 120,000 homes. Assume further that the breakdown of viewing is:

Station/program A	45,000 homes
Station/program B	36,000 homes
Station/program C	24,000 homes
Station/program D	15,000 homes
Total	120,000 homes

Based on a share-of-audience calculation, the following shares could be determined:

Station/program A	37.5 share
Station/program B	30 share
Station/program C	20 share
Station/program D	12.5 share
Total	100.0

As can be seen, it is possible but highly unlikely that one station/program could have 100 share of the total HUT audience.

The use of ratings and shares is an integral part of the Gross Rating Point system (GRP) which is used in determining and discussing media audiences. This subject is covered in more detail later in this chapter.

Continuity

Continuity can be defined as the degree of timing regularity in a media schedule. There are two extremes in the use of this tool. High continuity refers to a steady flow of advertising pressure throughout the campaign period. That's ideal. The opposite is low continuity, which means intermittent advertising pressure that creates a media schedule with blank holes (called a hiatus) in it. Neither strategy is right or wrong. In fact, most media planners end up compromising somewhere in between the two. Exhibit 8-9 illustrates these two strategies. The product is a ready-to-eat breakfast cereal with consumption 50 percent higher in the summer months.

As illustrated in the exhibit, plan A has a steady pressure of advertising throughout most of the year. Even though extra pressure is exerted in the summer months, advertising is fairly continuous throughout

the campaign period. Although plan B's over-all continuity is lower, it could be said to have strong continuity July through August.

Flighting

In Exhibit 8-9, plan B best illustrates this concept. There are two separate 13-week flights of spot TV—February through April, then June through August. Note there are five separate magazine flights in plan A. Flighting does not necessarily destroy continuity; it simply reduces the *degree* of continuity. Media planners strive for as much continuity as possible. Indeed, that is the very stuff a campaign is made of—its whole impact is greater than that of any single part.

How much continuity?

As much as you can afford. In most cases, budget is the limiting factor that forces a planner to stretch his or her dollars with flighting. For some products, a hiatus of three months is desirable. Ski equipment makers are probably unhurt by a three-month hiatus in the summer. However, most soft drink makers would keep advertising pressure up year round if they felt they could afford it, even though the warm months account for well over half of their sales. Most compromise with continuity and end up flighting in colder months to save up precious dollars for the summer.

The old retailer's saw still holds true for most national campaigns, "shoot when the ducks are flying." The theory is that unseasonal advertising pressure cannot easily change the consumer's shopping and buying habits. Double the current ad budget for Coke in January and you'll probably waste your money; advertising is simply not that powerful.

Exhibit 8-9. High-level plan A—$6 million (high continuity).

Medium	J	F	M	A	M	J	J	A	S	O	N	D
Net TV					XXXX	XXXX	XXXXX					
Spot TV	XXXXX	XXXX	XXXX	XXXXX	XXXX	XXXX	XXXXX	XXXX	XXXX	XXXXX	XXXX	
Weekly Magazines	XXXXX		XXXX		XXXX	XXXX	XXXXX		XXXX		XXXX	
Newspapers					XXXX	XXXX	XXXXX					

Low-level plan B—$3 million (low continuity).

Medium	J	F	M	A	M	J	J	A	S	O	N	D
Net TV												
Spot TV		XXXX	XXXX	XXXXX		XXXX	XXXXX	XXXX				
Weekly Magazines		X X	X X	X	X		XXXX	XXXXX	XXXX			
Newspapers						XXXX	XXXXX	XXXX				

Exhibit 8-10. April 1979–March 1980 flow chart, in gross rating points (o = 25 GRPs; ● = 40 GRPs; ■ = 100 GRPs).

	1979																																								1980												
	April					May				June				July					Aug.				Sept.					Oct.				Nov.				Dec.					Jan.				Feb.				March			
	1	8	15	22	29	6	13	20	27	3	10	17	24	1	8	15	22	29	5	12	19	26	2	9	16	23	30	7	14	21	28	4	11	18	25	2	9	16	23	30	6	13	20	27	3	10	17	24	4	11	18	25

Rows (symbols as positioned in the chart):

- **Network television (national):** three "o" marks (stacked) under each of May 20, May 27, June 3, June 10; three "o" marks (stacked) under Dec. 2 and Dec. 16.
- **Spot television (10 key markets):** "o" marks under May 20, May 27, June 10, June 24, July 8, July 22, Aug. 5, Aug. 19; "o" under Dec. 2 and Dec. 16.
- **Spot radio (10 key markets):** "●" over "■" under May 20, May 27, June 10, June 24, July 8, July 22, Aug. 5, Aug. 19; under Dec. 2 and Dec. 16.
- **Outdoor (10 key markets):** clusters of "●●" over "■■■" over "■■■" (stacked) under June, July, Aug., and Dec. periods.

| Total GRPs | 480 | | 1,260 | | 1,110 | | 1,110 | | | | 1,260 | |

Gross rating points

GRPs are a simple and very essential tool for your media planning bag. Sissors and Petray define the term:

> A measure of the total gross weight delivered by a TV or radio program or a spot schedule. *It is the sum of the ratings for the individual spots or programs.* One rating point means an audience of 1 percent of the coverage base. Hence, 150 GRPs means 1.5 messages per average home.

The media planner uses the term as a rough general description of his or her plan's weight or intensity. Exhibit 8-10 shows the hypothetical annual GRP levels for a major soft drink campaign.

How to calculate GRPs

GRPs are calculated by simply adding together all the ratings accumulated in your broadcast buy. GRPs are often expressed as a *weekly* total. (Monthly GRPs are also used. Always label your time period when using this tool.) Assume you are buying one 30-second commercial on each of the following TV shows in the third week of September.

Net TV schedule:	Average Rating*
ABC Monday Night Football	25
CBS Wednesday Movie	28
NBC Friday Movie	27
NBC Sunday, Wonderful World of Disney	25
	105 weekly GRPs

*Ratings are fictitious

Another way to calculate GRPs is to multiply your four-week reach by the frequency. R × F = monthly GRPs.

How many GRPs is enough?

No professional media planner would risk a pat answer to this question. The best guide is to look at your reach figure. There is a good rule of thumb on reach: try to avoid a four-week reach lower than 50 percent. A reach of 60 to 70 percent is considered more respectable. Anything higher than a reach of 70 is great if your budget will allow it and if you can live with the drop in frequency. Obviously, the higher the reach and frequency, the higher your GRP level. (R × F = GRP) As a rule of thumb, 25 weekly GRPs (100 per month) is considered low for a national campaign; 300 weekly GRPs (1,200 per month) is considered very strong. In making spot TV market buys, large expensive metropolitan areas such as Los Angeles make it extremely tough to build up high GRP levels when each rating point can cost over $300 for a prime-time 30-second announcement. For a show with a 25 rating, that's $7,500 for one shot in Los Angeles ($300 × 25 = $7,500).[10]

How many WGRPs can day network deliver?

Professional planners wanted to narrow the margin for error with the media numbers. Thus, teen GRPs, kid GRPs and women GRPs were invented. It's just a more accurate way to report the audience for a broad-

Exhibit 8-11. Weekly women rating points.

	Quarter			
	June	Sept.	Dec.	March
WGRPs day, network	35	35	35	35
WGRPs late, network	14	14	25	25
WGRPs spot TV	54	54	65	65
Total	103	103	125	125

Source: N. W. Ayer Media Facts, 1977-78.

cast program. Here's an excellent example from an Ogilvy and Mather media plan for a package goods product purchased by women 35 + , living in "A" counties with $15M + household income (see Exhibit 8-11). In Exhibit 8-11, notice how much higher the WGRPs (Women Gross Rating Points) are in the day network category opposed to the late network time. To calculate the WGRPs for this buy, the planner simply added up the Nielsen or Arbitron ratings for *women only* in each TV daypart considered for purchase. Then he compared all of the dayparts based on how many women each could deliver. If he reported total GRPs (men and women together) for late network, it would be inflated because of the *men* in the audience. Not a clear, honest picture for the client.

Combining media numbers with GRPs: TV, radio and outdoor can be added together

Note total GRP numbers at the bottom of Exhibit 8-10. It is common practice for media planners to add together all of their multimedia GRPs, radio + TV + outdoor, and so forth. Although it may be a boxcar figure, it does serve to compare how many gross impressions plan A will deliver over plan B. Or, how many gross impressions the new plan delivers as compared with last year's plan.

London Crumpets
(Actual product category and name withheld)
Fiscal Year 1980 Media Plan
Product description: A small, bite-size adult cookie that is used for snacks, after lunch or dinner, or anytime with coffee or tea. Retail price is 99¢ for a 12-ounce bag. London Crumpets has been on the market for six years and has shown consistent brand share growth in its category up until the past two fiscal years. The following plan was designed to halt the erosion of London's share points and revive its former posture in the marketplace.

Media Plan, Fiscal Year 1980
Executive Summary
Task
Maintain the current strength of the London franchise.

Media objectives/strategy

This discussion assumes that you have clearly defined and weighted your target prospects and that the geographic markets have been weighted or ranked. As your management team meets to discuss media objectives, you should have a clear picture of:

1. Product/brand
2. Primary and/or secondary target consumer
3. Consumers' shopping habits
4. Consumers' media habits
5. Major competitors
6. Competitive media strategy
7. Geographic priorities (distribution)
8. The creative objective (major problem)
9. Advertising objectives
10. Marketing objectives
11. Merchandising/promotion objectives

Setting media objectives/strategy without this information will be futile. So use the above checklist before proceding.

How to state media objectives/strategies

Media objectives/strategies must have meat and substance, yet the language should be lean. Above all, media objectives/strategies should state measurable goals within specific time frames whenever possible. When you are referring to brand shares, reach, or frequency, specific numbers (goals) should be clearly spelled out. This way it can be measured. In the interest of describing how to write media objectives/strategies, the following Ogilvy & Mather national media plan (developed for a client) will demonstrate how the professionals do it.

Available funds

Total advertising budget	$4,100.0M
Less production	350.0
Total media	$3,750.0
Less star talent fee (spokesman)	30.0
Working media budget	$3,720.0M

Media plan
A. Objectives
  1. Direct advertising toward current users.
  2. Increase current share from 12.0 to 13.0 during FY 1980.
  3. Encourage ongoing usage of the Brand.

B. Strategy
  1. Direct impressions toward all women proportionate to their London volume contribution with emphasis on the primary targets: women

35 + , living in $15M + households in "A" counties.

2. Allocate media dollars according to current London sales volume while maintaining competitive levels in high-volume cookie market areas.

3. Achieve at least a 75 reach with an average frequency of five among total women in key areas. Concomitantly, a reach of 50 will be sought among women exposed at least three times within any given four weeks of advertising.

4. Distribute advertising pressure according to quarterly volume contribution.

5. Maintain flexibility.

6. Provide continuous support within the quarterly investment allocation once the reach/frequency goals are met.

7. Employ media vehicles compatible with the copy requirements and over-all Brand's image.

C. Plan

	Dollars	Percent
Day network TV	$1,026.1	27.6
Late network TV	1,048.6	28.2
Fringe spot TV	1,645.3	44.2
Total	$3,720.0	100.0

D Delivery

1. Demographics—Slightly underdelivers upper-income category as a result of concentrating on television.
Geographics—Overspends spot TV markets by 11 percent to maintain competitive posture in key franchise areas.

2. National effort—Network television represents 56 percent of total media budget.

3. Reach/frequency—Delivery achieves goal in key markets.

4. Allocation requirements—Generally follows the quarterly sales volume.

E. Task accomplishment

1. The plan accomplishes the task of providing support to maintain current franchise of the Brand.

2. Minor deviations from demographic and geographic targets result from optimizing total plan delivery.

London Crumpets
Marketing and Copy Background

Overview

During FY 1978 London had a year of severe business decline.

Brand performance has shown loss of FY 1976 momentum and is now characterized by share erosion, volume misses, and weakened distribution.

Objective

Stabilize the franchise in key marketing areas.
National share and volume objectives:
Share: 13.5
Volume: 2,805,000 cases

Strategy

• Allocate marketing funds according to the Brand's consumption.
• Continue to place heavy emphasis on promotion, especially consumer.
• Implement a program of case rates designed to put London back in the feature cycle among major retailers.

London Crumpets
Long-term Copy Strategy

Objective:	• Best-quality cookie available for adults
Prime prospects:	• Upscale
	• College educated
	• Urban
	• Younger orientation
	• Higher self-image
	• Convenience oriented
	• Above-average living standard
	• Contemporary/active/involved
Competitive stance:	• Primary: Higher priced, non-chocolate cookies
	• Secondary: Other snack bits; crackers, etc.
Key benefit:	• Light, yet tastes rich; made with creamery butter. Can be served at parties or used any time as a snack.
Support:	• Imported from England
	• Product endorsements by celebrity spokesman
	• Product/process improvements
Tone and manner:	• Honest, straightforward
	• Lightly humorous
	• Human/sensory

London Crumpets
Media Objective/Rationale
Fiscal Year 1980

Direct advertising toward current users with the secondary objective of stimulating trial by non-users.

The goal is to maintain current share and gradually gain new share points.

Fiscal Year 1980 is expected to be a year of intense competitive pressure when cookies will dominate features and consumer promotion activity.

If advertising pressure is focused on current London users, some volume increase can be expected from heavier usage. Also, target demographics for users encompasses a large segment of non-users who are ideal prospects for increasing trial usage.

London Crumpets
Media Strategy and Rationale
Fiscal Year 1980

1. Prospect definition

   Direct impressions toward all women proportionate to their London volume contribution, with emphasis on the primary London targets.

   Women with the following characteristics:
   - Age 35 +
   - In $15M + households
   - Living in "A" counties

   See following demographic details.

2. Media allocation

   Allocate media dollars in accordance with the current London sales volume of each market.

   The media budgets of the individual markets will be prorated to the estimated volume contribution of each area.

   However, in the interest of strengthening the London franchise in key markets, and also recognizing

London Crumpets
Media Plan
Fiscal Year 1980
Demographic Targets

	Percent U.S. Women	Percent London Volume	Index
Total Women	100.0	100.0	100
Age			
Total			
18-24	18.0	13.9	77
25-34	20.4	17.9	88
35-49	23.0	21.3	93
50 +	38.6	46.9	122
Nonworking	56.6	60.4	107
18-24	8.4	6.0	71
25-34	10.4	9.7	93
35-49	11.1	11.0	99
50 +	26.7	33.7	126
Working	43.4	39.6	91
18-24	9.6	7.9	82
25-34	10.0	8.2	82
35-49	11.9	10.3	87
50 +	11.9	13.2	111
Household Income			
Under $8,000	38.1	28.6	75
$8–14,999	34.5	33.0	96
$15,000 +	27.4	38.4	140
Household Size			
1-2	39.9	38.0	95
3-4	35.8	37.7	105
5 +	24.3	24.3	100
County Size			
A	40.9	51.0	125
B	26.2	24.1	92
C	19.4	17.3	89
D	13.5	7.6	56

Source: MRCA Demographic Analysis.

the competitive spending environment, additional weights will be placed on the following areas.

	% Increase*	Index
Eastern Region	+ 85%	185
Detroit District	+ 85%	185
Chicago District	+ 65%	165
Los Angeles District	+ 65%	165

The chart below shows in detail the geographic targets based on London volume.

*Formula: Budget increase is estimated by multiplying the sales volume (percent) contributed by each region or district by the modification weights. Budget is then adjusted accordingly.

3. Communication goals
   A. Total reach/average frequency
      Provide at least a 75 reach with an average frequency of five among total women in the key areas.
   B. Effective reach
      Concomitantly, a four-week reach goal of 50 will be sought among women who have been exposed at least three times.

	Four-Week Reach/frequency Goals
Total reach/average frequency	75/5.0
Effective reach	50/3 +

London Crumpets
Fiscal Year 1980
Geographic Targets

	Percent Total U.S. Women	Percent Total London Volume	Brand Development Index (BDI)
Eastern Region			
Boston	5.28	6.60	125
New York	9.42	13.04	138
Philadelphia	7.75	13.34	172
Syracuse	3.38	5.91	175
Youngstown	4.78	6.55	137
Total Eastern	30.61	45.44	148
Southern Region			
Charlotte	5.55	3.83	69
Atlanta..............	4.03	3.24	80
Jacksonville	3.89	3.08	79
Detroit	4.76	8.52	179
Cincinnati	5.44	4.42	81
Total Southern	23.67	23.09	98
Central Region			
Chicago	6.44	5.35	83
St. Louis.............	3.57	2.91	82
Memphis	4.65	2.89	62
Kansas City	3.92	2.46	63
Dallas...............	6.46	3.60	56
Total Central	25.04	17.21	69
Western Region			
Minneapolis	4.15	2.01	48
Denver	2.40	1.30	54
Portland.............	2.77	1.80	65
San Francisco........	4.01	2.67	67
Los Angeles	7.35	6.48	88
Total Western	20.68	14.26	69
Total U.S.	100.00	100.00	100

Source: Nielsen

4. Distribute advertising pressure according to quarterly volume contribution.

Quarter	Percent Volume
June	24
September	23
December	26
March	27

5. Maintain flexibility.

It is recommended that all media activity be scheduled to run at the same time and that a substantial portion of the budget be placed in flexible media so the Brand can quickly react to:

a. Competitive activity, and

b. Key promotional events

6. Continuous support within the quarterly investment allocation will be sought once the reach/frequency goals are achieved.

Continuous advertising is desirable for the following reasons:

(a) There is sufficient evidence of advertising recall erosion among consumers during non-advertising periods.

(b) London Crumpets are bought on impulse (60 percent of all purchases). The daily traffic in stores includes many such purchases.

(c) Pressure against competition should be maintained.

Therefore, as soon as reach/frequency goals are achieved, advertising periods will be extended within the boundaries of the quarterly investment allocation. A total of 36 weeks of advertising has been set on judgment as minimum.

7. Employ media vehicles compatible with the copy requirements and over-all Brand's image.

A balance of highly efficient and effective media will be sought to ensure the most desirable combination of copy and media.

Fiscal Year 1980
Description of Media Plan

The Fiscal Year 1980 London media plan will use television as the sole medium for the following reasons:

1. The intrusive nature of the medium makes it the most effective vehicle for communicating the London message.

Fiscal Year 1980
Recommended Plan

Date: 12 February 1979

	June Quarter			September Quarter			December Quarter			March Quarter		
	April	May	June	July	August	Sept.	Oct.	Nov.	Dec.	Jan.	Feb.	March
		9		1	4	4	5	4		5		4
Day Net :30		35WGRP/Wk.			35W		35WGRP/Wk.	35W		35W		35W
Late Net :30		14WGRP/Wk.			14W	14W	25W	25W		25W		25W
Comb. Fr. :30		54WGRP/Wk.			54W	54W	65W	65W		65W		65W
Reach/frequency Spot area												
Total women		81/5.1			81/5.1			84/5.9			85/5.8	
Effective reach 3 + ...		53			53			59			60	
$15M Target women		77/4.5			75/4.3			80/5.3			80/5.2	
Effective reach 3 + ...		47			44			53			52	
Remainder U.S.												
Total women		57/3.4			57/3.5			61/3.8			63/3.7	
Effective reach 3 + ...		27			27			32			33	
$15M + Target women		51/2.9			51/2.8			56/3.5			56/3.4	
Effective reach 3 + ...		21			21			27			27	
Day network		$257.2			$231.1			$ 284.9			$252.9	
Late network		191.6			176.4			392.2			288.4	
Combination fringe		373.3			373.3			449.3			449.4	
Total		$822.1			$780.8			$1,126.4			$990.7	
Percent		22.1%			21.0%			30.3%			26.6%	

Day network	$1,026.1
Late network	1,048.6
Combination fringe	1,645.3
Total	$3,720.0
Percent	100.0%

2. It is highly efficient in reaching the target audience.
3. Judgmentally, at the current budget level, concentrating efforts on the primary medium should maximize the effectiveness of communication.

Daytime network television will provide the base upon which other national and local media efforts will be structured. This medium is the most efficient vehicle for reaching a broad national base of adult women.

Late-night network television will be used to extend reach nationally and increase the delivery of women in the higher income category ($15M +).

Fringe spot television will be implemented to align media delivery to targets, and tactically, to furnish additional support in London's key markets against competitive pressures.

Both network and spot television will be scheduled to run at the same time to maximize advertising pressure.

London Crumpets
Gross Impression Analysis
Fiscal Year 1980
(000)

	Day Network	Late Network	Fringe Spot	Plan Total	Percent Plan	Percent Target	Index
Total women	929,464	531,122	722,917	2,183,503	100.0	100.0	—
Age							
18–24	156,150	86,573	108,438	351,161	16.0	13.9	115
25–34	177,528	104,631	137,354	419,513	19.2	17.9	107
35–49	198,905	142,872	170,608	512,385	23.5	21.3	110
50 +	396,881	197,046	306,517	900,444	41.3	46.9	88
Household income							
Under $8,000	448,002	195,984	261,696	905,682	41.5	28.6	145
$8–14,999	310,441	198,108	234,225	742,774	34.0	33.0	103
$15,000 +	171,021	137,029	226,996	535,046	24.5	38.4	64
Household size							
1–2	370,856	215,104	329,650	915,610	41.9	38.0	110
3–4	340,184	182,175	166,271	688,630	31.5	37.7	84
5 +	218,424	133,843	226,996	579,263	26.6	24.3	109
County size							
A	308,582	246,972	471,342	1,026,896	47.0	51.0	92
B	276,980	151,370	153,981	582,331	26.7	24.1	111
C	187,752	72,764	78,798	339,314	15.5	17.3	90
D	156,150	60,016	18,796	234,962	10.8	7.6	142

London Crumpets
Fiscal Year 1980
Spot TV Market List

District/DMA	Percent Pop.	Percent Tgt.	BDI	36 Wk. Avg. WGRP/Week			
				Day Net	Late Net	Spot TV	Total
Boston							
Total Markets	5.10	6.34	124	33	12	39	84
Total District	5.28	6.60	125				
New York	9.42	13.04	138	32	20	69	121
Syracuse							
Total Markets	2.78	4.92	177	35	15	63	113
Total District	3.38	5.91	175				
Philadelphia							
Total Markets	7.67	13.16	172	35	14	73	122
Total District	7.75	13.34	172				
Youngstown							
Total Markets	4.53	5.99	132	39	18	52	109
Total District	4.78	6.55	137				
Detroit							
Total Markets	4.56	8.18	179	38	15	73	126
Total District	4.76	8.52	179				
Chicago							
Total Markets	5.34	4.60	86	32	30	51	113
Total District	6.44	5.35	83				
Los Angeles							
Total Markets	6.36	5.93	93	25	16	42	83
Total District	7.35	6.48	88				
Total Key Markets	45.76	62.16	136	33	18	59	110
Total Key Districts	49.16	65.79	134				
Rem. U.S. Key Markets	54.24	37.84	70	37	22	—	59
Rem. U.S. Key Districts	50.84	34.21	61				
Balance U.S.	100.0	100.0	100	35	20	—	—

London Crumpets
Fiscal Year 1980
Spot TV Market List

District/DMA	Budget				Percent Dollars	Index Target = 100
	Day Network	Late Network	Spot TV	Total		
Boston						
Total Markets	$ 48,535	$ 39,471	$ 162,400	$ 250,406	6.76	107
Total District	50,996	40,234	162,400	253,630	6.82	103
New York	84,335	116,744	307,748	508,557	13.69	105
Syracuse						
Total Markets	27,705	24,644	138,921	191,920	5.17	105
Total District	35,185	31,269	138,921	205,375	5.55	94
Philadelphia						
Total Markets	76,669	66,281	368,390	511,340	13.82	105
Total District	77,173	66,837	368,390	512,400	13.85	104
Youngstown						
Total Markets	48,011	44,872	140,700	233,583	6.31	105
Total District	51,243	48,917	140,700	240,860	6.47	99
Detroit						
Total Markets	48,515	40,833	228,482	317,830	8.59	105
Total District	51,490	42,442	228,482	322,414	8.71	102
Chicago						
Total Markets	47,991	91,635	137,462	277,088	7.49	163
Total District	60,376	106,862	137,462	304,700	8.24	154
Los Angeles						
Total Markets	46,010	61,502	161,467	268,979	7.23	122
Total District	53,983	67,216	161,467	282,666	7.60	117
Total Key Markets	427,771	486,002	1,645,300	2,559,073	69.06	111
Total Key Districts	464,781	520,521	1,645,300	2,630,602	70.93	108
Rem. U.S. Key Markets	598,329	562,598	—	1,160,927	30.04	82
Rem. U.S. Key Districts	561,319	528,079	—	1,089,398	29.07	85
Balance U.S.	$1,026,100	$1,048,600	$1,645,300	$3,720,000	100.00	100

London Crumpets
Total Women Frequency Distribution Analysis
Fiscal Year 1980
Spot Area

	June Quarter May	September Quarter September	December Quarter October	March Quarter January
Reach/Frequency	81.1/5.1	81.0/ 5.1	84.3/5.9	84.7/5.8
Number of exposures				
1+	81.1	81.0	84.3	84.7
2+	65.8	65.7	70.8	71.1
3+	53.2	53.2	59.2	59.5
4+	43.0	42.9	49.5	49.5
5+	34.6	34.6	41.2	41.1
6+	27.8	27.8	34.2	34.0
7+	22.3	22.3	28.4	28.0
8+	17.8	17.8	23.5	23.0
9+	14.1	14.2	18.8	18.0
10+	11.2	11.2	15.9	15.4
11+	8.9	8.9	13.1	12.6
12+	7.0	7.0	10.7	10.2
Weekly women Rating points				
Day network	35	35	35	35
Late network	14	14	25	25
Spot TV	54	54	65	65
Total	103	103	125	125

London Crumpets
Total Women Frequency Distribution Analysis
Fiscal Year 1980
Remainder U.S.

	June Quarter May	September Quarter September	December Quarter October	March Quarter January
Reach/Frequency	56.8/3.4	56.5/3.5	61.4/3.8	62.6/3.7
Number of exposures				
1+	56.8	56.5	61.4	62.6
2+	38.5	38.5	43.5	44.4
3+	27.3	27.4	32.0	32.5
4+	19.7	19.8	23.9	24.2
5+	14.3	14.5	18.0	18.1
6+	11.5	10.7	13.6	13.5
7+	7.6	7.8	10.3	10.2
8+	5.5	5.7	7.8	7.6
9+	4.0	4.2	5.9	5.7
10+	2.9	3.1	4.4	4.2
11+	2.1	2.2	3.3	3.1
12+	1.5	1.6	2.5	2.3
Weekly women Rating points				
Day network	35	35	35	35
Late network	14	14	25	25
Total	49	49	60	60

112

London
Media Rationale
Fiscal Year 1980

A. Daytime network television :30s
Daytime network television at a level of 35 WGRPs per week will be scheduled for 36 weeks beginning

28 April 1980.

1. Daytime television delivers the target audience more efficiently than other television dayparts.

Television Efficiency Comparison (:30)

	Daytime Network	Prime Network	Late-Night Network	Combined Fringe
Total women	$1.20	$ 2.71	$2.26	$2.32
Women 35 +	1.87	4.18	6.19	3.99
Women $15M +	6.56	10.44	8.50	7.63

2. Daytime television furnishes efficient national coverage while supporting the London high development areas. At comparable rating levels, the cost of daytime network is one percent less than day spot and delivers 34 percent more audience than the top 60 U.S. markets.

	:30 Cost	Percent U.S. Women
Day spot		
10 WGRPs top 60 markets	$8,592 (100)	73 (100)
Daytime network		
10 WGRPs	8,501 (99)	98 (134)

3. Daytime television offers a greater concentration of women viewers than the other television dayparts. In addition, on an equal dollar basis, daytime television furnishes the greatest absolute number of the London target audience.

Women Audience Composition

	Percent U.S. Adults	Daytime		Prime Time		Late Night	
		Percent	Index	Percent	Index	Percent	Index
Total women	52	81	(156)	57	(110)	56	(108)

Women Delivery (Equal Dollars)

	Daytime		Prime Time		Late Night	
	(MM)	Index	(MM)	Index	(MM)	Index
Total women	43.4	100	18.6	43	24.9	57
Women 35 +	27.8	100	12.1	44	9.1	33
Women $15M +	8.0	100	4.8	60	6.6	83
Women, "A" Counties	14.4	100	7.1	49	11.7	81

4. Thirty-five women rating points weekly are judged to be a desirable level of daytime network for London. This level provides adequate women delivery nationally and also serves as a strong base upon which to build other national and local advertising efforts.

	Total Women
Reach	42
Average frequency	3.2

5. Daytime television offers optimum Brand effectiveness as expressed by the media planning system.

Effectiveness Rating Delivery Index*	
Daytime	1.483
Prime time	2.163
Late night	1.902
Selected magazines	2.191

*Effectiveness Rating Delivery Index. This table indexes the delivery value of the four vehicles under consideration. It is the media delivery adjusted by the subjective weight (value) of the effectiveness of that particular medium.

B. Late-night network :30s

Late-night network television will be implemented for 36 weeks at a level of 14 WGRPs per week for the first two quarters of the fiscal year. This will provide one (1) announcement a week in each of the three (3) networks. For the balance of the year, 25 women GRPs weekly will be used in recognition of the Brand's quarterly volume contribution.

1. Late-night network extends the reach nationally among the $15M + household income group.
2. Late-night television usage is not as affected by seasonal variations as other dayparts. This gives the daypart excellent reach opportunities even during the summer months.

	Spring	Summer	Fall	Winter
Daytime	96	96	100	107
Prime time	95	89	107	111
Early evening	92	85	110	113
Late evening	100	100	96	104

C. Combined fringe spot television :30s

A combination of one-third early and two-thirds late fringe will be implemented at varying levels for 36 weeks in 32 London high-development markets.

1. This permits the opportunity to align the allocation of expenditures in accordance with the anticipated business opportunities in these markets.
2. The use of this medium further increases advertising pressure in key markets.
3. The flexibility of spot television allows quick reaction to competitive activity.
4. Spot television improves the delivery of the London target audience in "A" counties.

	Percent Total Audience Delivery			
	Day Net	Prime Net	Late Net	Spot TV
"A" counties	33.2	38.1	47.0	65.3
(Index)	(100)	(115)	(142)	(197)

London Crumpets
Alternative Media Plan, Fiscal Year 1980

This alternative plan was developed to determine the best media combination for satisfying the objectives of the Brand.

The alternative plan was selected and processed through the computer program for evaluating and estimating media (TEEM).

Media	Recommended Alternative	I	II	III
Daytime network	$1,026.1	$1,222.2	$1,362.7	$1,026.1
Late-night network	749.1	—	657.7	—
Prime-time network	—	—	1,699.6	1,048.6
Combined fringe................	1,579.7	2,010.6	—	1,645.3
Magazines.....................	365.1	487.2	—	—
Total	$3,720.0	$3,720.0	$3,720.0	$3,720.0

London Crumpets
Alternative Media Plans, Fiscal Year 1980
Summary of Findings

Alternative plans media mix	Remarks
Recommended alternative—Daytime network, late network, combined fringe, magazines	Provides special effort towards key target groups. Recommended plan contingent upon creative development of a magazine campaign.
Alternate I—Daytime network, combined fringe, magazines	Furnishes heavy-up in key markets. Rejected because of insufficient out-area support.
Alternate II—Daytime network, late network, prime network	Plan achieves reach, frequency, and effective reach goals nationally and in key markets. Rejected because of non-alignment of spending to geographic target. Also, duration of advertising activity is less than other plans examined.
Alternate III—Daytime network, prime network, combined fringe	Substitutes prime network for the recommended plan's late-night effort. Rejected due to loss in absolute number of gross impressions.

The following shows in detail the comparative delivery of the alternative plans.

London Crumpets
Alternative media plans, fiscal year 1980
Delivery Analysis
Gross Impressions (MM)

	Recommended Plan	Recommended Alternative	Alternative I	Alternative II	Alternative III
Total women	$2,183.5 (100)	$2,165.7 (99)	$2,208.2 (108)	$2,004.6 (92)	$2,032.6 (93)
W $15M + ...	535.0 (100)	544.2 (102)	557.6 (104)	405.8 (76)	481.3 (90)
W 35 + ...	1,412.8 (100)	1,397.3 (99)	1,427.2 (101)	1,286.7 (91)	1,318.9 (93)
W "A" County	1,026.9 (100)	1,006.5 (98)	1,035.3 (101)	733.9 (71)	932.4 (91)
Effectiveness Rating Delivery (000)	2,102.8* (100)	2,069.1* (98)	2,022.5 (96)	2,232.2 (106)	2,038.8 (97)
Effectiveness Rating Delivery Index	1.765* (100)	1.757* (100)	1.730 (98)	1.666 (94)	1.820 (103)

*Excludes *Woman's Day* "A" County edition.

Recommended Alternative Plan

The recommended alternative plan consists of a media mix incorporating daytime network, late-night network, combined fringe, and magazines.

This plan is contingent on the development of a magazine advertisement. Should an effective print campaign be developed during FY 1979, it is urged that the recommended alternative be implemented.

Magazines are funded by decreasing the amount of the recommended plan's weight in late night and, to a lesser extent, in combined fringe.

The incorporation of magazines is recommended for the following reasons:

1. It provides an opportunity to heavy-up among the London key demographic target: women in $15M + households.
2. Magazines are divided into two separate but coordinated efforts—national as well as demograph-

ic/geographic. This mix of magazines will concentrate print exposure in "A" counties where London sales potential is greatest as well as furnish national support for the Brand.

3. The use of magazines takes recognition of successful corporate and agency dual-media effectiveness testing.
4. There is no significant difference in effectiveness between the recommended plan and the recommended alternative:

	Recommended Plan	Recommended Alternative*
Effectiveness Rating Delivery	2,102,814	2,063,736
Effectiveness Rating Delivery Index	1.765	1.757

*Excludes *Woman's Day* "A" county

Fiscal Year 1980
Recommended Alternative Plan

Date: 5 March 1979

	June Quarter			September Quarter			December Quarter			March Quarter		
	April	May	June	July	August	Sept.	Oct.	Nov.	Dec.	Jan.	Feb.	March
		9		1	4	4	5		4	5		4
Day Net :30		35WGRP/Wk.			35W		35WGRP/Wk.		35W	35W		35W
Late Net :30		14WGRP/Wk.			14W		14WGRP/Wk.		14W	14W		14W
Comb. Fr. :30		54WGRP/Wk.			54W	54W	60W		60W	60W		60W
Magazines P/4C												
National												
Better Homes & Gardens .				BHG			BHG			BHG		
Good Housekeeping				GH			GH			GH		
American Home				AH			AH			AH		
Demo/Geographic												
LHJ Prime Showcase					LHJ	LHJ		LHJ	LHJ		LHJ	LHJ
McCall's Vip Zip					MC	MC		MC	MC		MC	MC
Woman's Day A. C.					WD	WD		WD	WD	WD	WD	
Reach/Frequency												
Spot Area												
Total Women		81/5.1			88/5.2	81/5.1	90/5.4		83/5.2	90/5.3		84/5.1
3 + ...		53			60	53	63		56	63		56
$15M + ...		77/4.5			87/4.4	75/4.3	89/4.8		79/4.6	89/4.7		79/4.4
3 + ...		47			54	44	58		49	58		48
Remainder U.S.												
Total Women		57/3.4			73/3.4	57/3.5	74/3.3		58/3.3	75/3.2		59/3.2
3 + ...		27			34	27	35		27	35		28
$15M + ...		51/2.9			71/2.6	51/2.8	76/2.9		53/2.9	76/2.9		53/2.8
3 + ...		21			25	21	32		22	32		22

	June Quarter	September Quarter	December Quarter	March Quarter
Day Network	$257.2	$231.1	$ 284.9	$252.9
Late Network	191.6	176.4	219.6	161.5
Combination Fringe.......	373.3	373.3	416.6	416.5
Magazines	— —	121.7	121.7	121.7
Total	$822.1	$902.5	$1,042.8	$952.6
Percent	22.1%	24.3%	28.0%	25.6%

Day Network	$1,026.1
Late Network	749.1
Combination Fringe.......	1,579.7
Magazines	365.1
Total	$3,720.0
Percent	100%

London Crumpets
Recommended Alternative Plan
Total Women Frequency Distribution Analysis
Spot Area

	June Quarter May	September Quarter September	December Quarter October	December	March Quarter January	March
Reach/frequency	81.1/5.1	81.0/5.1	89.5/5.4	83.2/5.2	89.8/5.3	83.7/5.1
Number of Exposures						
1+	81.1	81.0	89.5	83.2	89.8	83.7
2+	65.8	65.7	75.8	68.5	76.1	68.8
3+	53.2	53.2	62.5	55.9	62.7	56.0
4+	43.0	42.9	51.0	45.4	50.9	45.3
5+	34.6	34.6	41.3	36.7	41.1	36.3
6+	27.8	27.8	33.4	29.6	32.9	29.0
7+	22.3	22.3	26.8	23.7	26.2	23.1
8+	17.8	17.8	21.5	18.9	20.8	18.2
9+	14.1	14.2	17.1	15.1	16.4	14.3
10+	11.2	11.2	13.6	11.9	12.9	11.2
11+	8.9	8.9	10.8	9.4	10.1	8.7
12+	7.0	7.0	8.5	7.4	7.8	6.8
Schedule						
Day net. GRP/Wk.	35	35	35	35	35	35
Night net. GRP/Wk.	14	14	14	14	14	14
Spot TV GRP/Wk.......	54	54	60	60	60	60
Better Homes & Gardens	—	—	X	—	X	—
Good Housekeeping ...	—	—	X	—	X	—
American Home	—	—	X	—	X	—

118

London Crumpets
Recommended Alternative Plan
Total Women Frequency Distribution Analysis
Remainder U.S.

	June Quarter May	September Quarter September	December Quarter		March Quarter	
			October	December	January	March
Reach/frequency	56.8/3.4	56.5/3.5	73.5/3.3	57.8/3.3	74.5/3.2	59.3/3.0
Number of Exposures						
1 + ...	56.8	56.5	73.5	57.8	74.5	59.3
2 + ...	38.5	38.5	50.6	39.0	51.6	39.9
3 + ...	27.3	27.4	34.5	27.3	35.2	27.8
4 + ...	19.7	19.8	24.0	19.5	24.3	19.5
5 + ...	14.3	14.5	17.1	13.9	17.0	13.8
6 + ...	11.5	10.7	12.2	10.0	12.0	9.7
7 + ...	7.6	7.8	8.8	7.2	8.5	6.9
8 + ...	5.5	5.7	6.3	5.1	6.0	4.8
9 + ...	4.0	4.2	4.5	3.6	4.2	3.3
10 + ...	2.9	3.1	3.2	2.6	2.9	2.3
11 + ...	2.1	2.2	2.2	1.8	2.0	1.6
12 + ...	1.5	1.6	1.6	1.3	1.4	1.1
Schedule						
Day net. GRP/Wk.	35	35	35	35	35	35
Night net. GRP/Wk.	14	14	14	14	14	14
Better Homes & Gardens	—	—	X	—	X	—
Good Housekeeping ...	—	—	X	—	X	—
American Home	—	—	X	—	X	—

London Crumpets
Recommended Alternative Plan
Gross Impression Analysis
(000)

	Day Network	Late Network	Magazines	Fringe Spot	Plan Total	Percent Plan	Percent Target	Index
Total women	929,464	381,318	162,390	692,542	2,165,714	100.0	100.0	—
Age								
18–24	156,150	62,155	27,885	103,882	350,072	16.2	13.9	117
25–34	177,528	75,120	34,139	131,583	418,370	19.3	17.9	108
35–49	198,905	102,575	47,704	163,440	512,624	23.7	21.3	111
50 +	396,881	141,468	52,662	293,637	884,648	40.8	46.9	87
Household income								
Under $8,000	448,002	140,706	39,361	250,700	878,769	40.6	28.6	142
$8,000–14,999	310,441	142,231	65,652	224,384	742,708	34.3	33.0	104
$15,000 and above	171,021	98,381	57,377	217,458	544,237	25.1	38.4	65
Household size								
1–2	370,856	154,433	52,208	315,799	893,296	41.2	38.0	108
3–4	340,184	130,792	63,744	159,285	694,005	32.0	37.7	85
5 and above	218,424	96,093	46,438	217,458	578,413	26.8	24.3	110
County size								
A	308,582	177,313	69,035	451,538	1,006,468	46.5	51.0	91
B	276,980	108,676	43,778	147,511	576,945	26.6	24.1	110
C	187,752	52,241	29,441	75,487	344,921	15.9	17.3	92
D	156,150	43,088	20,136	18,006	237,380	11.0	7.6	145

Source: Ogilvy & Mather Inc., 1978. Edited and revised by permission.

Notes

1. *Technical Guide, 1976/1977 Study of Selective Markets and the Media Reaching Them,* Simmons Media Studies (New York: W. R. Simmon & Associates Research, 1977), pp. 36-40.
2. Jack Z. Sissors and E. Reynold Petray, *Advertising Media Planning* (Chicago: Crain Books, 1976), p. 32.
3. Marketing information for Bubble Yum provided by Jerral R. Pulley, executive vice-president, Life Savers, Inc.
4. W. T. Tucker and J. J. Painter, "Personality and Product Use," *Journal of Applied Psychology,* October 1961, p. 328; H. B. Bylund, "Social and Psychological Factors Associated with Acceptance of New Food Products," *Marketing Models, Quantitative and Behavioral,* edited by Ralph L. Day (Scranton, Pa., International Textbook Co., 1964), p. 146; Gary A. Steiner, "Notes on Franklin B. Evans' Psychological and Objective Factors in Prediction of Brand Choice," *Journal of Business,* January 1961, p. 60; Dorothy Cohen, *Advertising* (New York: Wiley, 1972), p. 354.
5. Arnold M. Barban, Steven M. Cristol, and Frank J. Kopec, *Essentials of Media Planning* (Chicago: Crain Books, 1976), pp. 34-35.
6. Sissors and Petray, *Advertising Media Planning,* p. 46.
7. Ronald Michman and Donald Jugenheimer, *Strategic Advertising Decisions* (Columbus, Ohio: Grid Publishing, 1976), pp. 190-91.
8. Jack Z. Sissors, Harry D. Lehew, and William Goodrich, *Media Planning Workbook: With Discussions and Problems* (Chicago: Crain Books, 1976), p. 31.
9. Barban, Cristol, and Kopec, *Essentials of Media Planning,* pp. 60-62.
10. *N. W. Ayer Media Facts, 1977-78.*

9 Sales Promotion— The Extra Step

Sales promotion and merchandising are often the most misunderstood and misused elements in an advertising campaign. Too often, it appears promotional plans are included only to "flesh out" the program or as an afterthought rather than as an integral part of the campaign. Sales promotion, however, may well be as important and valuable to the campaign planner as the more traditional campaign tools. Some experts now estimate the sales promotion investment by U.S. advertisers approximates that of measured media.

Sales promotion and merchandising techniques are not substitutes for media advertising forms. Confusion apparently arises because sales-promotion methods may include the use of media. For some tasks, traditional media advertising is best; for others, sales promotion usually results in the most effective campaign.

To understand sales promotion, we first start with some common definitions.

The difference between advertising and sales promotion
Useful distinctions

William A. Robinson, *Advertising Age* columnist and sales promotion consultant, defines sales promotion as "an activity in which . . . a short-term incentive is offered to the trade or the consumer to induce purchase of the product." By contrast, Robinson defines advertising as "rented media. You rent time on TV, you rent magazine space, to carry your message. The main purpose of advertising is to create a favorable image regarding the brand. It conditions customers' minds so that when they see a product in the store, they are favorably disposed to it."[1]

The American Marketing Association defines sales promotions as "those marketing activities other than personal selling, advertising, and publicity that stimulate consumer purchasing and dealer effectiveness such as display, shows and exhibitions, demonstrations, and various nonrecurrent selling efforts not in the ordinary routine.[2] John F. Luick and William Lee Zeigler say sales promotion is "a direct inducement which offers an extra value or incentive for the product to the sales force, distributors, or the ultimate consumer."[3] The Sales Promotion Executives Association's definition is, "Any activity which increases or speeds up the flow of goods and services from the manufacturer to the final sale." In addition, the SPEA regards the following items as sales promotion: direct mail, sampling, coupons, catalogs, and price lists, house organs, annual reports, consumer contests and incentive programs, sales contests and incentive programs, exhibits, packaging, signs and displays, premiums, gifts, specialties, product publicity, sales aids and presentations, sales meetings, and sales training.[4]

Clarence E. Eldridge differentiates advertising and sales promotion like this: "The role of advertising is to create favorable attitudes on the part of the potential buyers and to stimulate sales immediately or in the future. Sales promotion seeks to effect an immediate increase in sales."[5] A combination of the Robinson and Eldridge definitions will be used in this text. Advertising creates attitudes that may result in sales. Sales promotion is any technique that is used to generate immediate sales. This should sufficiently differentiate the two.

The importance of sales promotion

Sales promotion as a field has been growing rapidly in the United States. In some organizations, sales promotion is the primary tool used to generate sales. As a result, the number of sales promotion agencies or consultants who counsel, place, and implement sales promotion has increased dramatically. Robinson, using estimates from *Advertising Age* and A. C. Nielsen Company, set the U.S. sales promotion and merchandising investment at $35 billion in 1977,[6] compared to the *Advertising Age* estimate of measurable advertising of $37,990,000 for the same year.[7]

Eldridge cites three reasons for the increased use of sales promotion and merchandising:

1. Franchise-building advertising is a slow process. Many advertisers simply can't wait for advertising to have its effect in the marketplace. More direct-action-oriented approaches are being sought.

2. There is an increasing lack of discernible differences in many product brands. Thus, with no competitive advantage, advertising declines in respect to its power to move the public. Sales promotion offers an immediate differentiating influence.

3. The "cult of creativity" is increasing in advertising. Much advertising is designed simply to entertain, not sell. Sales promotion is designed primarily to achieve a sale and an immediate one.[8]

While some may argue with Eldridge's comments, the immediacy of sales promotion is no doubt appealing to many marketers who are faced with increasing costs and a need to achieve meaningful shares in a highly fragmented marketplace.

Perhaps the overriding reason for the advertiser's increased used of sales promotion and merchandising is a desire to gain more control over the total marketing program. Most consumer product manufacturing and distribution programs have been integrated. Today, marketing managers want integrated marketing programs as well. These integrated marketing plans extend the advertising and promotion program to all levels of the marketplace—from the sales force to the wholesaler to the retailer and the ultimate consumer. This approach maximizes marketing investments as opposed to piecemeal programs which may or may not be effective.

The purpose of sales promotion

Most experts agree that sales promotion offers primarily short-term incentives to purchase aimed at either the sales force, the reseller, or the ultimate consumer. There are, of course, exceptions such as trading stamps or long-term continuity programs exemplified by Betty Crocker coupons. Most promotion activities, however, have a definite starting and ending date and cover a relatively short period of time, further differentiating sales promotion from advertising.

Sales promotion often has another purpose—to obtain distribution either at wholesale or retail. Because many supermarkets now stock over 9,000 items and drug and discount stores often have 11,000 products on the shelves, just gaining store distribution is difficult; yet the success or failure of a product depends on it. Sales promotion can be used as an incentive to the trade to stock the product and, once stocked, as an incentive to the consumer to purchase. Sales promotion techniques may obtain distribution when more traditional media advertising cannot.

Richard E. Stanley cites four strengths of sales promotion and merchandising as a successful marketing tool.

1. The opportunity for the consumer or retailer to get something for nothing.

2. Sales promotion offers the "extra something to buy," over and above basic product benefits. It may be the fillip that pushes consumers to the final purchasing decision.

3. Sales promotion is a direct inducement to do something now. Because of the limited time frame often used, prospects are encouraged to act while the offer is available.

4. Sales promotion activities are flexible. They can be used at any stage of product development from new-product introduction to revitalization of existing products.[9]

Sales promotion generally works best in introducing new brands or in announcing significant improvements in existing brands. Sales promotion also seems to work well in improving product distribution or achieving additional reseller support. Existing brands may get lost in the maze of new products. Sales promotion can be used to remind the reseller or the consumer about the brand. Finally, sales promotion and merchandising are most effective when used to amplify ongoing media advertising campaigns. Sales promotion is the extra step. It can contribute to the success of the media campaign by providing the immediate stimulus to act.

Sales promotion limitations

Often, because the capabilities of a specific marketing tool are not recognized in advance, advertisers unfairly criticize the results of the use of that tool. Sales promotion techniques (as with media advertising), regardless of the creativity involved or the amount of money invested, can accomplish only certain objectives.

What sales promotion can do

Obtain trial of a product. Because sales promotion techniques are designed to provide short-term incentives to the consumer or reseller, trial of a new product, a reformulation of an existing product, or trial of a new category often can be achieved. While trial may be obtained, usually it is only initial trial. The product must provide the benefits promised to the consumer for long-term sales.

Establish a purchasing pattern by persuading initial triers to repurchase. If the product delivers the benefit promised, sales promotion can aid in obtaining repeat purchases. This may establish purchase patterns. For example, a continuing sales promotion program requiring consumers to save for a premium may effectively block competitive actions. The promotion provides the repurchase incentive to obtain the promotional item.

Increase consumption of a product. By identifying new uses for an old product, consumption can often be increased through sales promotion. A common sales promotion technique is the development and advertising of new recipes using the product as an ingredient. Sometimes these new recipes are compiled into a cookbook which is then used as a sales promotion feature. Similarly, a promotion that combines two products may help to increase the consumption of both. An excellent example is the promotion developed by the Puerto Rican rum industry and Coca-Cola who combined to promote the two products as a refreshing drink.

Neutralize competitive promotions. Sales promotion techniques are often used to help offset activities by competitors, particularly those which employ an especially effective competitive media campaign. Similarly, if competition has developed an effective sales promotion program, an offsetting merchandising plan may be designed specifically to hold present customers. Advertisers of leading brands, who seek to hold their share of market against invasion, often use sales promotion in this way.

What sales promotion can't do

Even the most brilliant sales promotional program cannot achieve some objectives:

Sales promotion can't build loyalty. Sales promotion can achieve trial of a product or service, but it is always a short-term incentive. Only satisfaction with the product or service can build brand loyalty. Promotional methods may keep customers buying in the short run; but once the promotion stops, customers may switch to another brand unless the product fills a real need. Business bought with promotion can often be lost to promotion.

Sales promotion can't reverse a declining sales trend. If the product has been in a lengthy sales decline or is in the latter stages of the product life cycle, sales promotion can provide only momentary sales gains or stave off the eventual demise. It cannot save a dying brand or product. An outstanding sales promotion program, for example, could not have saved the buggy whip industry any more than it could have rescued the ill-fated Edsel automobile of some years ago. While sales promotion is effective in many instances, it is not the panacea for all the ills of a product line or category.

Sales promotion cannot change the basic "nonacceptance" of a product. Quite the contrary, for if a product is of little value or does not provide a consumer benefit, sales promotion, rather than increasing sales, may well hasten the decline. For example, assume a manufacturer of premixed soups develops a new flavor which does not match the quality of the rest of his line. In an effort to beat competition to the market, he does no consumer testing. A promotion program is designed to obtain trial for the newly developed flavor. Customers who try the new soup flavor reject it. Not only do they reject the new flavor, they assume the same poor flavor is in the rest of the product line. Thus, the more trial the promotion achieves, the fewer prospects the manufacturer has. Under normal circumstances, without sales promotion, trial of the new flavor might not have been so great. Product quality might have been improved before it was too late. Thus, while sales promotion obtained trial of the product, the long term success of the promotion was actually negative.

With this overview of sales promotion and merchandising, we can discuss the more specific areas that might be included in the development of an advertising campaign.

Types of sales promotion

Three types of sales promotion can be differentiated according to the groups to whom the promotion is directed. These are consumer, trade, and sales force promotions.

Consumer sales promotion

The consumer market is the largest area of sales promotion and merchandising in terms of dollars invested. It is also the most innovative. Some of the more common sales promotion techniques are reviewed here with specific emphasis on how they might be used in an advertising campaign.

Promotion results must be measurable

All types of promotional programs have one thing in common—they must be measurable (quantifiable). It is no longer acceptable in most organizations to simply say, "We'll run a few coupons," or "How about including a contest?" There must be clearly defined measurable goals for the promotion. Otherwise, leave the promotional activities out. A poorly planned or poorly executed promotion may often be a detriment to the campaign rather than a help.

The rules are quite simple. Objectives must be set based on some measurable activity. For example, the objective of a sampling program might be to place the product in the hands of 45 percent of the prospective customers in a given area. By carefully developing a mailing list and through selection and distribution methods, this goal could be achieved. Another objective might be to move 90 percent of the old packages off the shelves of retail stores within the next two months, prior to the new package introduction. For this objective, a "two-for-one" promotion might be initiated to speed up the process. Through a store audit, it could quickly be determined whether the promotion was achieving its goal. The key point is that promotional objectives must be set in advance and be measurable. The quantification may take many forms but often a before-and-after measure, the return of coupons, redemption of premiums, or contest entries received are used as the basis for evaluation.

Objectives of consumer promotions

Six general objectives of most consumer promotions can be listed. All promotional campaigns should have one or more of the following as their objective:

1. To attract customers not presently using. The primary objective of many sales promotion programs is to attract new triers. This usually means some incentive is given users of competitive products to encourage them to try the brand. An alternative approach is to attract persons not using any brand in the particular product category. This is usually a more difficult task than a simple brand switch, although many successes have been reported.

2. To hold present customers. Most products rely on a stable base of users for much of their business. Therefore, it is usually as important to hold present customers as to attract new ones. Thus, while competitors attempt to take customers away with promotions designed to attract new triers, advertisers develop programs which are equally successful in holding present customers.

3. To load current users. One way to hold current customers is to "load them with the product" or "Take them out of the market" for a period of time. This plan encourages present customers to purchase a large enough supply of the product so they will not be purchasing again in the near future. This serves two purposes. First, it ensures that customers will continue using the advertiser's product since it is on hand. Second, with a sufficient supply of the product available, there is little likelihood present customers will respond to a competitor's promotional offer. Thus, the marketer has held his or her present customer.

4. To increase product usage. As was previously discussed, one of the primary objectives of sales promotion is to increase product usage. With a slowly growing consumer population, new or other uses must be found for the product to increase consumption. Continually attempting to take business from competition is a very expensive proposition and, in the long run, usually results in constant consumer brand switching which shows negligible increases for any brand. A better long-term strategy usually is to increase the user base for the product or service.

One of the most common methods of increasing product usage is through suggesting additional uses. For example, Arm & Hammer Baking Soda greatly expanded the sale of a fairly common staple through suggested new uses such as a refrigerator deodorizer, a washing compound, an oven cleaner, and others.

5. To trade consumers up to a higher quality or higher price level. An objective for many brands is to get consumers to "trade up" or buy a more expensive brand or model than that which they normally use. This is usually accomplished by means of a reduced price offer of some sort. Many automobile manufacturers, for example, often promote specially equipped models with stereo radio, air conditioning, bucket seats, and other options with a reduced or combination price. The objective is to get customers accustomed to these conveniences so their next purchase may be made at the regular price. Similarly, a bar soap manufacturer might attempt to move her present customers up to a higher price or level of quality through promotional activity such as multipacks, a new size, or the inclusion of free face cloths.

6. To reinforce brand advertising. Last, but certainly not least in the objectives of consumer sales promotion, is that of increasing awareness of or reinforcement of current brand advertising. A common example is a consumer premium tied to the advertising campaign such as the inflatable Dole banana, the Jolly Green Giant kite, or cowboy accessories sold through the "Marlboro Store," all designed to support the advertising campaign. In some instances, the advertising itself becomes an effective sales promotion tool, as in the use of advertising jingles which are turned into popular songs and sold as records.

Types of consumer promotions

It would be impossible to list all the various types of consumer sales promotion techniques available since new ones are being invented almost daily. Some authors such as Luick and Zeigler have separated promotion techniques into those designed for new products and those designed for existing or established products.[10] Others such as John S. Wright, Daniel S. Warner, Willis L. Winter, Jr., and Sherilyn K. Zeigler have identified a core of promotions which they suggest are the most common.[11] Stanley separates promotions into two groups—those which reach consumers in the store and those which the consumer receives at home.[12] Because of the varied types and increasing amount of sales promotion now used, these separations or distinctions become increasingly difficult. Thus, rather than attempting some artificial differentiation between types of consumer promotions, we will describe in some detail the eight most widely used techniques identified by Robinson.[13] Most other types of promotions are variations on one of these themes.

Note: No attempt has been made to list specific organizations that provide various sales promotion materials or services. To do so would likely mean this chapter would be soon outdated since sales promotion suppliers are so many and varied. The reader may obtain additional information on specific approaches and suppliers as the need arises from reference sources.

Sampling

With most new products, particularly package goods, one of the primary marketing objectives is to obtain trial usage. Because most prospective customers already use an established brand, simply getting a presently satisfied user of a competitive product to switch to a new brand may be a herculean task. One method that has proved successful over the years is sampling. It also appears to work successfully for product reformulations and the reinforcing of current brand usage for existing products.

Sampling can take many shapes and forms. For low-priced products, the least expensive sampling unit is often the regular product. For more expensive products or those in which several uses or servings are purchased at one time, a sample package may be developed. The purpose of a sample is to provide a sufficient supply of the product so the consumer can judge its merits.

While samples are normally distributed to prospects at no charge; another technique which is gaining importance is the sale of a trial package at retail. This is usually a special size of the product for which the advertiser charges a price to offset some of his or her costs. The trial-size offer has appeal to the retailer who receives a profit on the sales of sample goods rather than seeing them given away. The sale of the trial sample appears to be particularly appealing to advertisers whose products have a relatively high unit price such as cosmetics, drugs, and health and beauty aids.

The chief problem inherent in any sampling program is finding an effective yet cost-efficient method of distribution. Many methods are used, but four basic approaches are most common: through-the-mail, hand delivered to the prospect's door, as an on-pack with an existing product, and in-store sampling by demonstrators.

The through-the-mail method offers the advertiser the obvious advantage of being able to control fairly closely where and when the product is distributed. This permits demographic or geographic targeting. Cost and postal limitations on some products are usually the primary problems with through-the-mail. The problem of cost is the major disadvantage of delivery to the prospect's door. The opportunity to control where and when the samples are distributed and the fact that almost any product can be distributed are almost overwhelmed by the sheer cost of personal delivery. Cooperative ventures where several products are distributed at once often helps reduce the cost problem of door-to-door delivery.

The on-pack sample has the major advantage of low cost. The disadvantage, however, is that it is distributed only to those persons who purchase the product with which it is packaged. Thus, packing a sample of a new soy sauce with a brand of chow mein limits the product trial to purchasers of the specific brand of chow mein selected and not the entire market.

In-store sampling is becoming increasingly important in many areas particularly for food products. In these cases, persons, usually called "demonstrators," set up a table or booth, prepare the product, and offer samples to shoppers. This approach is particularly effective for food products because the consumer has an opportunity to taste the product prior to purchase. In addition, the "demonstrator" can often deliver a sales message during the sampling. The major disadvantages are the extremely high cost and limited number of stores in which the promotion can be conducted. It requires space, product personnel, and a great deal of planning. It can, however, be one of the most effective of all sampling methods.

New and unique methods of sampling through the media are being developed. Samples of the product often can be bound into a magazine or included with the local newspaper. This, of course, applies to only a limited number of small, inexpensive, nonbreakable products.

Sampling is a big business and brings dramatic results. Advertisers are willing to invest large sums of money to achieve trial. For example, a few years ago, Procter & Gamble, to introduce a new brand, distributed over a million one-pound samples of coffee in one geographic area of the country.

The campaign planner has several cost factors to consider in a sampling program. First is the cost of the sample itself. Next is the cost of distribution. Often special packages or promotional literature to accompany the sample must be printed. When a coupon is included to encourage trial, its cost must also be included. Sampling is expensive but can be worth it. Our best advice when you are planning a sampling program

Exhibit 9-1. Distributions of coupons by media.

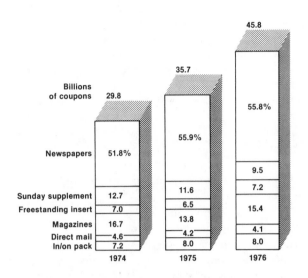

Source: A. C. Nielsen Company, *Researcher #4, 1977.*

is to contact one of the many special organizations which specializes in sampling.

In short, sampling works and works well. The key to successful sampling is to obtain cost efficiency while still distributing the product to the proper target market.

Coupons

Coupons are one of the oldest yet still one of the most effective sales promotion tools available to the campaign planner.

There are two types of coupons, manufacturer-distributed coupons and store coupons. Manufacturer-distributed coupons are those on which an offer is made on a particular brand by the manufacturer of the product. These coupons may be redeemed at any retail store that carries the product. For example, a coupon good for 10¢ off the purchase price on Open Pit Bar-B-Que Sauce could be redeemed at any retail outlet that stocked the product. Store coupons, on the other hand, are redeemable only at the store that offers the coupon. For example, if A&P placed a coupon in their newspaper advertisement offering 10¢ off on the purchase of Open Pit Bar-B-Que Sauce, that coupon would be good only at the A&P store, not at Safeway or Kroger. Stores develop their own coupons to generate promotional activity or, in some cases, to tie in with manufacturer promotions.

The basic advantage of the coupon is it allows the advertiser to reduce the price of his or her product at retail by a specific amount without relying on cooperation from the retailer. Coupons are used to induce trial of a new product or to gain trial of a new or improved product. They may also be used as distribution-forcing

devices, as competitive weapons against promotional activities by competitors, and as control techniques to limit the number of redemptions of certain types of promotions. While the primary purpose of coupons is to induce trial, they are also used to encourage repeat purchase of the product. For example, often a manufacturer will attach a coupon to the product good for a certain amount off on the next purchase of that product. This is a form of reward to the customer for use and encourages a repeat purchase.

Couponing, like sampling, takes many forms. The most traditional is a cents-off coupon distributed through media channels. Exhibit 9-1 illustrates the distribution of coupons by medium for a three-year period as measured by Nielsen Clearing House.[14] Other distributional techniques are in-packs and "cross-ruffs" in which a coupon for one product is either packaged with or printed on the package of another, usually complimentary, product. In a "cross-ruff," the couponed product may or may not be allied with the product carrying the coupon. Another popular method of coupon distribution is through cooperative mailings to selected homes. In these co-op mailings, an independent organization gathers the coupons of several marketers and mails them in a single envelope to consumer homes. The distribution cost is thus split among the participants.

The actual value of the coupon varies as widely as the products on which they are used. The range for package goods coupons is usually from 10¢ to 50¢, although there are no prescribed norms. The most popular coupon value is 10¢, although this tends to increase according to the retail price of the product.

The "buy one—get one free" coupon is increasingly popular. It is commonly used with existing products when the advertiser is attempting to take the consumer out of the marketplace for a period of time. A relatively recent innovation is the "self-destruct" coupon. Two coupons are printed together in an overlapping fashion. One coupon is for a lesser amount on the small size or purchase of one item, while the overlapping coupon has a greater value on a large size or multiple purchase. When one coupon is used, the second is destroyed.

Advertisers are constantly devising new couponing techniques (see Exhibits 9-2, 9-3, 9-4). For example, some retail outlets use a specially printed roll of cash register tape. On the back of the tape are printed coupons good for reduced prices at the store itself or at other retail outlets which may be located nearby. A food store might carry a coupon for a fast-food outlet on the back of its cash register tapes; for example.

Coupons are an increasingly popular method of consumer promotion, as is shown in the following charts developed by A. C. Nielsen Company. Exhibit 9-5

Exhibit 9-2. Self-destruct coupons from a newspaper are shown at the right.

Exhibit 9-3. Illustrated above is one page of a free-standing newspaper insert.

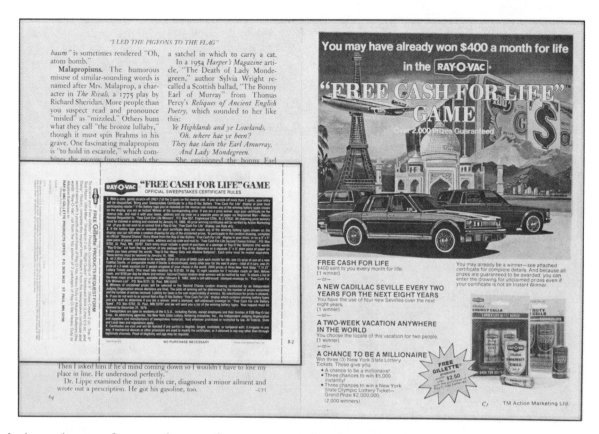

Shows the increasing use of coupons by manufacturers from 1972 through 1976. The 96 percent usage increase reflects not only an increasing number of coupons by manufacturers but an increasing number of companies using coupons as a promotion tool.

Consumers have an increasing interest in coupons, too. Exhibit 9-6, also from Nielsen, shows the number of households using coupons. In 1971 only about half

Exhibit 9-4. Pop-up coupon from the pages of the *Reader's Digest.*

Exhibit 9-5. Trend in coupon distribution; billions of coupons.

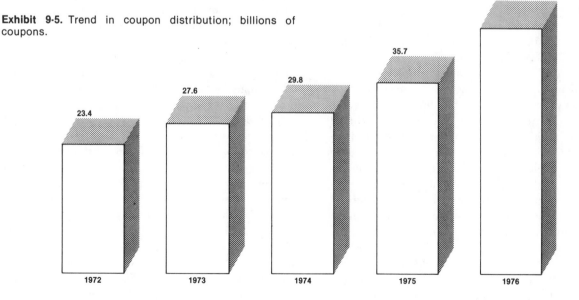

Source: A. C. Nielsen Company, *Researcher #4,* 1977.

Exhibit 9-6. Households using coupons (percent).

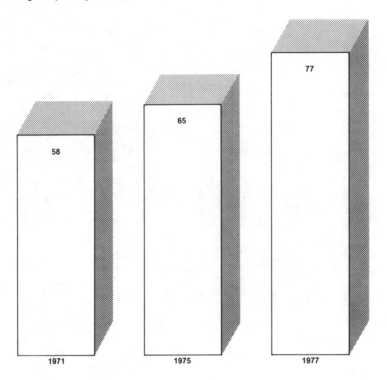

77

65

58

| 1971 | 1975 | 1977 |

Source: A. C. Nielsen Company, *Researcher #4,* 1977.

the households used coupons, while in 1977, more than three-quarters of all homes surveyed used or redeemed coupons. Consumer interest is definitely increasing.

One of the major difficulties in a couponing program is determining the estimated level of redemption the coupon may achieve. Few, if any, coupons are ever redeemed at 100 percent rate. In addition, the method of distribution of the coupon has a direct effect on the redemption. Exhibit 9-7 shows the average redemption rate for the various types of grocery product class coupons in 1976 as measured by Nielsen Clearing House (NCH). As can be seen, although newspapers accounted for the largest number of coupons, they had a low redemption rate, trailing only magazines.

Coupon promotion costs are not limited to the value of the coupon. Several other factors must be included as well. Traditionally, coupons redeemed through retail stores allow an amount for retailer handling. Currently, retailers receive 5¢ per retail coupon for handling regardless of coupon value. This amount is subject to change by agreement with the retailers or their trade organizations. In addition, a charge is made by the clearinghouse or other organization that gathers the coupons, reimburses the retailer, and bills the manufacturer. While costs vary tremendously according to type of coupon, distribution, and other factors, the rule of thumb is to include about 4¢ per coupon for this service. Thus, we see that a 10¢ coupon actually

will cost the manufacturer about 19¢ for each redemption made. (10¢ coupon value + 5¢ retailer handling + 4¢ clearinghouse = 19¢ total.)

Another consideration in couponing is the length of time during which coupons may be redeemed. In most instances, an expiration date is included on the coupon. A cents-off coupon is usually valid from six months to one year after distribution. While the majority of redemptions will occur in the first three months, redemptions may continue for the length of the coupon offer and sometimes after if retailers fail to honor the expiration date and continue to redeem the coupons at retail. Sufficient funds should be set aside for estimated coupon redemption when this type of promotion is being planned.

Misredemption is a major factor to be considered in any coupon redemption costs, i.e., incorrectly redeemed coupons or outright fraud. Misredemption can occur anywhere along the distribution channels from the consumer to the retailer to the wholesaler. For example, the consumer may ask that the coupon be allowed on the purchase of a competitive product or simply that the money be refunded. The retailer may accept out-of-date coupons or buy up large quantities of newspapers, cut the coupons, and redeem them without selling the product. Sometimes, criminals actually print up numbers of valuable coupons and sell them to unscrupulous merchants who in turn redeem them from the manufacturer. Misredemption requires constant policing. The major problem however is that misredemption is usually discovered only after it has occurred and there is little recourse for the advertiser. Most advertisers allocate a certain percentage of misredemption into their figures since little can be done about it.

A factor that affects the number of redemptions of coupons is the value of the coupon itself. For example, a coupon good for $1.00 off has much more appeal than one for 10¢. Other factors are the product category, whether the product is purchased regularly or occasionally, the amount of discount off the regular retail price, and the percentage discount off the purchase price which the coupon allows, to mention just a few. Most clearinghouses have developed estimates of redemption based on their experience with various types of coupons. These may be used to help determine the amount that should be set aside to help cover the cost of a couponing program.

Price-offs

A promotional tool often used in connection with an advertising campaign is the price-off or price pack. This promotion may take many forms. The two most common are a cents-off label or a two-for-the-price-of-one offer.

Since the FTC investigations of the early 1960s into misuse of these promotions, stringent rules have been developed on the use of cents-off labels and price packs. For example, the FTC has developed a series of "Guides," which are used as aids in developing adver-

tising and merchandising materials. The "Guide Against Deceptive Pricing" covers such areas as former price comparisons, retail price comparisons, comparable value comparisons, advertising retail prices that have been established or suggested by manufacturers or other nonretail distributors, and bargain offers based on the purchase of other merchandise. These "Guides" outline suggested methods of presenting offers fairly to the consuming public. Generally, the "Guides" requires that price comparisons be legitimate and bona fide based on former pricing of the products. Thus, if a two-for-the-price-of-one offer is made, the suggested price for both products must equal the former price for only one. The same is true for other types of promotional activities that involve previous, prior, or combination pricing. Exhibit 9-8 shows how price-pack deals in food stores declined sharply after the FTC rulings but are now beginning to increase.

These techniques offer the advertising campaign planner broad promotional opportunities. For example, with the cents-off label, a significant price reduction can be promoted to the consumer with the assurance the savings will actually be passed along and not absorbed in the retail channels. The price pack offers the same advantages as the retail coupon but has none of the accompanying redemption costs for retailers or clearinghouses. Additionally, accurate estimates of the promotion costs can be determined in advance. Finally, the use of special product labels can actually turn the package into a sales promotion tool at the retail level. This is increasingly important as self-service increases in the retail outlet.

Exhibit 9-7. Coupon redemption rates by media (percent).

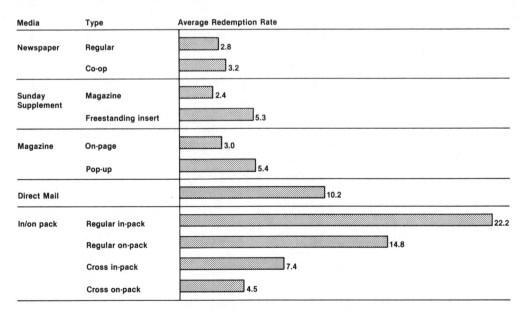

Media	Type	Average Redemption Rate
Newspaper	Regular	2.8
	Co-op	3.2
Sunday Supplement	Magazine	2.4
	Freestanding insert	5.3
Magazine	On-page	3.0
	Pop-up	5.4
Direct Mail		10.2
In/on pack	Regular in-pack	22.2
	Regular on-pack	14.8
	Cross in-pack	7.4
	Cross on-pack	4.5

Source: A. C. Nielsen Company, *Researcher #4,* 1977.

Exhibit 9-8. Trend in usage of price-pack deals in food stores, based on 14 product classes in which price packs have been used extensively.

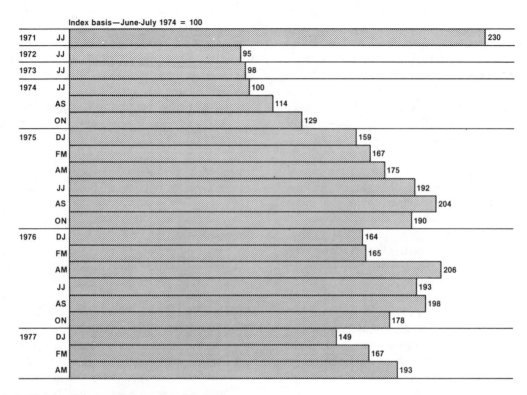

Source: A. C. Nielsen Company, *Researcher #4,* 1977.

The major disadvantage of the price pack is that, to be most effective, the offer must be advertised to the consumer. Without advertising, unless the consumer is shopping for the specific item, the reduced price may go unnoticed. Therefore, cents-off or price packs usually work best for established brands rather than new products, since consumers have a base against which to judge the price reduction on an established brand. In spite of this, promoters of new brands often make use of the price pack or cents-off label promotion.

In-pack premium

The mention of in-pack premiums immediately brings to mind ready-to-eat cereals. Yet, in-packs are still strong incentives for many other product categories.

The major advantage of the in-pack premium is that the product must be purchased for the consumer to obtain the premium. If a very desirable premium is available and promoted, substantial sales may be achieved that would not otherwise occur. Because all in-pack premiums will eventually be distributed, premiums are usually low cost or are built into the retail price of the product.

A form of in-pack premium is the continuity campaign where a series of premiums is collected by consumers over a period of time. For example, some detergent manufacturers have in-pack continuity programs that encourage the consumer to continue to purchase the brand time after time to obtain the full set of dishes, towels, or kitchen gadgets.

For campaign planners, the advantages of in-pack premiums are the known cost of the promotion and the opportunity to promote the premium. Each package is known to contain the premium and ensures that promotional expenditures will not be wasted by lack of premium availability at the retail level.

Recent events have discouraged some marketers from using in-pack premiums as heavily as in the past. First, of course, is cost. Finding a desirable premium at a reasonable cost becomes more difficult as prices continue to increase. Recent Federal Trade Commission and National Association of Broadcasters codes have placed stringent requirements on television advertising of premiums, particularly to children. The U.S. Food and Drug Administration also has quite stringent regulations about premiums packed with food products in terms of such factors as size, shape, and packaging of the premium. Thus, before deciding that an in-pack premium is an attractive promotional tool, the advertising campaign planner should seek the advice of an expert in the field.

Free premiums

The free premium usually consists of an item that aids or extends the use of the product. For example, a toothbrush may be banded to a tube of toothpaste or a mug used as the package for a chocolate milk mix. In effect, the offer is "buy this product and get this premium free." The major difference between free premiums and in-packs is the cost of the item.

A major advantage of the free premium is knowledge that the premium is available to the consumer in the retail outlets. Thus, little waste of media promotion occurs. In addition, the advertiser knows in advance the total cost of the promotion. The amount invested can be easily controlled through the number of free premiums made available and the promotional dollars spent to advertise the program.

In most instances, free premiums tend to have utilitarian value and are closely allied to the product being promoted. It is assumed that the premium will continue to remain with the consumer and serve as a reminder of the brand. Thus, many free premiums are imprinted with the name of the manufacturer, a brand, or logotype.

Because of the wide variety of free premiums, it is impossible to give rule-of-thumb estimates of costs. The campaign planner who wishes to use a free premium is advised to consult a premium-manufacturing firm or sales promotion organization.

Self-liquidating premiums

Self-liquidating premiums are items offered, usually with proof of purchase of the product, at a price which covers the out-of-pocket cost of the item. For example, a soup manufacturer may offer a set of specially designed soup mugs for proof of purchase of the product and a certain amount of money. The price paid by consumers covers the actual premium cost plus postage and handling. Because self-liquidating premiums are purchased in large quantities by the advertiser, the price is usually much lower than if the same item were purchased at retail. Thus, there is a savings to the consumer.

An alternative way to judge the value of a self-liquidating premium, other than counting the number of premiums redeemed, is the number of in-store or retailer displays that are gained through the use of the premium. Often, in fact, the goal of the self-liquidating premium is to gain retail displays with the actual distribution of the premiums a secondary consideration. The display of a self-liquidating premium with the product in a retail store can often move more mer-

chandise on an impulse basis than a well-planned advertising campaign.

Self-liquidators offer the advertiser several advantages. First, the cost of distributing the premium is borne by the consumer. Second, the premium is often tied directly to the advertising campaign or theme and is extended at no cost. An excellent example is the Virginia Slims cigarette theme, "You've come a long way, Baby," promoted through self-liquidating offers such as sweaters, blouses, bags, and similar items. Third, by purchasing in large quantities, the manufacturer can offer excellent values on products used as premiums.

The major disadvantage of the self-liquidating approach is the usual requirement by the premium supplier that the sales of a certain number of the premiums be guaranteed. If the premium is a success, there is no problem. However, if the premium redemption does not achieve the guaranteed number, the advertiser may find him- or herself holding a large supply of premiums that have little appeal to the consumer or that are tied to last year's advertising.

A major change in self-liquidating premiums has occurred in the past few years. Some advertisers are now promoting premiums that have no brand identification. Others have selected premiums with rather high prices. Usually self-liquidating premiums have been in the under-$20.00 category. Some advertisers have had success with more expensive premiums such as the KOOL cigarette sailboat at well over $500. The real success of a self-liquidating premium is usually the premium itself and the amount of promotion put behind the offer.

Contests and sweepstakes

Contests and sweepstakes generate a great deal of interest among consumers, especially if the prize structure is appealing. The major question, however, is whether running the contest will contribute to product sales. Most of the promotion supporting a sweepstakes or contest is directed only to the contest, not the brand. Unless the campaign is carefully planned, the brand's sales message may easily get lost in the excitement of the promotion. The contest or sweepstakes is a success, but the advertiser fails to achieve the desired sales goals.

While they are often lumped together in the same promotional category, a major difference exists between contests and sweepstakes. Contests are promotions in which participants compete for a prize or prizes based on some sort of skill or ability. Usually this consists of answering questions, completing sentences, or writing phrases or paragraphs about the product or its advantages, all of which require some form of talent. Sweepstakes, on the other hand, require only that the entrant submit his or her name to be included in a drawing or other form of awarding prizes. Because of the additional effort required of contest entrants, sweepstakes promotions usually draw more entries.

Contests and sweepstakes appear to work best in generating interest in a parity product or one that has no particular promotional advantage. They may also be used to help renew enthusiasm for the product at the retail level or to help in revitalizing an existing advertising campaign theme.

In addition, sweepstakes and contests do increase the readership of the advertising in which they are promoted. Consumers who have an interest in the promotion usually read the advertising more thoroughly than they do normal product advertising. Another advantage of a contest or sweepstakes is the opportunity to tie the promotion directly to the creative approach being used in regular advertising. For example, if a pineapple processor's advertising campaign is built around the sunny climate of Hawaii, a sweepstakes or contest built around trips to the islands would help reinforce the brand's sales message.

Finally, advertisers can often develop a large sweepstakes or contest prize list for a relatively small amount of money. Many manufacturers are willing to sell their products at less than retail cost to sweepstakes or contest promoters simply to obtain the additional advertising exposure their products will receive.

A major consideration in a contest or sweepstakes is preventing the event from becoming a lottery, illegal under state and federal laws. Lotteries have three basic elements: luck or chance, prizes or awards, and consideration on the part of the contestant. The consideration portion of a lottery is where problems usually occur. Any firm contemplating a contest or sweepstakes should consult qualified promotion and legal experts to ensure compliance with all federal, state and local regulations.

Although contest and sweepstakes promotions seem to rise and fall in popularity with advertisers, some factors remain fairly constant, e.g., sweepstakes are usually more popular with entrants than contests; cash and merchandise seem to generate the most enthusiasm as prizes. Oddly enough, offering too many prizes can create problems. Many contest developers suggest no more than a total of 100 prizes. Finally, the value of the contest or sweepstakes must be carefully weighed. With many states now conducting monthly legal lotteries with prizes up to and including $1,000,000 in cash, the prize structure of a contest or sweepstakes must be carefully planned.

Recent federal regulations require that all prizes offered in a contest or sweepstakes be awarded or that notification be made if all prizes are not to be awarded.

Prior to this ruling, advertisers offered large prize structures and gambled that only part of the prizes would be collected. Now, however, the total prize package is a known cost, plus the advertising support required to promote it properly.

Because development of contests or sweepstakes is such a highly specialized project, most advertisers and their agencies rely on the expertise of promotion specialists, such as D. L. Blair Company, Chicago, to develop and implement their programs.

Refund offers

Refunds are offers to return all or part of the product purchase price when a certain requirement is met such as supplying proofs of purchase. Many advertisers believe this type of promotion builds brand loyalty. They reason that, if the consumer uses the product a number of times to obtain necessary proofs of purchase for the refund, a purchase habit or brand loyalty will result. Also, when consumers take advantage of refund offers, the advertiser obtains their names and addresses. This helps pinpoint the user market and also offers follow-up sales opportunities.

In the 1977 study conducted by Nielsen Clearing House, the popularity of refund offers was found to be increasing substantially. Exhibit 9-9 shows that nearly 75 percent of the study respondents were aware of refund offers and 27 percent had participated. Of the 27 percent who had participated, nearly two-thirds had done so in the previous year. Consumers apparently like refund offers.

Two types of refund offers are used—those designed to obtain trial by offering to refund the product purchase price and those that reward present product users in an attempt to keep them brand loyal. Refund offers to generate new users normally appear in media advertising. Those that reward present customers are placed on or in the package of the product itself. In Exhibit 9-10, the Nielsen study shows how refund users learned of the offers.

Refund offers seem to work for all types of products. Exhibit 9-11 shows the various items for which respondents to the Nielsen study sent in for refunds. While the majority were given for food products, increasing activity was noted in such areas as toiletries, drug items, and even clothing.

A major advantage of the refund offer is the fact that many consumers purchase the product with the intention of claiming the refund but never do so. Thus, sales are achieved through the offer but refunds are not made. This is especially true for offers that require multiple purchases.

The primary disadvantage of the refund offer is that it actually amounts to a discount on the product. While

Exhibit 9-9. Popularity of refund offers (percent).

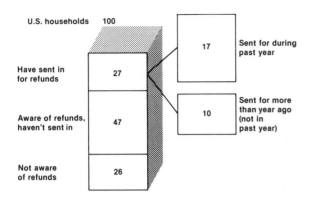

Source: A. C. Nielsen Company, *Researcher #4,* 1977.

the offer must be large enough to gain attention, making it too great may result in the majority of refunds going to present users so that no additional sales result.

Several cost factors must be considered in a refund offer. First is the value of the refund. Also, most offers are handled through organizations such as Nielsen who charge for handling the redemption plus the return postage. With a charge of approximately 11¢ for each redemption handled plus the return postage, 26¢ must be added to the value of the refund offer to determine redemption costs to the advertiser.

Obviously, from this brief overview, not all types of consumer promotion have been discussed. Such consumer promotional activities as the use of packaging,

Exhibit 9-10. How refunders learn of offers (percent).

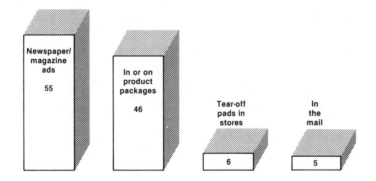

Source: A. C. Nielsen Company, *Researcher #4,* 1977.

Exhibit 9-11. Refunds from wide variety of products (percent).

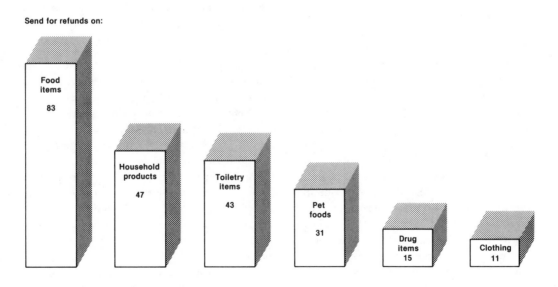

Source: A. C. Nielsen Company, *Researcher #4,* 1977.

in-store demonstrators, trading stamps, and other devices play an important role in the total sales promotion program for an advertiser. The eight types of promotions discussed, however, comprise the bulk of the activity at the consumer level.

Trade promotions

Trade promotions are often the key to a successful advertising campaign. Without retail distribution, even the most effective advertising cannot generate consumer enthusiasm, since the product is not available. Here we will review the basics of trade promotion.

Trade promotion goals

A key ingredient for success with any promotion is a clearly defined goal. This means the goal must be stated in measurable terms. For example, the objectives of a trade promotion program cannot be stated simply as "to get distribution." Rather, the goal should be stated as "to achieve distribution in retail outlets that account for a minimum of 65 percent of all-commodity volume (ACV)." Quantifiable results should also be projected for other types of trade promotion activities such as "achieving at least three facings in retail stores doing a minimum of $10,000 per week in volume in the top 50 markets." When the promotional goals are stated in such measurable terms, the success of the promotional program can be easily evaluated.

Trade promotion objectives

Most trade promotions have one or more of the following objectives:

1. To obtain trade support for advertising and merchandising activities
2. To gain new distribution
3. To build trade inventories
4. To improve trade relations

Obtaining trade support. As we review the various types of consumer promotions being used, it becomes clear that the success of many depends greatly on retail support. An advertiser, for example, may offer a special price pack and promote it heavily through the media. Unless the retailer stocks the price pack and makes it prominently available, however, the promotion will fail. The same is true for most other consumer promotions. To gain support, advertisers provide many forms of retail materials to back up their promotions such as trade deals, point-of-purchase materials, cooperative advertising funds, contests, and push money, among others. Numerous ways to judge retail support are available. One of the most common is to count the number of retailers or retail organizations that supported a particular promotion through pur-

chases, displays, features, or other measurable activities.

Gaining new distribution. Many trade promotions are designed simply to obtain new or additional distribution, particularly for a new product. Additional distribution is often the goal of existing products, too, as advertisers seek to maximize their media advertising investment by having the product available in as many locations as possible.

Retailers have limited space and usually seek products that offer the greatest margin and the fastest turnover. Trade deals, consumer promotion packs, featured items, and other approaches are all appealing since they can be converted into retail promotions. Because many products are at parity, retailers usually feature brands that offer them the greatest potential.

Building trade inventories. Advertisers constantly seek ways to increase the inventory of products stocked by the retailer. Full display shelves in retail stores usually mean greater sales. As the old saying goes, "If the product is not available, it is not sold." Advertisers use promotion, therefore, to encourage retailers to keep larger stocks of the product on hand so that it will be available and will also be promoted.

Improving trade relations. Manufacturers continually seek to improve relations with the trade. With the goodwill of the retailer, it is much easier to introduce new products, obtain promotional activity for existing products, and ensure continued distribution patterns. Most middlemen and retailers have a wide choice of products to stock and sell. The retailer usually favors the advertiser with whom he or she has a good rapport. Advertisers also recognize the importance of middlemen over whom they have little actual control. They try, therefore, to influence middlemen and gain support by offering substantial trade discounts, promotional materials, and other sales aids.

Types of trade promotions

It is impossible to list all the various promotions directed to the trade. The following, however, are the major types with others being a variation.

Trade deals. Trade deals are usually special price concessions, over and above normal discounts, granted for a limited period of time. They may be tied to a specific performance by the retailer or middleman such as larger-than-normal purchases; stocking of several sizes, flavors, or colors of the product; or incentives to lower the product price for a given period. Most trade deals are an incentive to the retailer to cooperate with the advertiser in some out-of-the-ordinary promotional way.

Trade deals are especially important in developing support for a new product, a new advertising campaign, or a promotional program. The size and type of the trade deal offered often has a significant impact on the success of the distribution at retail and thus the result of an advertising campaign.

The main advantage of a trade deal is the opportunity to gain retail support for the advertising campaign with special pricing. Another is the control the advertiser can exercise over the amount of "deal" merchandise available. By controlling the size of the deal to the trade, the advertiser has some control over the amount of money allowed as a discount. Finally, with a trade deal, the advertiser can promote when and how he or she chooses. The advertiser can make the deal available when promotion is needed and hold off when it is not required.

The primary disadvantage in trade deals is that, once "dealing" starts, retailers come to expect it in the future. Thus, when an advertiser wishes to develop a promotion without some kind of deal, he or she may find retailers unwilling to cooperate. In addition, trade deals have a tendency to become habit-forming, not just for the retailer but for the advertiser as well. Trade deals may be given when they are not really required to achieve the promotional goals. They then develop the force of habit, and retailers and customers alike wait for the "deal" rather than purchase at normal prices.

Deals also are expensive. The discount comes directly from the price of the product and is a direct reduction to the retailer. Deals have a direct effect on the profit-and-loss sheet. Advertising campaign planners often complain that trade deals absorb dollars that otherwise could have been used for consumer advertising. Because sales promotion provides a short-term incentive to purchase, trade deals cannot and will not build retailer or consumer loyalty. Finally, one of the major disadvantages of trade deals is that they may be absorbed in the retail channel. In other words, the retailer may simply absorb the trade-deal discount and not pass the proposed savings along to the consumer. Because the advertiser has no control over the retailer in these types of promotions, trade deals, especially if they are designed to offer a reduced price to the consumer, may often never achieve their goal.

Based on federal regulations, all trade deals must be offered to all retailers on an equal basis. That is, if a trade deal is made to one retailer or middleman, it must be offered on an equal basis to all retailers to whom the advertiser sells in a competing area. Offers may be made to various areas of the country or to noncompeting retailers on a selective basis. This practice is designed to prevent unfair trade discounting or pricing under the Robinson-Patman Act.

The five primary types of trade deals are buying allowances, free goods offers, count and recount offers, buy-backs, and advertising and display allowances.

BUYING ALLOWANCES. The buying allowance is a form of discount offered to retailers to encourage purchase of a certain quantity of product during a specific period of time. For example, a soft drink mix manufacturer may offer a $1.00-per-case buying allowance off the normal wholesale price from February 1 to March 15 to encourage retailers to stock the product for the upcoming heavy selling season. The physical handling of a buying allowance may take many forms. The most common is an off-invoice credit to the retailer or middleman.

FREE GOODS OFFERS. A somewhat different form of trade allowance is the free-goods offer. The soft drink mix advertiser mentioned above, instead of offering a buying allowance, might use a free-goods offer such as one case free with the purchase of ten during the February 1 to March 15 period. In this situation, the free goods are a discount to encourage the retailer or middleman to stock up prior to the selling season and to ensure the availability of a complete line of flavors.

Many manufacturers prefer the free-goods offer over case allowances for one simple reason: it costs less than the case allowance to the promoter. Free goods are priced at wholesale to the retailer, but the manufacturer is really only allowing the actual cost of manufacturing. With case allowances, the percentage deducted from the invoice includes the manufacturer's margin and thus actually amounts to more money.

In some instances, free goods are offered as an incentive on slow-moving products. Again, taking the example of the soft drink mix advertiser, to ensure the retail display of the full line, an offer of one case of fruit punch (a slow seller) might be offered with each ten cases of the more popular grape or cherry flavors.

COUNT-AND-RECOUNT OFFERS. Usually, this type of offer is made to help clear out the channels of distribution in retail stores. Let's use the soft drink mix advertiser example again. Instead of a buying allowance or free goods, the advertiser might offer a $1.00-a-case count-and-recount trade deal from March 15 until May 1. This is done to help get the product from the warehouse to the retail store in advance of the heavy selling season. It works this way. On March 1, the broker or advertiser's sales representative visits the warehouse or the retail stores of those accepting the count-and-recount offer. The merchandise on hand or in stock is counted. On May 1, at the end of the promotion period, the sales people again visit the warehouse or retail outlets and count the stock on hand. The difference between the opening and closing inventory is the amount subject to the count-and-recount deal. The retailer or wholesaler would be paid $1.00 for each case of the product sold during the period. Normally, the allowance is paid by check directly to the warehouse or the retailer.

BUY-BACKS. Another trade-deal variation, which often accompanies the count-and-recount deal, is the buy-back. The objective of the buy-back is to get the trade to restock the warehouse or retail stores immediately after the count-and-recount offer or to attempt to increase sales in the off-season. If the retailer has a stock of the product on hand, he or she will be encouraged to promote it and help move it out of the store. The soft drink advertiser, for example, might offer a buy-back allowance of $1.50 per case on the first purchase made by the wholesaler or retailer after the May 1 ending of the count-and-recount deal in the illustration above. The buy-back would be an additional discount of $1.50 on that one-time purchase. Usually, this type of promotion is limited to the amount of product sold during the previous count-and-recount promotion. Buy-back promotional discounts are usually paid directly to the warehouse or retailer by check from the advertiser.

ADVERTISING AND DISPLAY ALLOWANCES. These trade deals are designed primarily to encourage retailers to promote the trade-deal merchandise in their own retail advertising. This local feature by the retailer further supports the advertiser's national or regional campaign. Local retail promotions, particularly if they offer a reduced price, are usually very effective in moving merchandise. Generally, allowances take three forms:

1. An advertising allowance is a rebate paid to the middleman or retailer for advertising the manufacturer's product in local media. In the soft drink mix example, the advertiser might offer an advertising allowance of 50¢ per case on each case purchased from March 15 to May 1. The retailer, through purchases during that time, would then have a credit with the advertiser that could be used to purchase local advertising. Usually, retailers support their claim for the advertising allowance by furnishing proof of performance such as tear sheets of the ads or affidavits of performance that the advertising actually appeared. Many types and variations of the basic advertising allowance are used but all are tied to local advertising by the retailer in some way to support the sale of the advertised product. Advertising allowances are usually paid by check direct to the retailer.

2. Display allowances are just that. Retailers are given a predetermined allowance for developing a retail display of the advertised product. Guidelines for the display are set, e. g., the display must be of a certain size or contain a minimum number of cases of the product or amount of floor space to qualify. A photograph is used to certify to the manufacturer that the display was built. The display allowance may be a cash rebate, free goods, or contest prizes.

3. Merchandise allowances are offers made to retailers to secure advertising or displays of the advertised product. The merchandise may be a gift for the retailer or a variation of the free-goods offer previously described. Usually, the merchandise is something other than the product being promoted.

Point-of-purchase materials. Advertiser-developed point-of-purchase material for use in retail stores is a major promotion category. Point-of-purchase materials may range from a simple shelf-talker in a food or drugstore to an elaborate, long-term, moving display for a liquor retailer. Point-of-purchase pieces, originally offered to retailers for displays, often become permanent store fixtures such as clocks, wall ornaments, product dividers or headers, and other items.

Point-of-purchase materials come in many shapes and sizes. Illustrations of the more popular types of materials in use today are shown in Exhibit 9-12.

Most point-of-purchase materials are offered or shipped to retailers with little or no restrictions. Because of this, it is estimated approximately half of all POP materials are never used. There are simply too many advertisers sending too much material to a limited number of retailers. In spite of the problems of getting point-of-purchase materials used, their value cannot be doubted. The advents of self-service shopping in all types of retail operations points up the increasingly important role this type of material plays in supporting advertising campaigns at the retail level.

A strong advertising campaign can often be increased many-fold through the use of effective point-of-purchase advertising materials. It is especially effective when the media advertising campaign theme is carried through to retail POP materials.

Cooperative advertising. While often maligned as being unmanageable and a form of discount and source of dispute between retailer and manufacturer, cooperative advertising is still an excellent way to bring the national campaign to the local level. In many cooperative advertising agreements, the advertiser agrees to pay 50 percent of the cost of the advertising placed locally by the retailer in support of the advertised brand. While many cooperative agreements are set up on a 50–50 basis, they vary widely according to the product category, the amount of advertising done by the manufacturer, the value of local retail advertising to the sale of the product, and other factors. The usual agreement is for newspaper space. Increasing numbers of advertisers, however, are including radio and television in their co-op programs and some even

Exhibit 9-12. Point-of-purchase materials come in many sizes. Immediately below is a poster, actual dimensions 20″ by 13½″.

Dimensions of the plastic shelf strip below are 10⅛″ by 1⅜″.

The shelf talker illustrated here is actually 20″ by 4″.

split the cost of circulars and flyers.

The major advantage most advertisers find in cooperative advertising is local media support for a national or regional campaign. Also, since retail advertising is price-specific, the advertiser gains the benefit of a local price feature by the retailer. In most instances, this price feature is impossible in national campaigns.

The chief disadvantage of cooperative advertising is a limitation on the degree of control that the advertiser can exert over retailers or middlemen who develop the retail advertising. In some cases, less-than-professional-looking advertisements are run under the cooperative program, or the advertisements appear in undesirable media. Usually, unless there is full understanding, the advertiser must share the cost even if it appears that full value was not received. Another problem is the national-local rate. Often co-op agreements are set up on a shared cost based on the national rate in the media. If the retailer receives the lower local or retail rate, the advertiser may find he or she is paying 75 percent or even more of the actual cost of the advertising. Also, cooperative advertising is sometimes agreed to by the advertiser to offset competition. Often, the same money might be better spent in some other way. Finally, according to federal law, once a cooperative advertising program is initiated by an advertiser, it must be made available to all retailers under similar conditions. Thus, once a cooperative advertising program is started, it is usually most difficult to stop.

Dealer loaders. A dealer loader is designed to do exactly what the name implies—load the dealer with a product. One type of dealer loader is packing the product in a display such as a wheelbarrow, wagon, or other valuable premium. The premium and product are used as a display unit. When the product has been sold, the retailer keeps the premium. In addition, self-liquidating premiums (previously discussed), which are used as retail displays, are also used as dealer loaders. In this case, after the promotion is over, the dealer keeps the premiums included in the display. Dealer loaders may take almost any form from a small, impersonal gift to sporting goods, clothing, or even expensive foreign trips for the retailer and his or her family. Dealer loaders are often tied to a specific-size purchase with the value of the loader proportionate to the value of the order. This type of promotion is frequently used to support a new advertising campaign with the loader tied to the theme of the campaign. As with other types of trade deals, if a dealer loader is offered, it must, under federal regulation, be made available to all retailers on a proportionate basis.

Contests. Dealer contests have grown in size and importance over the years. Today it is not unusual for retailers to have opportunities to win very expensive prizes in contests sponsored by advertisers. Contests are usually tied to specific achievements by the retailer such as purchases, total sales, sales based on quotas, sales increases over previous periods, or sales of a new or existing product line. As a general rule, for a contest to be effective, the retailer must be given a reasonable opportunity to win.

Contests often work better with independent retailers than with chain stores. Many chain-store operations have very strict rules about contests, premiums and gifts that may be given or awarded to their store managers. In these instances, clearance is required from the chain's headquarters office before any type of contest can be conducted with their employees.

Contests generate great dealer interest and support while they are going on, but often don't have long-lasting effects. Once the contest is over, the retailers tend to return to their regular promotional activities. It is likely, though, that trade relations are improved through a contest. With the growth of contests and expanding prize structures, many retailers enter only those they have a good chance of winning, or which offer a particularly lucrative prize.

Push money. Often called "spiffs or PM," push money is money paid by the advertiser directly to sales people to promote specific items in the product line. A refrigerator manufacturer, for example, might offer "PM" or "spiff" on a certain model. During the time the promotion is in effect, the retail sales people are encouraged to personally promote that particular model since they will be rewarded with an additional cash prize. Usually, "spiffs or PM" works only for those products in which the retail sales person is a key selling ingredient. The device is not effective for products sold in self-service situations or those with a low selling price.

In nearly every case, the use of "PMs" requires the cooperation and approval of the store manager or the headquarters office of the retail store. Because offering money to employees is regarded as an inducement, retail management must be consulted prior to the offering of such a program to their employees.

While push money is still used, the legality of the practice has been questioned, and many advertisers are reviewing their use of this promotional tool.

Sales meetings. Probably the most widely used trade promotional tool is the sales meeting, which is conducted for retailers by the advertiser's sales representative or the broker sales force. Theoretically, all retail store personnel should attend these meetings. In many larger chains, however, these persons aren't available. Thus, sales meetings are often conducted for retail headquarters personnel or merchandising managers who, in turn, hold sales meetings for the retail people on the floor. Obviously, with this approach, something may be lost in the translation of the message. Nevertheless, sales meetings are an important way to merchandise and promote to the trade, especially when a new product, a new promotion, or a new advertising campaign is being introduced.

Sales meetings take many forms, from a simple meeting in a hotel room with a small group to a formal, traveling, professional show. The determining factor is the importance of the announcement to the advertiser and the middleman. The advertising campaign is usually a key feature of a sales-meeting program. Special emphasis is often given to the geographic areas represented by the retailers present. Thus, part of the development of many consumer-product advertising campaigns is a brief outline of how the material will be presented to the retailers and the sales force.

Promoting to the sales force

The final but certainly not the least important part of advertising campaign promotion is obtaining the support of the sales force, whether advertiser, employee, broker salesperson, or independent sales representative. Enthusiastic support of the campaign by the sales force can often make a major difference in overall results.

Results must be measurable

As in consumer or trade promotions, results from sales-force promotion must be measurable. This is usually a simple matter of developing goals for the sales force, then measuring against those goals. With the introduction of a new advertising or promotion program, for example, each member of the sales force is given a sales quota. Quotas may be based on the territory, increases over existing businesses, new distribution, or other objectives. Sales quotas are often tied to personal incentives in the form of either money or prizes.

While the advertising campaign planner usually is not involved in the development of sales quotas, he or she should be aware that they are used and that supporting materials may be needed.

Objectives of the promotion

Most promotions are designed to build sales-force enthusiasm for the campaign. This is often difficult because sales forces vary so widely. One advertiser may have a sales force composed entirely of company employees. Another may use broker representatives exclusively. Still others may have commission representatives who also represent 15 to 20 noncompetitive advertisers. And others may have a com-

bination of all the above. Just getting all these sales people enthusiastic about the advertising campaign so they will stress it to retailers may be a most difficult task.

Salespeople who truly believe their company is supporting their sales efforts with advertising and promotion usually work harder to make the program successful. In fact, in some instances, advertising campaigns are developed as much for the benefit of the sales force as they are for the trade and the consumer.

Sales-force goals of trade-level support take many forms. Goals may be set, for example, to obtain a certain number of tie-in advertisements from retailers. Others may be designed to obtain a certain number of displays in stores. Often, gaining new distribution in the sales areas is the primary goal. Although the objectives vary depending on advertiser needs, the sales force usually has three goals:

1. To obtain additional sales to the trade
2. To obtain additional distribution among either present or new retailers
3. To gain retail support for the campaign in the form of tie-in advertising or merchandising features

While the campaign planner is usually not responsible for the development of sales-force promotional objectives, sometimes such a program is requested.

Types of promotion to the sales force

Promotion directed to the sales force takes many forms. The choice usually depends on the type of sales force, the methods of communication, and the closeness with which the advertiser works with his or her salespeople. Some fairly standard techniques are used and they are briefly reviewed here. The campaign planner is sometimes expected to develop sales-force promotional materials, particularly for the smaller advertiser. This seems like a natural extension, since elements of the basic advertising campaign are often used as a basis for the promotional program.

Sales meetings. Like trade sales meetings, these can range from brief one- or two-hour meetings to full-scale production numbers at a distant resort. Much depends on the size of the manufacturer, the type of product, and the importance of the campaign. Generally, one of the key ingredients of these sales meetings is the presentation of the advertising campaign. Thus, the advertising campaign planner is often included in the program for such sales meetings.

Sales manuals. The sales manual is a descriptive booklet designed to help salespeople do a better job of selling. It is usually designed for internal use. The manual may contain product information, background materials, price lists, models, and other information that will assist in presenting the product line to prospects. The advertising campaign, advertising materials, and promotional program are usually integral parts of a sales manual.

Sales portfolios. Sales portfolios are usually developed as an external selling tool for the sales force. The portfolio may take any form, from loose-leaf binders to booklets to brochures to flyers. They are often designed to be left with the prospect. The portfolio contains information on the product being promoted, price lists, the advertising campaign, order forms, and other selling materials. The importance of the campaign, the type of market, and the needs of the sales force dictate the type of sales portfolio to be created. Often, the campaign planner is called on to help develop the sales portfolio because of knowledge of the market, the advertising campaign, and the advertising plan.

Sales letters. Sales letters, expressing the theme of the campaign, are used to announce sales meetings and to keep personnel enthusiastic during the course of a promotion. These sales letters often contain information that can be used in follow-up calls on prospects by the sales force.

Notes

1. William A. Robinson, Correspondence and personal conversations, May 1978.
2. American Marketing Association, Committee on Definitions, *Marketing Definitions: A Glossary of Marketing Terms* (Chicago: American Marketing Association, 1960), p. 20.
3. John F. Luick and William Lee Zeigler. *Sales Promotion and Modern Merchandising* (New York: McGraw-Hill, 1968), p. 4.
4. Sales Promotion Executives International, New York, Folders, brochures, and other printed material.
5. Clarence E. Eldridge *Marketing for Profit* (New York: Macmillan, 1970), pp. 125-38.
6. William A. Robinson, Correspondence, April 27, 1978.
7. *Advertising Age,* 9 January 1978, p. 9.
8. Eldridge *Marketing for Profit,* pp. 125-38.
9. Richard E. Stanley, *Promotion* (Englewood Cliffs, N. J.: Prentice-Hall, 1977), pp. 308-32.
10. Luick and Zeigler, *Sales Promotion,* pp. 37-65.
11. John S. Wright, Daniel S. Warner, Willis L. Winter, Jr., and Sherilyn K. Zeigler. *Advertising*, 4th ed. (New York: McGraw-Hill, 1977), pp. 630–47.
12. Stanley, *Promotion,* pp. 308-32.
13. William A. Robinson, Personal conversations and lectures, 1977–78.
14. A. C. Nielsen Company, "A Look at Sales Promotion," *The Nielsen Researcher,* no. 4, 1977, pp. 2–14.

10 Evaluating the Advertising Campaign

A crucial step in the development and execution of an advertising campaign is providing a mechanism for evaluation. For major campaigns, two evaluations may be made: (a) concurrent evaluation during the time the advertising is running and (b) final evaluation at the conclusion of the campaign. Concurrent testing provides an opportunity for fine tuning the specific elements in the marketplace. Modifications or changes can be made to ensure success of the total program. Evaluation at the end of the campaign is needed to determine if the objectives or goals were achieved.

In this chapter, we will review the problems of advertising campaign measurement, what should be measured and how, and the most common methodologies used.

While the emphasis will be on measurement methodologies for the total campaign, some of the more popular individual advertisement or commercial evaluation techniques will also be discussed. For more complete information on specific techniques, a research text or the various testing organizations should be consulted.

What is being measured

It is all too easy to fall into the trap of attempting to measure the total marketing effort for the product rather than the effects of the advertising messages. As pointed out in chapter 4, the advertising goals of a campaign should be expressed in terms of the communication effect, not necessarily actual sales of the product or service.

The question of whether to measure sales effects or the communication effects of advertising was probably best summarized by Gail Smith in, "How GM Measures Ad Effectiveness."[1]

No one denies that the ultimate objective of advertising is

to raise the level of performance for a product and hopefully to reap a benefit in terms of increased sales, but it does not necessarily follow that sales figures constitute a measure of advertising. To say so is roughly equivalent to saying that the measure of Mickey Mantle's prowess as a baseball player is whether the Yankees win or lose. As talented as he may be, I doubt if Mr. Mantle would appreciate being measured in those terms. He contributes, but he is not the only factor. The same principle holds of advertising; it is a marketing force, it contributes to the sale, it does not ensure it — ever. Therefore, we prefer not to be saddled with that particular concept.

Thus, with minor exceptions, a basic rule is: Measure the communication effects of advertising, not the sales effects, unless you can control all of the marketing variables.

While we strongly urge the evaluation of the campaign by communication effects, the actual evaluation must be based on what the advertising goals and objectives were. If they were stated as being measurable in terms of sales, the measure of the campaign must be sales. Similarly, if the goals and objectives of the campaign were stated as communication objectives, then those are the yardstick.

The overriding importance of setting realistic and measurable goals for the campaign is more evident than ever.

Problems in advertising campaign measurement

According to Kenneth A. Longman, three basic problems appear in advertising evaluation:

1. People are notoriously unable to answer questions about whether an advertisement or commercial motivated them to purchase a certain product.
2. Relatively few people are actually motivated to action through exposure to advertising; i.e., an ad

that motivates 3 percent of those exposed is usually considered to have been successful.

3. Most people have difficulty in separating the effects of the advertising campaign from the many other factors that might have influenced their purchase, such as past experience with the product, prior advertising exposure, exposure to sales promotion or store materials, previous exposure to the product in the store, and the effect of competitive advertising.

The problem of relating advertising to sales, therefore, is not unidimensional but multidimensional. It is a difficult task for people to sort these factors out and draw a direct cause-and-effect relationship for advertising.[2]

Simon Broadbent identifies other measurement problems such as the difficulties created by forces in the marketplace. A single product's advertising is usually a very small factor when compared to past and present promotion, distribution, competition, and so forth. Therefore, it becomes even more difficult to isolate specific advertising results.

The second evaluation problem is the advertising time span. According to Broadbent, the first effects of advertising lift the product to a level of acceptability. Additional advertising builds on that acceptability. This is usually a slow process where major changes are not quickly apparent. In campaign evaluation, however, dramatic changes in sales or communication effects are usually desired, because these can be identified as a sign of success. Success may be there, but it is not quite so apparent.[3]

Finally, the prospect's memory creates a problem in evaluation. H. S. Zeilske found that consumers tend to forget advertising rather quickly. In one test, only 63 percent of the sample could remember a given piece of advertising immediately after receiving 13 successive weekly exposures. Four weeks later, only 50 percent of those exposed remembered the advertising, and, after six weeks, less than one-third could recall the test material.[4] Thus, while an advertising impression is made initially, it apparently is forgotten rather quickly.

What we are measuring and why

The first step in measuring communication effects is to determine what those effects are and what evaluation tool will be used. We have suggested the use of the Robert J. Lavidge and Gary A. Steiner "Hierarchy of Effects Model" as described in chapter 3.[5]

Lavidge and Steiner see the movement from "unawareness" to "purchase" of a product as a series of six distinct steps. The first step is "awareness" and the second "knowledge," both of which relate directly to information or ideas about the product or service. The third step, "liking," and the fourth step, "preference," are the "feeling" steps which deal with attitudes about the product. The fifth step, "conviction," and the sixth step, "purchase," are "action" or behavioral steps which result in the actual purchase of the product.

While Lavidge and Steiner have six specific steps in their model, from "awareness" to "purchase," these are usually collapsed to the four that are used in our evaluation model for advertising campaigns. They are: (1) awareness/knowledge (recall), (2) liking (attitude change), (3) preference, (4) conviction/brand to be purchased or brand bought last.

Awareness and knowledge

The lowest level of communication effect of advertising is awareness or knowledge of either the product or service being advertised or the advertising message itself. When the product is new or unknown, the objective of the campaign may be simply to make the consumer aware that it exists. This is the simplest measure, and, therefore, is the most widely used.

For a known or existing product, the advertising task usually is to develop awareness or knowledge within the target market about a specific benefit of the product or service. This measure does not necessarily attempt to determine whether the message has a communication effect. The assumption is made that, if the consumer is aware of the message or has gained knowledge about the product, the advertising has achieved its basic goal.

Under the assumption that the advertising message or the product was unknown prior to the start of the campaign, the awareness measure can be made at any time after the campaign starts. The usual quantification is determining how many persons are aware or recognize the product, the campaign theme, or one of the promises made.

Recall

The second level of advertising effectiveness is recall. This simply refers to that fact that persons exposed to the advertising campaign can repeat or play back certain portions or ideas they saw or heard. They "recall" the advertising message. Again, no measure is made of the value of the advertising message or the impact it might have on the target market.

Two forms of recall are used in advertising evaluation, unaided and aided.

In the unaided-recall method, respondents are asked if they remember having seen or heard advertising recently for any brand in a certain product category. No further clues are given to help identify the sponsor, the brand, or the message. In aided-recall measures, certain clues are given to help the respondent remember advertising. For example, rather than asking only if advertising for a certain product category had been seen or heard, the question asked might be phrased to determine if the person could recall which brand or what advertiser used a certain graphic device or made a certain claim in his or her advertising. Thus, the hints or suggestions "aid" in recalling the advertising.

While both aided and unaided recall are used in evaluating an advertising campaign, unaided recall is believed to be the stronger. Because the respondent is asked only about the product category and is asked to spontaneously recall or remember the advertising, the assumption is that a longer-lasting impression has been made.

The strongest effect of the campaign at this level is specific information about the product or service to the consumer. Thus, if a consumer learns from advertising that only one brand of cough drop has the advantage of dual action, i.e., it's both antiseptic and anesthetic, and that the product with these properties is Brand Z, then knowledge has been communicated. It is assumed the message communicated will have an effect on the future purchase behavior of the consumer, although the relationship is somewhat tenuous.

Recognition, recall, and knowledge of the product, the message, or the benefits probably make up the bulk of the content of all campaign evaluation.

Liking and attitude change

The third level of advertising effect is *liking* the product or service. Liking assumes the consumer is aware and has some knowledge either from the advertising or from actual use. Often, it is difficult to separate advertising knowledge from experience, which makes the measure more difficult.

In respect to "liking," we assume that advertising has had an effect on the consumer's mental condition or that some sort of attitude change has occurred. The consumer has moved beyond the awareness or knowledge stage and has formed a positive opinion about the product. Liking does not mean that the consumer will purchase the product. It means that positive feelings exist.

An example of liking a product is to have a consumer name several acceptable brands of products in a category. The assumption is made that, if the products are acceptable, they are liked. (Remember the "evoked set" discussed in chapter 3.) While liking is an important step in evaluating the results of an advertising campaign, this measure still does not assume a purchase action. A consumer may like many products but purchase only a few.

Preference

The next factor to be considered is preference. This simply means that, among a certain number of products or brands within a category, one is preferred over the others. In terms of campaign measurement, the assumption is made that the advertising message has created a level of acceptance for a specific product, so that among available alternatives the advertised product is preferred and would likely be purchased.

Because preference indicates that, all things being equal, certain brands would probably be purchased, preference is one of the stronger measures of the effect of advertising. If advertising is the major decision factor in creating product preference, the campaign is usually considered successful whether or not actual sales result.

Purchasing behavior

The final and most powerful effect of advertising is directly affecting behavior or moving a consumer to a purchase. Usually conviction and behavior are difficult to measure because of the many variables involved. There are some instances, though, in which purchase behavior can be traced directly to the advertising message such as in direct response.

In the conviction measure, as in all others, it is assumed that members of the target market have seen and reacted to the advertising message. The consumer has become aware of the product or service advertised, has developed a liking, has moved up through the preference stage, and is now prepared to take or has taken the final step of conviction to purchase or has actually purchased the product.

In the Lavidge and Steiner model, conviction and purchase behavior are in the conative or motivation area of behavior. Because a person often cannot accurately describe a conviction, some of the measures in this evaluation require questions of purchase intention or past purchase behavior. Thus, attempts are made to identify advertising as the force that created a switch of brands or stimulated the purchase of a product or service in the past or what might occur in the future. Intent to purchase is also assumed to be a strong indicator of advertising success.

Most questions in the area of conviction deal with what was purchased. A given purchase is compared with past or usual behavior to determine if a change occurred. If change, such as a brand switch did occur or if there was an indication that a brand switch might occur on the next purchase, an attempt is made to link this behavioral change to the advertising. While the link is often questionable, it is used as a form of evaluation, especially if the reason given for the brand switch is implicit in the advertising message.

Many behavioral or psychological models can be used to evaluate advertising. The Lavidge and Steiner "Hierarchy of Effects" model or parts of it have gained widespread industry acceptance. The model provides a practical and useful, if somewhat arbitrary, method of advertising campaign evaluation.

Methods of measuring the results of a campaign

With an understanding of the particular advertising campaign results that should be measured, we now face the problem of how to make the measurement. While the design and implementation of questionnaires are extremely broad and complex topics, some generalizations can be given on ways in which campaign evaluations can be made. Generally, awareness, recall, attitudes, and brand usage are the primary topics which are investigated.

Measuring awareness

Awareness is generally regarded as the measurement of knowledge without reference to source. While the primary interest in campaign evaluation is knowing if there is a relationship between the advertising and consumer knowledge, this is usually not possible. Four methods of measuring awareness are used.

1. *Yes-or-no questions.* Example: "Have you heard of Fred's Flour" Yes _____ No _____. While the yes-no questions are simple to administer and tabulate, no information is gained beyond the direct answer.

2. *Open-end questions.* Example: "What companies can you name that package flour?" Here, more information is obtained than that in a yes-no situation, but no relationship to the advertising campaign is developed.

3. *Checklist questions.* Example: "Which of the following products does Fred's Company manufacture?" Flour _____ Rolling pins _____ Automobiles _____ Electronic computers _____. Here the answers are easily obtained and the range of answers is restricted. As in the open-end and yes-no questions, again no connection with the advertising campaign is developed.

4. *Rating scales.* Examples: "How would you rate Fred's Flour in comparison with other brands of flour you have used." Better _____ About the same as _____ Not as good as _____. With this approach, a measure of familiarity is achieved, but differences among the persons doing the rating make it difficult to combine answers or interpret the exact results. Additional scales or other approaches are sometimes used to make this form of measurement more reliable.

Measurement of awareness through the above techniques is usually quick and fairly low in cost since it can be done through the mail or by telephone interview. The results are easy to tabulate and generally straightforward. These advantages are balanced by the lack of knowledge of a significant change in awareness, e.g., awareness may have been higher before the campaign than after. This change is not measurable with a straight awareness approach. In addition, it is difficult to determine the source of the awareness. Awareness may or may not have come from the advertising campaign. While awareness is important to the evaluation of the campaign, it is the simplest of all measures and does not, in most cases, provide a direct relationship.

Measuring recall

In campaign evaluation, measuring recall is determining the amount of knowledge among consumers that can be directly related to the advertising and identifying the campaign as the source of that knowledge. Recall is normally used to determine the extent to which advertising messages have been retained by consumers. Although tenuous, the assumption is made that recall of an advertising message and purchase behavior are related. Thus, recall is believed to be an important measure for the advertising campaign.

Two types of recall are measured, aided and unaided.

Unaided recall. Example: "Can you recall any brands of flour being advertised in the last few weeks?" In this instance, the respondent is given no clues as to what brand is being investigated or what additional questions might be asked. The respondent must recall any or all advertising messages he or she might have seen in the past and relate them to the question. The assumption is made that advertising remembered without any direction from the interviewer is stronger than that in which information is given.

Aided recall. Example: "Do you remember seeing or hearing any advertising for Fred's Flour recently?" Here the respondent's reply is aided by the brand name. Thus, rather than trying to remember all flour advertising, the respondent can concentrate on the particular brand. Care must be taken that not too much aid is given or the respondent may resort to guessing rather than recalling.

The major advantage of measuring recall is that it allows you to measure at least one aspect of the advertising campaign. If the respondent remembers the campaign message or portions of the actual advertising, a direct correlation can be made. The main problem, which was alluded to previously, is that recall and purchase behavior may not be directly connected. In other words, the person may *recall* the message. But that message may have no effect when the purchase decision is made. Moreover, many campaigns are quite similar over the years. Thus, the respondent may recall a previous advertising message and put it into the context of the present campaign. In these cases, it is extremely difficult to identify or isolate specific campaign features.

Measuring attitudes

Recall tests and attitude tests are often combined in an attempt to determine if there are major differences between those consumers who remember the advertising message and those who don't. In addition, attitude tests are often used to measure changes in consumer perception of a product or the degree of acceptance of various claims made through advertising when they are used over a period of time.

Five basic techniques are used to measure attitudes and relate them to advertising campaigns.

1. *Direct questions.* Example: "How would you describe the use of Fred's Flour for baking?" Here, only a favorable or unfavorable attitude toward the product is measured. The level or degree of feeling is not possible with this type of question. As a result, this is often combined with the next type of question which is a rating scale.

2. *Rating scales.* Example: "How would you describe the self-measuring spout on Fred's Flour package?" Very easy to use _____ Easy to use _____ Neither easy nor hard to use _____ Hard to use _____ Very hard to use _____. While the scales are easy to apply and tabulate, the main problem with this type of question is the view of the respondent. A "Very easy to use" answer by one person may be the same as an "Easy to use" response from another. In other words, the scale does not discriminate sufficiently to permit a precise line to be drawn between the various attitudes.

3. *Checklists.* Example: "Which of the following are most important to you when you purchase flour?" Price _____ Package _____ Pre-sifted _____ Reputation of manufacturer _____. Here, the attributes under study may be easily ranked by the respondents and easily tabulated by the advertiser. The primary problem, however, is that one is never sure that the most important factors have been isolated and listed on the questionnaire. In addition, the meaning of each of the questions is not always as clear as one might want them to be. For example, does "Reputation of manufacturer" mean the same thing to all respondents?

4. *Semantic differential tests.* Example: "Would you say the user of Fred's Flour is:

A good cook   __ __ __ __ __   A poor cook
Extravagant   __ __ __ __ __   Price-conscious

Paired opposite descriptive words or phrases are separated on a scale. The respondent is allowed to check the place on the scale where he or she would place the product. In this way the respondent's attitude toward the product is determined. The scale is easy to use and the results are simple to tabulate. The major problem with this type of measure is that the scale may not be interpreted by all respondents in the same manner.

5. *Partially structured interviews.* Example: "I'd like for you to tell me some of your feelings about baking and the ingredients you use such as flour, butter, and milk." Here, the attempt is made to allow the respondent to discuss the general topic area and reveal attitudes about the product without using a specific set of questions. While the interviewer knows the general areas about which information and attitudes are sought, the use of the unstructured interview allows the respondent an opportunity to indicate areas of interest which might not have been previously considered.

Attitudinal tests are regarded as quite important in advertising campaign evaluation. A favorable attitude is considered to be an indication that the person is more likely to purchase a product than if he or she has an unfavorable attitude. As a result, changes in attitudes are regarded as more important in campaign evaluation than awareness or recall. Unfortunately, there is little evidence that a favorable attitude will always result in behavioral change, such as purchase of a product. In addition, the use of attitude measurements is open to question because it is most difficult to obtain an accurate measure of people's attitudes about any subject.

Measuring brand usage

Brand usage is the final measure of the effectiveness of an advertising campaign. While we have stressed that advertising should be considered only on the basis of communication effects, many advertisers try to trace the results directly by measuring such things as movement of goods through store audits, pantry audits, and consumer panels. When consumer interviews are used, they consist primarily of a series of questions about past, present, and future brand usage. For example,

1. "What brand of flour do you normally purchase?" Fred's _____ Harry's _____ Aunt Ethel's _____ Brand X _____.

2. "What brand of flour did you buy last?" Fred's _____ Harry's _____ Aunt Ethel's _____ Brand X _____.

3. "What brand of flour do you think you will buy next?" Fred's _____ Harry's _____ Aunt Ethel's _____ Brand X _____.

By using this type of consumer questionnaire, primarily used on a pre-test-post-test basis, we can measure changes in purchasing habits. When these changes are combined with tests of awareness, recall, and attitudes, determination of the effects of an advertising campaign is sometimes possible. While the relationship is somewhat tenuous, the attempt to relate advertising to sales is sometimes fruitful when all variables can be controlled.[6]

How to measure the campaign

Traditionally, campaigns have been evaluated at the conclusion of the schedule. With increasing media costs and changing market conditions, however, many advertisers now evaluate the advertising campaign while it is in progress. Because advertising pretesting was discussed earlier, only concurrent testing and posttesting are discussed here. In addition, market testing—a totally separate form of evaluation which is often used prior to the introduction of a national advertising campaign—will be reviewed.

Concurrent testing

Concurrent testing simply means the advertising campaign is evaluated as it is running in the marketplace. There are several advantages in this technique: (a) it gives an opportunity to quickly determine if the campaign is reaching the intended market, (b) it helps to determine whether the messages being sent out are being interpreted as intended, and (c) it measures the effects the messages are having on the target market.

If any of the measures reveal that the campaign is not on target, adjustments can be made to correct the problem immediately; one need not wait until the end of the schedule.

Three basic methods of gathering information about an advertising campaign on a concurrent basis are available: coincidental surveys, consumer diaries, and advertising tracking studies.

Coincidental studies. These are attempts to measure consumer exposure to the advertising while it is appearing. The technique is particularly effective with broadcast. The most common type of coincidental study is the telephone interview. For example, assume an advertiser wants to determine if his or her advertising message is reaching the correct target audience. Telephone calls to members of the target market are made while his or her advertising is being broadcast on either radio or television. By determining what stations or shows are being seen or heard, the advertiser can determine through a survey whether or not the target audience is hearing the message and, if so, what information or meaning is being received. Because coincidental surveys are designed to furnish only very basic data, little information is obtained other than a quick

reading of message distribution and general information content.

Consumer diaries. These are used by some advertisers to record the behavior of persons in their target market. For example, customers or prospects may keep diaries of such activities as media usage, purchases, exposure to competitive promotions, and use of coupons. By reviewing the diaries, an advertiser may determine if his or her advertising message is being exposed to the target market and what effect this exposure has. If the respondents are exposed to the advertising message and no attitude or behavior changes occur, the advertiser may decide the message is not effective. There are obvious limitations on the amount of information that can be obtained through diaries, but the methodology often serves as an early warning system for spotting potential strengths or weaknesses in an advertising campaign.

Tracking studies. These usually consist of consumer interviews during the course of the campaign. The purpose of these studies is to determine the levels of exposure and effect that are being achieved by the advertising campaign. Because it is commonly agreed that advertising effects build over time, the tracking studies are usually conducted in "waves" or according to a predetermined schedule. An example may help to explain the tracking concept and the manner in which it is conducted.

Assume that on March 1 a new advertising campaign for Brand P is started. In the advertising plan, tracking studies incorporating a telephone methodology have been planned for April 1 and June 1.

On April 1, a series of random telephone calls is made to consumers. The sample size is sufficiently large so that reasonable assumptions may be made about the results. The questions asked are such things as, "Have you seen or heard any advertising for the (Brand P's) category?" If advertising in the category has been seen or heard by the consumer, the next question is, "What brand was it for?" This is followed by such additional questions as, "In what medium was the advertising seen or heard?" "What did the advertising say?" "What brand do you normally buy?" This first study establishes a benchmark for the campaign. In addition, the study spotlights such items as lack of exposure with prospects, misunderstanding of the message, and misidentification of the sponsor that might be occurring. Based on this first "wave," the advertiser can then make any necessary adjustments.

Again, on June 1, another series of random telephone calls is made asking the same questions. Under the assumption that the samples are comparable, comparisons can be made between the first and second "waves" or studies to determine any changes which might have occurred. In addition, it can be learned if the changes made after the first study have corrected any of the problems previously found.

Tracking studies of this kind can be conducted at any time during the campaign at normal intervals of about 60 days. For some product categories, a shorter or longer time period may be required.

Telephone studies are the most common form of tracking although tracking may be done through personal interview or diaries or by other means. Other means of concurrent testing are available but these three are primary.

The major advantage of concurrent testing is the rapid accumulation of information. Based on this information, campaign decisions can be made quickly and efficiently. The major disadvantage is the limited amount of information that can be obtained. Also, since concurrent testing takes place during the campaign, a quick reading may often not accurately reflect what the final results might be.

The Post-test

The traditional campaign evaluation approach is the post-test, which is conducted at the conclusion of the campaign. While data gathering through panels, diaries, personal interviews, telephone surveys, and other means is common to both the concurrent and the post-test, the primary purpose of this measure is to evaluate the final results of the campaign against the predetermined advertising goals or objectives.

In a standard post-test, consumers in the target market or area in which the campaign was conducted are questioned about the advertising and the effects of the message on their opinions, attitudes, and behavior. These results are then weighed against the objectives and goals of the advertising campaign to determine if satisfactory results were achieved for the advertising investment.

The major problem in post-testing is lack of information on changes that may have been caused by the advertising campaign. Unless concurrent testing has been done, little may be known about consumer attitudes toward and opinions about the product prior to the time the advertising messages were placed in the media. It is difficult to determine, therefore, if advertising had the desired effect or if the attitude and opinions found in the post-test were already present. A measurement technique called the *pre-post test* is often used to solve this problem.

In the pre-post testing technique, advertisers conduct a pretest in the market before launching the advertising campaign. This provides a benchmark for later evaluation. By knowing what attitudes and opinions were held by consumers prior to the start of the campaign, a comparison can be made with the findings after the campaign has run.

For example, assume the advertising goal for a specific campaign was to raise the awareness level about a particular product benefit within the target market population by 25 percent. Without a pretest, it would be difficult to determine if the goal had been achieved at the end of the campaign or if that level was already present. Assume further that a pretest was conducted in the market and an awareness level of 16 percent was found among the target group. Thus, for achievement of the goal of 25 percent increase, awareness of the product benefit at the end of the campaign would have to measure at least 20 percent (a 25 percent increase over the 16 percent base). If, after the campaign had been run, it was found that the awareness level of the specific product benefit was 32 percent among the target population, the campaign could be judged very successful; the advertising goal was only a 25 percent increase in awareness and a 50 percent increase was achieved.

The post-test and pre-post technique can be used to evaluate almost any campaign objective. The chief distinction of the methodology is that the study is conducted after the campaign has been run and there is no opportunity for change or revision. This inability to change or revise is also the chief disadvantage.

Test areas and control groups

A useful way to evaluate a specific advertising campaign on a limited basis is through test areas and control groups. This technique is widely used to evaluate the advertising campaign for new products. It is usually conducted prior to a widespread use of the campaign or a national roll out.

Cities or areas are selected for the test and matched as closely as possible. For example, three different areas might be selected to test an advertising campaign. A similar group of three areas matching as nearly as possible the geographic, demographic, and product-usage patterns of the test cities would then be identified. The advertising campaign being evaluated would be conducted in the three test areas. The three matching markets would receive no advertising and would serve as controls. At the end of the test campaign, studies and comparisons of advertising effects would be made between the test and control markets to determine differences. Because the areas were matched as closely as possible, it can be assumed the advertising campaign in the advertised markets would be the reason for any differences found.

The major advantage of the test-and-control approach is the comparatively low cost of placing and evaluating the campaign in a few limited areas as opposed to widespread use without testing. In addition, if necessary, changes can be made in the materials after the test results are obtained. The major disadvantage of this evaluation method is the difficulty of matching the control and test areas and the possibility that competition may "read" the test and learn what is planned for the future.

Syndicated and custom research techniques

A number of syndicated research services specialize in the evaluation of advertising campaigns and individual advertisements. Because these services vary so greatly in methodology, only the major techniques are discussed. Those who wish to investigate specific techniques should consult the individual organization offering the services.

Syndicated print techniques

The most common technique for evaluating print advertisements or campaigns is that employed by Daniel Starch and Staff. Although Starch studies are designed primarily to evaluate individual advertisements in magazines, the technique can be adapted to other forms of print.

The Starch technique consists of a recognition-and-recall test. First a list of magazines which respondents believe they have seen before is compiled. Based on their acknowledged exposure to the publication, respondents are taken through the magazine page by page and are asked questions about each advertisement one-half page or larger. The basic question is whether the respondent recalls having seen or read any part of the advertisement. Based on the response, a rating is made of the reader's involvement with each advertisement recognized. Every advertisement in the issue is scored. Advertisers may then compare the score of their advertisement to the scores of others in the same product category or to all advertisements in the magazine.

Other organizations such as Gallup & Robinson offer evaluations of print advertisements and nearly all follow some form of the recognition-and-recall technique.

Starch and Gallup & Robinson syndicated services are widely used by many advertisers. Some advertisers and agencies, however, have reservations about this form of measurement. They cite the fact that these techniques measure only the recall of the advertisement by the reader and not the selling effectiveness or the persuasive ability of the ad as a whole. In some cases, the argument goes, the very devices used to gain memorability and recall in a Starch or Gallup & Robinson study may work against developing a strong sales message. That is, an advertisement by its unusual nature may be remembered for itself but the product or

sales message forgotten. At best, Starch and Gallup & Robinson scores measure only one aspect of print advertising—the ability to be recalled. This should be kept in mind when you are considering this approach to advertising evaluation.

Syndicated broadcast techniques

Many more services are available to evaluate broadcast advertising, primarily television, than print. Almost all, however, use one of three basic methodologies for commercial testing: (a) on-air systems; (b) in-theater systems; and (c) forced viewing. All are used extensively for pretesting as well as evaluation. All were discussed in chapter 7.

Custom research

The following custom research methodologies are those which are most commonly used in advertising campaign evaluation rather than for evaluation of individual advertisements. There are, no doubt, other methods in use but these appear to be the most popular.

Personal interviews. These are usually considered the most accurate of all advertising campaign evaluation techniques. Whether the evaluation centers on past purchase behavior, understanding of present campaign messages, or questions about competitive activity, the personal interview is usually able to elicit the information from the respondent.

Personal interviews may take many forms from traditional door-to-door to mall intercepts. The major advantage is the opportunity for face-to-face discussion and clarification of answers to the questions asked. The major disadvantages are the extremely high cost of personal data gathering and the inability of interviewers to make contact with people not at home or to contact respondents in certain urban areas.

Consumer panels. These have been widely used to gather all types of advertising information. Panels consist of respondents who agree either to keep records or to answer inquiries on an on-going basis. Questions asked the panel may take almost any form. The major advantage of the panel is the high rate of return from the respondents, since they are usually committed to the techniques. The major disadvantage is the lack of selectivity among the respondents. In addition, the panel response technique consists of polling those who have agreed to participate. This group may or may not be representative of the whole population.

Mailed questionnaires. Sending questionnaires is a relatively low-cost method of obtaining an evaluation of an advertising campaign. The mail questionnaire offers many advantages—from selection of the sample to wide geographic distribution for response. Usually, more detailed questions can be asked in a mail survey than any other form. The main disadvantage is the length of time needed to carry out the study and the often low return response rate. Mail surveys, for evaluating advertising campaigns, in spite of the problems continue to be a widely used form of data gathering.

Telephone interviewing. This is an increasingly popular form of data gathering for campaign evaluation. The telephone call has many of the advantages of the personal interview, yet it is much less expensive. It can be used in areas where personal interviews cannot be made and, often, respondents will answer questions by telephone they will not answer any other way. The obvious disadvantages of telephoning are inability to show advertising materials and asking very complex questions. The innovation of WATS (Wide Area Telephone Service) has enabled advertisers and researchers to poll people on advertising campaigns all over the country from one central location.

Most commercial research organizations can develop an evaluation plan using either one or a combination of the above techniques. The cost of the evaluation will vary widely based on the size of the sample, the geographic area to be covered, the type of product, and the methodology employed. For example, a post-campaign study for a widely used consumer package-goods brand with 1,000 telephone interviews in each of two markets would cost from about $5,000 to $7,000.

Some research organizations offer a syndicated form of custom research for campaign evaluation. Usually, this methodology requires the advertisers to submit one, two, or more questions about the campaign to the research organization. That organization has several noncompetitive advertisers who have done the same. The questions are then combined into a usable format, and a certain number of consumers are contacted and the questions asked. Because several advertisers have combined, the price is usually much lower than that for an individual study. Another form of evaluation study is for a research organization to investigate several product categories through consumer studies, compile the data, and then offer this information to the various companies at a flat rate.

Sales results. While our primary emphasis has been on the communication effects of the campaign, advertisers often also use sales or marketing information for evaluation. The chief methods are internal sales data and syndicated or custom research.

Internal sales data are used to learn if product sales are responding to the advertising campaign. This effect can be measured either through comparisons to previous periods or against sales goals which have been set for the brand. A widely used source of information

comes from broker or sales force reports.

Syndicated or custom research usually consists of the subscription to such auditing services as The Nielsen Retail Index or SAMI. Nielsen makes bimonthly studies of retail food and drugstores to obtain information on distribution levels, penetration of the product into different types of stores, share of national case volume, share of in-store distribution, product movement, and activities of competitors. SAMI offers a service that measures warehouse withdrawals by food and drugstores thus indicating the popularity of the product at retail.

While many marketing variables are involved in the sale of the product, if sales measurement techniques such as The Nielsen Retail Index are used, one can sometimes determine if the failure or success of the product can be related to the advertising campaign.

Other methods of advertising campaign evaluation such as personal observation and expert opinion are sometimes used. The methods listed above, however, make up the bulk of the data gathering and evaluation techniques.

In summary, the methodology used for campaign evaluation may vary according to such factors as available funds, type of campaign to be evaluated, geographic area, type of product, and advertising media used. Thus, there is no one best way or predetermined methodology that should be used for any given campaign or any type of advertiser. The evaluation should be developed to fit the needs of the advertiser and the marketplace.

The major point of any advertising campaign evaluation is to be sure the technique measures the objectives stated in the campaign strategy. If the intent is to measure advertising awareness, the methodology used should be keyed to fit that goal. If, on the other hand, the goal of the campaign is to increase product preference, the evaluation methodology may be vastly different. Like the development of an advertising campaign, there is no hard and fast rule for evaluation. As the saying goes, it all depends.

Evaluating the evaluation

For purposes of evaluating the evaluation, certain questions should be asked about the research itself. While numerous considerations can be cited for any research study, Broadbent suggests four areas:

1. Is the sample representative? Obviously, the respondents in the evaluation sample should be members of the target market to whom the advertising campaign is directed. The advertising may do an excellent job of communicating the sales message to women 35 to 49 years of age. But that's of little value if the target group for whom the advertising is intended is young men 18 to 24. The groups simply aren't that much alike.

2. Does the respondent understand the questions you're asking? Too many times, in follow-up interviews, it has been found that respondents didn't actually understand the questions they were asked. As a result of this misunderstanding, garbled—or even worse— misleading or incorrect information was obtained. To be able to reply with the information sought, the respondent must understand the question being asked.

3. Are the conclusions drawn from the advertising campaign evaluation substantiated? Leaping to conclusions is prevalent in campaign evaluation. Because so much time and effort have gone into the campaign, the creators are sometimes inclined to explain away problems or to assume, as accepted, things that may not be true. The research conclusions reached in the campaign must be based solely on the information gathered and reported with a minimum of explanation required.

4. Was the sample large enough? A frequent problem in campaign evaluation is finding enough respondents who have seen or are familiar with the advertising to make an adequate evaluation of it. The problem becomes crucial for products that have a small market share, are purchased infrequently, or have a limited media schedule. Yet, for meaningful conclusions to be drawn, the sample base must be of a sufficient size to be statistically accurate.[7]

Test marketing

While not specifically a method of campaign evaluation, the test market is essentially a trial of the proposed campaign on a reduced scale. As such, test markets could be regarded as a form of pretesting or a form of campaign evaluation. Because the test market gives us an opportunity to see how the campaign will work on a small scale, it is placed in the evaluation area in this text.

Many reasons exist for using a test market. Three of the major ones are:

1. A trial of the campaign. With marketers attempting to take more and more of the risk out of advertising, the test market offers an excellent opportunity to try out the campaign. By testing the campaign in a smaller market or on a reduced scale, the advertiser has the opportunity of seeing how it might work and of making any needed fine-tuning adjustments before moving the campaign into the larger more expensive broad-scale market.

2. An opportunity to try variations. Where alternative campaigns have been developed, test markets allow an advertiser to try the variations in an actual market setting to determine the best choice. For example, two or more campaign themes may have been developed,

each of which has performed about the same in a pretest format. The test market allows the measure to be made in a "real-world" setting and the results to be evaluated.

3. A way to reduce the financial risk. With the increasing cost of media and the need to reduce advertising investments as much as possible, the test market gives the advertiser an opportunity to try a campaign in a controlled risk situation. A failure in a test market is not nearly so costly as one on a national scale.

Types of test markets

While test markets may be developed for many reasons, three essential purposes predominate:

1. Product test. The product test is an opportunity to learn how the product or service is accepted by consumers prior to a national or broad-scale introduction. While preliminary laboratory tests may have proved successful, the acid test for a new product is the response or results in the actual marketplace.

2. Advertising test. Like the product test, the advertising test is an opportunity to try the advertising campaign on a reduced scale prior to a rollout. As mentioned previously, the advertising program may be fine tuned as a result of test market results or alternatives evaluated on their success or failure in a test market.

3. Media weight tests/spending level tests. Advertisers often use test markets to evaluate various levels of media weight or various levels of advertising spending. The use of these tests gives the advertiser the opportunity to determine the most effective and efficient spending level for achieving the advertising goals.

How to develop a test market

Two basic steps are needed in developing a test market plan. First, the broad-scale or national plan must be developed. This is the advertising campaign that would be used provided the test market plan is successful. In other words, all parts of the major program must first be developed in detail. The second step is to reproduce this broad-scale program in miniature, in other words, the major plan is then scaled down to fit the test market or markets selected. This is usually done through a translation of the broad-scale program in the form of a percentage of expenditure or investment. For example, if the proposed national advertising investment for the campaign is planned at $5,000,000, the test-market expenditure would be determined based on the test-market size as a percentage of the national program. In this case, if Fort Wayne, Indiana, was selected as the test market, and the population of Fort Wayne was determined to be 1 percent of the planned size of the national campaign, then the investment in Fort Wayne would be $50,000

($5,000,000 × .01 = $50,000). Other relationships may be used, but population, size of the test market as a part of the broad-scale plan, and percentage of media costs are often used as methods for determining the amount to be invested in the test market. In addition to the estimated advertising campaign costs, other investments such as sales promotion programs, and consumer incentives are scaled to fit the test market. The entire broad-scale plan is miniaturized to fit the test market; it represents what the larger plan would be on a proportionate basis.

Developing a test market plan

Three major factors should be considered in developing a test market plan.

1. Test market size and location. The proposed test market must be large enough to be reasonably representative of the broad-scale market. While test markets should be small enough to control and evaluate, they must be large enough and have enough of the pertinent market variables for the campaign to get a fair test. The test market should be of sufficient size so that the national competitive climate is represented. The same competitors should be present in the test market with approximately the same competitive weight as that found in the national market.

The test market must also be capable of satisfactorily reproducing the national media plan. For example, if the national plan calls for the use of newspaper supplements, the test market must provide newspaper supplements for an adequate test. Attempting to test a media plan on a reduced scale with other media forms can often be misleading in respect to what national results might be.

While the test market must be large enough to give the campaign a fair test, it must be small enough to reduce the financial risk to worthwhile proportions. For example, New York City might represent the national program exactly, but it would make a poor test market simply because of the amount of investment required to conduct the test.

2. Duration of the test. A second major factor is determining the length of a test market. This decision is usually based on the minimum amount of time required to accurately measure the results. Thus, there is no hard and fast rule on how long a test market should run. Two major factors are usually considered: (a) The test should run long enough to permit checking the initial levels of product distribution, trade stocking, and displays. With some products, this could be a matter of days and, with others, weeks or even months may be required to take the product through the distribution channels. (b) There should be sufficient time to allow for the formation of a clear assessment of the level of

consumer trial and the proportion of repeat purchases. In other words, a short test might be misleading as consumers try the product initially but fail to make repeat purchases. Advertisers frequently have read the results of a test market incorrectly because their interpretation was based on initial purchases. The lack of repeat purchases after the first trial was not evaluated and, as a result, what appeared to be a successful product was, in reality, a failure. The same is true of the advertising campaign. Initial awareness might be very high, but knowledge and preference might not develop. Unless sufficient time is allowed for the test market to show the full results of the campaign, the results could be misleading.

3. Measurement and control of results. The final factor in the determination of the relative success of a test market is the ability to measure the results. Closely allied with that is the control the advertiser has over obtaining or gathering the results of the test market. It does little good to develop a test market and then not be able to obtain the necessary test results or not be able to control some of the factors in the market that would prevent an accurate appraisal. For example, attempting to use a test market in which obtaining sales figures for the product is very difficult only compounds the problem. If a test market is to be used, the measurement and control of the results of that test are vital.

Test market problems

While test marketing is gaining favor with advertisers in most categories, two major problems must be recognized.

1. Competition reading test. In most good test markets, it is as easy for competition to obtain information about the test market as it is for the advertiser. Because all marketers use many of the same techniques and often the same syndicated information sources, it is a simple matter for a competitor to watch a test market while it is in progress. When this occurs, the competitor often knows the success or failure of the campaign as quickly as the advertiser. With this knowledge, a competitor often is able to react and generate a campaign which would offset an advertiser's success. Usually, no matter what steps are taken, a competitor can read a test market and learn from either its success or mistakes. This is the major disadvantage of test marketing.

2. Competition destroys the test market. Competitors may also take market actions that will give a false reading to the test market. For example, if a campaign is developed with a strong competitive price story, a competitor might lower his price in the test market to make the results inconclusive. A competitor often prefers to destroy the test market with competitive activities rather than risk facing the results of the successful test. In other words, if the test proves successful, the cost to the competitor to combat the results would be greater on a broad-scale basis than on a test alone. Thus, the competitor chooses to muddy the test rather than allow the advertiser to develop a successful approach.

In spite of the cost of development and the risks involved, test markets are an excellent way to learn how an advertising campaign would perform in a "real-world" setting at a reasonable cost.[8]

Evaluating a test market

There are fundamental differences between advertising campaign evaluation in a test market for a new product and an on-going campaign for an established product. Much of the preceding discussion has assumed either that the product is established or that the advertising is sufficiently widespread so that a test situation is not the case. A brief overview of the evaluation of a test market advertising campaign follows.

Advertising awareness is usually the major evaluation measurement in a test market. Because the product is new and, in some cases, may be the first of its kind in the market, just making consumers aware of the product or the benefit may be the key ingredient for success. Because advertising usually has the double task of obtaining consumer product awareness and registering the product name among many confusing competitors, simple awareness may be a justifiable advertising evaluation measure, provided it has been stated as an advertising goal.

Distribution of the product can also be an advertising goal in a test market. Because new products have no track record in the marketplace, retailers are sometimes hesitant to stock them until they are in demand. Thus, the use of consumer advertising to "pull" the product through distribution channels is often stated as an advertising objective.

When advertising is powerful enough to have customers ask for the product, particularly to the extent that retailers feel it necessary to stock it, the campaign is usually considered effective. Similarly, if advertising in a test market fails to sufficiently convince customers so they go to the store and purchase the product after distribution has been achieved, then retailers may discontinue the product. While distribution was obtained, the advertising was not powerful enough to generate a consumer behavioral change.

Sales may well be a logical evaluative basis for an advertising campaign in a test market, all other factors being equal. Many test products are unknown and rely almost entirely on advertising for achieving awareness, and, ultimately, sales. In these cases, traditional market variables that impinge on an existing product may not be present for a test product. Thus, it may be possible to gauge the strength of the advertising campaign on the basis of sales in a test situation. This seems to be particularly true for a product that is the first entry in a new category or is the newest brand in an existing product category.

Notes

1. Gail Smith, "How GM Measures Ad Effectiveness," *Printer's Ink,* 14 May 1965, pp. 19–20.
2. Kenneth A. Longman, *Advertising* (New York: Harcourt Brace Jovanovich, 1971), pp. 29–33.
3. Simon Broadbent, *Spending Advertising Money* (London: Business Books, 1975), pp. 212-13.
4. H. S. Zielske, "The Remembering and Forgetting of Advertising," *Journal of Marketing*, January 1959, pp. 239-43.
5. Robert J. Lavidge and Gary A. Steiner, "A Model for Predictive Measurements of Advertising Effectiveness," *Journal of Marketing*, October 1961, pp. 61.
6. Harry Dean Wolfe, James K. Brown, and G. Clark Thompson, *Measuring Advertising Results*: Studies in Business Policy #102 (New York: Industrial Conference Board, 1962).
7. Broadbent, *Spending Advertising Money,* pp. 210-43.
8. Gordon Medcalf, *Marketing and the Brand Manager* (Oxford, England: Pergamon Press, 1967), pp. 202–207.

11

How to Make Winning Presentations

Ron Hoff, creative director for Foote Cone & Belding, interviewed several senior agency persons in New York and Chicago to find out exactly what bugged them about presenters. The following "dirty laundry list" tells what is wrong with most presentations. After citing the problems, the rest of this chapter gives specific proven solutions.

David Ogilvy:

"Most presenters are incoherent."

"I don't know what they're talking about."

"Why doesn't anybody start with a short summary of the problem, the research, the strategy, the promise, the media . . . *three minutes worth.*"

". . . listen before you talk."

"I don't know whether to read what he's *showing* or listen to what he's *saying.*"

". . . no evidence that the presenter has taken great pains with his presentation."

Arthur Schultz:

"They just don't sell; lack of support for what you're recommending."

"We often repeat what somebody else just said. 'What I think David was trying to say. . . .' "

This chapter was condensed from the writings of three senior advertising executives. Drawing from years of experience in internationally famous agencies, they have agreed to share the secrets of their success (and failure) in making client presentations. The late Andrew Kershaw was chairman, Ogilvy and Mather, when he wrote *How To Make Agency Presentations.* Ronald Hoff, executive creative director, Foote, Cone & Belding/New York, is author of a national workshop course, *Agency Presentations.* Paul Repetto, who spent 20 years in the advertising business with N. W. Ayer and Foote, Cone & Belding/Los Angeles,is author of an *Advertising Age* workshop lecture on *Agency Presentations.* Credit to these authors is given in context throughout chapter 11.

"Jargon. It's embarrassing."

"Don't paraphrase slides. Read them word for word."

David Ofner:

"No explanation at the start of *why we are gathered here.* No clear agenda."

"No sense of direction. Imprecise."

"Our presenters lack presence, authority."

"We don't know how to win. . . ."

John O'Toole:

"The purpose of personal presentations is to leave the prospect with the feeling that each of the presenters, with whom he will probably be spending more time than his wife, is the brightest, most professional, most capable person available in the agency business. Precious few of our presenters leave that impression."

Harvey Clements:

"We don't pay attention to lighting. Should be carefully set up and tested."

"We don't plan for involvement by the audience."

"Too many extraneous slides."

"Don't tell the audience how wonderful you think the recommendations are. If the stuff is good, they'll know it."

David Berger:

"The general failing is treating the presentation as yours, instead of the audience's. Presenting what *you* did rather than what *they* need."

"In terms of research this means emphasizing the study rather than the problem and the solution. In terms of media it means counting gross rating points instead of conveying a sense of *how much* advertising people will encounter."

"In terms of account management this means conveying the fact that you did your homework rather than what the listener needs to know."

"In terms of creative it means presenting how hard you worked rather than how the selling problem is being attacked."

Bryan Putnam:

"Too many presenters—amount of detail."

"Presentations in an informal way."

Chuck Winston:

"Too much time on everything."

"We answer the same question over and over. We seem to think that *one* answer for one question is somehow painfully inadequate."

After the critics had spoken, Ron Hoff boiled their grievances down into three cardinal sins.

- Imprecise
- Unorganized
- Deadly dull

Checklist for preparation

It's easy to avoid these sins if you *prepare*. Look over the following list and spend your time working on areas in which you need to improve.

- Allow enough time for preparation or suffer doom.
- Focus on the lion.
- Treat the client as a person, not an advertising pro.
- Focus attention on the subject.
- Do's and don'ts on opening and closing.
- Approach the client's problem from his point of view—sales.
- Select your presenters carefully.
- The production—pay attention to details.
- How to show off your work.
- Visual aids—getting past the optic nerve.
- Questions—the sudden-death round.
- You can't over-rehearse.
- A checklist of 119 questions and tips.

Allow enough time for preparation or suffer doom

The marketing, media, and creative are dynamite. Now it's time to present this delicate newborn child to the client. Will the client agree with you? Will he or she see the brilliance? Will he or she embrace it and love it? Only if you put the same loving care into *presenting* the work as you did in creating it. You can't rush it. Remember, the presentation is a finished commercial for your agency. The presentation *is* the agency. To wing it without solid preparation is a waste of everyone's time.

In too many cases, the presentation is treated like a bastard child. It gets whatever scraps of time are left

over once everything else is done. Perhaps in one day or a night a hundred slides are shot, developed, and then thrown into a carousel. We rationalize that the stuff is so great, it won't matter how we present it, the client will rave over it. Foolish thinking. Most clients expect to see evidence of great care and concern on their behalf. Magnificent work can easily be ignored if it is presented in beggar's clothing.

Focus on the lion

Invariably there is one key person whose blessing is crucial to your success. One in the group you present to will be the *lion,* the others the lambs. Seek the out the lion and be sure to give him or her plenty of eye contact during the presentation. Also, tailor your presentation especially for the lion.

Andrew Kershaw tells how:

In one case, not so long ago, our intelligence came from a former Ogilvy and Mather employee—now working in a division of the prospect company. He characterized the prospect as a martinet, with a great attachment to rigid methods and rules. Another source said that our prospect had been heard to praise our house advertisements, to which he referred as "The Tablets."

Putting this to good use, we built our presentation on the theme of "discipline in advertising." We got the business.

Kershaw emphasizes that intelligence should be verified by two or more reliable sources. You take a very big chance tailoring your whole presentation based on one person's judgment. Especially if you do not know that person very well.

Treat the client as a person, not an advertising pro (according to Paul Repetto)

It's simply more realistic to admit that advertisers are less interested in advertising per se than we are. Their minds are cluttered with a host of other marketing problems besides advertising. Advertising is not their daily bread, it's *our* daily bread.

Repetto points out two very important problems that result. First, the client has other things on his or her mind. Plus, the client feels uneasy "sitting on the bench" as the supreme judge of advertising. The client knows deep inside that he or she is not really the expert; you are. So, he or she feels threatened. The client is sitting in front of peers—wide open and vulnerable. A person's natural strategy in this situation is to shield him- or herself, *to take a defensive posture.* Repetto gives the following admonition:

Failure to recognize the fact that you are in an adversary role with the key person kills more presentations than any other single factor.

Reduce the tension—use a warm-up

Andrew Kershaw recalls the time when he was the

client prospect and Ogilvy and Mather was the presenting agency. "We had the *warm-up* in David Ogilvy's office and then he led me into the conference room. . . ." Ogilvy clearly understood this potential adversary relationship. One reason for his great success is his understanding of human relations. He has a natural talent for putting people at ease. And that's the first step in overcoming this adversary relationship.

Focus attention on the subject

Paul Repetto suggests that a good way to start the presentation is with an agenda. Not a handout, that's distracting. Have the agenda on a poster board and say, "Here's what we're going to cover this morning." Now, you've done two important things. The client knows business has clearly started. The agenda rivets his or her attention to both you and the business. Equally important, the agenda helps reduce tension. Because now the client gets a clear picture of what's going to happen. No shocking surprises. The client knows you aren't trying to be manipulative. The client feels you trust him or her and respect his or her intelligence.

Restate the assignment (according to Paul Repetto)

Another simple way to reassure the key person is to restate the assignment, *using exactly the same words he used when he gave it to you.* First off, this reestablishes his authority and helps him feel secure in that role. Secondly, it tells him that you've heard him. And thirdly, it establishes the agency as the problem-solving partner of the client rather than the adversary.

Do's and don'ts on opening and closing

Andrew Kershaw offers some tips:

- Don't start with a funny story. That's amateurish.

- Don't start until after the beginning. (The actual beginning is not the real start.) How much warm-up time is needed is a very subjective thing. You have to feel your way along.

- Don't offer profuse thanks and claim what a privilege it is. It is undignified. But be polite and pleasant.

- A good way to start is with a businesslike agenda.

- You can find charming, gentle, and warm ways to introduce your team by name, rank, and function.

- When the "beginning" is over, *start with something memorable.* Your initial impression is critical. If it is dull, you will probably never win the audience over.

On closing

- Do not let the meeting end with a whimper or peter out with a recital of trivia.

- Make the closing memorable. The final impression must *move* the key person closer to agreeing with you.

- Put your strongest presenter at the end.

- Do not end with a peroration. A flowery rhetorical plea for the account sounds like a desperate prayer. Close confidently; boldly.

- A reprise is acceptable. Restate the client's original assignment and reinforce how you fulfilled it.

- Make your closing dramatic.

- The leave-behind or plans book must be well typed and contain all the important matters discussed during the presentation. Include a synopsis on each agency person who will be assigned to the account. Give full details on their experience, skills, and special strengths.

- The leave-behind should contain a list of names of present clients with addresses and phone numbers. Suggest that the prospect phone them for more information.

Approach the client's problem from his point of view

Ron Hoff believes that many advertising people have not learned to speak the client's language.

Your priorities are mixed up when you insist on cramming 107 of your objectives down the client's throat when his greatest interest is *his* objectives.

What kind of objective are we talking about? Marketing objective? Advertising objective? I submit that the *best* presentation technique is to state the *one* objective that is foremost in the client's mind. Advertising is generally judged in terms of sales—in terms of brand share. That's what this business is all about. When sales fall off, advertising agencies get fired. Don't present a whole slew of objectives. Present one . . . and write it from the client's point of view. Get to the heart of it. Don't mince words.

I recall going to a lot of agency Plans Board meetings. Invariably, by the end of the meeting, the walls would be loaded with objectives. Marketing objectives, advertising objectives, research objectives, creative objectives, media objectives—pretty soon it all turned into mulligan stew and you couldn't tell the potatoes from the tomatoes.

I submit to you that this does nothing but confuse everybody. When all the excess verbiage is ruthlessly boiled out of everything, your primary mission usually boils down to one basic objective. Be sure you give that objective center stage with bright flood lights on it.

Keep your language simple

Paul Repetto is fond of a little thing Arthur Kudner wrote to his son. It's all that needs to be said about communicating something important.

Never fear big, long words. Big long words name little things. All big things have little names. Such as life and death, peace and war, dawn, day, night, hope, love, home. Learn to use little words in a big way. It is hard to do, but they say what you mean. When you don't know what you mean, use big words. They often fool little people.

Select your presenters carefully

The art director may be exceptional in his or her field. Even brilliant. However, he or she may be a lousy speaker; nervous in front of people. Don't force the art director on stage just because he or she masterminded the creative strategy. Ideally, the client would like to see the people who will be working on his or her account. But exceptions can and should be made for people who do not feel comfortable presenting and who do not want to learn how to present.

Andrew Kershaw recommends that you not select the presenters until you know who will be in the audience and how many. People feel uncomfortable if they are outnumbered by the agency.

> All the agency people chosen to be present should have some functional role to play in the presentation. It is awful to watch someone sit silently during a presentation, a stuffed dummy, an obvious makeweight.

The production—pay attention to details

The first thing you must memorize about production is the *Presentation Law of Physics:*

> Agency equipment always breaks down *during* the client presentation. It is programmed that way by mad engineers at the factory.

There are thousands of stories about equipment failures killing presentations. And losing business. And they're all true. The tragic part is how wasteful and stupid we are by not having oil in our lamps so we are ready for any surprise. We deserve to lose the business when the client looks back and sees the projectionist with his pants down and no spare suspenders.

Kershaw admonished his people to "beware goofing on the staging." You can do everything right. Spend 100 work-hours getting the advertising ready. But one slip and "the audience will *forget the content* and remember only that the slide was upside down."

Here's a checklist based on Andrew Kershaw's experience in stage management. Don't start the presentation without it.

- Study the presentation room well in advance.
- Know where electrical outlets are.
- See if the room can be darkened.
- Is there a screen available?
- Can the lights be dimmed? Who will operate the light switches? Make sure the lighting has been tried and rehearsed.
- Avoid presenting in total darkness. If you can't see the whites of their eyes, and if they can't see yours,

you are asking for trouble—or snores.

- If the room lights cannot be dimmed, get some appropriate table lamps or floor lamps with low wattage bulbs.
- Do you need an easel to display your ads? Most ledges in board rooms are too narrow to hold ads.
- Your projectionist must always have spare bulbs and batteries. Make sure he or she has them. It's even a good idea to have a spare projector at the ready in case a slide jams and you can't fix it.
- You will need a pointer. Make sure everyone knows how to use it.
- Carefully arrange tables and chairs in advance. Avoid lining up prospect and agency people as opposing armies, glaring at each other across the table.
- Decide if a mike is necessary. Pray that it is not. But if the room is too large, make sure you test the sound system and have an engineer on hand in case of failure.
- Check out the lectern if you use one. Test the lights, test the lip that holds your papers, test the width for turning your pages. Test its height; you do not want to look diminuitive behind it, nor should you loom like the Green Giant.
- Provide your audience with note pads, pencils, and clean ash trays.

Ogilvy and Mather's presenter's survival kit

1. Long extension cords with multiple plug-in capacity
2. Projection bulbs for carousel and movie projector
3. An exciter lamp for movie projector
4. Push pins
5. A gum eraser
6. Black and colored felt pens (for fixing typos in charts)
7. An emergency splicer
8. Rolls of masking tape, Scotch tape, and duct tape

How to show off your work

Ron Hoff believes in creating excitement from the moment the client walks in the door. A good way to do that, according to Hoff, is "to show where the campaign will go without doing the whole campaign. Do a batch of headlines, blow them up, mount them, and place them around the room. It will look like you've done a ton of work—and the client will get the feeling the campaign could go on forever."

You can do the same thing with television. Display one board (or a reasonable facsimile thereof) and write brief synopses of follow-up commercials. Blow them up (include a visual of the key frame for each commercial) and display them about the room.

Andrew Kershaw was a believer in creating excitement, too. "If permitted, decorate the walls with ads. Show annual reports, merchandising, posters, booklets, brochures. Make it look exciting."

"Once we made a presentation thousands of miles from home," continued Kershaw. "We erected a temporary wall to display our work in the boardroom. We were successful with the wall but not the account. This proves you can try too hard."

Visual aids—getting past the optic nerve

The quickest way into the human brain is through the eye. It's a person's most efficient learning tool. However, the eye is a very impatient organ. Like any of the other physical senses, it needs stimulation to remain alert and fixed in one spot for very long. One study reported that the average adult eye must be stimulated every nine seconds or it will lose interest. That's a pretty big challenge. Especially when you con-
(Above three unique to O&M.)
thinking about other serious marketing problems, personal problems, dental appointments, a daughter's injury, a son's overnight engagement. As Tom Murry of Murray-Chaney Advertising once said, "The world is not about advertising. It's about people." And that applies to clients as well as consumers. You've got to be compelling if you expect to get past the optic nerve and into the grey matter.

Ron Hoff has written a tablet of valuable "scripture" on making and using slides. If you follow these laws, you'll not only keep the client awake, but he or she will be absorbing your precious information and moving closer to conversion.

The ten commandments of making and using slides

1. Limit words per slide: 15 to 20, best. Think of the slide as a *billboard.*
2. Use several *simple* slides in place of one complicated slide.
3. Use *titles* with caution. Good, brief slides don't need them.
4. Dark backgrounds are best. Blue. Black. Red. White on dark blue for *ease* of reading, recall. Sans serif best.
5. Nobody ever complained about words on slides being *too large.* Design slides for "back row."
6. Use color functionally, sparingly. Emphasis, not ornamentation.
7. Don't leave slide on screen *after* you've discussed it. If a lengthy bit of information follows after the slide, go to black.

8. Operate slides *yourself.* White tape on forward button.
9. Always check to make sure slides are right side up, not upside down and backwards. Check it yourself immediately before the presentation starts.
10. Rehearse with everything *exactly* as it will be.

Andrew Kershaw gives the following advice on the use of slides and charts: Study it before and after the visual aids are done.

1. Read everything on the slide exactly as written the instant the slide appears. Having done so, you can give any additional information. Don't show a slide and discuss something else. What the eye sees, and what you say, must march together.
2. Never turn your back on the audience to read a slide or chart. Have note cards or a transcript so you don't have to read from the screen.
3. Visual aids are supposed to help you. When charts fall all over or slides jam or get shown upside down, they are not aids at all—they destroy communication: These things can be prevented by adequate rehearsal.
4. Learn to use a pointer. It is a marvelous instrument. When it is used properly, the audience is riveted to it. And it enables you to maintain a respectable distance from the screen or chart, and you will not be in the line of vision of the audience.
5. White lettering on blue or red or green background is usually most legible. (That is because the room is at least partially darkened: it is not inconsistent with the rules about illegibility of reversed type.)
6. Never show a storyboard in a presentation. Put the frames on separate slides with accompanying words on a tape recorder.
7. If in the course of your talk you refer to a booklet, merchandising piece, package, or direct mail piece, always show it to the audience. Then, if possible, hand it to the audience to look at more closely.
8. When you show ads, always read the headline. And read the subhead, too, especially if it is a good one. But never read all the copy—it takes too long.
9. If you play a radio commercial, an ingenious idea is to accompany the commercial with silent-film footage (or a series of slides) of a highway, taken from the driver's seat, to simulate the effect of a car radio. People will know where to look—and it adds a touch of showmanship.

10. A presenter makes his life a lot easier if he sticks to just one kind of visual aid—to switch from slides to charts to film is asking for trouble.

11. Proofread your material several times. It is an invariable law of presentations that charts and slides always contain a typo or two, misspellings, a wrong figure. (A good trick for spotting errors is to read the words on each slide from back to front.) If an error should slip through undetected and cannot be corrected before the presentation, always point it out. Don't let the audience spot it.

12. Set *early* deadlines or suffer. Waiting until the last minute to make your visual aids is a 90-proof formula for failure. Allow plenty of time to make changes, fix typos, and rehearse.

Questions—the sudden-death round

When major agencies compete for accounts, this is where many *eliminations* occur. For example, if six agencies are invited to present, odds are that, based on the presentation alone, two or three will be dead before the questions and answers begin. Assuming that your presentation is right on target, you've still got the highest hurdle left.

An astute client will perform exploratory surgery during the Q&A. The client will make careful incisions into the following areas, and then observe how the agency body responds:

Personnel. Are they bright people? Do they have character? Do they articulate well without a script? Do they answer directly? Are they honest? Are they dignified? Do they like each other? Do they accept their leader? Will they respect our authority? Can we get along with them? Like them?

Substance. Are we hiring professionals? Are they *experts* in their particular fields? Do they know more about advertising than we do? Can they give solid, logical support for the advertising budget they want from us? Do they really understand our product from our point of view (profit and consumer satisfaction)? From the consumer's point of view (problem solving)? Do they show sparks of genius and originality in media and marketing decision making as well as creative strategy?

Aggressiveness. Are they confident in themselves? Do they believe they can deliver the objectives they have set? Do they demonstrate the kind of aggressiveness that is needed to battle for brand shares in our highly competitive market? Are their goals high enough, yet realistic? Will they work toward *our* profit as well as their own?

Sound frightening? Most surgery is. But there are some excellent ways you can prepare for a client's delicate scalpel. Your confidence will increase tenfold if you will give heed to the following advice from Ron Hoff. It's based on years of winning experience, and just enough losing to know how to avoid it.

How to cope with questions

Most politicians have a system you might want to consider. They have their staffs write down every question that might be asked during a press conference—and they make sure they have the answers. The day before your presentation, spend an hour *anticipating* the questions you may get. Write them down.

- "Who is the biggest competitor? What's our share of market?"
- "Will legal let you say that? Have you asked?"
- "Why a :60? It would be better as a :30?"
- "Does it have enough brand identification?"
- "How much will that commercial cost? Have you thought about shooting in Europe?"
- "Where's the big idea?"
- "Does your theme line clearly position the product?"
- "Have you tested the theme line? What do people think it means?"
- "How did you determine your budget?"
- "Do you think 75 GRPs will deliver enough prospects?"

If you can honestly say, "We looked into that very question—and here's what we found . . . ," you're not going to get much argument from your audience.

If somebody asks a question that you *should* know the answer to but don't—say, "I should know the answer to that but I don't." *Write the question down* so that everybody can see you have every intention of looking into it.

Another tip. Find out about the people you'll be presenting to. Do a little digging. What kinds of questions are they likely to ask? Do they have any pet peeves? Ask around. The more you know about your audience, the better able you'll be to control the situation.

Appoint a leader for the Q&A session

There's always the one question everybody is dying to answer. And they all jump in together. So the whole agency dies right there on the spot. Grim, yet so common. Be sure someone is responsible for fielding the questions. This person can easily establish authority at the outset of the Q&A by asking for questions. Then, as questions come, he or she can nod or gesture to the best agency authority on that subject. It maintains order and keeps the impulsive jaws from flapping.

Don't hitchhike on each other's answers

A sure sign of agency weakness is for Sue to "clarify" what Rick was saying. It may be acceptable to add something to a response now and then, but never say, "What Rick was trying to say is. . . ." That's inviting sudden death.

You can't over-rehearse

How to defeat nervousness

There are two important secrets. First, be in complete command of your material. Know exactly what's coming up—what you want to say—how you want to say it—the points you want to register. Rehearse until you're sick of it. The better you know your material—the more you've rehearsed—the less likely you are to be nervous.

Incidentally, if it's possible to rehearse in the same room where you'll be performing, so much the better. The more uncertainties you can remove from your presentations, the fewer butterflies you'll have.

The second secret is one that requires lots of persuasion. Before you get up to talk, tell yourself you know your subject better than anybody in your audience (and you had better). Convince yourself that you're better at what you do than anybody in the place—and that you're going to outshine everybody on the program. Pump yourself up—get your adrenalin going. Tell yourself you're going *to be the best and you will be.*

And, of course, *you've* got to be sold on the material you're presenting, or your audience won't be. This is particularly important if you're presenting work that you didn't create yourself.

Criticism

How do you handle it? (I've got a big answer to this one.) The best attitude for a presenter is one of good-natured confidence. Don't be overbearing. Don't be a clown. If you're good-natured, your audience probably will be, too. If you're confident, it gives your audience confidence in you.

But don't be so confident that you're intractable. Don't give the impression that the words are embedded in stone and the pictures are sacrosanct. David Ogilvy has a good point. He says, "Most clients like to have the feeling that they contribute something to the advertising." If the suggestion sounds feasible, say you'll try it. Don't fall in love with your own words—there are 600,000 words in the English language and the possible combinations are endless. Don't act as if you've been mortally wounded if somebody questions your work. Listen before you leap. The true professional gives reasoned responses rather than rash rebuttals.

A checklist of 119 questions and tips (by Andrew Kershaw)

First things

1. Did you get briefed?
2. Have you gathered intelligence?
3. Have you studied the people attending?
4. Do you know your competition?
5. Have you learned the prospect's needs?
6. Are you sticking to the ground rules?
7. Do you plan to include a little surprise?
8. Will you finish on time?

Matching audience and performers

9. Will the performers outnumber the audience?
10. Have you matched the prospect by rank?
11. Did you find a part for all in attendance?
12. Have you given your best presenters a dramatic role?

Stage management

13. Have you tried to present in *your* offices?
14. Away from home, have you checked out, *in advance*: Electrical outlets? Sound system? Projection equipment and method? Lighting? Darkening of room?
15. Have you arranged for these props: Easels? Space for display of ads, etc.? Lectern? Pointer? Pins, tape, and spare bulbs? Note pads? Pencils?
16. Refreshments: How and when?
17. Have you thought about seating?
18. Did you avoid exotic staging?
19. Have you rehearsed slides and film on equipment in presentation room?

Constructing the presentation

20. Did you combine showmanship with business?
21. Have you remembered that informal is more difficult than formal?
22. Are you appealing to self-interest?
23. Are you flattering prospects by treating their problems as unique?
24. Are you giving evidence of special efforts?
25. If you are in a speculative presentation, are you doing it properly?
26. Is the creative work the high point?
27. Is the boss introducing the team?
28. Have you found an unusual way to recite the facts about the agency?

29. Were you going to show an organization chart? Don't.
30. Are you relating your strong points to the prospects' needs?
31. Are you showing relevant experience?
32. Or how you make up for its absence?

How to use case histories

33. Are they brief?
34. Are the cases relevant?
35. Don't use involved case histories.
36. Visual illustrations are vital.
37. Have you selected up-to-date cases?

How to select creative material

38. Did you pick relevant advertising?
39. Did you include humor and emotion?
40. Are you showing categories that appeal to your audience, e.g., cars to males?
41. Show some famous old campaigns.
42. Please be careful with long copy.
43. Use foreign examples with discretion.
44. Don't show a standard reel: make one up for each prospect.
45. Did you find dramatic ways of showing material?
46. Do not give elaborate explanations for each commercial.
47. Do you plan to play games to get them involved?

How to use visual aids

48. Remember to read the slide.
49. Don't turn your back to the audience.
50. Do you have the text of the slides and charts in your script?
51. Have you rehearsed the handling of visual aids?
52. Are you comfortable with the visual aids?
53. Use the pointer.
54. Have you checked the size of the type: is it legible?
55. Flip-charts are good only for small audiences.
56. Don't present storyboards.
57. Read headlines, not body copy.
58. Radio needs special care.
59. Watch the lighting.
60. Use only one kind of visual aid for each presenter.
61. Did you check the slides and charts for typos?

Show that your agency is different

62. Talk about discipline.
63. Magic lanterns.
64. Stability of staff and clients.
65. Describe growth with clients.
66. Show dedication to creative excellence.
*67. Talk about Creative Council.
*68. Explain One Agency Indivisible.
*69. Draw attention to International Management Supervisors.
70. Say you believe in first-class business.
71. Talk about your agency chief.
*Items unique to O&M.

How to start and how to close

72. Be prepared to warm up, but no funny story.
73. Make the start memorable.
74. Are you opening with a film or a reel?
75. Tell them "Why you should pick us."
76. Is the ending memorable?
77. Ask for the order.
78. Are you ending with a film or a reel?
79. Have you organized the leave-behind?

Question time

80. Encourage questions.
81. Be truthful, simple, to the point.
82. Listen to the question.
83. Don't hedge or waffle.
84. Don't minimize problems: acknowledge them.
85. Make them laugh.
86. Don't knock the competition.
87. Don't criticize current advertising.
88. Watch for signs of boredom.
89. Make sure you don't all reply at the same time.
90. Don't make promises you can't deliver.
91. Be ready to offer a list of names of clients.
92. Be ready to deal with the usual objections.

The rehearsal

93. Rehearse.
94. Rehearse again.
95. You cannot have too many rehearsals.
96. Did you use rehearsals to change the format?
97. Have you cut scripts?
98. Did you consider changing the order?
99. Remember that informality is achieved through rehearsals.
100. Rehearse your ad libs.

101. Watch the timing.
102. Make everyone rehearse.

How to become a better speaker.

103. Encourage courses in public speaking.
104. Listen to yourself on a tape recorder.
105. Watch yourself on video tape.
106. Edit your script.
107. Use quotes or memorable expressions.
108. Do memorable things.
109. Be careful with humor.
110. Stand up.
111. Have you devised a good introduction?
112. Are you disarming and reassuring?
113. Watch your dress, your mannerisms, and your hands.
114. Don't smoke or chew.
115. Gesticulate.
116. Remember to watch for changing moods of the audience.
117. Be ready to improvise.
118. Learn to use your voice.
119. Don't expect applause.

12

Frito-Lay Rold Gold Award Winning Campaign

A team of senior students in advertising at San Jose State University* won first place in the 1977 Annual American Advertising Federation Student Competition. The team competed against some 75 colleges and universities nationwide. Their written advertising plan, as presented to Frito-Lay, Inc. in Washington, D. C., is reproduced in this chapter.

About a year after the national competition, Frito-Lay decided to use the creative strategy presented by the winning team on sales truck posters promoting Rold Gold pretzels (see page 166). This is a first for the AAF student competition and demonstrates the open-mindedness of Frito-Lay executives who were willing to go with a winning campaign idea, even if it came from outside. The authors hope that future AAF "clients" will be bold enough to consider the same action.

Tips on successful preparation for AAF competition

1. Solid rationales crucial

After reviewing several professionally written plans, the authors note how some agencies support every decision with sophisticated logic. Yet, others are quite loose. However, in student competition, it's suicide if you don't justify *everything* in writing. *Judges will assume you are ignorant until proven intelligent.* At the regional level, none of the judges will be actual clients. You must assume they know very little about the assigned product and do everything possible to educate them. Expect both regional and national judges to come from Missouri. Why? Why? Why? They want proof that you arrived at a decision by reason, not by throwing darts. How well you support your decisions with logic and/or numbers often spells the difference between

winning and losing. Have your books open and ready to show your methodology during the Q & A.

2. Anticipate judges' questions—have Q&A leader

With limitations on the size of books, every detail cannot be justified in writing. As veteran Ron Hoff points out in chapter 11, you should rehearse with a list of questions you expect to be asked. Also, have someone appointed as a Q&A leader. If it turns into a free-for-all, some anxious soul will butt in where he or she doesn't belong and make your agency look stupid. Or, even worse, every question gets answered with five different bits of wisdom, each worth about two cents. Again, you look stupid.

3. Set early deadlines—expect Murphy's Law to prevail

One of the authors lost in the Coca Cola-Sprite competition almost by default. Students were still arranging slides in the carousel at 3:00 A.M. the morning of the District 12 competition. A defective dissolve unit was never discovered because there were too many other fires to put out. The defective dissolve unit malfunctioned about five minutes into the presentation. For twenty minutes the judges watched a tragicomedy of mismatched slides and dialog. An agonizing, inexcusable way to lose an account.

4. To be remembered—communicate brilliance in writing

Consider that your written plan is buried in a stack of up to fifteen books. That's 750 pages! Like wading through *War and Peace*. How on earth do you get remembered? First, substance. Nothing can help if that's not present. However, substance can get buried

---

*Dennis Martin, co-author of this book, served as faculty advisor for the San Jose State student team.

by poor writing and/or weak format. *Many brilliant campaigns have been lost to the world because the agency could not articulate the brilliance.* Write with clarity. Use short sentences. Use paragraph subheads that say something. That sell! Use white space to make a big point. Underline main ideas. In short, advertise.

5. Stand-up presentations—sudden-death round

Rehearse. Rehearse. Rehearse. Those precious minutes of rehearsal often separate the good from the great. Indeed, your agency may look great on paper, but when you open your mouth, you die. And who wins? An agency that merely looks *good* on paper (a notch below *great*), but they do an exceptional job of presenting. Is that fair? Yes. Because the client wants to be *sold.* He or she wants to be lavished with attention . . . with sincere interest in *his* problems. The client wants to be persuaded to make a decision. And the agency that focuses on the client's problems and *promises solutions he can understand, in a memorable way,* will win the business.

Exhibit 12-1. Creative strategy formulated by winning AAF student competition team was subsequently used by Frito-Lay on truck posters illustrated here.

AAF Advertising Campaign

Prepared for Frito-Lay, Incorporated

ROLD GOLD PRETZELS

by

Gabardine, Herringbone & Tweed
San Jose State University

GH&T
Gabardine, Herringbone & Tweed

Robert M. Weber — President

J. Arthur Renaud — Marketing Director

Jerry T. May   — Media Director
Wade Goertz   — Media Assistant

Holly Bourne   — Creative Director
Enn Purdmaa   — Copy Chief/General Editor
Kathleen Saunders — Research/Copywriter
Marna Levin   — Art Director
Marc Shur   — Art Director

Lori Runge   — Sales Promotion Director

Denise Collins   — Production/Traffic Director

Kate Turmes & Luci Ackhart

TABLE OF CONTENTS

SITUATION ANALYSIS

Product History

From its origin over 10 centuries ago as a monks' reward to children, the pretzel has grown to a $128 million business in the Unites States alone. The pretzel was first introduced in America during the 17th Century as a soft, doughy twist. However, when an anonymous Pennsylvania baker overbaked a batch -- the hard pretzel as we know it today was born.

Company History

The origin of the Frito-Lay Company can be traced to three parent companies: Num-Num Food Industries (which acquired the ROLD GOLD trademark through a merger with the American Cone and Pretzel Co.); the Frito Company of Dallas; and the H.W. Lay Co. In 1959 Num-Num Foods merged with the Frito Co. and two years later, the Frito name fused with Lay. In 1965, Frito-Lay joined PepsiCo.

PRODUCT EVALUATION

Distribution: Heartland/Non-Heartland

ROLD GOLD is distributed nationally from El Segundo, California; St. Louis, Missouri; and Canton, Ohio. Grocery stores receive the bulk of distribution intensity, with minimal effort directed toward liquor and convenience outlets.

Distribution is split into 12 Heartland and 21 Non-Heartland divisions. In the Heartland, ROLD GOLD holds an 8.6% share-of-market ($8,716,500), while Non-Heartland share-of-market is 37.5% ($10,283,500) in annual retail sales.

Notably, ROLD GOLD's All Commodity Volume has decreased in the West and Southeast, traditionally strong Non-Heartland areas for the brand. This loss can be attributed to increased encroachment by regional and private-store brand and ROLD GOLD's lack of advertising support.

ROLD GOLD Distribution by Zone (ACV)

Zone	1974	1975	1976
Northeastern	47	50	54
Western	60	58	56
Midwestern	60	58	62
Southwestern	65	67	72
Southeastern	72	70	70

Category and Brand Growth

The overall category growth for pretzels has increased an astounding 57% over the last five years (1971-1975). Within this time span, the ROLD GOLD brand has grown 67%. However, while both the category and brand indexes have increased, ROLD GOLD's dollar share-of-market (in supermarkets has declined 1.7%.

A comparison between category and brand growth is less pronounced in Non-Heartland areas (17% category growth, compared to 15% ROLD GOLD growth), due to less private and regional brand intrusion. In Heartland areas, however, the difference between category and brand is more widespread (19% category compared to 3% ROLD GOLD growth), due mostly to the fact that 66 of the 88 total pretzel manufacturers are located in the Heartland.

	HEARTLAND			NON-HEARTLAND	
	Category	Brand		Category	Brand
	78.6	44.7		21.4	55.3
Growth	19%	3%		17%	15%

ROLD GOLD's national competitor, Mr. Salty, is currently the largest manufacturer of hard pretzels. Annual sales approach $26 million and represent a 20% share of national retail sales. (Snack Food Bluebook, pg. 66). ROLD GOLD's sales are $19.5 million, representing a 13.5% share of supermarket sales.

In-Store Positioning

From a survey of 22 San Jose supermarkets, it is encouraging that ROLD GOLD is consistently shelved in the snack food section, positioned next to other Frito-Lay products. The average shelf-facing for ROLD GOLD was 4. Only private store brands fared better (with an average of 4.5). The other national brand, Nabisco's Mr. Salty, is usually located in the "cookies and crackers" section with other boxed Nabisco snacks. Its average facing of 2.5 may reflect the fact that Mr. Salty is produced in only two configurations (twists and sticks), while ROLD GOLD offers five variations.

A primary retail trade survey of San Jose, California supermarket managers revealed that in-store positioning is determined primarily by regional office schematics with regard to space and traffic considerations.

Price

ROLD GOLD is competitively priced against Mr. Salty, yet both national brands are priced slightly higher than regional and private brands.

Primary research indicated that price is not a major consideration in the brand selection process of consumers.

Recognizing the nine ounce twist as ROLD GOLD's critical size, the following chart outlines price comparisons within the category, (as surveyed in the San Jose market).

PRICE COMPARISON CHART

BRAND	SIZE	AVG. PCKG. PRICE	PRICE/OUNCE
ROLD GOLD	9 oz.	56.6¢	6.28¢
Mr. Salty	10 oz.	58.4¢	5.84¢
Granny Goose (regional)	9 oz.	55.5¢	6.16¢
Tem Tee (regional)	9 oz.	39¢	4.33¢
Private Brands (average)	9 oz.	47.7¢	5.46¢

Packaging

ROLD GOLD is packaged in a flexible cellophane bag with a see-through panel. While most regional and private brands are similarly packaged, Mr. Salty is packed in a box.

Primary consumer research revealed that while price was relatively inconsequential, packaging is a major consideration in purchasing pretzels. Of the 319 survey respondents, 90 percent preferred flexible packaging:

- 60% preferred a clear flexible bag to facilitate product inspection prior to purchase.
- 28% considered a flexible bag to contain "fresher" product than boxes.

Because package appearance is crucial to the success of an "impulse" product, it is important to note that our focus group unanimously disliked the actual design of the ROLD GOLD package, citing a lack of eye-appeal and aesthetic characteristics.

"A package design must be appealing and stand-out enough
to arrest the attention of passersby. Design must invite a
second look at the package and its contents...In a test employing more than 50 different color transparencies of a standard
design, the ones which 'stood-out' best were the designs most
successful on retail counters and shelves." (American Management Report, #65, 1967)

Notably, the ROLD GOLD package design does not conform with other
Frito-Lay packages.

- The Frito-Lay name is not displayed on the package. Our
consumer studies reveal that Frito-Lay company is well
known and respected for producing quality snacks.

- All other Frito-Lay packages are related in some way.
The brand names either rhyme (Fritos, Cheetos, Doritos),
include the company name (Lay's Potato Chips, Frito Lay's
Natural Style Potato Chips), or are similarly designed.

MARKET EVALUATION

Consumer Survey

Our consumer survey sample was scientifically drawn from Census Tract
Information gathered from the Planning Commission of San Jose, California.
Supermarket locations were matched with demographic information in respect
to household income extracted from TGI (Target Group Index) data on "pretzel
users". A total of 319 shoppers, who identified themselves as pretzel consumers, were interviewed. (Complete survey appendixed)

Target Demographics Based on Survey

Married Female -- 67%	High-School Graduate -- 86%
Caucasian -- 78%	Household Income $10-19,999 -- 45%
25-49 Years of Age -- 78%	Employed Part-Time -- 56%
2-4 in Household -- 86%	Suburban -- 60%

According to the survey, the largest purchaser of pretzels is the wife
(89%); while the major household consumer of pretzels is the husband (51%).
Usually, the wife was found responsible for brand choice unless otherwise
specified by the husband or other family members.

Focus Group

To extract a greater depth of knowledge of consumer attitudes toward
pretzels, a ninety-minute interview of 10 pretzel consumers was conducted.

The subjects' demographic profiles were aligned with those of the primary
consumer survey. The highlights of this interview are as follows:

- Misassociation of the ROLD GOLD name
- Eye-appealing snack

- Product appearance dictates good taste
- Salty "satisfying" flavor
- Stand alone as a snack food (more than a beer companion)
- Frito-Lay products have an excellent reputation for quality
- Consumer does not associate ROLD GOLD with Frito-Lay
- Consumer disliked ROLD GOLD package design

(Complete report appendixed)

Syracuse Telephone Survey

To uncover possible variations in consumer attitudes and behavior in the Heartland, as opposed to the Non-Heartland, a random survey of 50 pretzel users was conducted in Syracuse, New York. The questionnaire was a condensed version of the original San Jose consumer survey.

Responses from Syracuse pretzel consumers were, for practical purposes, almost identical to those gathered in San Jose. No discernible explanation for the Heartland/Non-Heartland statistical schism emerged.

- Only 20% of respondents indicated a favorite brand, with only two people mentioning ROLD GOLD.
- No one knew who made ROLD GOLD.
- The "salty" flavor was described as the most favorable product attribute.

(Complete survey appendixed)

Retail Trade Survey

Personal interviews with 15 San Jose, California supermarket managers were conducted.

The survey indicated a concensus that supermarkets are required to increase purchasing of a particular brand commensurate with the degree of a manufacturer's consumer advertising effort. According to Alpha-Beta's Northern California Senior Buyer, supermarkets are virtually forced to increase purchasing when a manufacturer advertises or promotes either a new or established product. The survey highlights are listed below:

- Actual purchasing is decided by store buyers and is determined by discounts, bulk rates, manufacturer advertising and promotional allowances.
- In-store locations of products is determined by corporate schematics, while actual shelf space is alloted according to package size and consumer demand.
- Consistently, summer and fall are the highest sales seasons for pretzels.
- Most store managers feel coupons are a consumer purchasing motivator.
- Frito-Lay's sales force offers adequate service.
- Pretzels are a profitable item.

(Complete survey appendixed)

PROBLEMS/ISSUES

PROBLEM STATEMENT

In light of ROLD GOLD's low brand awareness and name misassociation, how can ROLD GOLD best be positioned a) in the consumer's mind, and b) against competitors.

RECOMMENDATION

Position ROLD GOLD against all other pretzels by establishing a strong brand image. At the same time, generate high brand awareness among pretzel users, in particular, and other snack food users, in general.

RATIONALE

Determining the position of a firm's product or service within the consumer's mind is crucial to future marketing activity. Products which are physically indistinguishable, (as ROLD GOLD is to other brands of pretzels), may be perceived quite differently in the attitudinal framework of the consumer.

Our primary research indicates that consumers do not see any objective differences in pretzels. <u>Subjective differences, therefore, must determine brand preferences</u>. (Salty flavor, eye-appeal, shape, crunchiness.) These salient features can be attached solely to the ROLD GOLD name.

> "Position is a brand's subjective characteristics, as perceived by consumers, in relation to competing brands."
> (<u>Journal of Advertising Research</u>, February 1976)

<u>86.5% of all pretzels consumed are brands other than ROLD GOLD</u>. By positioning ROLD GOLD against competitive brand pretzels, (rather than against all snack foods), increased volume will be generated by conquest of these brands. Current ROLD GOLD users will increase consumption - as will consumers of other snack food items in an inevitable spillover effect.

Other important reasons for positioning ROLD GOLD against competitive pretzels, rather than the entire snack food industry are:

- To penetrate the snack food market, a dual barrier of convincing consumers of other snacks not only to switch to pretzels, but to a particular brand, would arise.
- Considering the proliferation of so called "snack foods", it would be extremely difficult to define and monitor competition.
- Difficulties would arise in gauging advertising impact upon a $12 billion total snack food industry.
- Sales potential of the product would be difficult to project within such a diverse and overwhelming field.
- By positioning primarily against the pretzel category, cannibalization can be minimized.

SUB-PROBLEM

Despite ROLD GOLD's remarkable success in "pushing" their product through the distribution chain, share-of-market is dropping. Is it time to consider "pulling" the product through the retail channels?

RECOMMENDATION

ROLD GOLD should combine "push" and "pull" promotional strategies in both Heartland and Non-Heartland areas.

RATIONALE

"Most firms in most industries attempt some sort of compromise between these polar positions (i.e., push and pull strategies)." (Handbook of Modern Marketing)

Despite the exclusive use of the push strategy, ROLD GOLD has shown a 67% growth in the last five years. However, to curtail the 1.7% loss of market share suffered during that period, the introduction of the pull strategy should immediately be employed in accordance with the long term marketing plan. This method is designed to stimulate continuous demand among consumers; whereas the push method generates mainly short-term incremental growth.

Within the snack food industry, this concept was success-fully employed by Nabisco "after discovering an underpromoted cookie and cracker business. Whereas Ritz crackers has been showing minimal growth rates, implementation of a (combined push/pull) strategy rocketed growth rates to 16 percent annually." (Business Week, Sept. 27, 1976)

Our primary retail trade research further substantiates Ritz' promotional strategy. When enough consumers ask for a brand name, retailers said they couldn't refuse to stock it.

While "pulling" the consumer into the marketplace with advertising, the "push" strategy can be effectively used within the supermarket securing shelf position. End-of-aisle constructions, point-of-purchase displays, and secondary locations complement advertising in reinforcing consumer "impulse" decision making.

SUB-PROBLEM

With ROLD GOLD operating on a bottom-line net profit margin of 19.4%, as set forth by Frito-Lay, what is the best method for budgeting promotional ex-penditures?

RECOMMENDATION

Utilize the "payout planning" method so that advertising monies are charged against the brand.

<u>RATIONALE</u>

The payout concept of budgeting considers advertising as an investment, making a direct connection between advertising expenditures and profits.

Payout planning is an accepted method in the consumer packaged-goods field, employed by companies such as General Foods, Proctor and Gamble, and Borden. Using this method, companies work on a break-even schedule of three to four years, with a corporate philosophy of investing advertising funds ahead of sales. Advertising expenditures are accumulated and charged against the brand; the break-even point is not considered achieved until revenues from sales of the brand are sufficient to cover advertising expenditures in the current fiscal period as well as from the previous two years.

This approach puts a realistic burden on advertising and sales promotion costs by accumulating expenditures over the entire introductory period. The alternative method of starting with a new budget request each year ignores the drain on corporate profits by previous years' expenditures.

The payout planning method is particularly effective for introducing a "new" brand to the market or for promoting a previously unadvertised product. Considering the minimal promotional budget allocated ROLD GOLD, payout planning principles particularly apply.

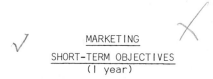

MARKETING
<u>SHORT-TERM OBJECTIVES</u>
(1 year)

1. Establish a positive brand image and awareness for ROLD GOLD in key markets.

2. Capture an increased market share of 50% in selected Heartland and Non-Heartland markets.

<u>LONG-TERM OBJECTIVES</u>
(3 years)

1. Continue building positive brand image and awareness for ROLD GOLD.

2. Increase market share to 21% nationwide, (minimum).

3. Establish ROLD GOLD as the <u>number one</u> pretzel in the nation.

<u>STRATEGY</u>

1. • Position ROLD GOLD against competitive brand pretzels

2. • Utilize a push/pull promotional strategy to establish positive brand image and awareness. As a result, an increase in consumer demand will stimulate retailer demand, thus increasing distribution.

3. • Avoid wasting money in "lean" markets by rolling-out promotional programs in key market areas where both category and brand development (indexes) are high.

> "The high cost of advertising has forced marketers to look at promoting and selling their products on a more efficient market-by-market or regional basis, heavying-up in markets where sales are biggest or have the most potential." (Advertising Age, February 21, 1977)

4. • Effectualize a minimum 21% share-of-market forecast within a three year period (to $35.7 million in retail sales annually). Figures show the pretzel category as growing an average of 11% annually, regardless of minimal promotional activity. By 1980, pretzel sales are expected to exceed $170 million in relation to adjusted past yearly increases.

5. • Capitalize on the Frito-Lay reputation by featuring the name on a package re-designed in light of consumer preference.

6. • Budget promotional monies by the payout planning method.

II. MEDIA OBJECTIVES

1. Increase brand awareness by concentrating in media which will provide <u>maximum reach</u> of ROLD GOLD's target audience:

Married Female	High-School Graduate
Caucasion	Household Income $10-19,999
25-49 Years of Age	Employed Part-Time
2-4 in Household	Suburbanite

2. Determine the product's seasonality and exert media efforts accordingly.

3. Direct media efforts toward divisions with highest sales potential for both brand and category development.

4. Select media which will provide the most efficient combination of reach, frequency, and continuity within our established budget.

5. Co-ordinate media efforts for maximum advertising and sales promotion continuity.

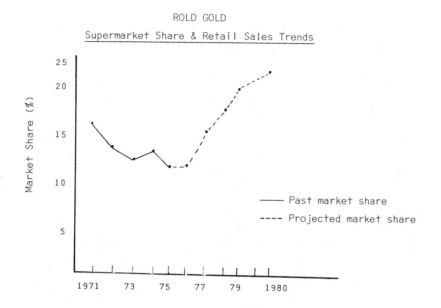

ROLD GOLD
Supermarket Share & Retail Sales Trends

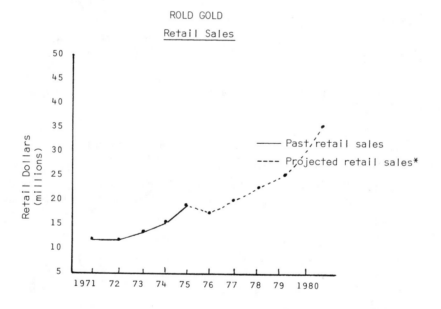

ROLD GOLD
Retail Sales

*ROLD GOLD retail sales have increased over 60% in the past five years (1971-75). Our agency projects that by adopting our marketing & promotion programs, ROLD GOLD will enjoy a 55% retail sales increase (minimum) in three years - (increasing from $19.5 million to $37.5 million retail sales annually).

MEDIA STRATEGY

Our media strategy is based upon the stated marketing and media objectives as well as estimated communication needs to meet these objectives.

(1) The ROLD GOLD campaign will be introduced into carefully selected markets for one full year beginning in September of 1977. Constant monitoring and post-evaluation (occurring at four month intervals) will gauge successes and insure that the marketing and media objectives have been achieved. Consequently, the campaign will be adapted for a roll-out into additional divisions.

Evaluation Period I runs from September to December when 52% of the total media budget is expended. Evaluation Period II runs January through April when 16% of the total budget will be allocated. Evaluation Period III runs May through August consuming the remaining 32%.

Nielson Store Audits will be employed to insure the company's overall marketing efforts are on target. Starch Reports will be used to evaluate the campaign's advertising strategy and media placement.

(3) The use of Spot Television as the primary medium provides the greatest impact, while reaching at least 90% of the target market at the onset of the campaign, and maintaining an 80% reach throughout.

(4) Consumer Magazines, will be purchased on a regional basis to allow for greatest flexibility in directing the message to the specified target market.

(5) Outdoor Advertising offers geographic flexibility and continuity within the campaign.

(6) Advertising and sales promotion will work hand-in-hand to stimulate product awareness and consumer demand for ROLD GOLD. This will also increase retailer demand and distribution.

(7) A contingency fund will be set aside to capitalize on favorable market developments. Subsequent to evaluation periods, additional divisions will be added.

MARKET SELECTION

Non-Heartland Divisions	Heartland Divisions
San Jose	Syracuse
San Diego	Pittsburgh
Richmond	Detroit
Omaha	Cleveland
Kansas City	
Portland	

RATIONALE

The campaign is designed to run initially in the ten market divisions for one year. Each selected market has proven sales potential in both brand and category development, while closely matching demographic points with the target audience – as indicated from primary and secondary research. – Also, each Frito-Lay sales zone is represented with these ten selections.

The proportion of Heartland to Non-Heartland divisions is based on the total number of divisions in each of these categories – 12 Heartland and 21 Non-Heartland – and the fact that ROLD GOLD is traditionally stronger in the Non-Heartland divisions.

Additional rationale for introducing the campaign on a key market basis, rather than on a national level, are:

• By introducing the campaign in selected divisions we are in the best position to gauge whether sales (and market share) forecasts for the national plan are attainable.

• The high cost of national advertising is prohibitive for a previously unadvertised product.

• Since ROLD GOLD operates on bottom-line profit margin, advertising funds will be earned. Proven successes in the key markets will justify additional advertising monies allocated to the brand.

	CDI	BDI	ROLD GOLD Share-of-Market
San Jose Division (Western Zone)	48	65	19%
San Diego Division (Western Zone)	59	163	34%
Portland Division (Western Zone)	47	58	20%
Omaha Division (Midwestern Zone)	50	92	24%
Pittsburgh Division (Midwestern Zone)	215	173	11%
Cleveland Division (Midwestern Zone)	173	86	8%
Syracuse Division (Northeastern Zone)	159	78	8%
Kansas City Division (Southwestern Zone)	71	136	30%
Richmond Division (Southeastern Zone)	51	105	29%
Detroit Division (Midwestern Zone)	120	160	20%

Precise market share figures for all Frito-Lay divisions were calculated from the <u>Pretzel Heartland vs. Non-Heartland</u> chart (supplied in the ROLD GOLD case) by comparing "% Brand" dollar values with "% Category" dollar values.

For example:

San Jose Division - 2.1% (of category sales), or $2,688,000*

2.6% (of brand sales), or $407,000*

*By correlating these figures, it is determined that in the San Jose division ROLD GOLD holds an 18.8% share-of-market.

MEDIA SELECTION

Television

Advantages:

- Spot TV allows for <u>market-by-market penetration</u>.
- Spot TV is <u>highly selective</u>, facilitating <u>demographic matching of target markets by programming</u>.
- Spot TV offers the <u>most efficient combination of reach and frequency</u>.

Disadvantages:

- Message must penetrate the viewer's pre-attentive processing.

Recommendation

<u>Use spot television as our primary medium to deliver ROLD GOLD'S message</u> <u>efficiently with desired reach and frequency</u>.

Consumer Magazines

Advantages:

- <u>Selectively targets prospects</u>.
- <u>Space can be bought geographically</u>.
- Consumer magazines are a <u>prestige medium</u>. <u>Housewives</u> consider magazines a <u>highly credible source of information</u>.

Disadvantages:

- Early closing dates limit flexibility in timing.
- Messages cannot be communicated as frequently or immediately.

Recommendation

<u>National consumer magazines will be used on a regional basis; saving</u> <u>money, minimizing waste, and achieving a detailed targeting of markets</u>.

Outdoor

Advantages:

- <u>Fast, efficient way to build high awareness</u>.
- Outdoor can be tailored to <u>obtain specific reach and frequency</u>.
- It is an <u>excellent impulse trigger</u>; ideal for reminding the prospect <u>at a time when the desire for the product is apt to be recognized</u>.
- The prospect need not <u>buy or tune-in the medium; it is inescapable</u>.

Disadvantages:

- Short message or copy length.
- Lacks extreme selectivity

Recommendation

Outdoor advertising is recommended to strengthen our overall advertising strategy. A "supermarket" buy will be made in ROLD GOLD's selected markets providing maximum coverage at high volume stores.

Radio

Advantages:

- Provides local coverage.
- Offers a good follow-up medium for sales promotions.
- Timing of the commercials can be pinpointed.
- Cost per thousand is relatively low.

Disadvantages:

- Food is more effectively advertised in a visual medium.
- Radio is often played as an extraneous accompaniment to other activities.
- The message is fleeting; a radio can be turned off easily, once the message is delivered it is gone.

Recommendation

Due to radio's disadvantages, we recommend its use only in self-liquidating sales promotional activities.

Direct Mail

Advantages:

- Direct mail is a highly selective medium allowing strict geographical control.
- It is an excellent co-ordinator for sales promotion efforts.
- It is a personal medium that is selective in reaching prospects.
- There is no waste circulation.

Disadvantages:

- High costs are involved due to its high degree of selectivity.

Recommendation

Direct mail will be used to co-ordinate sales promotional activities between major retail buyers and the regional salesforce.

Newspapers

Advantages:

- Allow for relative flexibility within markets.
- Consumers actively seek editorial and advertising information.
- News content of the newspaper injects the element of immediacy into advertising.

Disadvantages:

- Newspapers have poor reproduction in black and white, while color has mechanical limitations.
- There is a short life-span and little pass-along readership in newspapers. Consumers usually only have one exposure to the advertisement.

Recommendation

Newspaper color reproduction is poor for food products. This medium cannot be used to its full effectiveness in displaying the product. Therefore, newspapers will not be purchased.

Trade Publications

Advantages:

- Trade magazines parallel consumer magazines reaching a more select audience.

Disadvantages:

- Most supermarket buying is directed through main or branch offices with individual retailers having little influence on buying decisions. *(Primary retail trade survey) This contributes to a high waste factor.

Recommendation

Due to the effectiveness of Frito-Lay's sales force and the selectivity of direct mail in reaching major retail buyers, trade publications will not be purchased.

 SPOT TELEVISION

Prime time spot television is recommended as the primary medium. Prime time spots will provide ROLD GOLD with the means of reaching the housewife efficiently. At the same time, it will reach all members of the family during the evening; when ROLD GOLD would be particularly appealing as a snack while the family is watching television.

EXPENDITURES BY MONTH

	Total Monthly GRP's	SPOTS/MO.	COSTS	REACH	FREQ.
SEPTEMBER	300	64	$106,500	88-95	7.4
OCTOBER	200	48	71,000	85-87	7.1
NOVEMBER	150	32	53,250	82-86	6.9
DECEMBER	200	48	71,000	85-87	7.1
JANUARY	75	16	26,625	71-75	3.9
FEBRUARY	75	16	26,625	71-75	3.9
MARCH	75	16	26,625	71-75	3.9
APRIL	75	16	26,625	71-75	3.9
MAY	200	48	71,000	85-87	7.1
JUNE	200	48	71,000	85-87	7.1
JULY	100	24	35,500	78-82	5.4
AUGUST	50	12	17,750	64-68	3.3
			$603,500		

EXPENDITURE BY DIVISION

DIVISION	COST-PER-RATING POINT	ANNUAL COST-PER-MARKET
San Jose (SF)	$90	$154,000
San Diego	22	37,400
Richmond	11	18,700
Portland	28	47,600
Omaha	10	17,000
Kansas City	30	51,000
Syracuse	12	20,400
Pittsburgh	36	61,200
Detroit	64	108,800
Cleveland	52	88,400
		$603,500 Total

SPOT TELEVISION BUYS: Based on 30-second spots
(100% prime-time)

Estimated 4-Week Reach of TV Homes at Various GRP Levels				
PRIME TIME 100%				
WKLY GRP	Prime Spots	% Reach	Frequency	# Station
50	3	64-68	3.3	1
75	4	71-75	3.9	2
100	6	78-82	5.4	2
150	8	82-86	6.9	3
200	12	85-87	7.1	3

(Source: TELMAR SPOT TV)

HEARTLAND:

4 Markets
6800 GRP's total   Total cost = $241,400

NON-HEARTLAND:

6 Markets
10,200 GRP's total   Total cost = $362,100

TOTAL SPOT TELEVISION COSTS = $603,500
TOTAL GROSS RATING POINTS   17,000
TOTAL ROLD GOLD MARKETS   10
SOURCE: (AYER MEDIA FACTS: 1976)

183

PROGRAM LISTINGS (San Jose Division Listings)

PROGRAMS	TIME ZONE	NETWORK	PRETZELS ROLD GOLD (% viewers)*	PRETZELS ALL ADULTS (% viewers)*
MONDAY				
NFL Football	6:30 - 9:00	ABC	28.9%	26.1%
The Jeffersons	8:00 - 8:30	CBS	19.0	19.7
Maude	9:00 - 9:30	CBS	20.4	21.4
TUESDAY				
Happy Days	8:00 - 8:30	ABC	24.2%	20.2%
M*A*S*H	9:00 - 9:30	CBS	27.6	24.5
WEDNESDAY				
Baretta	9:00 - 10:00	ABC	20.8%	17.5%
Good Times	8:00 - 8:30	CBS	24.6	24.5
THURSDAY				
Welcome Back Kotter	8:00 - 8:30	ABC	20.7%	18.6%
The Waltons	8:00 - 9:00	CBS	21.8	22.6
Streets of S.F.	9:00 - 10:00	ABC	24.4	24.1
FRIDAY				
Sandford & Son	8:00 - 8:30	NBC	29.5%	22.5%
Police Woman	10:00 - 11:00	NBC	22.2	28.3
SATURDAY				
Starsky & Hutch	9:00 - 10:00	ABC	23.7%	21.1%
Sat. Nite at Movies	9:00 - 11:00	NBC	22.5	18.8
All in the Family	9:00 - 9:30	CBS	31.7	30.6
SUNDAY				
Six Million $ Man	8:00 - 9:00	ABC	24.1%	20.5%
Kojak	9:00 - 10:00	CBS	24.1	24.4
Rhoda	8:00 - 8:30	CBS	21.3	20.7

*(Based upon TGI Figures: 1976)

 CONSUMER MAGAZINES

Consumer magazines will be purchased as a secondary medium. Selection criteria is based on matching demographic characteristics of ROLD GOLD'S target market with the highest percentage of target market readership. (Data was formulated by juxtaposing Target Group Index Information.)

SELECTED PUBLICATIONS	TARGET MARKET CIRCULATION
Better Homes and Gardens	472,000
Family Circle	795,000
Woman's Day	125,000
	1,392,000 per issue

In addition to these magazines, a selected buy will be made in T.V. Guide. The low CPM and high reach of this publication make it a very desirable media selection. T.V. Guide will be bought on alternate weeks from television, insuring maximum reach and continuity during the months of January thru April.

T.V. Guide	2,239,000 per issue

While the CPM is an important consideration in any media buy, it is equally important to realize the actual cost-per-user. The following chart illustrates a breakdown-per-magazine.

	Market Circulation	CPM Subscriber	% Pretzel* Readers	# Reached	CPM Pretzel User
Better Homes & Garden	472,000	9.69	24%	112,000	$40.51
four color $4574. per page					
Family Circle	795,000	8.14	21%	116,155	$55.77
four color $6479. per page					
Woman's Day	125,000	9.29	21%	26,750	$43.43
four color $1162. per page					
TV Guide	2,475,000	2.64	34.0	727,942	$ 8.97
B & W $6530. per page					

TOTAL MARKET CIRCULATION PER MONTH

     5,870,000

TOTAL PRETZEL EATERS REACHED

     1,778,233

   *(Extracted from TGI data on pretzel users)

Magazine Buys Based on Full Page, Four Color Rates:

<u>Better Homes and Gardens</u>   Total Cost: $22,870
    Five insertions in four markets
(Cleveland - Syracuse - Kansas City - San Diego)

<u>Family Circle</u>   Total Cost: $32,395
    Five insertions in five markets
(Pittsburgh - Omaha - Richmond - San Jose - Detroit)

<u>Woman's Day</u>   Total Cost: $ 5,810
    Five insertions in one market
(Portland)

<u>TV Guide</u>   Total Cost: $52,240
    Eight insertions in all markets

                      Total Costs: $113,315

	San Jose	S.D.	Rich	Port	Omaha	KC	Syra	Pitt	Det	Cleve
SEPTEMBER	FC	BH&G	FC	WD	FC	BH&G	BH&G	FC	FC	BH&G
OCTOBER	FC	BH&G	FC	WD	FC	BH&G	BH&G	FC	FC	BH&G
NOVEMBER										
DECEMBER	FC	BH&G	FC	WD	FC	BH&G	BH&G	FC	FC	BH&G
JANUARY	TV Guide	TV Guide	TV Guide	TV Guide	TV Guide	TV Guide	TV Guide	TV Guide	TV Guide	TV Guide
FEBRUARY	TV Guide	TV Guide	TV Guide	TV Guide	TV Guide	TV Guide	TV Guide	TV Guide	TV Guide	TV Guide
MARCH	TV Guide	TV Guide	TV Guide	TV Guide	TV Guide	TV Guide	TV Guide	TV Guide	TV Guide	TV Guide
APRIL	TV Guide	TV Guide	TV Guide	TV Guide	TV Guide	TV Guide	TV Guide	TV Guide	TV Guide	TV Guide
MAY	FC	BH&G	FC	WD	FC	BH&G	BH&G	FC	FC	BH&G
JUNE	FC	BH&G	FC	WD	FC	BH&G	BH&G	FC	FC	BH&G
JULY										
AUGUST										

<u>OUTDOOR</u>

    It is recommended that outdoor advertising be used to strengthen the overall advertising strategy. Outdoor advertising is an effective medium for ROLD GOLD pretzels:

- Fast awareness builder.
- Research indicates eight out of 10 female supermarket shoppers are now employed at some regular job. · Outdoor, by frequently reaching the mobile market, provides the best opportunity of covering this target group. (Dupont Study - Supermarket Buying Habits)
- Outdoor advertising complements spot TV coverage.
- Outdoor has proven ability to quickly build brand identification and awareness.
- Outdoor affords a full-color, larger-than-life reminder just before the impulse buyer enters the supermarket.
- ROLD GOLD can dominate a market at a low cost-per-thousand.

The markets selected for outdoor coincide with the 10 introductory markets. A 30-sheet poster panel will be scheduled in all 10 markets - providing a "100" showing scheduled for all 10 in September 1977, with a "50" showing in May 1978.

OUTDOOR

#100 - September 1977

Market	Boards			Cost-per-Month
	Unlit	Lit	Total	
San Jose 640,000	12	52	(64)	$12,080
Portland 533,700	20	70	(90)	$14,440
Omaha 629,400	6	46	(52)	$ 6,290
Richmond 792,600	17	27	(44)	$ 6,050
San Diego (1,082,100)	24	56	(80)	$14,560
Kansas City (1,215,600)	--	90	(90)	$16,650
Detroit 1,755,400	--	200	(200)	$46,000
Cleveland 2,700,400	8	128	(136)	$25,360
Pittsburgh 2,246,400	52	102	(154)	$22,147
Syracuse 820,900	74	21	(95)	$ 8,280
TOTALS (18,016,500)	213	792	(1005)	$171,857

OUTDOOR

#50 - May 1978

Market	Boards			Cost-per-Month
	Unlit	Lit	Total	
San Jose	6	26	(32)	$6,040
Portland	12	32	(44)	$7,220
Omaha	3	21	(24)	$3,080
Richmond	6	13	(19)	$3,005
San Diego	12	28	(40)	$7,280
Kansas City	--	45	(45)	$8,325
Detroit	--	100	(100)	$23,000
Cleveland	37	11	(48)	$12,680
Pittsburgh	25	51	(76)	$11,740
Syracuse	4	6	(10)	$4,040
TOTALS	105	333	(438)	$86,410

Total Population: 18,016,500

Total Reach: 98%

Total Cost: $258,267

Total CPM: $14.33

MEDIA SCHEDULE

AND

BUDGET

MEDIA BREAKDOWN BY MONTH

	MAGAZINES	TV	OUTDOOR	TOTAL
SEPTEMBER	$12,216	$106,500	$171,000	$289,716
OCTOBER	12,216	71,000		83,216
NOVEMBER		53,250		53,250
DECEMBER	12,216	71,000		83,216
JANUARY	13,068	26,625		39,793
FEBRUARY	13,068	26,625		39,793
MARCH	13,068	26,625		39,793
APRIL	13,068	26,625		39,793
MAY	12,216	71,000	$ 87,600	170,483
JUNE	12,216	71,000		83,216
JULY		35,500		35,500
AUGUST		17,750		17,750

Cadillac
ROLD GOLD
Fleetwood Brougham d' Elegance
MEDIA BUDGET
(Sept. '77 - Aug. '78)

	$ Expenditures	% of Total
SPOT TV	$603,500	63%
Production	$ 35,000	
CONSUMER MAGAZINES	$113,315	12%
Production	$ 8,000	
OUTDOOR	$258,267	25%
Production	$ 11,000	
TOTAL BUDGET:	$1,029,082	

MEDIA SCHEDULE

	SEPT	OCT	NOV	DEC	JAN	FEB	MAR	APR	MAY	JUNE	JULY	AUG
SPOT TV	300 GRP	200 GRP	150 GRP	200 GRP	75	75	75	75	200 GRP	200 GRP	100 GRP	50 GRP
CONSUMER MAGAZINES	FC BH&G WD	FC BH&G WD		FC BH&G WD	TV GUIDE	TV GUIDE	TV GUIDE	TV GUIDE	FC BH&G WD	FC BH&G WD		
OUTDOOR	100 SHOWING								50 SHOWING			
RADIO					⟶							
SALES PROMOTION								✕				
$ SPENT	289,716	83,216	53,250	83,216	39,793				170,483	83,216	35,500	17,750
% OF BUDGET	29	8	6	8	4	4	4	4	18	8	4	3

ADVERTISING/CREATIVE
OBJECTIVES AND STRATEGY

INTRODUCTION

"The average consumer now sees 900 commercials a month, and most of them slide off her memory like water off a duck's back. For this reason you should give your advertisements a touch of singularity, a burr that will stick in the viewers mind."*

This "burr" comes from knowing the product from the consumer's viewpoint and letting this knowledge shape creative effort. Our consumer research has highlighted the following:

Product Benefits

1. ROLD GOLD pretzels have <u>eye-appeal</u>.

2. Appearance dictates <u>good taste</u>.

3. ROLD GOLD pretzels have a salty, satisfying flavor.

4. ROLD GOLD pretzels are <u>versatile; more than just a beer companion</u>.

5. Frito-Lay products have an <u>excellent reputation</u>.

Product Disadvantages

1. Lack of consumer brand awareness and competitive product differentiation.

2. ROLD GOLD name is misassociated by consumer.

3. Consumer doesn't associate ROLD GOLD with Frito-Lay.

*<u>Confessions of an Advertising Man</u>, Ogilvy, David

ADVERTISING OBJECTIVES

1. Generate strong brand awareness by persuading pretzel consumers to choose ROLD GOLD rather than arbitrarily selecting a brand.

2. Create a sharply defined image for ROLD GOLD based on product benefits.

3. Link Frito-Lay reputation of excellence with ROLD GOLD.

CREATIVE OBJECTIVES AND STRATEGY

1. Make ROLD GOLD name easy to remember through:

    • clear identification of POLD GOLD as a pretzel
    • repetition of name
    • use of identifying slogan

2. Associate salient product qualities solely with ROLD GOLD by illustrating:

    • eye appeal
    • salty satisfying flavor
    • versatility

3. Give ROLD GOLD pretzels a likeable "personality" by:

    • presenting ROLD GOLD in "fun" situations
    • associating ROLD GOLD with "fun" people
    • identifying ROLD GOLD as a Frito-Lay product

COPY PLATFORM

Basic Promise

ROLD GOLD pretzels are the best pretzel because of consistent appearance and flavor.

Basic Audience

Married Female	High-School Graduate
Caucasian	Household Income $10-19,999
25-49 Years of Age	Employed Part-Time
2-4 in Household	Suburban

Basic Execution

The misassociation of the ROLD GOLD name will be illustrated in amusing scenarios, enforcing correct identification of the product and awareness through repetition, visual description of product qualities, and association with "fun" people.

Basic Product Features

1. Eye-appeal

    Primary research indicates the consumer is attracted by variety of shapes, golden-brown color, and sparkling salt crystals.

2. Satisfying flavor

    Primary research indicates consumer enjoys the crunchy, salty, taste of pretzels.

3. Versatility

    Primary research indicates the consumer considers pretzels as a snack for all occasions, by itself, or with other "fun" foods or beverages.

CREATIVE PRE-TESTING

Objective

To determine the communication effectiveness of the three proposed 30-second television commercials.

Execution

To meet this objective, a questionnaire was administered that tested six different measures of communication effectiveness: Perception of the message, believability, negative impact, positive impact, after image, and influence on attitude.

In brief, the methodology employed was as follows:

A focus group of eight women and two men fitting the ROLD GOLD demographic target market evaluated the advertisements.

To prevent the possible bias of the respondents, each 30-second commercial was presented under these controls; 1) the three storyboards were graphically illustrated by the same artist, 2) one interviewer presented each concept with equal verbal expression, 3) Concept B - "ROLD GOLD puts you on the right snack" was staggered between the two executions for Concept A - "ROLD GOLD...the only pretzel worth its salt".

After each storyboard was presented, the consumer completed a recall questionnaire. A half-hour discussion followed, in an attempt to delve deeper into respondents' attitudes.

Concepts

CONCEPT A: "ROLD GOLD, the only pretzel worth its salt.", was executed in two different approaches.

EXECUTION 1: "The Mistaken Identity" theme educates the consumer on the correct meaning of ROLD GOLD by playing on the name humorously. It features eye-appeal and good taste.

EXECUTION 2: "The Bungling Burglars" theme educates the consumer by associating ROLD GOLD pretzels with items of value, again humorously.

CONCEPT B: "ROLD GOLD puts you on the right snack."

EXECUTION: "Detectives find the right snack" theme was executed showing ROLD GOLD pretzels as the perfect snack for anytime or place, emphasizing product benefits.

Focus Group Results - Summary

CONCEPT B: "ROLD GOLD puts you on the right snack."

The majority of the respondents considered this theme boring, repetitious, and over-used on television.

CONCEPT A: "ROLD GOLD, the only pretzel worth its salt."

EXECUTION 2:   The Bungling Burglars

The theme "ROLD GOLD, the only pretzel worth its salt" was unanimously well received. However, the respondents found the execution typical. It did not portray originality, believability, nor did it facilitate retention of the ROLD GOLD name.

CONCEPT A: "ROLD GOLD, the only pretzel worth its salt."

EXECUTION I: The Mistaken Identity

All respondents found this execution of the theme "ROLD GOLD, the only pretzel worth its salt" credible and enjoyable.

- Eight out of 10 respondents recognized and remembered the ROLD GOLD theme.
- Mistaken identity of the ROLD GOLD name successfully portrayed the consumers' associations with it.
- They found the characters fun, attractive, and enjoyable.
- Theme line recall was excellent. (Respondents noted the entire slogan on the recall test.)

THEME

ROLD GOLD, the only pretzel worth its salt

This theme best fits the copy platform and effectively communicates our message because:

- It clearly identifies ROLD GOLD as a pretzel.
- Consumer identifies salt as crucial to both appearance and taste. Using the word "salt" links the visual and taste sensations with ROLD GOLD pretzels.
- It challenges all competition, claiming exclusive quality among all pretzels with the words, "the only pretzel worth its salt".

Ultimately the use of this theme eliminates the need for separate, costly Heartland and Non-Heartland themes.

Consumer research showed less than 20% brand preference in both Heartland and Non-Heartland. Response among the 20% who had a preference was highly fragmented. Also primary research illustrated that pretzel eaters enjoyed the same product features regardless of geographic location.

Therefore, recognition and positive association with the ROLD GOLD name is essential in both heavy and light consumption areas. In heavy areas, our theme will promote brand recognition and preference by claiming superiority, while in light consumption areas, our theme will create brand recognition (inevitably fostering brand preference).

EXECUTION RATIONALE

At present, the name "ROLD GOLD" doesn't mean pretzels to consumers. They misassociate the name ROLD GOLD with tobacco, cannabis, or other items unrelated to pretzels: 1) Because this misassociation of the ROLD GOLD name requires consumer education, and 2) the potential of being the first pretzel to engage in heavy promotion and advertising is an advantage in itself.

The ROLD GOLD name is limelighted throughout our campaign. The execution capitalizes on various misassociations, accomplishing consumer education and awareness. It then extends beyond awareness to a positive identification of the name by creating a sharply defined personality for ROLD GOLD.

SALES PROMOTION OBJECTIVES

1. To assist advertising in creating <u>strong brand awareness</u>, and a <u>sharply defined image</u> for ROLD GOLD, in the marketplace.

2. To inform, equip and motivate each link in the distribution chain, thus securing shelf space for ROLD GOLD in major grocery outlets.

3. <u>To secure secondary display locations</u> for ROLD GOLD in retail outlets.

4. To <u>motivate</u> the Frito-Lay sales force.

SALES PROMOTION STRATEGIES

1. Instigate a tie-in promotion with a national brand soft drink.

   A. Create a p.o.p. tie-in display to stimulate impulse purchases and enhance brand visability.

   B. Create a tie-in couponing promotion with a soft drink product to boost sales and encourage retailers to stock ROLD GOLD.

2. Offer a self-liquidating premium to the consumer.

3. Launch a two week radio promotion in each key market.

4. Offer a promotional allowance on all cases of ROLD GOLD pretzels.

5. Utilize direct mail as a "door opener" for the Frito-Lay sales force, and an introduction to the advertising campaign directed at trade buyers.

6. Supply Frito-Lay sales people with a presentation package covering the ROLD GOLD campaign.

7. Incorporate an incentive program for the Frito-Lay sales force.

SALES PROMOTION EXECUTION

Tie-In Promotion

In September, a tie-in promotion with Pepsi-Cola will be executed. It will run the first three weeks of the advertising campaign for ROLD GOLD. The advantages for this type of tie-in are as follows:

- Pepsi-Cola is a popular national brand soft drink which is known by most people. By matching Pepsi with the product, ROLD GOLD's brand visability will increase.
- A soft drink will serve as an alternative to the traditional "pretzel and beer" image.
- Pepsi-Cola will pay for one-half of the production costs. This was verified by the promotional director for Pepsi-Cola in San Francisco.

A. The p.o.p. tie-in display:

Will feature nine ounce bags of ROLD GOLD twists and sticks. It will also feature six-pack 12 ounce cans of Pepsi.

Description: The cardboard end-cap display will carry the theme, "ROLD GOLD, the only pretzel worth its salt". The products will be stacked in cut case cartons. Pepsi-Cola will also be featured on the display.

Costs: $3.50 per display

According to our primary research, tie-ins are the most acceptable form of end-aisle displays for retailers.

B. Couponing:

ROLD GOLD and Pepsi will also be tied-in to a couponing promotion. A 15 cent coupon redeemable on six-packs of Pepsi cans, will be stuffed in ROLD GOLD packages. Conversely, six-packs of Pepsi cans will carry 15 cent coupons redeemable on nine ounce bags of ROLD GOLD twists and sticks.

Costs: $1.77 per thousand coupons

- 3 million Pepsi coupons
- 1 million ROLD GOLD coupons

Couponing of this nature increases sales, at the same time encouraging retailers to stock ROLD GOLD pretzels. Pepsi-Cola is a major national brand soft drink, sold in almost every major grocery store chain. When a customer receives a coupon for ROLD GOLD with their Pepsi, they will return to that store to buy the pretzels. The retailers will then feel they must stock the product to meet the demand. The district manager for Northern California Safeway, cited this as an excellent buying motivational strategy. The couponing will also fall during the first three weeks of the campaign, incorporated with the p.o.p. display.

Self-Liquidating Premium

To emphasize ROLD GOLD as an "anytime" snack, a pretzel jar will be offered to the consumer as a self-liquidating premium. The 16 ounce clear glass jar will carry the ROLD GOLD LOGO in golden filigree lettering. Clear glass displays product's eye-appeal. Because the premium is a kitchen decoration always in the consumer's view, it will serve as a constant reminder of the ROLD GOLD brand name.

Two labels from any ROLD GOLD package will be required along with payment. The premium will be promoted in consumer magazines.

Self-Liquidating Radio Promotion

The theme for the radio promotion will be "The ROLD GOLD Rush - for the Only Pretzel Worth its Salt". The promotion will be sold as a package to one "Top-Hit" 5,000-50,000 watt radio station in each key market. According to TGI figures, "Top-Hit" stations constitute target market listenership. Stations chosen will attract the 25-49 age group.

Non-Heartland Divisions	Heartland Divisions
San Jose - KLOK	Syracuse - WHEN
San Diego - KCBQ	Pittsburgh - KDKA
Richmond - WLEE	Detroit - CKLW
Omaha - KFAB	Cleveland - WGAR
Kansas City - KCM	
Portland - KEX	

The radio promotion will be tested during the first year. The promotion will be evaluated for its effect on brand awareness, and reintroduced in following years in additional markets.

The promotional package will cost $1200 and will be sold for $1500 to cover shipping costs and contingencies. The promotion will fall in the second week of April, 1978; which precedes the third wave of the media schedule. The package will include:

- A $500 gold nugget grand prize.
- 100 "pretzel twisters" (riddles based on product's history).
- T-shirt giveaways for correct riddle answers ($350).
- Bumper sticker giveaways available at radio stations and all major retail outlets that carry ROLD GOLD pretzels. (Frito-Lay salesmen will distribute the bumper stickers at the retail outlets) ($250).

The Contest:

Contestants will phone in to answer the "pretzel twister". There will be one winner for each correctly answered twister. His/her name will then be automatically entered into the Grand Prize Drawing, which will culminate the two week promotion.

Each radio station will administer the promotion with only two stipulations: 1) Two "pretzel twisters" must be given in the morning between 6 am and 10 am, and one between noon and 2 o'clock. According to TGI, this is when listenership is highest among our target market. 2) Not more than 100 names can be entered into the drawing in order to improve the entrants chances.

According to the promotional director at radio station KLOK in San Jose, this type of promotion is viable because it involves the consumer. Value of prize doesn't necessarily raise or lower participation.

A self-liquidating promotion of this type allows a company to utilize a mass medium at no expense.

Trade Promotional Allowances

According to primary research, the major motivation for trade buyers' purchasing decisions are promotional allowances. Grocery retailers will be offered a 10% discount on each case of ROLD GOLD pretzels. This offer will run from August 2 to 22, 1977.

Direct Mail

The direct mail effort will serve as a door-opener for Frito-Lay sales-people. It will include a cover letter and a four-color, three panel brochure, describing the profitability of stocking the ROLD GOLD pretzel product line. It also serves as an introduction to the advertising and sales promotion campaign.

Direct mail will be sent to: 1) Home office management of major grocery store chains, and 2) Store and district managers of major and independent supermarkets during the last week in July of 1977. This will allow time for home offices to plan display spaces for ROLD GOLD. According to primary research, the majority of supermarket chains plan their displays according to home office schematics.

The brochure will outline:

- Frito-Lay quality and ROLD GOLD excellence
- Marketing support for ROLD GOLD
- Advertising and media plans
- Sales promotion support

Presentation Package

The Frito-Lay sales force will be equipped with a complete sales package, detailing the entire campaign and explaining how ROLD GOLD can be profitable for retailers.

Incentive Program

Because the ROLD GOLD sales force will play an integral role in the success of the campaign, a sales incentive in the form of a sales contest will be offered.

The contest will be held during the month of August, coinciding with the company's distribution push. The top salesperson in each of the selected markets will be awarded a $250 gold nugget.

TOTAL BUDGET

Media:

Spot TV	$603,500	
Magazines	$113,315	
Outdoor	$258,267	
		$975,082 (92.3%)

Sales Promotion:

P.O.P. Displays	$ 2,625	
Coupons	$ 3,540	
Direct Mail	$ 5,500	
Sales Package	$ 3,000	
Sales Award	$ 2,500	
		$ 17,165 (1.6%)

Production Costs:	$ 54,000 (5.1%)
Contingency Fund:	$ 10,000 (1.0%)
TOTAL	$1,056,247 (100%)

APPENDIX I

CONSUMER SURVEY

Total Number of Respondents: 319

Sex: Male 32.9% (105)   Marital Status: Married 78.3% (250)

Female 67.0% (214)   Single 21.6% (69)

Size of Household: Employment:

1 - 6% (20)   Full-time 28% (90)
2 - 24% (76)   Part-time 45% (145)
3 - 29% (92)   Unemployed 26% (84)
4 - 25% (80)
5 - 9% (31)   Age:
6 - 4% (14)
7 - 1% (4)   18-24 7% (25)
8 - less than 1% (1)   25-34 54% (165)
9 - less than 1% (1)   35-49 32% (100)
                                50-64 6% (18)
                                65 up 1% (6)

Income: Education:

$25,000 or more 12% (37)   College Graduate 20% (64)
$20,000 - 24,999 19% (62)   Attended College 28% (89)
$15,000 - 19,999 31% (98)   High School Grad 42% (133)
$10,000 - 14,999 22% (70)   Other   10% (33)
$ 5,000 - 9,999 13% (40)
 under $4,999   3% (12)

1. Do you buy corn chips?   2. Do you buy pretzels?

yes *69% (221)*   no *31% (98)*   yes *100% (319)*

Include them on a shopping list?   Include them on a shopping list?

yes   no   yes   no

3. Do you buy potato chips?   4. Do you ever use "cents off"
                                          coupons while shopping?
yes *90% (287)*   no *10% (32)*
                                          yes *66% (210)*   no *34% (109)*
Include them on a shopping list?

yes *19% (61)*   no *81% (258)*

5. Who in your family eats the most corn chips?
    Children *38% (121)*;   Husband *27% (86)*;   Wife *35% (112)*
    Who in your family eats the most pretzels?
    Children *29% (92)*;   Husband *51% (162)*;   Wife *20% (65)*
    Who in your family eats the most potato chips?
    Children *34% (110)*;   Husband *29% (93)*;   Wife *36% (116)*

6. Who in your family picks the corn chips you eat?
    Children *3% (10)*;   Husband *7% (23)*;   Wife *90% (286)*
    Who in your family picks the pretzels you eat?
    Children *1% (4)*;   Husband *10% (32)*   Wife *89% (283)*

7. Do you have a favorite brand of pretzel?

yes *17% (53);*   no *83% (266)*

Reason: Fresher *2% (5);* Price *1% (4);* Shape *less than 1% (2);*

Name Brand *less than 1% (3)*

8. When you have guests in your home do you serve corn chips?

yes *91% (291);*   no *9% (28)*

When you have guests in your home do you serve them pretzels?

yes *88% (280);*   no *12% (39)*

9. How often do you buy pretzels?

Less than once a month *37% (119);* Once a month *48% (152);*

2-3 times a month *13% (40);* Once a week *2% (5);* 2-3 times a week *less than 1% (3)*

10. How many packages of pretzels do you buy at once?

1 - *92% (293);* 2 - *5% (15);* 3 - *3% (10);* 4 - *less than 1% (1)*

11. What kind of package do you prefer for potato chips?

bag *89% (284);* box *6% (20);* no preference *5% (15)*

12. What kind of package do you prefer for pretzels?

bag *90% (287)* box *4% (12);* no preference *6% (20)*

Reason Why:

Can see if broken *19% (60);* Freshness *7% (22);* no reason *6% (20)*

13. When would you say you eat pretzels the most?

Watch TV *54% (172);* Parties *39% (123);* Lunches *5% (15);* "Just snack" *3% (9)*

14. What beverage goes best with pretzels?

Beer *44% (145);* Soft Drinks *38% (120);* Alcohol *6% (10);* Milk *6% (21);*

Juice *4% (13)*

15. What other foods do you eat with pretzels?

Dips *36% (123);* Cheese *6% (20);* Other Snacks *18% (58);* None *37% (118)*

16. What is your favorite brand of pretzel?

Don't Know *81% (258)*   Other *4% (13)*

Mr. Salty *3% (11)*   ROLD GOLD *3% (8)*

Granny Goose *1% (4)*   Nabisco *less than 1% (3)*

Frito-Lay *less than 1% (2)*   Bachman *less than 1% (1)*

17. Where do you usually find it in the store?

Snack Food Isle *76% (241);* Don't Know *9% (30);* Cookies/Crackers *9% (29)*

End Isle *6% (19)*

18. If your favorite pretzel is not in stock would you:

Buy another snack food *66% (210);* Buy another pretzel *31% (100);*

Go to another store *3% (9);*

19. When choosing pretzels, what do you consider important?

Taste *19% (62);* Price *16% (50);* Shape *5% (15)*

20. Why do you like pretzels?

Salty *63% (201)*; Crunchy *19% (60)*; Taste *9% (30)*; Other *9% (28) NOTE: Under this category, there were so many "other" reasons it was not practical to list them all since none had more than two responses.*

SYRACUSE TELEPHONE SURVEY

Total number of respondents: *50*

1. Do you buy pretzels? yes *50* ;   no *27*

2. What is the name of your favorite pretzel?

   Mr. Salty *2*;   Charlie Chips *1*;   Hanover *3*;   Bachman *2*;   Peppridge *1*;   ROLD GOLD *2*;   Don't Know *39*

3. Can you name the manufacturer of your favorite pretzel?

   Nabisco – Mr. Salty *2*;   Don't Know *9*

4. Are you familiar with Frito-Lay? yes *50* ;   no *0*

5. Do you feel that Frito-Lay makes good snacks? yes *50* ;   no *0*

6. What do you like most about pretzels? Salty *14*;   Shapes *12*;   Taste *10*;   Crunchy *9*

FOCUS GROUP RESULTS

1. CONSUMER'S MENTAL IMAGE
   A. Felt pretzels stood alone as a snack food.
      1. Not necessary to eat with anything else.
      2. Satisfying as a complete snack.

   B. Pretzels hold a youthful, wholesome image.

   C. Associated pretzels with activities.
      1. Sports   3. Traveling
      2. Picnics   4. Entertaining

   D. Associated with refreshing, cold beverages.
      1. Cold beer and soft drinks
      2. Disliked hot beverages with pretzels

2. CONSUMER'S DESCRIPTION OF PRETZELS
   A. Satisfying flavor
      1. Crunchy;   2. Salty;   3. Filling

   B. Wholesome snack
      1. Non-greasy;   2. Low in sugar

   C. Eye-Appealing Snack
      1. More descriptive than other snacks
         A. Form;   B. Variety of shapes
         C. Glaze;   D. Decorative display
      2. Color
         Preferred medium brown shade

3. <u>CONSUMER'S PACKAGE PREFERENCES</u>
    A. Preferred Bag over Box
        1. Ability to see product
        2. Ease of storage and packing
            A. Preferred pliable bag that was eacy to roll down and store.

    B. Box initially attractive
        1. Bright colors and photo of product
        2. But lacking bag attributes
            A. O.K. for sticks
        3. Disliked Mr. Salty Character on Nabisco package
            A. Character name reminded them of peanut

    C. Enjoyed useful information on package
        1. Product history;   2. Receipes;   3. Trivia

4. <u>CONSUMER BRAND PREFERENCE</u>
    A. No preference
        1. Appearance strongest buying factor

    B. Frito-Lay
        1. Youthful, innovative image
        2. Associated expertise with corn chips and other salty snack foods
        3. Concluded that Frito-Lay should produce quality pretzels

    C. Nabisco
        1. Traditional, eastern image
        2. Associated expertise with cookies

5. <u>CONSUMER SUGGESTION FOR PRETZEL USE</u>
    A. Active events
        1. Traveling;   2. Picnicing;   3. Sports activities

    B. Childrens' Snack
        1. With lunch;   2. Teething Babies;   3. Easy, no mess;
        4. Good reward - not sweet

    C. Change of Pace

    D. Decorations
        1. Art projects;   2. Christmas Decorations

6. <u>CONSUMER'S ATTITUDE TOWARDS ROLD GOLD PRETZELS</u>
    A. Name
        1. Disliked name;   2. Associated name with tobacco, cannabis;
        3. Name non-descript;   4. Did not associate with Frito-Lay

    B. Package
        1. Design unimaginative, simplistic
        2. Preferred Frito-Lay logo to be more visable
            A. Would positively influence purchases
        3. Liked color-bright yellow
        4. Liked see-thru panel on bag

RETAIL QUESTIONNAIRE RESULTS

Total Number of Respondents: 15

1. Who purchases products from manufacturers?

    A. Buyers   B. Manager   C. Dept. Head   D. Other _____
       (10)   *(2)*   *(3)*   *(NA)*

2. What are the purchasing decisions based on?

    A. Advertisements *(3)*   B. Samples *(NA)*   C. Price *(4)*
    D. Bulk rates *(5)*   E. Discounts *(4)* F. Service *(3)*

3. What trade publications do you read?

    7 publications were noted, with no significant leader.

    A. Of those which ones are the best?
    Progressive Grocer (4); Chain Stores Age (1); Supermarket News (4)

4. How do you decide on the location of a product within your store?
    Office Schematics (13) from Central Buying and Marketing Dept.
    in regards to Space and Traffic

    A. Decide what position on the shelf the product is placed? Eye Level? Etc.?
    Profit (2); Size (6) and Movement. Decided by Marketing Dept.
    Office Schematics (3)

5. What is your policy on point of purchase displays? Like? Dislike? Etc.?
    Like (8); Dislike (2) Main office decision. Have limited appeal.
    Will feature if the size is right and profitable.

6. How do you feel about coupons as a purchasing motivator?
    Good (8); Poor (1); Fair (1) Helps sell items. Most consumers
    are using them these days.

7. Do you find the service of the Frito-Lay sales force adequate?
    Yes (7); No (3) Could be better (1) Retailers who found service
    inadequate was due to lack of stock

8. Do you determine the position for Frito-Lays snack-food product line?
    If YES, what prompts this decision? *(3) Reasons: Product movement,*
    service, space available

    If NO, how is the decision made? *(12) Reasons: Head Office decision*
    by Merchandising specialists as per reasons above

9. Do you determine the number of shelf-facings assigned to a manufacturers product line of:

   Bagged snack foods?   YES*(5)*   NO*(6)*   If no, who *Main Office*

   Boxed snack foods?   YES*(4)*   NO*(6)*   If no, who *Main Office*

10. What factors influence this decision?

    A. Advertisements *(1)*   B. Consumer Demand *(9)*   C. Discounts *(3)*

    D. Bulk rates *(1)*   E. Price *(4)*   F. Other *(2)*

    If Other, Please explain   *Profit*

11. How do you decide on the fully stocked end-aisle displays of one product line of snack foods?

    All factors mentioned question 10. Not a retailer policy

    Does the manufacturers advertising influence this decision?

    Yes*(13)*   NO*(1)*   Other *Sometimes (1)*

12. Do you ever display snack-foods with appropriate, complimentary beverages in high traffic areas?

    Yes*(10)*   NO___

    IF YES, what factors influence this decision? Manufacturers' discount? Manufacturers' promotion? Etc.?

    Manufacturers' discounts (5); Manufacturers' promotion (5); Demand, Quantity, Profit

13. Do you find that snack foods sell better during a certain season?

    YES*(14)*   NO -

    If Yes, please rank in order of season: 1) Fall 2) Winter 3) Spring
    4) Summer   *Fall (3); Winter (1); Spring (0); Summer (7)*

14. Are pretzels a profitable product line in your store?

    YES*(14)* NO*(1)*

    If Yes, what brand/brands   *All Brands*

15. Under what circumstances would you consider featuring pretzels on an end-aisle display? *Gross Profit (3); Movement Price Demand (2); Promotion Allowances (3); Discount, Tie-in with beverages (4)*

16. Under what circumstances would you consider placing a free standing point of sale display for pretzels? *Special Price (2); New Product Introduction Profit (3); Movement and Demand Created (2); Tie-in with Beer and/or Soft Drink Promotional Allowances (4)*

<u>ERRATUM</u>

Mathematical discrepancies arise in the ROLD GOLD case provided by Frito-Lay. Certain figures are impossible to correlate, and are conflicting.

- The case claims ROLD GOLD supermarket sales totaled $19.5 million in 1975, representing a 13.5% of supermarket sales.

- The case also indicates <u>total retail</u> sales for the pretzel category totaled $128 million during the same fiscal period.

Since 19.5 is 13.5 percent of 144, total category sales would have to exceed $144 million, thus discounting the validity of the given data.

This hinders accurate sales projections for both the brand and category, and share-of-market comparisons within the category.

Pursuant to contacting AAF headquarters in Washington, D.C., Gabardine, Herringbone & Tweed received a memo instructing us to use the figures as supplied by Frito-Lay and to disregard secondary data.

Assuming competing agencies are in compliance, GH&T has worked-to-rule.

APPENDIX II

TELEVISION CAMPAIGN

ROLD GOLD Pretzels   TV   :30
"Mistaken Identity"

Video	Audio
Open with MS of man at party tearing open product bag. Elderly lady in the background.	Background music and party SFX
CU of man pouring product into bowl. Old lady smiles.	Man: (confidently to himself) "ROLD GOLD...who could resist.
ECU of man holding up pretzel for inspection.	
A smile of approval lights up his face as product glistens.	
Man crunches into pretzel.	SFX: crunch
Cut to MS of man and statueque woman dangling a long cigarette holder. Old lady in background.	Man: "Care for a ROLD GOLD.." First woman: (cuts him off in mid-sentence)"...No, thank you...I prefer my own brand."
Woman takes long, icy drag off her cigarette and blows smoke in man's face.	
Cut to MS of man standing with frizzy haired girl. Old lady in background.	Man: (changing tone) "Like some ROLD GOLD pre..." Second woman: "...Nooo m-a-n. Like I'm not into that scene anymore. What's your sign anyway?"
Cut to MS of perturbed man standing with Zsa Zsa Gabor type fondling necklace. Old lady still in background.	Man: (cautiously) "Could I offer you ROLD GOLD pre..." Third woman: "...Diamonds, dahling ...only diamonds."
CU of man shrugging. Old woman moves forward and takes pretzel from bowl.	
ECU of old lady holding up pretzel for scrutiny.	
She winces a knowing smile as product again glistens.	Old Lady: "ROLD GOLD!...The only pretzel worth its salt!"
She takes a bite.	SFX: crunch

Video	Audio
MS of old lady linking her arm through man's as she shoulders up to him starstruck. Super: Frito-Lay presents	Anncr (VO): "Frito-Lay presents..." Music and SFX out
Cut to stop motion tag of stick pretzel... Super: ROLD GOLD	VO: "ROLD GOLD..."
...Forming into twist. Super: ROLD GOLD...the only pretzel worth its salt.	VO: "...the only pretzel worth its salt."
Animated sparkle gleams from salt crystal.	SFX: ping!
Close of ECU of product package.	Out.

```
ROLD GOLD Pretzels                   TV      :30
"The Will"


Video                              Audio

Open with LS.  Zoom over four      Open with sobbing and mumbling.
respondents at last will and
testament hearing.

Camera stops at lawyer sitting     Lawyer:  "...and to my dear sister..."
in front of portrait of deceased.

Pan to sobbing woman in black.     Lawyer:  "...for her persistent
                                            affection, I leave Samson..."

CU as she sucks up her breath      Lawyer:  "...my beloved goldfish."
in indignation...                  Woman:   (wails in self-pity)

Pan to shifty looking couple       Lawyer:  "...and to my niece and
whispering furiously.                       nephew, who have no doubt
                                            eagerly awaited this moment..."

ECU of lawyer looking from         Lawyer:  (makes "raspberry" sound)
will, shrugs...

Pan to placid looking young        Lawyer:  "...and finally, to my loyal
grandson.                                   grandson and only relative
                                            worth his salt.  I leave my
                                            fortune in...ROLD GOLD."

MS of group glaring jealously      (silence)
as grandson shrugs in
appeasement.

Cut to lawyer rolling in wheel-    (whispering)
barrow stuffed with bank bags.

MS of respondents converging       (oohing and aahing)
on wheelbarrow.

MS of greedy nephew tearing        SFX:  tear
open bag.

Hold shot of product glisten-      (gasps of shock)
ing.

CU of sobbing sister...then        Sister:  "PRETZELS???!!!"
faints

CU of nephew biting into           SFX:  CRUNCH
pretzel.                           Nephew:  "Hmmmmmm!"

MS of niece flashing anger         Niece:  (admits in surprise) "He mighta
at nephew as she grabs product             been cheap, but he sure had good
and takes bite.                            taste!"

Cut to lawyer holding pretzel      Lawyer:  (answers confidently)
in one hand and draping a                   "Certainly...ROLD GOLD...
consoling arm around grandson.              the only pretzel worth its
Same super.                                 salt."
```

PRINT CAMPAIGN

<u>PRINT AD</u>

Full Page

ILLUSTRATION: MISERLY OLD MAN COUNTING STACKS
                OF PRETZELS

HEAD: INVEST IN ROLD GOLD

COPY: In 1929 -- at a time when everything else seemed like a
       bad investment -- ROLD GOLD became America's favorite
       pretzel.

       Just look through the clear-view package. You can see why.

       ROLD GOLD's sparkling glaze and golden-brown color means
       a fortune in flavor. And a salty, crunchy taste that's
       perfect...for parties, picnics, or just watching T.V.

       And the Frito-Lay seal says quality. Everytime. You can
       bank on it - ROLD GOLD...

TAG LINE: ...The only pretzel worth its salt.

<u>PRINT AD</u>

Full Page

ILLUSTRATION: ONE YOUNG BOY OFFERS ANOTHER A BIT OF HIS
              ROLD GOLD PRETZEL.

HEAD: A share of ROLD GOLD is an investment in good times.

COPY: At parties or picnics, with T.V. -- or just good friends --
       ROLD GOLD's sparkling glaze and golden-brown color means
       a fortune in flavor.

       And a salty, crunchy taste that's priceless.

       The Frito-Lay name on every clear-view package means only
       one thing - ROLD GOLD...

TAG LINE: ...the only pretzel worth its salt.

SALES PROMOTION CAMPAIGN

<u>SALES PROMOTION PRINT AD</u>

Full Page

ILLUSTRATION: GLASS JAR FULL OF PRETZELS WITH ROLD GOLD
               BAG LEANING AGAINST IT. COUPON BELOW.

HEAD: Protect your ROLD GOLD investment

COPY: With this 16 ounce pretzel jar. Featuring ROLD GOLD
       elegantly lettered in golden filigree. An attractive
       decoration in any kitchen.

       Now -- by special offer from Frito-Lay -- it's yours.

       Here's how to order.

       Just send two ROLD GOLD proof of purchase seals and $4.95
       along with the coupon below.

       And Frito-Lay will send you the only jar worth its pretzels.

Bibliography

Aaker, David A. and Myers, John G. *Advertising Management: Practical Perspectives.* Englewood Cliffs, N. J.: Prentice-Hall, 1975.

A. C. Nielsen Company. "A Look at Sales Promotion." *The Nielsen Researcher,* no. 4, 1977.

Advertising Age, 9 January 1978, p. 9.

————, 27 February 1978.

————, 8 May 1978.

————, 22 May 1978.

American Marketing Association. *Marketing Definitions: A Glossary of Marketing Terms.* Chicago: American Marketing Association, 1963.

Barban, Arnold M.; Cristol, Stephen M.; and Kopek, Frank J. *Essentials of Media Planning.* Chicago: Crain Books, 1976.

Barton, Roger, ed. *Handbook of Advertising Management.* New York: McGraw-Hill, 1970.

Bloom, Derek; Jay, Andrea; and Twyman, Tony. "The Validity of Advertising Pretests." *Journal of Advertising Research,* April 1977.

Bodeau, Robert. "Advertising Media: An Appraisal." *Journal of Advertising,* Winter 1976.

Boone, Louis E., and Kurtz, David L. *Contemporary Marketing.* Hinsdale, Ill.: Dryden Press, 1977.

Boone, Louis E., Kurtz, David L. *Dialogues in Marketing—Taped Conversations.* Hinsdale, Ill.: Dryden Press. Produced by Joe Cappo, *Chicago Daily News,* in cooperation with J. Walter Thompson Company.

Boyd, Harper W., Jr., and Westfall, Ralph. *Marketing Research : Text and Cases.* 3d ed. Homewood, Ill.: Richard D. Irwin, 1972.

Boyd, Harper W. Jr.; Westfall, Ralph; and Stasch, Stanley F. *Marketing Research: Text and Cases.* 4th ed. Homewood, Ill.: Richard D. Irwin, 1977.

Boyer, Dwight. "Flights of Fantasy." *Cleveland Plain Dealer,* Sunday News Magazine, 8 February 1976, pp. 20-22.

Britt, Steuart Henderson. "Are So-Called Successful Advertising Campaigns Really Successful?" *Journal of Advertising Research,* June 1969.

Broadbent, Simon. *Spending Advertising Money.* 2d ed. London: Business Books Limited, 1975.

Buell, Victor P., and Heyel, Carl. *Handbook of Modern Marketing.* New York: McGraw-Hill, 1970.

Burton, Phillip Ward. *Advertising Copywriting.* 3d ed. Columbus, Ohio: Grid Publishing, 1974.

Burton, Philip Ward, and Miller, Robert J. *Advertising Fundamentals.* Columbus, Ohio: Grid Publishing, 1976.

Bylund, H. B. "Social and Psychological Factors Associated with Acceptance of New Food Products." *Marketing Models, Quantitative and Behavioral.* Edited by Ralph L. Day., Pa.: International Textbook Co., 1964.

Caples, John. *Tested Advertising Methods.* Englewood Cliffs, N. J.: Prentice-Hall, 1974.

Cohen, Dorothy. *Advertising.* New York: Wiley, 1972.

Colley, Russell. *Defining Advertising Goals for Measured Advertising Results.* New York: Association of National Advertisers, 1961.

Cravens, David W.; Hills, Gerald E.; and Woodruff, Robert B. *Marketing Decision Making: Concepts and Strategy.* Homewood, Ill.: Richard D. Irwin, 1976.

Criteria for Marketing and Advertising Research. New York: Advertising Research Foundation, 1953.

Daniels, Draper. "The Second Meaning of the Word Creative." *Journal of Advertising,* Winter 1974.

Dean, Joel. *Managerial Economics.* Englewood Cliffs, N. J.: Prentice-Hall, 1951.

Dirksen, Charles T.; Kroeger, Arthur; and Nicosia, Francesco M. *Advertising Principles, Problems, Cases.* 5th ed. Homewood, Ill.: Richard D. Irwin, 1977.

Dunn, S. Watson, and Barban, Arnold M. *Advertising: Its Role in Modern Marketing.* Hinsdale, Ill.: Dryden Press, 1974.

Eldridge, Clarence E. *Marketing for Profit.* New York: Macmillan, 1970.

Engle, James F.; Wales, Hugh G.; and Warshaw, Martin R. *Promotional Strategy.* rev. ed. Homewood, Ill.: Richard D. Irwin, 1971.

Evans, Richard H. "Planning Public Service Advertising Messages." *Journal of Advertising,* Winter 1978, pp. 28-34.

Friedman, Hershey H., and Friedman, Linda. "Advertising Myopia." *Journal of Advertising,* Spring 1976, pp. 29-31.

Garfinkle, Norton. "The Marketing Value of Media Audiences—How to Pinpoint Your Prime Prospects." Paper read at Association of National Advertisers Workshop, 19 January 1965. Quoted in Sandage and Fryburger, *Advertising Theory and Practice.*

"G. F. Portfolio Plan—Communicate to Grow." *Advertising Age,* 23 February 1976.

Gibson, James J. "A Critical Review of the Concept of Set in Contemporary Experimental Psychology." *Psychological Bulletin,* November 1964.

Glim, Aesop. *How Advertising Is Written and Why.* New York: Dover, 1961.

Haley, Russell. Quoted by Ramond in *Advertising Research: The State of the Art.* New York: Association of National Advertisers, 1976.

Headen, Robert S.; Klompmaker, Jay W.; and Teel, Jesse, E., Jr. "Increasing the Informational Content of Reach and Frequency Estimates." *Journal of Advertising,* Winter 1976, pp. 18-23.

Heighton, Elizabeth J., and Cunningham, Don R. *Advertising in the Broadcast Media.* Belmont, Calif.: Wadsworth Publishing, 1977.

Higgins, Denis. *The Art of Writing Advertising.* Chicago: R. R. Donnelley, Advertising Publications, 1965.

Hilliard, Robert L. *Writing for Television and Radio.* New York: Hastings House, 1976.

Hoel, Robert F. *Marketing Now.* Glenview, Ill. Scott, Foresman, 1973.

Houston, Franklin S. "Pooled Marketing and Positioning." *Journal of Advertising,* Winter 1976, pp. 38-39, 44.

Hurwood, David L., and Brown, James K. *Some Guidelines for Advertising Budgeting.* New York: The Conference Board, 1972.

Kleppner, Otto. *Advertising Procedure.* Englewood Cliffs, N. J.: Prentice-Hall, 1966.

Kotler, Philip. *Marketing Management.* Englewood Cliffs, N. J.: Prentice-Hall, 1967.

Kotler, Philip. *Marketing Management: Analysis, Planning, and Controls.* Englewood Cliffs, N. J.: Prentice-Hall, 1976.

Kurtz, David L. *Marketing Concepts, Issues, and Viewpoints.* Morristown, N. J.: General Learning Press, 1972.

Lavidge, Robert J., and Steiner, Gary A. "A Model for Predictive Measurements of Advertising Effectiveness." *Journal of Marketing,* October 1961.

Littlefield, James E. *Readings in Advertising.* St. Paul, Minn.: West Publishing, 1975.

Longman, Kenneth A. *Advertising.* New York: Harcourt Brace Jovanovich, 1971.

"A Look at Sales Promotion." *Nielsen Researcher.* Northbrook, Ill.: A. C. Nielsen Co., 1977.

Luick, John F., and Zeigler, William Lee. *Sales Promotion and Modern Merchandising.* New York: McGraw-Hill, 1968.

McNeal, James U. *An Introduction to Consumer Behavior.* New York: Wiley, 1973.

McNiven, M. A. *How Much to Spend for Advertising.* New York: Association of National Advertisers, 1969.

Malickson, David L., and Nason, John W. *Advertising—How to Write the Kind That Works.* New York: Charles Scribner's Sons, 1977.

Mandell, Maurice I. *Advertising.* Englewood Cliffs, N. J.: Prentice-Hall, 1974.

Medcalf, Gordon. *Marketing and the Brand Manager.* Oxford, England: Pergamon Press, 1967.

Norins, Hanley. *The Complete Copywriter.* New York: McGraw-Hill, 1966.

N. W. Ayer Media Facts, 1977-78.

"Ogilvy IAA Man of the Year." *Advertising Age,* 22 May 1978, p. 97.

Peckham, J. O. Sr. *The Wheel of Marketing.* Privately printed, 1975.

Ramond, Charles. *Advertising Research: The State of the Art.* New York: Association of National Advertisers, 1976.

Riesz, Peter C., and Shuchman, Abe. "Response to the ADA Crest Endorsement." *Journal of Advertising Research,* February 1974, pp. 21-25.

Rogers, Everett, and Shoemaker, F. Floyd. *Communication of Innovations,* 2d ed. New York: Free Press, 1971.

Roman, Kenneth, and Maas, Jane. *How to Advertise.* New York: St. Martin's, 1976.

San Augustine, Andre, J., and Foley, William F. "How Large Advertisers Set Budgets." *Journal of Advertising Research,* October, 1975.

Sandage, C. H., and Fryburger, Vernon. *Advertising Theory and Practice,* 9th ed. Homewood, Ill.: Richard D. Irwin, 1975.

Schuster, M. Lincoln. *The World's Great Letters.* New York: Simon and Schuster, 1940.

Scott, James D., ed. *The Creative Process.* Ann Arbor: University of Michigan, Bureau of Business Research, 1957.

Sharing for Understanding. Proceedings of the Annual Conference of the American Academy of Advertising. Edited by Gordon E. Miracle. East Lansing, Mich.: American Academy of Advertising, 1977.

Sissors, Jack Z.; Lehew, Harry D.; and Goodrich, William. *Media Planning Workbook: With Discussion and Problems.* Chicago: Crain Books, 1976.

Sissors, Jack Z., and Petray, E. Reynold. *Advertising Media and Planning.* Chicago: Crain Books, 1976.

Smith, Gail. "How GM Measures Ad Effectivess." *Printer's Ink,* 14 May 1965.

Sosanie, Arlene K., and Szybillo, George J. "Working Wives: Their General Television Viewing and Magazine Readership Behavior." *Journal of Advertising,* Spring 1978, pp. 5-13.

Stanley, Richard E. *Promotion.* Englewood Cliffs, N. J.: Prentice-Hall, 1977.

Steiner, Gary A. "Notes on Franklin B. Evans' Psychological and Objective Factors in Prediction of Brand Choice." *Journal of Business,* January 1961.

Technical Guide, 1976/1977 Study of Selective Markets and the Media Reaching Them. New York: W. R. Simmons & Associates Research, 1977.

Trout, Jack, and Ries, Al. "The Positioning Era Cometh." In *Readings in Advertising.* Edited by James E. Littlefield. St. Paul, Minn.: West Publishing, 1975.

Trout, Jack, and Ries, Al. *Positioning "Positioning."* Chicago: Crain Books, 1972.

Tuck, R. I. J., and Firth, Jill. "Can Research Join in the Creative Process?" In *Market Research to Advertising Strategy and Vice-Versa.* Estoril, Lisbon, Portugal: ESOMAR, 1973.

Tucker, W. T., and Painter, J. J. "Personality and Product Use." *Journal of Applied Psychology,* October 1961.

Twedt, Dik Warren. "Some Practical Applications of 'Heavy-Half' Theory." In *Proceedings, Tenth Annual Conference.* New York: Advertising Research Foundation, 1964.

Wedding, Nugent. "Advertising as a Method of Mass Communication of Ideas and Information." *Journal of Advertising,* Summer 1975, pp. 6-10.

West, Herbert. "Why You Need a Master Strategy Blueprint." *Advertising Age,* 18 January 1957.

Wolfe, Harry Dean.; Brown, James K.; and Thompson, G. Clark. *Measuring Advertising Results: Studies in Business Policy 102.* New York: Industrial Conference Board, 1962.

Wright, John S. "The Advertising Marketing Marriage." *Journal of Advertising,* Spring 1974, pp. 28-33.

Wright, John S.; Warner, Daniel S.; Winter, Willis L. Jr.; and Zeigler, Sherilyn K. *Advertising.* New York: McGraw-Hill, 1974.

Young, James Webb. *A Technique for Producing Ideas.* Chicago: Crain Books, 1940.

Zielske, H. S. "The Remembering and Forgetting of Advertising." *Journal of Marketing,* January 1959.

Index

DISCHARGED

DISCHARGED

OCT 2 7 1981
DISCHARGED

DEC 8 1982   DISCHARGED
MAR 5 1980

DISCHARGED

DISCHARGED
FEB 1982   DEC 3 1988

MAR 1 8 1982

DISCHARGED

OCT 2 6 1982
DISCHARGED

DISCHARGED

DISCHARGED
MAY 1983   APR APR 1980

DISCHARGED

DISCHARGED   DISCHARGED

MAY 1 3 1992

DISCHARGED

NOV 2 1 1986   NOV 1 6 1992
DISCHARGED

DISCHARGED

DISCHARGED

DISCHARGED